ASIDE ARTHUR CONAN DOYLE

PAUL R. SPIRING is both a Chartered Biologist and Physicist and he is employed by the Department for Children, Schools and Families (UK) to work for the European School System in Germany. Recently, he was appointed Head of Biology at the European School of Karlsruhe. Paul is co-author of two previous books entitled *On the Trail of Arthur Conan Doyle: an Illustrated Devon Tour* (Brighton: Book Guild Limited) and *Bertram Fletcher Robinson: a Footnote to The Hound of the Baskervilles* (London: MX Publishing Limited). He is also the author of *BFRonline.biz*, a website that is dedicated to commemorating the memory of Bertram Fletcher Robinson. Paul is a member of numerous societies including The Devonshire Association, The Conan Doyle (Crowborough) Establishment, The Sherlock Holmes Society of London, La Société Sherlock Holmes de France, The Sydney Passengers and The Crew of the S.S. May Day.

Frontispiece. *The Chronicles of Addington Peace* by Bertram Fletcher Robinson (London: Harper & Brother, 1905).
**COPYRIGHT BRITISH LIBRARY BOARD.
ALL RIGHTS RESERVED (012632.cc15)**

ASIDE ARTHUR CONAN DOYLE

TWENTY ORIGINAL TALES

BY

BERTRAM FLETCHER ROBINSON

Compiled by

Paul R. Spiring

First published in 2009
© Copyright 2009
Paul R Spiring

The right of Paul R Spiring to be identified as the compiler of this work has been asserted by him in accordance with the Copyright, Designs and Patents Act 1998. All rights reserved. No reproduction, copy or transmission of this publication may be made without written permission. No paragraph of this publication may be reproduced, copied or transmitted save with the written permission or in accordance with the provisions of the Copyright Act 1956 (as amended). Any person who does any unauthorised act in relation to this publication may be liable to criminal prosecution and civil claims for damage.

ISBN- 9781904312529

MX Publishing Ltd, 335 Princess Park Manor,
Royal Drive, London, N11 3GX
www.mxpublishing.co.uk

Book Jacket design by Staunch
www.staunch.com

Cover Illustration. Bertram Fletcher Robinson (seated centre) with Arthur Conan Doyle (behind his left shoulder) aboard *Steamship Briton* during July 1900.
COURTESY OF BRIAN W PUGH

Dedication

This book is dedicated to the memory of
Simon Hollas (see below). He was a
very special member of a very
special family. Those of us that met him
will never forget the laughter.

Simon Hollas,
(31st May 1973 – 23rd November 2008).
COURTESY OF PAULA BRINE

Acknowledgements

I would like to thank the following individuals and organisations for their assistance with the preparation of this volume of stories; Hugh Cooke (European School of Karlsruhe), Graeme de Bracey Marrs (Robinson family), Madeline & Paula Brine (Hollas family), Alistair Duncan (Author: *Eliminate the Impossible* and *Close to Holmes*), Shelah Duncan (British Library), Meade-King, Robinson & Company Limited (Liverpool), Julian Morgan (European School of Karlsruhe), Arthur Robinson (Robinson family), Su Rumford, Philip Weller (The Baskerville Hounds, The Dartmoor Sherlock Holmes Study Group and The Conan Doyle Study Group), Dr. Frances Willmoth (Jesus College, Cambridge University), Jeffrey M. Young and especially Brian W. Pugh (The Conan Doyle [Crowborough] Establishment) for his assistance with the revised *B. Fletcher Robinson Bibliography*.

CONTENTS

Introduction – x

1
Black Magic:
The Story of the Spanish Don.
1

2
The Laughter of Dr. Marais.
A Story of the Breton Coast
13

3
The Trail of the Dead:
The Strange Experience of Dr. Robert Harland.
I.-The Hairy Caterpillar.
(with J. Malcolm Fraser)
22

4
The Trail of the Dead:
The Strange Experience of Dr. Robert Harland.
II.-The Mystery of the Lemsdorf Ham.
(with J. Malcolm Fraser)
31

5
The Trail of the Dead:
The Strange Experience of Dr. Robert Harland.
III.-The Chase in the Snow.
(with J. Malcolm Fraser)
42

6
The Trail of the Dead:
The Strange Experience of Dr. Robert Harland.
IV.-The Anonymous Article.
(with J. Malcolm Fraser)
52

7
The Trail of the Dead:
The Strange Experience of Dr. Robert Harland.
V.-The Ammonia Cylinder.
(with J. Malcolm Fraser)
62

8
The Trail of the Dead:
The Strange Experience of Dr. Robert Harland.
VI.-The End of the Trail.
(with J. Malcolm Fraser)
74

9
The Battle of Fingle's Bridge:
How the Ferns and the Rushes
Fought the Gorse and the Heather,
And What Came of the Battle.
84

10
Fog Bound
(with J. Malcolm Fraser)
91

11
The Debt of
Heinrich Hermann
101

12
The Chronicles of Addington Peace:
I.-The Terror in the Snow.
110

13
The Chronicles of Addington Peace:
II.-Mr. Taubery's Diamond.
124

14
The Chronicles of Addington Peace:
III.-Mr. Coran's Election.
135

15
The Chronicles of Addington Peace:
IV.-The Mystery of the Causeway.
146

16
The Chronicles of Addington Peace:
V.-The Vanished Millionaire.
156

17
The Chronicles of Addington Peace:
VI.-The Mystery of the Jade Spear.
167

18
The Mystery of Thomas Hearne.
A Tale of Dartmoor.
177

19
The Return of Oliver Manton
188

20
How Mr. Denis O'Halloran
Transgressed his Code
194

Footnotes and Sources – 199

Source Acknowledgements – 208

B. Fletcher Robinson Bibliography – 209

INTRODUCTION

The relationship between Bertram Fletcher Robinson and Arthur Conan Doyle was mutually advantageous. It is probable that the two men were first introduced by Fletcher Robinson's uncle, Sir John Robinson at the Reform Club in London during the mid 1890's. All three men were fellow 'Reformers' and Sir John was both a prominent member of the managing committee and Doyle's friend. However, Doyle wrote that his friendship with Fletcher Robinson was not actually 'cemented' until July 1900.

Thereafter, Fletcher Robinson acted as 'assistant plot producer' to Doyle's most popular story, *The Hound of the Baskervilles* (1901). He also provided Doyle with a central idea to the plot for a second Sherlock Holmes tale entitled, *The Adventure of the Norwood Builder* (1903). Later, Doyle sought assistance for a story entitled *The Lost World* (1912) from Fletcher Robinson's former school-friend, Percy Harrison Fawcett. This link may have inspired Doyle to use the then deceased Fletcher Robinson as a model for the heroic narrator of that story, Edward E. Malone.

In return, Doyle was seemingly content to patronise Fletcher Robinson's work. For example, *The Lady's Home Magazine of Fiction* (1904), *Home Magazine of Fiction* (1904/05), *The Detroit News* (1905), *Oelwein Daily Register* (1906) and *The Penny Magazine* (1907) each feature Fletcher Robinson stories with an editorial note that alludes to his association with Doyle. Similarly, during 1906, Peter Fenton Collier of New York published a compilation of twelve tales collectively entitled *Great Short Stories, Volume 1 (1): Detective Stories*. This book includes one story by Fletcher Robinson together with an introductory note by the editor, William Patten in which, he too refers to an association between the author and Doyle. Given that Doyle also contributed two items to that same book, it appears that he was fully aware of Patten's comment and did not object to it.

Fletcher Robinson and Doyle remained close friends until the former's death on 21st January 1907. Between 1901 and 1907, the two men continued to meet at the Reform Club and also at meetings of 'The Pilgrims' and 'Our Society' in London. During that same period, Fletcher Robinson spoke or wrote in high praise of Doyle on at least four separate occasions. Moreover, Doyle is known to have invited Fletcher Robinson to play golf near his home at Hindhead during October 1906. He also sent flowers to Fletcher Robinson's funeral together with an affectionate message that read 'In loving memory of an old and valued friend'. Later, Doyle lamented that the premature death of Fletcher Robinson was a 'loss to the world'.

Aside Arthur Conan Doyle was compiled as a tribute to a friendship that has long been overshadowed by ignorance of the facts. It is my belief that this book would have been welcomed by Doyle as a fitting tribute to Fletcher Robinson whom he described as a 'fine fellow'. The stories contained herein are published as they first appeared within the original periodicals and also in their correct chronological sequence. I do not feel qualified to comment upon the literary value of these stories. Instead, I defer to the opinion of Doyle; a man who achieved so much, met many, and evidently spotted something of unique value in both Bertram Fletcher Robinson and his work.

Paul R. Spiring
December 2008

BLACK MAGIC:
THE STORY OF THE SPANISH DON.
BY B. FLETCHER ROBINSON.

AYBE 'twas not 'xactly what a man might call a ghost, sir; but, to my mind, 'twas something worse."

"The story, Jake, the story!"

"But if I was to tell you, sir, you'd be saying, like they rascal boys on the jetty, that 'twas only another of old Jake's lies for to get a mug of ale."

"You know perfectly well I should say nothing of the kind."

From bitter experience I had learned that Jake, unlike certain distinguished pianists and tenors of my acquaintance, could never be brought to exercise his powers by importunate requests. So, having lodged my formal protest against further delay, I handed my tobacco pouch to the weather-beaten veteran by my side, and while he filled and lit his pipe, stared down into the little Cornish harbour that lay, bathed in the warm June sunshine, at my feet. From the headland where we sat it formed a quaint and pleasing picture—of fishing boats resting from their battles with Atlantic surges, their blue-jerseyed crews idling beside them, of picturesque red-tiled roofs, split by the narrowest of crooked streets, of tangled nets hung out to dry, and empty baskets heaped in corners. At last my patience bore fruit. From out the blue smoke-rings that curled slowly up through the still air beside me, the voice of the old sailor arose once more.

You must know, sir, that about two and forty, or it may be three and forty, year gone, I was a foremast hand on a trading brig they called the *Hampden*, as was lying inside the mouth of a river on the Guinea coast. What was the name of it as writ down on the chart I don't call to mind; but we sailors used to call it the Mootrer River, which was what the Frenchies had christened it after a boat's crew had been cut up there by the niggers. I don't say as how we spoke the name correct, but 'twas as near as we could get to it.

A bad place it was; nothing but mango swamps, where the fog rose that thick at night as you felt as how you could carve a pipe bowl out of it, and mud banks with red-backed crabs scuttling in and out of their holes for all the world like rabbits in a warren, and 'squeters that I'll take my affy-davy were nigh the size of humming birds. The river was smelly and oily-looking, with green stuff growing out into it, and enough dead niggers to keep the sharks and the crocodiles busy. Then, to top all, there was the malarious fever hanging round, and watching to catch us after sunset. No, sir, 'twas not a place we visited for our constitoosians.

There was a factory, as they call it, about two miles up the river, where the bank was near ten feet high, and the situation consequently less pizenous. It was a rummy old place of one storey, with a verandey in front, and a sort of warehouse at the back, with a six-pounder gun mounted on the roof, as a sign of good faith to the niggers. A white man was never reckoned to last more than three years on an average; though they did say as how a Scotchman, who was a famous hard drinker, once lived there no less than five years in a state of delirium tremendous afore he blew his brains out. He had made a bet as he wouldn't die of the fever, and he told his friends in his will to be very careful to see that the money was paid to his relatives.

We cast anchor opposite the factory, and commenced to unload that part of the cargo as was consigned to it, into flat-bottomed boats full of niggers. A mixed cargo 'twas called, and very mixed it were; rum and old muskets and powder and cotton cloth, for the most part, with a lot of other queer consarns I can't call to mind. The hands were so mighty anxious to be away, that the mate, who was a sight too fond of hazing us and very free with his langvidge when roused, never had to give us no encouragement. He'd stand on the poop sliding out his orders in a melancholius way, with as sweet a mouth as if he had been colloguing with the wife of the owner in her best parlour up at Clapham. He always allowed as the Mootrer took the heart clean out of him. As for the hands, they'd take a squint now and again over the bulwarks at the crabs under the mangoes, and the sharks which were jostling themselves out of the water round the scupper-hole of the cook's galley, and then they'd turn to hoisting the cases out of the hold as if their lives depended on getting the job done quickly—which by the same token was pretty much what they did depend on in that season of the year.

By noon of the fourth day, we had got the cases over the side, and had taken in a many barrels of palm oil, with ivory and the like things which come from those parts. Mighty glad we were, for the second mate and the cook were down with fever already, and what with the fear of us catching it ourselves, and what with the bad cooking, we were all very down on our luck. I suspect it was about two bells in the first dog watch—begging your pardon, sir, that is five o'clock—when the skipper comes on to the bank by the factory and hails the brig. He had been ashore colloguing with the chief factor, a poor, washed-out beggar of an Englishman, who we reckoned had taken the berth to save his burial expenses at home. We had hoped as we should up anchor there and then, but the skipper he gave no orders, and what the foc'stle said of him and the Mootrer makes me blush to think on. But, as they say, "hard words don't break no bones," and there we were for another night of it.

The next day what does the skipper do but go ashore early, and we glimpsed him and the factor mixing their pegs in the verandey as cool as might be. Another man was down with the fever, which left us short-handed, and we were all getting pretty mad at such darned tomfoolery. I remember old Tom Burton, that went by the name of "Biscuits," seeing that biscuits were biscuits in those days, and Tom was most always dry, and not so clean as might be—I remember how old Tom allowed as he hadn't signed on to serve in no blooming fever hospital, and that if the skipper wanted to treat the ship's crew to a 'oliday, he should have brought up opposite to Southend or Rosherville Gardens. The first mate got wind of this, for, as you may guess, the grumbling didn't get no quieter when he was around, and presently he calls us aft and tells us that we were waiting for two passingers from up the river, and that we should put to sea so soon as ever they came aboard.

That night, sir, it chanced that old Biscuits and I had the first anchor watch, and I will not deny that what with the heat and what with the extry allowance of rum that had been served out to us to keep off the fever, we were not altogether maintaining what one of these here Board of Trade Enquiries would call a sharp look-out, though 'twas a part of the coast where in those days a man trusted more to pistols than to Providence. To tell the honest truth, we were lying under the starboard bulwarks with an old sail over our heads to keep out the fog and the dew and the 'squeters, which last were like devouring lions. I was dreaming as a shark had fastened on to my leg, which same was caused by Biscuits' foot, he suffering from heat rash, and twisting in his sleep, when all of a sudden I sat up with a scream buzzing in my ears. I tell you, sir, I was only half awake, but it seemed the very kind of cry as I'd heard once afore in a razzle dazzle at Callao, when a little fat German got his discharge with six inches of steel between his shoulders.

"Biscuits," says I, pulling him by the ear to wake him, "wot was that?"

"Wot was wot?" he sings out rather sharp, for I had nipped him harder than I had the meaning.

"I thought I heard something," says I.

"Oh! you thought, did you?" says he, feeling his ear cautious like. "Then, don't you go thinking again, young feller, unless you want me to 'it you over the 'ead."

I didn't see as he had call to turn nasty, so I left him, cussing to hisself, and went and leant over the bulwarks. The moon was up, and the sky as thick with stars as weevils in a biscuit. We lay about the middle of the river, and I could see the whole breadth of it—nigh on two hundred fathoms it was, I reckon—with the currents twisting and curling like so many snakes, and great oily eddies rising in the middle. It was mortal hot, and the smell of the mud came off they swamps till it nigh turned my innards. There were a lot of queer noises about, as there always are in Africa after sundown, like things creeping and stirring in their sleep, and the tree frogs were croaking and chirruping fit to bust themselves.

"'Tis only a long-eared man as could hear anything of a night like this," said Biscuits, sarcastic like, as he came and stood beside me. "Blessed if it ain't a regular sing-song they frogs are having!"

He had hardly got out his words, when from under the mangoes, opposite the factory and just abreast of where we lay, there came a hail for a boat. It kind of startled me, coming so sudden; but, for all that, I couldn't help looking at Biscuits out of the corner of my eye, triumphant like.

"'Tis a rummy start," says he, with his eyes a-staring. "What a white man—for a white man it is by the voice of him—can be doing in they mango swamps at this time of night beats me. I reckon I'd better call the skipper."

With that he goes below, and in less than no time brings up the skipper, who must have turned in in his togs, for he was ready dressed —boots and all. He came over to where I was standing, and took a squint at the land through his night glass.

"'Tis like enough to be the passengers, my lads," says he; "though I can't make 'em out. So haul the gig alongside, and tumble in."

He slipped down into his cabin, and by the time we had got the boat alongside—it had been swinging astern—he was on deck again, with a couple of cutlasses under his arm, which he handed over to us; not that there was anything surprising in that, for 'twas all the protection a trader was like to get on that coast, with so many murdering blacks about.

We pushed off, and he steered to where, as near as we could reckon, the man had hailed us. When we gets to about two boats' lengths from the shore we lay on our oars, and the skipper stood up in the stern sheets.

"Are you there, gentlemen?" he hollas out.

At that a man steps out from the shadow of the bushes. The moon was shining down fair upon his face, for all the world like a lime-light at a theater, and I could make him out as plain as could be. A rummier-looking chap I never set eyes on. He was a sort of a freak —what a doctor gent has told me they call an Albiner. His hair, or as much of it as could be seen under his big hat, was just as white as wool, and the same with his eyebrows and a straggly little beard he had; but whether by breeding or the sun, the skin of his face was 'most as dark as a nigger's. A double-barrel gun was slung across his back, and he had a big knife—what the Frenchies call a *cootoo de chaise*—at his belt. There didn't seem to be no one with him, and there he stood, with the mud above his ankles, looking at us, and we at him.

"At length you have roused yourselves," says he, after a bit, speaking his English with the twang of a furriner. "It was time; I grew tired of the mud bank."

From the way he stared, I saw the skipper had never set eyes on him afore, and wasn't too pleased with the look of him. His hand went groping back to his flap pocket, and I glimpsed the brass butt of a pistol. Howsomever, he spoke him fair enough.

"I am sorry, *Señor*, to have kept you waiting, but your runner did not tell me when to expect you. Your terms were too good to refuse; but I feel it my duty, before you come aboard, to tell you I must call at two stations further south before sailing for Europe. This may be of inconvenience. Will you not wait for another ship?"

"My good *Capitan*," says the other, smiling till his teeth, which were very white, shone in the moonlight, "my desire is to leave this river so accursed. I trouble not myself where your so excellent vessel shall proceed so long as she does not remain."

The temper of the skipper was never what you might call rated A1 at Lloyd's, and the don seemed to rub him up the wrong way, somehow.

"Then the sooner you come aboard the better!" he snaps out. "But where's your friend? The message said two of you."

"My *camerado*! Ah! 'tis a sad story. But yesterday we two march side by side, and he laugh and make much joke. I say 'Be careful how you walk in this ground of swamp so full of snake,' and he answer me, 'There is no need; they will run away before we come.' We walk and we walk, and of a sudden one turn under his foot and bite him, once, twice here." He bent down, and touched his knee. "In a half of an hour he was dead, in many twists. Oh! it was not a pleasant sight—by no means. It is sad to see a *camerado*—in twists."

He clapped his hand over his mouth, as if to smooth his moustache, and, though his eyes were solemn enough, I couldn't, somehow, stop thinking that his mouth was grinning and his teeth shining under his fingers.

"What have you done with him?" says the skipper.

"He is already beneath the ground. It should have been to me a pleasure to have brought him to you; but, alas! the climate!"

The skipper looked mighty oneasy. I think he kind of suspicioned that there was a screw loose somewhere—but what was the square thing to do wasn't clear to him. So he stood biting his nails and scowling at the don, and the don stood in the mud, as cool as cold storage, smiling back at him.

"Well, I suppose there's nothing more to be said?" says the skipper at last. "I suppose you've got some traps somewhere, haven't you?"

"UNSLUNG HIS GUN, AND GOT IT UP AT THE READY" (*p*. 182).

At that the fellow turned about, and called out in some heathen lingo; and out from the mangoes straggled over a dozen niggers, walking two and two. Each pair on 'em had a stoutish pole, passing from shoulder to shoulder, and a package slung to it, which seemed mighty heavy from the way the pole gave as they walked. They came down to the edge of the water, and stood looking at their master. Mortal feared of him they seemed, and he had only to cock his eye at 'em to make 'em squirm like whipped puppies.

"Why, what the deuce have you got there?" sings out the skipper. "I never said I'd ship a cargo."

"*Señor Capitan*," says the don, "I am ready to pay for any trouble that I may so regrettably cause. If I did not tell you of these trifles, pray accept my apologies the most profound; but, in the name of all the saints, allow my people to place the cases in your boat with speed, for I grow to dislike this mud bank exceedingly."

He off with his big hat, and bowed to the skipper, who looked as if he'd like to ask him what he meant by it. Howsoever, I suppose he didn't see his way to refuse to take the man's things, and in a minute or two the niggers had waded out and stowed the cases in the bottom of the boat. They were so astonishingly heavy that, by the time they had finished, we lay lower in the water than I cared for. It was not a river one would choose for the " good old annual "—and the skipper, he sings out:

"I tell you what, *Señor*, we'll have to make two trips of it. I'll send back the boat for you later. Give way, my lads."

We were watching for the order, and pulled the first stroke with a will, but, before we could get in another, the Spaniard had sprung waist-deep into the river, and was holding on to the stern of the boat, with his eyes as green as a tom cat's. The skipper he whips out the pistol, and claps it to his head.

"Let go, my man!" he holloas, "or, by heaven, I'll blow your ugly head in."

The don was in a tight place, and he had the sense to know it. He let go of the boat, and, as he did so, an eddy caught us and swung us round. We all lost sight of him for a moment; and when we next brought our eyes to bear, dern me! if he hadn't unslung his gun, and got it up at the ready! Biscuits and I were too startled to row, and just lay on our oars, looking first at him, and then at the skipper, the pair on 'em facing each other—for all the world like two of these here furrin duellists one reads of. I can't but admit but that I was in a blue funk, for the skipper was the worst shot with a pistol that I ever did see, and the don could have plugged the three of us as easy as shelling peas. But, praise the powers! Mr. Spaniard drops his muzzle with a laugh, and sings out quite cheerily:

"*A'dios*, my brave *Capitan!* I have thrown myself on the honour of the English. But I beg of you, do not make delay."

And with that, I'm blowed if he didn't kiss his paw to us, like an actor fellow in a play.

We weren't long in making the ship, and soon slung the cases on board. The skipper took it into his head to send us back by ourselves to fetch the don. Neither Biscuits nor I liked the job, but there! in course it had to be done. We found him waiting, quite affable, and when we were helping him on the deck, he tipped us a bit of Spanish gold. After that he went below, and we saw no more of him that night.

As soon as it was light, we up anchor and dropped down the river. You can guess how pleased all hands were to feel the heave of the open sea and hear the surf booming on the bar behind us. There was a light, north-easterly breeze, and, so soon as we were clear of the coast, the old *Hampden* was headed south under all the canvas we could crowd on her.

The don didn't show on deck in the forenoon. The boy whom Biscuits allowed as we ought to call the steward, seeing as how we had become a passinger boat, he told us that the fellow had got all his cases stowed in his cabin, and was sitting on the top of them like a hen on a setting of eggs; but boys are liars by natur', and we did not take much notice of what he said. About six bells in the afternoon watch, the don came up and walked on the poop for a while, looking sharply about him all the time, as if he fancied we might be up to some little game with him. Now and again he took a squint over the port bulwarks at the coast which had sunk to a dun-coloured line in a sort of red brick glare, and seemed pleased at the pace of the brig. There wasn't much to lay hold on against him, but the foc'stle set him down as a rummy sort of chap.

It was that night, sir, as we first sighted the thing that was to cause so much trouble on board. It all comes back to me now, as plain as if it happened yesterday, with me still a foremast hand on the old *Hampden*, which has been firewood these twenty years. Eight bells had just struck—twelve o'clock land time—and the four of us of the starboard watch that were fit for duty had tumbled up from below, rubbing our eyes and yawning. The skipper was speaking to the mate afore he turned in, and called me aft on some job or other. The moon had sunk away to the west, leaving a little yellow blob of colour above her in the sky; and though the stars were out in thousands, there must have been a haze above us, for they were shining sickly like, as if something had disagreed with 'em. As for the sea, it was as black as pitch, save where the wake astern was glowing in the darkness. Maybe you have seen that same fiery water, if you've been south of the line, sir. 'Tis caused by what I once heard a doctor gent say was the animal-coolies, which give out a fosforus light when disturbed. Old Biscuits was at the wheel, and I could make him out by the light of the binnacle, munching his quid like an old cow chews her cud. As I was saying, the skipper and the mate and me was standing close together when we heard a step behind us, and there was the don.

"It is dark, my *Capitan*," says he.

"That's so," says the skipper, looking him up and down, as if he wanted to know what the dickens he was doing out of his bunk at that time of night.

"I have to-night a feeling unpleasant," says the don, softly, waving a see-gar he had in his hand. "I desire much the company of friends. Where, I say to myself, shall I find my friend the so excellent *capitan?* Upon deck, observing his duty, without a doubt. I come, and be'old I discover him!"

He laughed softly to himself, and then went and leant over the rail astern. The skipper scowled at the mate, who was doing all he knew not to grin, and then he turned to me, and asked me what in thunder I was loitering there for? But just as I turned to go forward I heard a shout, and the don bolted right into the middle of us, and brought up against the mate with a bang.

"*Madre de dios*," says he, all of a tremble, pointing astern, "what is that which follows?"

The skipper and the mate ran to the rail, with me a foot or two behind, knowing my place; and there we all stood, staring into the darkness. For a dozen seconds there was nothing to be seen; then, of a sudden, about a half-mile astern, came a regular explosion of light on the water—a flash so fierce and bright as made me, who had seen such things time out of number, catch my breath with a snort. It was a great curve of fire, flaming and storming along after us, just as it might have been one of these here torpedo boat destroyers, filled up with lighted kerosine—though, bless ye, sir, them things were never dreamed of in those days.

"It is a boat in pursuit!" sings out the don, grabbing the skipper by the arm.

"Boat be blowed!" growls the skipper, shaking him away. "You go down and take a tot of rum, man. It'll steady your nerves."

With that he and the mate walks forward, laughing with each other, leaving me and the don alone.

"I think, sir," says I, very respectful—being mindful of the gold piece, and expecting, it might be, another—"I think, sir, 'tis a great fish passing through a drift of weed, which is always full of the animal-coolies that make the blaze. I have often seen the likes of it before, but never, by the same token, as fiery as to-night."

All this time the thing was coming upon us fast. The breeze had dropped, and we weren't making more nor two knots; so it overhauled us, hand over fist. The don was shaking like a flag in half a gale of wind, and I began to feel a bit curious as to what it could be myself. It was not before it was about a dozen lengths away that I could make it out.

"Why, 'tis only a shark!" I says; "though the biggest I ever set eyes on."

"What does it here?" he stammers out.

"Blest if I know, sir. It may be the cook has been heaving some extra ripe junk overboard—Lord knows there was plenty in the last cask—or maybe it's come for someone, as we sailors believe sometimes."

I said that thinking on the three poor fellows we had below, shivering with fever they had caught in that cursed Mootrer River; for I'd heard as one of them was as like as not to be slid off a grating with a shot at his toes in a day or so; and some say there's never a sailor dies in these seas without a shark to come to his funeral. But, dern me! if I'd hardly got the words out of my mouth when that Spanish devil came at me like a madman. By a stroke of luck, he had left his knife below, and I gived him a tap on the chest that sent him back against the rail, where he stood gasping out a string of foreign swear words as long as my arm and twice as thick.

"*Por vida del demonio*, but you shall answer me for this," he says at last, with an ugly look.

"I'm sorry, sir," says I, "but 'twas your fault not mine."

With that I walked forward, for I felt as how his company was onsettling to the nerves. The men they asked me what had been up, and I told them that either the don had had a drop too much liquor, or else his top hamper wanted staying forward; for what had made him so mad with me was clean out of my reckoning.

'Twas my trick at the wheel in the forenoon watch, and when at eight o'clock I went aft I was mighty pleased to find that the don was still below. Howsoever, I don't suppose I'd been at the spokes more than ten minutes before I glimpsed his ugly head popping up out of the companion; and up he came, looking very yellow about the gills. He took a squint over the rail, and I heard him give a sort of little chuckle to hisself. After that he commenced walking up and down, up and down, with now and again a look at me out of the corner of his eye, as if he was trying to make up his mind to something. He was just so soft-footed as a cat, and each time he passed behind me I began to fancy he was stealing up on me, and that the first thing I should find would be six inches of knife in my back. I declare, sir, that when the old skipper came rolling aft, asking me, by this and that, what I meant by my lubberly steering—indeed, the ship's wake was like a corkscrew —'twas the pleasantest sound I had ever heard.

Before my trick was ended the don had

"'IT IS A BOAT IN PURSUIT!' SINGS OUT THE DON" (p. 183).

slipped below again, and when a hand came aft to relieve me I just cast my eye over the rail to see if the shark was still keeping us company. I couldn't see nary a sign of him, but somehow or other I knew that he was there, watching us—and waiting. You may think 'tis a lie, sir, though it be the sober truth. But I felt he was there, and the thought of it was like a drop of cold water trickling down my back. So presently I up and asked the skipper if I might try my luck at catching him. I got a bit of pork from the harness cask, which one might have thought would have drawn every shark for miles, 'twas so powerful, and baited a shark hook and dumped it overboard, taking a couple of turns with the end of the line round a belaying pin. But, bless you, sir, he never made no sign. I was looking down into the flurry of the wake in a melancholius way, when I heard a laugh in my ear, and there was the don!

"You waste your time, so valuable, my friend," says he. "He is like the fetish idol of the negro over there in Africa. He love the humans; nothing else, only humans."

Passinger or no passinger, I had had enough of the man and his fool talking.

"Now, look here, sir," I says. "If I were to tell the hands what you say, 't would be mighty onpleasant for you. Sick men, like to die, we may have aboard, but that counts little in the ways of Providence; for if that ugly brute astern has come for someone on this here brig, 'tis as likely you as they."

With that I walked forward, a little out of breath maybe, and left him with something to digest.

Now, as to what happened that same night, I cannot rightly speak, seeing as how it was my watch below. Even with what we knew afterwards, we never could quite make out the rights of the matter. Biscuits saw as much of it as anybody, and this is what he told me.

It was the middle watch, and he was stationed as look-out on the foc'stle—an easy job in those waters, where you didn't sight a sail once in a week. The great African moon was low in the west, and the glitter on the sea was fair dazzling to the eye, while on the planks of the deck the shadows lay in broad, dark pools, just so black as ink. As was usual with old Biscuits, he was doing anything but his duty, for he'd got his back against the capstan and was squinting lazily aft, past where the mate, leaning on the rails looking down into the waist, was scratching his head to keep himself awake, to where the hand at the wheel showed in the glimmer of the binnacle. The lad was an Irishman—Malone by name—who had had a touch of the fever, and was still a bit weak and queer; but so precious short-handed were we that the moment a man could crawl out of his bunk, back he had to go to duty. There was a fairish breeze blowing, but in quick, irregular puffs, difficult to steer by. The other two hands on deck were curled up in some corner, fast asleep.

Somehow or other, Biscuits said, his eyes kept on wandering to the long level shadow under the port bulwarks between the mate and the wheel, and presently he began to think he could see something lying or crawling there. The shadow lay so plaguy thick that he couldn't make out nothing for certain; but that was his idea. However, as the minutes slipped by and he saw nothing more, he set it down to his constitoosion, for Biscuits was by no means a blue ribboner, and had seen some queer sights in his time. Indeed, what next happened put the whole thing clean out of his head, and it was not until some days afterwards that he remembered about it. For all on a sudden there came a puff of wind from a fresh quarter, and the brig was taken aback forrard. The mate woke with a start, and tumbled down the ladder into the waist, bawling out orders to flatten the head-sheets, and so forth. There was a good bit of row and confusion with the watch below tumbling up, men singing out to each other, the yards squealing, top-sail sheets rattling, and coils of rigging flung about. The ship refused to pay off as she should have done, and the mate sprang back into the poop, taking many things to witness that he'd be the death of the lubber at the wheel. But the spokes were spinning all ways—Malone had disappeared!

When Biscuits heard the mate sing out in his surprise, which he did pretty freely, he ran aft as hard as he could, to see what was up. He found the mate standing open-mouthed, and staring at the wheel as if he thought Malone had hid himself in the binnacle. Next minute, however, he ran to the rail, for it was certain that overboard was the only place the poor chap could have gone, though how in the world he had managed to get there was a mystery. Biscuits followed him, and they made out the lad almost at once, his head showing black in the very middle of the stream of moonlight, not forty yards away. But even as the mate was turning to give the order to get out a boat, the water all about Malone became, in the way of speaking, a twisting pool of fire, in the middle of which they saw him shoot up from the sea with all of his lower limbs hid, as with an apron, in huge, grey jaws. Over the oily waves came a horrid scream, which broke sudden in the middle, as the poor chap was jerked under the water; and Biscuits sat down on the deck and covered his face with his hands, for he had liked the lad, and he knew that the tiger of the sea had got his own.

Of course, everyone on board had something to say as to how Malone went over the side. He had been a bit queer and narvous since his fever, and the skipper allowed he had committed suicide; and most of us agreed with him. Anyhow, we were all mighty down about it; for many a night had the lad kept the foc'stle in a roar with his Irish yarns, and he was regular popular amongst us. The skipper got out his rifle to try a shot at the murdering devil astern, but the brute had disappeared.

The next two days passed with fairish winds and all well. The sick men, now that we had dropped the land, took a strong turn for the better, and most of us had nigh forgotten about poor Malone; for 'tis God's providence that gives sailor men short memories. The don, too, was far more sociable-like, and handed about his see-gars most affable. It was about noon of the third day, and I and another man were at work in the waist on some job or other, with the mate on the poop watching us. I heard the mate sing out above us, and looking up, I saw the don beside him with a face like spoiled tallow. He had grabbed the mate by the arm with one hand, and was pointing astern with his other.

"Good Lord! man," says the mate, "what's the matter now?"

Fear, they say, is catching, and the don was in such a mortal funk that I think the mate was a bit shook himself. They both walked quickly aft, but in about half a minute the mate came back alone, and leant over the rail, grinning down at us in a sickly sort of way, as if he had been badly startled and didn't want to show it.

"Don't stand gaping there, you lazy lubbers!" says he, with other words as I will suppress. "'Tis only that cussed shark come back again."

Now, the skipper was a man mightily fond of his grub, even in the tropics, which shows a fine constitoosian. He always had a square meal about seven, and if it wasn't ready for him to the moment there was the very devil to pay. That evening, about five minutes past the hour, he came on deck in a tremenjous temper, saying as how his supper wasn't ready, and asking where in thunder was the boy. Since the cook had been down with fever, the boy had had to do his work, and one of the hands ran forward to the galley to call him. However, he wasn't there, nor was he in the foc'stle, nor was he in the cabins aft, where I went to look myself. The skipper took a reef in his langvidge, and began to look a bit anxious-like, while we all turned to and searched the brig. The old *Hampden* wasn't like one of these here floating hotels of liners, with their parlours and bar rooms and passages and corredoors, and in less nor ten minutes we had made certain that the boy wasn't aboard. The skipper he stamps about the deck, saying that there was a curse on the brig; but, by the same token, when he heard Biscuits remarking of the same to another hand, what did he do but up and swear he'd put him in irons for mutiny and murmuring on the high seas. At last he went below, looking very pale about the gills, and with a sight less appetite than when he came on deck; which was fortunate, seeing as how there was no one left on board who had much of an idea of cooking.

You can guess, sir, as things weren't particularly pleasant forward. We were all shook, and shook badly. It seemed only a question who would be the next, and the hands took to looking at each other suspicious-like, and watching and skulking in corners. Though it had gone again, we knew nigh enough what was waiting astern for any man ten seconds after he struck the water, and the very thought of it turned some of us youngsters queer in the innards. The sick men had got wind of the trouble, and if they were left alone but five minutes they would set up a screaming, like a parcel of women, for the fear of they didn't know what. To top all, the next day was a dead calm, and the next, and the next, with the sun standing over the foremast like a red-hot shield of iron in the copper-coloured sky, with a heat that made the tar in the seams fairly boil, and sent the men cursing into every bit of shade they could find. 'Twas a rare time for grumblers, and that we were all.

'Twas at midnight on the fourth day after the boy had disappeared, if I remember rightly, that I went aft for my trick at the helm. Since the sun had set there had been a puff or two of wind from the eastward, but the ship had hardly steerage way on her. A sickly haze spread over the water, and the moon shone down over the fore topsail as big as two. Half an hour more, and the breeze had dropped entirely; so the mate, after a long look round him, slipped away below to mix himself a drink, leaving me alone on the poop. Forward I could glimpse the look-out on the foc'stle, dozing against the bulwarks. What with the slow, huge heave of the water as it washed past, glittering here and there under the moon, and what with the heat, which was suffocating, I felt like a fellow in one of those dreams after a heavy supper, which you kind of know as you've dreamt afore.

The deuce of a bit can you move, but you've a notion that something horrid is on the way to you. I was loosening myself at the neck, when I saw the head of our passinger come peeping up the companion. He took a squint round him, and then came up and went edging by me to the rail astern. As he passed I caught a glimpse of his face, and, by the powers! it gave me a rare turn.

the mate, so I took a turn of a rope round the wheel, to keep it steady, and slipped softly back to take a peep over his shoulder.

Lord knows how he heard me; but afore I could get nigh enough, he whipped round, and faced me.

"So, my friend, it is you," says he, quiet like, though he was shaking with the fear

"WHEN HE KNEW I SAW HIM HE PULLED UP DEAD" (*p.* 188).

The sides of his mouth were drawn down, and his eyes were a-shining with that kind of light—half rage, half fear—as you see in a rat when you find him nabbed by the leg in a gin. I didn't half like his being behind me, seeing as how he had a kind of grudge against me. To make matters worse, he presently began talking to himself in his furrin lingo. It was mortal strange to hear, for he carried on as if he were begging and praying of someone, and now and again he would pull up short, as if waiting for an answer. All this he did, leaning out over the rail, and looking down into the water astern. What he saw there was beyond my knowledge, and, after a minute or two, I began to get regular curious. There was no sign of

that was on him. "Come, then, and let me show him to you."

With that he catches me by the arm, and lugs me to the rail.

"Manuel! Manuel!"

He was leaning out over, and calling softly, as I might hail a friend across the street.

"Manuel! Manuel!" says he again, with his fingers working and beckoning.

"Manuel! Manuel!" he hollas a third time, and then I saw his arm stiffen and point.

I sighted it almost as soon as he; a something that was rising in the blackness under the stern—a something that I could make out by reason of the glow of that same shiny water as I told on afore. 'Twas like a fiery shadow, so to speak, slowly rising upward and upward, growing larger as it came. And then, before I could settle the meaning of it, there shot of a sudden out of the sea, not ten feet beneath us, the head of that devil's fish, with the moon shining all grey upon it, and the ripples running off it like lighted brandy from a pudding at Christmas-time. You may think I was mad or drunk, sir; which I was neither. But its *eyes*—they were not shark's eyes at all. As I live, they were human, and with a lust of murder in them that 'twas unholy for to see.

I don't think as how I was ever what you may rightly call a narvous man, sir; but I jumped back with a kind of choking in the throat, though the don never so much as moved till after it had sunk again. Then he let out a laugh—such a laugh as is not meant for man to make of hear.

"See you, my friend?" says he. "That is how Manuel gaze at me when the blood choke him. I tell you it is he that does wait for me day after day. *Madre de dios*, he is driving me mad!"

I was in a plaguy funk, sir, but, being sorry for the poor beggar, I tried my best not to show it.

"Come, come, sir," says I, touching him on the shoulder, "don't you take on like this. Maybe 'tis the heat as has been too much for you. Go below, sir, and get the skipper to mix you something cooling."

I had hardly got the words out of my mouth, when he swung round on me, making a snapping noise with his teeth more like a mad dog nor a man.

"It is Manuel, I tell you! Manuel, whom you would have heard when I stab him there on the river bank had you not all slept like pigs. As he lay coughing the blood, he swore that he would for his revenge follow me, and that I should never the gold enjoy. He had the black magic of the negro —the fetish—over there in Africa. He has that shark possessed. To his spirit I offer humans—first the man, then the boy. But it is for me that he still waits—for me!—for me!"

He dropped down upon the deck, and lay there foaming, with the rage and the fear on him, like a man in a fit.

It all came on me like a flash—the cry I had heard on the anchor watch in the Mootrer; the death of Malone; the disappearance of the boy. I tell you, sir, I staggered right back with everything in a mist around me, I was so flumgasted. I guessed I should have fallen if I had not fetched up again the port bulwarks, and that shook the sense into me. It was good for me it did so, for the first thing I saw was the don half way toward me with his knife in his hand.

When he knew I saw him he pulled up dead, and there we stuck watching of each other. How long it was I don't know. Seconds, I reckon, though they went slow enough to me. Then all on a sudden his hand slipped back over his shoulder, something sang like an arrow through the air, and a knife crashed into the bulwarks behind me, though not without slicing me along the ribs as it passed. Two inches more, and I had been a dead man. The next thing he was upon me, and I was struggling for my life with him.

I was a handy youngster in those days, sir; but the fellow was strong in the madness that was on him, and I felt he was the better of the two. In less than no time he had me jammed agin the bulwarks, and began to slowly hoist me up and over, though I clung to him like a leech. I tried to holloa, but he had slipped a hand to my throat, and there was precious little breath left in me. Over his shoulder I could make out the hand on the foc'stle, who had woke up at last, rubbing his eyes and staring at us like a cow over a gate. At last he started running towards us, holloaing for all he was worth. However, it was little good he was like to do me, for by that time the don had nigh choked the life out of me, and I felt that I should have gone to what waited astern before help could come. 'Twas the despair of it that put a new thought into my head. With the last strength that was in me I got a purchase with my feet, which were now almost on a level with the top of the low bulwarks, and heaved upward and outward at the don. It took him fair by surprise, and the next moment we both of us plumped into the water.

What with being half strangled, and what with the water I swallowed, it was touch-and-go with me whether I should sink or swim; but by paddling with my hands I just managed to keep myself afloat. It may seem foolish to you, sir, but at first I felt more pleased on having dragged that murdering devil over the side than afraid of the death that must come to me. I remember staring up in a dazed fashion at the stern of the old brig, as it slowly drifted away, and listening to the shouts of the hands as they came running up on to the poop. I didn't know what had become of the don, until suddenly I heard someone set up a screaming, and caught a glimpse of his white head under the counter of the brig. He was carrying on in a mazed fashion, digging his nails into the planks, and trying to clamber up the side, all the time yelling for help in half-a-dozen strange lingoes, in a way that made your flesh creep to hear.

Gentlemen have many a time asked me what I thought on during—well, what next happened. 'Twas little I could tell them. It may have been through a hail from the brig, or it may have been through instinct; but, whichever it was, all at once I knew that it was coming, and so turned to face it. It's a terrible thing to feel the fear of death upon one, sir; and it takes different men in different manners. As for me, I was that weak that I could do no more than wait with the beginning of a prayer in my throat, and my legs numb with the thought of what happened to Malone. As the swell carried me up I sighted it full two hundred yards away by the line of fire it drew through the shiny water. Fast enough have I seen those brutes travel, but this one shot across the space between for all the world as a shuttle flies. A noise of shouting came to me from the brig, but I took no heed, but watched it come. I saw it top the next long roller and come sliding down upon me, with a sort of steadfast purpose in the rush of it that was strange to look upon. Twenty yards, ten yards, five yards—and it passed me; passed me, sir, though the water about me was rank with the blood from my cut over the ribs, and I lay fair in its path. Then, as I rose to the heave of the sea, I got a sight of that Spanish devil, with the moon shining on his white hair, beating madly with his fists at something which seemed to have nipped him clean across the middle, same as an otter might hold a trout. And that was the last I knew, for at the sight of it I fainted clean away, and was as near gone to Davy Jones as might be afore Biscuits fished me into the bow of the gig with the boat hook.

* * * * *

"Did you ever see the shark again?"

"No, sir."

"And the Spaniard, had he spoken the truth?"

"Every word as true as gospel, as far as we ever heard. What the rights of the matter were I never knew, but there was nigh on four thousand pound worth of gold dust in his cabin, all told; and they found the bones of his comrade, picked clean enough by the beasts, not a hundred yards from where we took him off the bank of the Mootrer. Don't ask me any more about it, sir, for, as to the fetish and that, I don't know what to believe, save that there are a many wonders in the great deep. You haven't another pipe of 'baccy on you, have you, sir?"

THE LAUGHTER OF DR. MARAIS.
A Story of the Breton Coast.
BY B. FLETCHER ROBINSON.

"EUGENIE—at last!"

"They watch me so closely, Henri. Even for half an hour it is hard to slip away. You are not angry with me?"

There was the light of love and the trust of love in the grey eyes raised to his. He kissed her—the best of all possible answers to such a question; and they laughed together nervously, as young lovers must do to whom the world of passion is a strange new thing.

"Have you been thinking about me, Henri?"

"And talking too, sweetheart, indiscreet that I am. I was telling the sea how I loved you, until I remembered what a grim old traitor he was. So I gave up the sea and tried a cormorant that swept out of nowhere to perch quite near me. But it proved a bad confidant—gone before I had well begun."

"I am glad it did not hear. They are evil-looking birds, and—they make me think of him."

She nestled closer to him with a little shiver of fear. With his protecting arms around her they stood together in silence, gazing over the heaving waters. Behind them the tall lichen-patched boulder hid them from curious eyes on the tall winding cliff path. There was no sign of human life, save the smudge of smoke blurring the clear air over the shoulder of the hill—that marked their little Breton seaport.

"Have you anything to tell me?" he asked suddenly.

"There is no change. When he calls my aunt flatters him, and lies to him, as she has done for the last six weeks. It is always the same story; the honour that he has done me; her surprise when she first heard the news; the eagerness with which I am looking forward to the marriage. And he sits in the chair by the window laughing at her, and now and again glancing at me with those cruel, greedy eyes of his. Yesterday I met him with a basket on his arm. He had two little rabbits in it, and he showed them to me with some jest of their being martyrs in the cause of experimental science. When I pleaded for them—for indeed my heart was sick—he talked of school-girl sentiment, and turned away laughing. You are a doctor, too, Henri. I do not know if these things must be. But you would hide them from me, would you not?"

"Great Heavens, this is intolerable!" The man had broken from her, and was striding up and down the narrow ledge. "I will speak to your aunt this very day. If she will not give you to me, I will act for myself. This torture is not to be borne."

"No, no, Henri!" She had stayed him in his walk and was clinging to his arm again, her face raised in anxious appeal. "You must be patient. We have still a month of hope left to us. Surely the good God will hear my prayers. I fear the doctor more than I can tell you, Henri. I have looked into his soul and know the evil things that dwell there. He will pursue with a hatred in his black cruel heart that will stop at nothing—nothing. Oh, my dear, my dear, something tells me that when he learns the truth his vengeance will follow us—to the grave."

The young man sank down on a slab of rock and covered his face with his hands. The meshes of the net that Fate had woven were closing round them fast. It was this man of whom they spoke, this celebrated professor, this Doctor Jean Marais, whose discoveries had set scientific Europe by the ears, that had picked him out of the ruck of struggling Paris students, and given him the small appointment which stood between him and absolute want; and when the health of his benefactor broke down it was he, Henri Marsac, who had suggested his native town as a place of rest for the great doctor, remaining himself in Paris, buried in his work. At that time there had been no word of love between Eugenie Rougon and himself, nothing save those ancient signals of glance and flush, by which means Dame Nature warns young people of their danger. For he was miserably poor, and even her aunt—anxious as the grumbling old tyrant was to be quit of the orphan she had been obliged to rear—would have

✱ Copyright, 1902, in the United States of America.

laughed at him for a fool if he had talked of marriage.

And then this amazing thing had happened. Doctor Jean Marais, the middle-aged cynic, the merciless experimentalist, the human icicle—as all supposed him—had fallen in love with this grey-eyed girl, pressing his suit with relentless vehemence. Her aunt, delighted at so rich a match, had accepted him in her niece's name, almost before Eugenie had realised that she had him as a lover. Poor girl, she had no place of refuge from them, no one to whom she might turn for help; and so the young man had come to his home only to find that the marriage day of this strange pair had been settled. A chance meeting with Eugenie, a few words of veiled regret, and she had fallen on his neck, imploring him to save her. They had met often since then. But they had formed no plans, and the net drew closer with wasting days. His small appointment was held at the will of his rival; Eugenie was penniless; to fly would be to starve; he groaned aloud in his agony of mind.

And even as he did so there rose a fearful cry beside him, through which there ran an intensity of quivering horror, that for the moment held him in his place, nerveless, motionless. He looked up. The girl was standing over him, her little hands stretched out as though to save him from a blow, her eyes fixed over his shoulder as if held by some terrible and malignant spectacle. She seemed to be struggling with words of protest or appeal. A light froth rose to her lips. Suddenly her eyes grew white under the long lashes, her head dropped, and with a dull sound she fell backward on the rock. In an instant he was by her side, lifting her head, stroking her hands, crying to her by name. He stared wildly round, but there was nothing to be seen save a single black cormorant gliding down the breeze below them. He felt for her heart with trembling hands. It had ceased to beat; he was alone with the dead.

* * * * *

II.

"COME in, come in."

Professor Jean Marais stood in the centre of Madame Rougon's little parlour. A case of instruments lay open on the table before him. His back was to the lattice window, through which the dying sunset still glowed faintly. His head was thrust forward from between his narrow shoulders, and his beady eyes set close together across a long, thin nose, peered expectation from behind their glasses. There was something feline about his pose, something suggestive of an animal about to spring.

"Ah, it is you, Henri! So early a visit of condolence shows a kindly sympathy. I thank you, my dear young friend."

Henri Marsac had stayed near the door. One hand had clutched the back of a chair, and so fierce was its grasp that the strained fingers shone out white as ivory in the gathering shadows.

"I saw Madame Rougon at the door; she tells me that you have just completed a second examination. Have you any opinion to give?"

"She is dead, Henri, quite dead; but you surprise me with your question; surely you already knew the answer, for I am told that it was you who found her on the cliffs."

"Yes, it was I who found her."

"Have you any theory as to how the accident occurred?"

"Doubtless she was gathering flowers—and fell."

"Indeed? I had expected more discernment in my favourite pupil. Will it surprise you to learn that she died in a fit?"

"Professor, I cannot discuss this case." He had turned towards the door, when the soft musical voice of the scientist followed him and stayed him.

"One moment, my dear young friend; there is a matter on which I greatly desire your opinion. Whispers have reached my ears; perhaps old women have gossiped, and I have heard the echoes. Now, indeed, there has come an end to all things, true or false, yet scarcely a satisfactory end. You, I believe, have known Eugenie from a child; you were to each other as brother and sister. Her spotless name must be almost as dear to you as to myself. Why was my plighted wife upon the cliffs this morning? Could it, indeed, be true that she had a secret lover? Had she so far forgotten herself as to give him a rendez-vous alone on the cliffs—where, I understand, you found her?"

"Before God, Professor, Eugenie was as pure and white as the angels amongst whom she stands."

"Exactly; I do not doubt it. But you do not answer my question."

"My apologies, Professor," said the young man, his white face turned resolutely to the questioner, who was peering eagerly at him like some evil bird of darkness

"IN AN INSTANT HE WAS BY HER SIDE, LIFTING HER HEAD."

through the gloom of the fading twilight; "I do not believe she had a lover."

"Saving, of course, myself. I am indebted to you, Henri. You have raised a great load from a mind that has already suffered much to-day. By the way, I understand that you possess a humble relation who acts as undertaker to this thriving community?"

"It is my cousin."

"I shall see that he is employed. You will forgive me if I do not detain you, but her aunt requires my help and consolation. I notice that this house of death causes you a natural distress. Adieu, my young friend; I thank you for your sympathy in the name of her who is lost to us."

Trembling as if from some great physical torture, Henri Marsac stumbled down the narrow stairs into the street. What did this cruel being know? What did he suspect? For himself Marsac was absolutely careless; he had but one desire, to return and take his master by the throat, to tell him all, to crush and bruise that mask of a face that hid its owner's secrets so well. But he feared for her. She had always been first in his thoughts—she was so still. A blemish on her name, a rumour spread with malignant skill—it would be a method of revenge too obvious to be neglected by a merciless enemy. For her sake he must be silent.

At the turn of the street he stayed for a moment looking back at the little house where she lay. In the confusion of his thoughts it seemed the bitterest wrong of all—that this man, who for long months had made her life a hopeless misery, could come and go, profaning even her death chamber with his presence, whilst he was a stranger—an intruder—who could be turned from the doors.

The after-glow of the sunset still flushed the horizon as Marsac left the town and walked slowly along the cliffs towards his father's cottage. Presently he halted and sat down on the close smooth turf of the cliff verge, his elbows resting on his knees, his head supported by his clenched fists. Hour after hour slipped by unnoticed, the moon grew out of the darkened heavens, and her silvery beams passed over the sea towards him; a rising wind drew hollow murmurs from the breakers on the rocks beneath. From the distance below the moon, a vast army of clouds gathered on the sky-line and moved majestically upwards towards the zenith, light veils of streaming vapours, the advance guards of the cloud battalions going before. But still Marsac sat motionless, gazing seaward. What had drawn from her that frightful cry, that still haunted his ears? Why had she fallen dead before him? All was confused, inexplicable. He felt as if he had passed into a nightmare land of evil dreams.

At last through the chaos of his thoughts there came a wild desire which grew and mastered him. He would see his dearest love once more; he would see her alone, without the profanation of that man's presence or of the old woman's, his ally. Thus was it only fit that they should say farewell, the last long farewell before the coffin-lid closed down upon her, so sweet and true, and tender. He rose and walked swiftly back along the path towards the town.

It had become a tempestuous night, and the wind drew strange creaks from the old roofs above him as he passed through the narrow streets. Here and there an oil lamp in an ancient bracket flickered madly under the stronger gusts. He saw no one, for the hour was late and the last cabaret had long been shut. He reached the house, and stood gazing up at the narrow curtained windows from which no glimmer of light shone. Her room was in the rear, looking out upon a small straggling garden. He groped his way round the crumbling wall, scaled it, and moved cautiously amongst the neglected flower beds that sprinkled the rough turf. A single bar of yellow light stabbed into the darkness from an upper chamber. It would be from the candles that they had set around her where she lay. Was there also some watcher by the dead? That was a risk he must run. A window ledge, a loose shutter, a strand of ancient ivy gave foot- and finger- hold, and he was standing on a rusty iron balcony that projected from the room.

The lower half of the window was open, and softly clutching the loose curtains he stooped to peer within. But even as he did so there came to his ears a choking laugh—a low malignant chuckle that might have been followed by the clanking of a madman's chains. The sheer horror of it sent Marsac reeling back against the edge of the balcony, as if he had been struck in the face. For a moment he clung there panting, his hand at his throat. A chill crept up his spine and through his hair. And then like the brave man he was, he sprang into the room, her name upon his lips—to the rescue!

The meagre candles were guttering down.

around the white bed, which stood out, a pool of light, in the gloom. Across the white purity of the clothes that covered the body there stretched what at first seem to Marsac a heavy shadow; but even as he watched the shadow moved, it defined itself, it became the head and shoulders of a man, the Professor, Jean Marais. He was on his knees at the further side of the bed, his long arms with bent and clawlike fingers stretched over the body. His distorted face was turned towards the window with an expression of fear mingled with an indescribable ferocity, as of a man surprised in some inhuman deed. But the next moment he had recognised Marsac, had staggered to his feet, and steadying himself against the wall, stood facing the young man.

"What devil's work are you about, Dr. Marais?"

"That, Henri Marsac, is a question I must ask of you."

"And this time you shall have your answer," he cried passionately. "I have come to say farewell to the dead girl who loved me."

"These are strange words."

"But true words, by Heaven. Listen to me, Doctor Marais. If she who lies there could rise from her bed of death, you would see her come to my arms, turning from you as from some foul reptile crawling on the ground."

A gust from the gale without came blustering through the open window; two only of the candles flickered back into light.

"STILL MARSAC SAT MOTIONLESS, GAZING SEAWARD."

The waiting shadows sprang forward blotting out the figure of the Professor; but Marsac could still see the livid face thrust forward, peering at him with a curious significance.

"Do you think I did not know, my candid lover? Do you think I have not marked your skulking and prowling after the forbidden fruit? I too have a secret to tell, perhaps several secrets. What was it, think you, that she saw down there on the rocks? What was it that stopped that false heart of hers? It was I —I, above your head, leaning over to make an end of your pretty lies with a nice clean knife at your neck. Oh! but I have not done with her—or with you. I have my revenge ready to my hand; and such a revenge, one for which a devil might dream."

He threw back his head, and the room of death echoed once more to his laughter. It was grotesque, repulsive, horrible.

"Do you think she hears us now?" he shouted, his mask of indifference gone, the veins ridging his yellow forehead, his hands gesticulating furiously. "Do you think she knows what is in store for her? Do you know that I could make you kneel before me, my handsome Henri, crawl before me, grovel before me, begging for

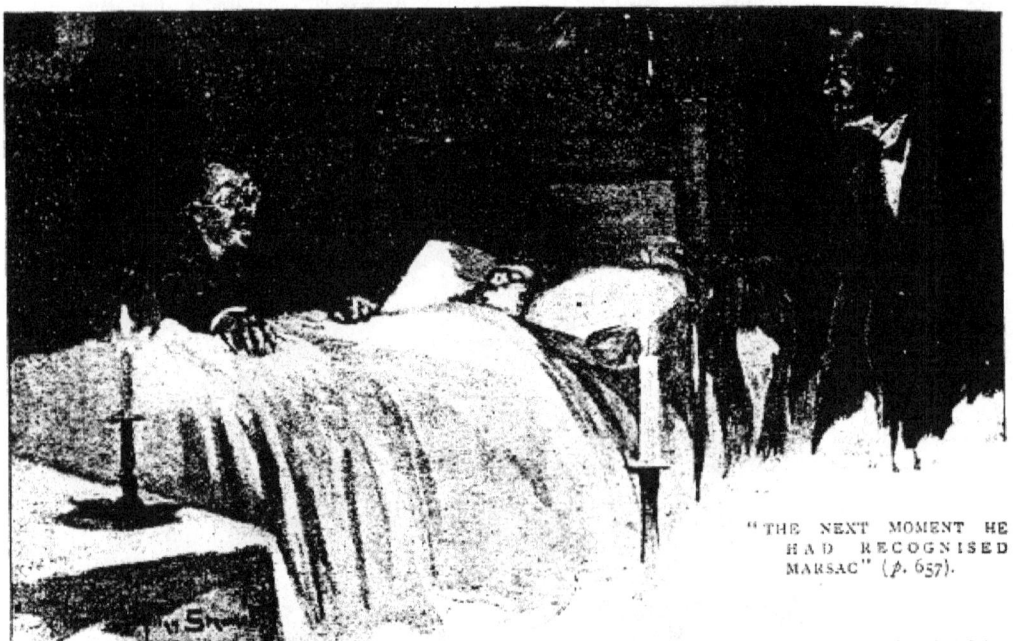

"THE NEXT MOMENT HE HAD RECOGNISED MARSAC" (*p.* 657).

mercy? I, Jean Marais, have the power of life and death, I am omnipotent, I am——"

But Professor Jean Marais did not finish his sentence, at least in an articulate manner. Instead, he started clucking like a hen, pinching his throat the while. He dropped forward on his knees, his distorted face showing an instant over the coverlet of the bed; then he disappeared, and there came a sound of drumming heels on the carpetless floor. But soon that ceased, and all was still.

III.

"IS that you, Marie?"

"Yes, Professor."

"What are you doing there?"

"Nothing, Professor."

"I can see that for myself, old fool; I mean, what are you doing in my room?"

The old woman looked at the ceiling, as if she expected to find an answer there. Receiving no inspiration from its dingy whitewash, she rose slowly with a crackling of silk and approached the bed.

"Marie."

"Yes, Professor."

"Why have you got your best dress on?"

Doctor Marais had raised himself on his elbow, and was peering at his housekeeper with a look of anxiety. He seemed to be struggling to recall, or rather rearrange, his memory.

"I would not go," she said, pulling out a large handkerchief and slowly dabbing at her eyes, "I would not leave my master when he was so ill, even for an afternoon; though there were many neighbours who would have been proud to sit with so celebrated a gentleman."

"But where should you go?"

"Why, to the burying, Professor, the burying of Eugenie Rougon."

The immediate collapse of her master seemed to annoy the old woman. She grumbled her complaints, as she fanned and bathed the pinched, livid face till the eyelids fluttered, and the eyes crept out beneath them.

"Go away."

"But, Professor——"

"If you don't obey, you will leave my service to-morrow."

She went. After all, if he died it was no matter; if he lived he would assuredly carry out his threat should she disobey him. Some women learn sense after careful training.

The character of Jean Marais was not one that lent itself readily to remorse. Indeed, it was totally lacking in that humanity which brings a man into sympathy with the sufferings of his fellows. Yet the facts that now faced him were so peculiarly gruesome that even he shrunk from their realisation. From the first he had known that his hungry passion for Eugenie was not returned; but until ten days before he had not imagined that he had a successful rival. His vague suspicions drawn from chance gossip had finally been crystallised by the successful shadowing of his pupil, Henri Marsac. With a murderous ferocity in his heart, he had crawled over the rocks towards the lovers. But the scream of Eugenie that told him he was discovered also recalled the fact that he was attempting a vulgar crime, for which he would be undoubtedly guillotined. He therefore slipped away, unseen by Marsac, purposing some more finished method of revenge.

He had been pacing his room, sullen and furious, when a servant brought him the amazing news that Eugenie had been carried home dead. He rushed across to the house of Madame Rougon, and made a close examination of the body. It puzzled him. A second examination followed, in which he used the needle test of Floquet, the diaphanous experiment of Richardson, and yet further methods of his own. There was no doubt about it: the girl was still alive!

Criminals are mostly made by chance. To conceal his knowledge as a method of revenge did not at first occur to the Professor, or, if it did, he thrust it behind him. But unfortunately Marsac, who never guessed the true cause of that tragedy on the cliff, did not keep away. Before the eyes of the Professor, as he talked with him, there rose picture after picture wherein was shown the joy of the lovers at their meeting, their kisses and embraces, their cries of delight. He forgot that he had been forcing a marriage on the girl; he only remembered that she had betrayed him, and that Marsac had betrayed him. No, by Heaven, they should not meet again, these two; all believed her dead, and dead she should be. He left the house, the secret still his own.

Late that evening he returned—why, he did not know. All arrangements were in his hands; he could come and go as he pleased. He mounted to the room where she lay. The condition of trance was still more obvious to the expert eye. Even Marsac could notice it—if he were there. He laughed aloud at the thought of what his rival would suffer when he knew—and know he should, some day. Then someone burst into the room—it was the man himself. But it was a different Marsac from the respectful student, a Marsac that taunted him and maddened to a point which almost drew from him an exultant confession of the revenge he was taking. Then a thing undefinable happened—a thing that resulted in his waking two days later in his own bedroom, feeling remarkably weak and ill.

To the logical mind, argued Dr. Marais, the thing was settled. She was in her grave and the matter was at an end. But upon this proposition there sprung a crop of exceptionally unpleasant suggestions that refused to be put aside; again and again he drove away these imaginings, but each time they returned with an added horror of detail. Great heavens! Such thoughts were better suited to the visions of the delirious and insane! It was a vault, not a grave. He was sure of that. Indeed, he remembered that the Rougon vault had been shown him in the little church. She might even yet be alive. Such things had been before.

He crouched upon the bed, staring into the gloom of the gathering night. Pah! how the room smelt. It was like fresh-turned mould; and his night shirt, it clung like a shroud. He must have lights, scores of lights, an illumination. He stretched out his hand for the bell, and started as it touched some cold substance. It was a bottle half full of brandy—there was light enough to see that—and a glass beside it. Dr. Marais was a temperate man, but he filled the glass to the brim, and drank it with quick, eager gulps. He stepped out of bed and tottered across towards his dressing table. The spurt of the match showed him his clothes neatly folded upon a chair. He began to dress himself with trembling fingers.

IV.

"MOREOVER, it is sacrilege," said the sexton, crossing himself.

"It is the accomplice that we must discover," muttered the gendarme, curling his moustache.

"The mystery is how he had the strength to do it," said the at doctor, stooping and replacing a piece of sacking over the face of the thing that lay at their feet.

It was the first dawn, and the wind whispering amongst the trees that fringed the churchyard, blew raw and cold. The sexton glanced at the flush to the east and snuffed out the candle in his horn lantern. The gendarme walked over to the vault, glanced at the stone slab that had been prised aside, and slowly returned. The doctor bit his nails and meditated.

"Yesterday afternoon," he said to the gendarme, "I left Professor Jean Marais in his bed. He was in a state of collapse, following upon a slight seizure, and his mind wandered. This morning at four o'clock I am roused, and brought here to be told that my patient has died, after breaking open a tomb and stealing a body. I should be glad of an explanation."

"Well, doctor, it was the sexton who saw it and ran for me."

"Saw it, saw what?"

The arm of the law turned to the arm of the church.

"Tell the doctor your story," he commanded.

"It must have been about one this morning, Monsieur," said the sexton nervously. "I can't swear to the hour, but it was about then. It was my window that woke me. I hadn't latched it properly, and the wind had unfastened it, and then banged it to, breaking a pane. I slipped out of bed to see to it. My room looks out on the churchyard, and as I was closing the latch I saw a light among the trees. I opened the window again and leant out, listening. Someone was at work there—in the lull between the gusts I could make out the rasp of iron on stone as distinct as might be.

"I was badly scared, but I wasn't going to have such goings-on among my trees. I dressed myself and slipped out of my cottage, nobody knowing—me being a widower these ten years come Easter. I crept in at a side gate and moved cautious like across to where I had noticed the light. What puzzled me was that, now, barring the wind, I couldn't hear or see a thing."

The sexton paused, and, raw morning though it was, wiped off the perspiration with an unsteady hand.

"I had marked the spot from my window, the Rougon vault, where they had the burying yesterday. But the nearer I got to it the less I liked the whole business. If I had had a little holy water, I should have felt more comfortable, for I couldn't help thinking that the devil had got a hand in it. There was a good moon, but with the drifting clouds it wasn't a light you could trust to as a stand-by. And I wanted a good light—I did, indeed.

"I was picking my way amongst the headstones, and peering into the shadows, with half a mind to run for it, when I heard something that seemed to take the heart clean out of me. It was a faint noise of laughing, but not real laughing neither. It came up from somewhere down below my feet like the crackling of thorns under a pot, as the *curé* says. 'What it is,' said I, crossing myself for the black fear that was on me, 'I don't know; but where it is I do know. It's down in the Rougon vault.' And I hardly got the words out when there came a glint from the moon, and I saw that the covering slab had been prised aside—not so difficult a job as it sounds, mark you, for it had been moved yesterday, and the masons were coming to cement it down again this morning.

"The sight of that slab and of a crowbar lying beside it heartened me up a good deal. 'Devils don't use crowbars,' said I, and with that I crept over and peeped down into the vault. Something was crouched on the last of the little flight of steps with a lantern set beside it, and presently it threw back its head, laughing, and I saw that it was a man. I can't tell you what the face was like, Monsieur, though I am not likely to forget it. But if a living man can suffer the pains of hell, that man had them on him then. I couldn't stand it, Monsieur, and just made a bolt of it towards the town, till I ran into Jacques here."

"And what did you do, Jacques?" asked the doctor of the gendarme.

"I sent for Monsieur the doctor, and returned with the sexton to the churchyard. I was not afflicted with fears like him. I drew my sword, and making him —as one accustomed to tombs—bear the lantern in front of me, I followed him into the vault. The coffin of Eugenie Rougon had been broken open, and the body removed. Across it lay the Professor, quite dead. The accomplice—for he must have had one, if not more—had escaped. If Monsieur will pardon me, it is well known that these doctors will stop at nothing to obtain subjects for experiments."

"You can't seriously mean that you suspect the celebrated Professor Marais of common body snatching?"

"I have no doubt about the matter."

The doctor shrugged his shoulders expressively.

"I should stop theorising and get to business if I were you, Jacques. Have you looked for any further clues?"

"It is not necessary to teach me my business," said the gendarme, with an air of offended dignity. "Before you arrived I had made a careful examination. I found a crowbar, a chisel, a hammer, a lantern, and this letter which was clutched in his fingers."

He held out a sealed envelope towards the doctor, who examined it curiously in the light of the sun that peeped up in a warm red glow over the hills to the eastward. There was no address.

"He must have brought it with him," said the doctor. "If he had found it in the coffin he would surely have opened it."

"Unless he died before," suggested the sexton.

"A good idea," said the doctor, breaking the seals.

They gathered round him as he spread out the paper on the slab of a grave. The gendarme did not attempt to conceal his feeling that the doctor had robbed him of an undoubted prerogative. But he made no open complaint. The doctor read aloud:

"I have written this" (the letter ran) "that my cousin, H. S. Marsac, the builder, may not be inconvenienced should this place ever be opened. He knows the facts of the case, and has consented to carry out my wishes. For this I thank him.

"Let it be known, then, that this empty shell stands as the punishment of an act that might well stand alone in the annals of crime. Professor Jean Marais had endeavoured to force into a marriage my wife that is to be, Eugenie Rougon. It is not necessary for me to explain the circumstances further than by saying that the Professor, when asked to pronounce an opinion on the apparent death of this lady, announced that she was certainly dead, though he well knew that she was alive. This he did from motives of revenge, on the discovery that he had in me a successful rival. Later I surprised him by her bedside, and his words aroused in my mind a suspicion of the truth. His sudden illness enabled me to investigate the tests that he had been even then conducting. They showed me he had doubts about her death —that she was alive. On the following day, aided by my cousin, I was able to revive her, and to take her quietly from the house.

"This I did that Professor Marais might imagine, upon his recovery, that he had succeeded in his inhuman design. Whether it is possible for remorse to touch so hard and cruel a heart I do not know. Yet I cannot imagine that a being can exist, who, sooner or later, will not be tormented by the thought of such a crime. But of this I am assured, that if he is not thus punished in this world, he will receive no mercy in the world to come.

"HENRI MARSAC."

The three men straightened themselves and stared at each other.

"A churchyard is not a fit place for these tricks," said the sexton.

"I believe they have almost brought themselves within the law," said the gendarme.

"THE THREE MEN STRAIGHTENED THEMSELVES AND STARED AT EACH OTHER."

THE TRAIL OF THE DEAD:

THE STRANGE EXPERIENCE OF DR. ROBERT HARLAND.

By B. FLETCHER ROBINSON and J. MALCOLM FRASER.*

I.—THE HAIRY CATERPILLAR.

IT is with no intention of delighting the curious that I put my pen to paper. Only at the urgent desire of many members of my own profession have I undertaken a task necessarily disagreeable, and do now recall the details of a case which I take to be without parallel in the records of criminology. In the mental state of the afflicted being there was, indeed, little that was abnormal. Manias that are similar to his fill our asylums. But that laborious studies in the byways of science, rather than in her more frequented paths, had placed at the will of his disordered brain weapons of a deadly potency, transformed a personal misfortune into a great and urgent public danger.

I spent four years at Cambridge, where, though my degree was a high one, I found too many distractions to make such progress as I could have wished in my profession. Yet my interest in medicine grew steadily, and on leaving the University I determined, having both the means and the time at my disposal, to seek out a spot where I could throw myself into my work without the interruptions of old friends and old associations. The high reputation of Heidelberg attracted me, and hither I migrated.

Sufficient for myself. The man who was to be associated with me in my strange quest I will describe with equal brevity. My cousin, Sir Henry Graden, Kt., M.D., F.R.S., F.R.G.S., was a man of remarkable personality—a surgeon of brilliant gifts that had made for him a European reputation, yet an eccentric—or so the world held him—who lacked the steady application necessary for complete success. He would throw himself into the solution of a problem, or the prosecution of a new experiment, with the utmost zeal; yet on achieving the desired result he would shake off the atmosphere of the hospital and laboratory and start on some wild-goose chase that might include the ascent of an unclimbable peak, the capture of a rare species of wild animal, or the study of a little-known tribe of savages. In person he was of great stature, and heavily, almost clumsily, built, with a rugged, weather-beaten face, keen yet kindly grey eyes, and brown hair, somewhat grizzled about the temples. In age he was well past the forties. In dress and deportment he might pardonably have been mistaken for a prosperous Yorkshire grazier. Indeed, he was wont to complain that he acted as a magnet to all the tricksters of London; though, from the shrewd smile with which he accompanied his protests, it was easy to see that he thoroughly enjoyed the diversion of turning the tables on his discreditable opponents.

It was towards the end of my second year at Heidelberg. An autumn sun had sunk to rest in a golden haze over the wooded hills, and the night, luminous under a harvest moon, lay upon the old town. I was sitting at my table, on which a shaded lamp threw its yellow circle, arranging the notes of the lectures I had that day attended, when there came a knock at the door behind me. I cried a sulky invitation, for I feared the appearance of one of my preposterous student friends, with his jargon of the duel and the beerhouse. But the next moment an enormous hand had dragged me into the realisation of my duties as a host by standing me on my feet amid the clatter of a falling chair.

"Why, Cousin Graden!" I cried, for indeed it was he who had thus treated me. "What cyclone has blown you here?"

"Egad! I believe it's the truth I've heard," said he, throwing himself on to a sofa that cracked again under his weight—he was a famed breaker of furniture was cousin Harry Graden. "They told me that you'd shut yourself up for nigh on two years—work, work, work—as if there was no young blood in your veins, and no green world lying around you, with not a yard of it that isn't

---

* Copyright, 1902, by B. Fletcher Robinson and J. Malcolm Fraser, in the United States of America.

worth all the most learned dissertations ever written."

I knew his favourite doctrine. It would have been as foolish to argue with him as to attempt to uphold the necessity for the Union with an Irish Home Ruler.

"But what are you doing here?" I repeated.

"It's to Berlin that I'm bound, to read a paper before a society that is good enough to be interested in some notes I took recently on the Kaffir witch-doctors. I'd a few days in hand, so I thought I would take a peep at my dear Heidelberg and, incidentally, at my worthy cousin, Robert Harland."

He rose and stalked about the room, clucking to himself like a contented hen.

"Same beer jugs and china pipes; same wainscot, a shade darker maybe; same old oak beams, a thought more smoky; same schlägers above the mantelpiece."

He took down one of the student's duelling-swords and slipped his hand into the heavy hilt. Raising his long arm into the orthodox attitude, he swept the keen thin blade in hissing circles.

"Do you ever tramp on the sawdust, and drum with the schläger, and bleed in the tank, Cousin Robert?"

"Not I. Though I have heard of your triumphs in the past, you man of blood!"

"And who has been gossiping?"

"Professor Von Stockmar. He asked me to supper the second day I arrived, for the sole purpose, as I believe, of impressing me with the fame of a certain duelling desperado of a student, one Henry Graden, who flourished in Heidelberg twenty years ago."

"What, Von Stockmar? Little Hermann? What a good fellow he was! Did you ever hear him sing a song about—but, of course, that's not possible. So little Hermann's a professor, is he? Are you under him?"

"No; I am with Professor Marnac."

Graden walked across to the fireplace and slowly filled a huge china pipe that lay thereon. He lit it and, turning his back to the empty grate, sent forth such puffs of smoke that he spoke as from out a cloud, mistily.

"He has made himself a great name, this Marnac. How do you stand with him, Cousin Robert?"

"I don't quite know. I was a great favourite of his in my first year."

"And now? Have you quarrelled?"

"Well, not exactly; it's a foolish story."

"The foolish stories are often of greater interest than the wise ones."

"Well, Cousin Graden," said I, leaning back in my chair and lighting a fresh cigarette, "if you want to hear it, I'll tell it you, and as shortly as may be. It began by the publication some six months ago of Professor Marnac's celebrated book, 'Science and Religion.'"

"Humph! a strong effort, full of suggestions," he grunted; "but brutal, callous, and revolutionary. It had a mixed reception, I believe."

"It had; and nowhere more so than in this University. Von Stockmar followed in by a pamphlet of unsparing criticism, which split the students into two bodies—the Marnac men and the Stockmar men. It was a pretty quarrel, and gave an excuse for a score of the inevitable duels."

"Did Marnac attempt a reprisal?"

"He did, and in the unusual form of reading aloud Von Stockmar's attack upon his theories to the class, of which I am a member. He appealed to us for sympathy. His agitation was remarkable. I declare that he snarled over his opponent's name like a dog over a bone; and a most unpleasant scene ended in a fit, from which we aroused him with difficulty."

"But this does not tell me how you came to be involved," he cried sharply, striding over to the table and plumping himself into a chair facing me.

"Have patience, my impetuous cousin. From the first I had always found a friend in Von Stockmar. I liked him, and we met frequently. The second day after the scene in the lecture-room I was walking with the cheery little man when we chanced upon Marnac. He gave me an ugly look, but said nothing. That night, however, he came to these rooms and abused me roundly. He reminded me of the interest he had shown in my work, called me a traitor to his party, and in other ways behaved with a childish absurdity. Naturally, I refused to give up a valued friend."

"You did right. But surely the affair has blown over?"

"To the contrary, the antagonism—on Marnac's side, at least—has grown still more bitter. Whenever I chance to be present, he misses no opportunity of attacking 'my dear friend,' as he calls Von Stockmar, in the most cruel and vindictive fashion. My position at his lectures is, I assure you, becoming most unendurable."

"You are too sensitive, Cousin Robert. The absurdities of a vain and jealous——"

Graden checked his unfinished sentence

"'We neglect our visitor.'"

with his nose cocked in the air like a gigantic terrier. Surprise and suspicion were in his expression and attitude. Then he rose slowly, as with an effort, and leant forward across the table, his knuckles resting on its edge.

"We neglect our visitor," said he gravely, and at his words I turned sharply in my chair.

In the shadows about the door, yet outlined with sufficient clearness against the black oak of the wainscot, a face stared in upon us. Around the head, crowned with a black skull-cap, fell a thick growth of white hair that was saint-like in length and beauty; the beard was of the like venerable purity. In a man of his apparent age the cheeks were curiously rosy, while the hand that held open the door was small as a woman's and delicate as old ivory. For a moment I thought that the eyes, exaggerated by the convex pebbles of great gold glasses, turned upon me with an expression of malicious satisfaction. Yet this was but an impression, for the gloom hung heavily about him where he stood, and my sight had not been unaffected by nights of study.

"Will not the gentleman step in?" Graden continued, with a reproach at my unhospitality in his voice.

Professor Rudolf Marnac—for it was he who thus honoured us—slid his diminutive figure through the door and advanced, with a courteous inclination, into the lamplight.

"My dear young sir," said he, in the soft musical English with which it was his custom to address me, "I should not have intruded myself at this late hour but that I am the bearer of painful news which I felt it right to communicate to you. Your friend, Hermann Von Stockmar, died this evening of acute inflammation of the lungs."

"Died?" I cried in bewilderment. "Why, I passed him in the street at midday looking well and hearty."

"Yes, it is even so, Mr. Harland. One moment a steady flame illuminating this University with its light; the next, a sigh from the conqueror Death and it is extinguished. The active brain is still; the pen, trenchant, incisive, destructive, is laid aside for ever."

It was an impressive homily; but from so open and vindictive a foe it seemed singularly inappropriate.

"You seem surprised," he continued. "I fear that encounters in the cause of science may have led the public to believe that poor Von Stockmar and I cherished personal animosities. If that is so, I trust you will use your influence to contradict it. My sorrow is already heavy enough—without that unwarrantable suspicion."

The Professor seemed deeply affected. Removing his spectacles, he pulled from his side pocket a large silk pocket-handkerchief. As he did so, a tinkle caught my ear. A square box of some white metal had fallen to the floor. It rolled into the lamplight, where the lid flew open. The Professor hastily clapped on his glasses; but already Graden had retrieved the box and was presenting it to him.

"There was nothing in it, sir," said he, for the Professor had stooped and was examining the carpet minutely.

"I thank you, I thank you."

"Pray do not mention it. Cousin Robert, if you and the Professor will excuse me, I will step across and take a last look at poor little Hermann. Where are his rooms?"

Before I could answer, the Professor was on his feet.

"Pray accept me as your guide," said he, moving towards the door. Graden bowed his thanks like a polite elephant. I followed the pair down the stairs.

It was growing late, and the narrow streets of the students' quarter were well-nigh deserted. A moon, like a polished shield, hung over the old castle above us, picking out each turret and parapet in silver grey against the sleeping woods that swept upward to the sky-line. Across our path the gabled house cast broad, fantastic pools of shadow. A wind had risen with the moon, and sighed and quivered in the roofs and archways. Once, from a distant beerhouse, came the faint mutter of a rousing chorus, but soon it was swallowed and carried away by the midnight breezes.

We had not far to walk, and in five minutes the Professor was tapping discreetly with an ugly devil-face of a knocker on Von Stockmar's door. Presently the bolt was drawn, and Hans, the grey-bearded servant of the dead man, stood in the doorway, a lamp held high above his head. He blinked upon us moodily, with eyes dimmed by old age and recent tears, till, catching sight of Graden's huge bulk, he stepped forward with a snort of surprise, flashing the light in his face as he did so.

"By Heavens! but it is Heinrich der Grosse!" he stammered. "Ach! Herr Heinrich, but have you forgotten Hans of the Schlägers, servant of the honourable corps of the Saxo Borusen?"

THE HAIRY CATERPILLAR.

"No, no," said Graden, shaking the veteran by the hand. "So our little Hermann took you for his servant, as he promised? This is a sad day for us both, old friend. Tell me, how did it happen?"

"Do not ask me, Herr Heinrich. My mind wanders—I, who served him nigh on twenty years and was as a father and mother to him."

The worthy fellow put down the lamp in the little hall into which he had led us, and mopped his eyes with a hand that trembled with emotion.

But Graden persisted in his quiet way and soon extracted the details. It seemed that it was the custom of the dead Professor to take a nap after his midday meal. That afternoon, however, his sleep was unduly prolonged, and at four Hans, who knew he had an engagement about that hour, slipped in to wake him. His master was lying on the couch in his bedroom, where he was wont to take his siesta. But he was in a curious, huddled position and breathing stertorously. Hans failed to rouse him, became alarmed, and hurried off for a neighbouring doctor. That gentleman diagnosed the case as a sudden

"With a swift sideways turn of the head, he caught sight of our faces in the doorway."

and severe chill which had settled on the lungs, causing violent inflammation. Everything possible was done, but by eight he was dead. Beyond the remarkable violence of the seizure, the doctor had said, there was nothing unusual in the symptoms. Overwork had doubtless undermined the constitution and rendered it vulnerable to a sudden attack.

"And while he was asleep — had he visitors?" asked Grayden.

"The street-door is never locked during the day."

"But would you not have heard the steps?"

"It was my custom to sleep, too. Herr Professor allowed it."

"So. I should like to take a last look at your poor master, friend Hans. By the way, Cousin Robert, where is our guide, the learned Marnac? I did not see him leave the house."

"Perhaps the Professor Marnac has already gone to my master's room, the second to the right on the first floor," suggested the old servant.

In two strides my cousin was on the steep and narrow stairs. For a man of his age and size he mounted them with a surprising activity. Indeed, when I gained the landing he was already standing at the door of the room. He held up his hand with a warning gesture. I stepped up to him softly and peeped over his shoulder.

By the side of an old sofa placed against the wall of a room, half bed-chamber, half study, Professor Marnac crouched on his hands and knees. A lamp stood on the floor at his elbow. He was working with feverish haste, yet with a certain method, moving the lamp onward as his examination of the section lit by its immediate rays was completed. It was an odd sight, this silver-haired figure that crept about, peeping and peering, like some species of elderly ape. So absorbed was he that it was nigh on a minute before, with a swift sideways turn of the head, he caught sight of our faces in the doorway and rose to his feet.

"I can find no trace of it," said he, smoothing back his hair with a sigh. "It is excessively annoying."

"Of what, may I ask, sir?" I queried.

"Of my signet-ring, Mr. Harland. A valued possession which I would not lose for fifty pounds."

"Pray let me assist you," said I, stepping forward and raising the lamp, which the Professor had replaced on the table.

"No, no, Mr. Harland. Enough has been done; in the presence of death we must forget such trivialities. Besides, although it was on my finger when I entered the house, it may have been dropped in the hall or on the stairs. I do not doubt that Hans will find it."

The Professor spoke in so resolute a fashion that politeness did not demand that I should press the matter. My cousin had already passed behind a great screen of stamped leather that cut off the bed from the rest of the apartment. Marnac had stepped after him, and I, though at a slower pace, followed them. To be honest, the events of the evening had disturbed me not a little. I had grown suspicious, uneasy; and this annoyed me in that I was without reasonable cause for such a frame of mind. Granted that the Professor had displayed oddities of demeanour, yet he was notoriously an eccentric. And if my cousin had become taciturn, if his politeness rang insincerely, the death of his old friend——

"Stand back, Herr Professor! stand back, I say!"

It was Graden's voice, stern and decisive. I sprang to the corner of the screen and peered into the darkened alcove beyond.

Upon his death-bed pillows the calm and simple face of poor Von Stockmar gleamed like a mask carved in white marble. But neither of the two men who confronted each other across the body looked upon it. Graden, a grim and resolute figure, stood holding a common wooden match-box in his huge hands. He had opened it carelessly, for cheap sulphur matches were scattered on the sheet before him. Marnac's face I could not see, but in the pose of his back and shoulders there was something feline—something suggestive of an animal about to spring.

For a second or two the three of us stood in silence. My cousin was the first to break it.

"Pray do not let us detain you, Professor Marnac," said he. "Should we chance upon your ring, believe me, it will be safe."

The Professor straightened himself with a little gesture of submission and stepped back into the lamplight. His hand was on the latch, when he turned upon us—for we had followed him—with a face deformed with the most malignant fury.

"*Au revoir*, my friends," he cried. "I wish you a pleasant evening."

And then a fit of laughter took him— smothered, diabolical merriment that broke out in oily chuckles like water gurgling from a bottle. The door closed upon it. We stood listening as it grew fainter, fainter, until it died away in silence on the lower stairs.

"Turn the key, Cousin Robert. But, no; after him, lad, and bolt him out of the house. He'll be burning it down, else."

Graden was inexplicable; but I ran to

obey. As I reached the hall, I heard the clang of the street door and the squeaking of the bolts as Hans shot them behind the departing visitor.

When I re-entered the room, I found the screen pushed back against the wall, and my cousin, in his shirt-sleeves, leaning over the bed. He barked at me over his shoulder to sit down and keep quiet, and I humbly obeyed him. Once or twice he turned to the lamp which he had at his elbow, and I caught the glimpse of a magnifying-glass.

his head sunk forward, his eyes on the floor. I watched him expectantly.

"It's a great gift, is observation," he began. "It makes just the difference between mediocrity and success in game-hunters and novel-writers, in painters of pictures and explorers of the unknown lands, where a man has never a map to help him. And this same trick of observation has given me some very remarkable results this evening; and how remarkable you will realise when I set them out in proper order. You've a

"A round, fluffy ball rolled out and lay motionless."

Presently he rose, and, carrying the lamp in his hand, commenced a circuit of the room, lingering now and again to examine some object. At the dressing-table he paused for several minutes, using the magnifying-glass repeatedly. But shortly afterwards he threw himself into a chair beside me with the air of a man whose work is done.

"It's no disrespect to our little Hermann that I mean," said he, pulling out a big briar, "but smoke I must."

He sat there puffing for a minute or two,

logical head, Cousin Robert, and I want you to give me your fullest attention. Contradict me if I overstate the case.

"Fact the first: That a certain celebrated scientist, Rudolf Marnac, had an ill feeling —a very ill and evil feeling—towards a certain brother-professor, one Hermann Von Stockmar. Fact the second: That Von Stockmar died suddenly."

"Of a natural cause, as certified by a competent physician," I added quickly.

"Exactly. Fact the third: Marnac, who

considers you a deserter to the Stockmar camp—as, indeed, I gather from your own story—appears in your rooms to inform you of the sudden death of his enemy. Now, why should he do that?"

"He is an eccentric. A sudden whim, perhaps. We were very intimate once, you must remember."

"Though hardly so now, from his manner of regarding you when he first announced himself this evening."

"He might have caught what we were saying. Listeners hear no good of themselves, but that does not tend to improve their tempers."

"Well, let that pass. It brings us to fact number four: He tells a deliberate lie."

"A lie! But when?"

"The man was worth studying. When I first saw him this evening, I ran my eye over him. I especially noticed his hands—their suppleness, their delicate colour, their long, prehensile fingers. I do not doubt that he is very proud of them. He wore no ring —it is not the custom of those who deal with germs to so adorn themselves. What was he looking for so anxiously in this room, if it were not a ring? Why did he leave us in the hall that he might conduct this search before our presence disturbed him?"

"I cannot suggest an explanation; but really, Cousin Graden, you seem to be weaving a most unnecessary tangle. I cannot imagine what result you expect to obtain."

"A conviction for murder."

I stared at him in the most profound amazement.

"Yes, murder, Cousin Robert; as deliberate and cold-blooded a doing to death of an innocent man as has ever befouled a corner of God's fair world."

He rose from his chair and ploughed heavily up and down the room. The veins started in his forehead; his huge hands knotted themselves tensely.

"Listen. This afternoon a man lay asleep on that couch in the corner. We know the manner of man—a keen investigator, an indefatigable worker, an honest fighter; but one who had never done in all his life a mean or ignoble action. There comes a creak upon the stairs, the door is opened softly, a head peers in. He—the murderer—enters the room. He knew the custom of the house in this warm September weather: the doors open, the old servant asleep, the master taking his regular siesta. How far is he a criminal, how far a lunatic? Is this act premeditated, or the sudden tempting of opportunity? Who can say? It is enough that in his diseased imagination he has come to regard the sleeper as an enemy who maliciously set himself to destroy his theories and to bring ridicule on the laborious work of years. His desire for revenge against his critics at home and abroad is concentrated on the man before him.

"How the THING came into his possession I cannot guess, though that should be a point easily discovered. He himself may have obtained it from Africa, or it may have come into his hands by chance, as the chief of the Entomological Museum. But he has it safe enough, shut up in the tin box which fell from his pocket in your rooms. The spring of the lid was defective, you may remember; it is that same defective spring that will hang him.

"He stands over there, listening and watching. There is no sound; the sleeper will not wake. He opens the case upon the dressing-table and lifts the THING with tweezers — for every hair of it has its poison. With scissors he cuts off some score of hairs, catching them in the crease of a folded sheet of notepaper. He replaces it in the case and closes the lid. Like an ugly shadow he flits across to the couch, kneels by its side, and one, two, three times blows the hairs from the creased paper across the intake of the sleeper's breath. He turns, snatches up the case from the table, and is gone. In five hours Professor Von Stockmar is dead of inflammation of the lungs. There is not a doctor in all Germany who would challenge that diagnosis. In nine hours Professor Rudolf Marnac is accused by me, Henry Graden, of murder."

"But this deadly THING!" I cried, with a sinking horror at my heart. "This beast, reptile, insect—what is it? Where is it now?"

For answer he thrust his fingers into his pocket and drew out the same wooden match-box that I had seen him with by the bedside of the dead man. He slid it half open and tapped it sideways on the table under the lamp. A round, fluffy ball rolled out and lay motionless. Suddenly a little black head protruded, a score of tiny feet paddled into motion, and across the table there crept a hairy caterpillar—a loathsome, disreputable object, for across its back lay a ragged scar, where the hairs had been shorn away.

"Do you recognise the species?"

In a faint-hearted way I leaned across to grasp it, but with a sudden motion he brushed my hand aside.

"I see you do not," said he grimly. "It is common enough in South Africa."

With the end of a match he carefully pushed the insect back into the box, and replaced it in his pocket.

"The luck was against Marnac," he continued. "Not for one moment do I suggest that otherwise I should have suspected the truth. To begin with, the defective spring of the case allowed the caterpillar to escape while he was bending over poor Hermann. After he had done his devil's work he slipped it back hastily into his pocket. He never realised what had occurred until, upon accidentally pulling it out with his handkerchief in your lodgings, he found it empty. It was for that reason he accompanied us here, for that reason he searched so anxiously. What became of it did not matter so long as it was not found in this room; though, as a matter of fact, there was very small danger, even then, of it affording a clue.

"And now we come to a stroke of abominable ill-luck, of which Marnac has every right to complain. I found the caterpillar on the sheet of the bed, where it had crawled in its wanderings. But that was not the worst of it, for I happened to be the one man in all Heidelberg who knew of its peculiar properties; who knew that its hairs are slightly poisoned, sufficient indeed to raise a nasty rash on the hand; who knew that the old-time Hottentots employed it for removing their enemies by blowing the hairs into their lungs. I took out a match-box, emptied it, and collected the caterpillar. I was closing the box when I looked up and saw Marnac watching me with a shocking expression, which could scarcely have distorted the face of a perfectly sane man, however provoked. Nearly every murderer has a screw loose somewhere; but, in my opinion, Marnac is in an unusually bad way. It may turn out more of an asylum than a gallows business, after all."

"But the details of the scene you picture; how did you obtain them?"

"I am a quick thinker, and the events of the evening began to arrange themselves in a sort of sequence, crowned by the discovery of the caterpillar. The inference to be gathered from them was obvious. I examined the nostrils of the dead man, and found four of the caterpillar hairs caught therein. On the dressing-table lay an ordinary pair of nail-scissors. Two hairs were jammed where the blades met. On the creased sheet of paper, which I found behind the couch, there was no sign; but the use to which it had been put was plain. From Hans I knew the custom of the house: the sleep after the midday meal, the open doors, the opportunity. Is the matter plain to you?"

"What are you going to do?" It was all that I could say.

"Nothing to-night. To appear at a German police-station at this hour with such an extraordinary story would be—for two foreigners, at least—the height of absurdity. Besides, there is no hurry; Marnac won't budge. He'll sit it out, never fear."

One o'clock clanged out from the steeples as I bade good-night to Graden at the door of my lodgings. He had already secured a room in a neighbouring hotel.

"Have you a lock on your bedroom door?" said he.

"I believe so."

"Well, use it to-night. We've an ugly customer to deal with; and the worst of it is that, unless I am much mistaken, he knows how much we know."

I watched him as he rolled away, a gigantic figure in the moonlight, waving the thick stick he carried. Never had my stairs seemed so uncomfortably dark, never had they creaked behind me so mysteriously. It was with a sigh of relief that I gained my room and by a quick glance assured myself that I was alone.

It seemed that I had only just dropped off into dreamland—for, indeed, sleep had been hard to woo that night—when a knocking at my door brought me from my bed. I unlocked and opened it. Cousin Graden filled the foreground.

"I didn't think he'd throw up the sponge," said he. "But he has, none the less. Marnac has bolted!"

"And you?"

"I shall follow."

So commenced those strange wanderings which I shall entitle "The Trail of the Dead."

THE TRAIL OF THE DEAD:

THE STRANGE EXPERIENCE OF DR. ROBERT HARLAND.

BY B. FLETCHER ROBINSON AND J. MALCOLM FRASER.*

II.—THE MYSTERY OF THE LEMSDORF HAM.

HOW Rudolf Marnac, the venerable savant, brought about the death of his rival and critic, Professor Von Stockmar, of Heidelberg University, I have already explained. I have, moreover, related the accident by which my cousin, Sir Henry Graden, the famous explorer and scientist, chanced to be visiting me, a student of medicine at the German University; and I have endeavoured to outline the steps by which the baronet arrived at the discovery of the crime that had been committed. I have now to tell of the pursuit of Marnac, the murderer, a pursuit as strange in its outset as it was terrible in its conclusion. For this, the first adventure in the chase of this inhuman monster, it may be said that I have chosen a fanciful title. Yet "The Mystery of the Lemsdorf Ham" is too appropriate to be neglected for that reason.

At the first the Heidelberg police met our theory of Von Stockmar's death with incredulity. When they moved in earnest, it was too late; all trace of Professor Marnac had been lost. It was discovered that he had taken from his rooms a small travelling valise and a considerable sum in ready money; but beyond these facts nothing was known; even his manner of leaving Heidelberg was a mystery.

For myself, the weeks that followed were in every respect intolerable. From a peaceful student I found myself transformed into a secret ally of the police, an unhappy being whose privacy was liable to be disturbed at all hours by some inquisitive official. Even worse, the authorities had detained my cousin, and those who are intimates of Sir Henry Graden will understand that I suffered at his hands. In the capture of the murderer—as we knew Marnac to be—he took a passionate interest. He was for ever in my rooms, denouncing the authorities for their delay, advancing theories, or cursing his own inaction. The lieutenant in charge of the Heidelberg police went in absolute terror of the Englishman, and, indeed, refused all interviews in which he was not adequately protected by his satellites.

On a calm October morning I was sitting reading by my window, thankful of the momentary quiet I enjoyed, when the door burst open and my cousin came frolicking into the room. I admit the absurdity of the expression when applied to a middle-aged giant of sixteen stone; but frolicking describes it. Without a word of apology he seized my book, a new edition of Smallwood's "Digestive Organs of Molluscs," and flung it into the fireplace. It was too much.

"Henry Graden," said I, starting up indignantly, "you are my cousin, but you presume on that relationship. These schoolboy antics are insupportable."

"Capital, Robert! capital!" he answered, regarding me with a comical expression. "By Gad! there's stuff in the boy! You'd like to punch my head, I suppose?"

I was somewhat ashamed of my outburst, and picked up the book, which was greatly damaged, before I replied.

"It's all very well, cousin Graden," I said, sulkily enough. "But between you and the police, I am worried to death."

"Good! Then you can have no objection to leaving Heidelberg this afternoon."

"Leave Heidelberg? Why should I leave Heidelberg?"

He strode over to where I stood and laid his great hand on my shoulder with a touch that implied an apology.

"A schoolboy you called me just now. That's just what I am, a schoolboy let loose in the playground. The police have raised their embargo. An address which will bring me when they have need of my evidence—that is all they ask. Now, I want a travelling companion—a man I can trust. You can guess my errand, Cousin Robert. Before a week is out I shall have my hand on him, I shall, by Heaven! You will come

---

* Copyright, 1902, by B. Fletcher Robinson and J. Malcolm Fraser, in the United States of America.

with me? Good lad, I knew it. The train leaves at three. I'll call for you."

"But where are we going?" I shouted, running to the door; for already he was down a score of stairs.

"St. Petersburg. You have a passport?"

"Yes—but Cousin Graden, Cousin Graden, I say——"

It was no use. I heard the street door slam behind him. St. Petersburg—and the winter coming on. Eugh! I had always detested cold. But next to escaping misfortune it is best to possess a philosophic mind. I commenced to pack my bag with my warmest underwear.

At thirty-five minutes past two, Graden sent up word to say that he had a cab waiting my pleasure, and in three minutes more my luggage was upon it. Half-way down the main street we chanced upon Mossel, the fat lieutenant of police. He glanced at us keenly with, as I thought, a certain suspicion. Graden saluted him coldly, muttering maledictions upon him for a stupid ass. There was no great friendship between the two. I paid the cab while my cousin saw to the tickets. Five marks provided us with a subservient guard and an empty carriage.

"And what are your plans for this intolerable Petersburg expedition?" I asked, as the train thumped its way out of the station.

"We are not going to St. Petersburg. We are going to Lemsdorf."

"To Lemsdorf! I have never heard of the place."

"No more had I an hour ago. Allow me to discover it."

He pulled a red-bound Baedeker out of his pocket and fluttered through the pages.

"Here we have it—'Lemsdorf: fourteen to fifteen hours from Berlin. Rising town in West Prussia. 12,000 inhabitants. Large dye-works. 'Prinz von Preussen,' 'Goldner Adler' hotels well spoken of. Cab from the station, 75 pg. Little of historical interest. Excursions to Denker and the Huren, a wild and desolate district with several large lakes, on the Russian frontier.' Not altogether an inviting prospect at the latter end of October, eh, Cousin Robert?"

"I did not imagine we were going there for pleasure."

"Pessimist! Do neither the 'Prinz von Prussen' nor the 'Goldner Adler,' 'well spoken of,' as Baedeker describes these hostelries, attract you? Then the dye-works, they are sure to be interesting."

"Henry Graden," cried I with determination, "you try me too far! I am as eager as yourself that this criminal should be brought to justice. For this reason alone I have every right to know the why and wherefore of an expedition which will entail upon me, as I see clearly, the most extraordinary discomforts."

"It seems a pity, my dear cousin, that Nature, which endowed you with so many admirable qualities, should have omitted the saving grace of humour," he rejoined. And then changing his tone to a greater sobriety: "You shall hear all that I know or conjecture. It will, at least, help us on our journey.

"First, as to the facts at my disposal. For myself, I had heard much of Rudolf Marnac, but only as a Heidelberg professor of distinction, whose stupendous effort, 'Science and Belief,' had set educated Europe by the ears. From you I learnt of his quarrel with Von Stockmar, a quarrel originating in the latter's attack on the work in question, of which Marnac was inordinately vain. Then came the chain of facts that proved—to our mind, at least—that Marnac had murdered his colleague with a diabolical ingenuity. Could such a crime be inspired by a quarrel so trifling? It was almost past belief. Further evidence was necessary; and this evidence the investigations of the police have supplied.

"When I learnt that his father, Jean Marnac, had died in a Paris asylum, I began to see my way. But it was the statements of his servants that cleared my last doubt. An eccentricity which at one time amused them had of late been changed to a violence that filled them with terror. He had presented them with copies of the book, elaborately bound. A housekeeper who had served him for twenty years was loaded with abuse and discharged because the old creature admitted that she could not follow his arguments. He was the victim of a partial mania. Such cases are not uncommon.

"Whither had this dangerous creature fled? It seemed a mystery insoluble. He was well provided with money; on all topics but one he was admirably sensible. The police admitted that he had beaten them. But only yesterday I obtained a clue. It may be valueless; but for myself, I think otherwise. At least it is worth the journey I am asking you to make in my company.

"At my urgent request the police admitted me to his rooms. His papers they had already examined, without result. I found that he possessed a fine library. I am a book-lover, and my first step was to examine it. Tucked away in a corner of a shelf, yet within easy reach of his customary chair, I found a volume. It was typical of the man that it should be elegantly bound. Within were collected the hostile criticisms with which his book had been loaded. The more severe were scribbled over with the vilest epithets. Von Stockmar was personally threatened, as was also a certain Mechersky, a professor of the Imperial University at Petersburg. I abstracted the volume. You may like to examine it."

He drew it from the capacious pocket of his travelling ulster and gave it to me. The cover was of the choicest morocco; upon it, in gold, were emblazoned the arms of the University. It was a triumph of the binder's art, yet I handled it with a singular feeling of disgust.

The interior was oddly divided. The greater part consisted of clippings from papers and magazines, neatly gummed upon blank pages. But here and there were interpolated pamphlets, held in their place by elastic bands. In contrast with this orderly arrangement, scarcely a page but was defaced by pencilled remarks, satirical or abusive. I ran through them hastily until I came upon the article which bore Mechersky's name, extracted apparently from some French review. Its severity seemed to have lashed Marnac to fury. It was covered with a maze of pencillings. But my attention was soon centred on a portion of the text which, being underlined in red, stood out from the page with some prominence. "The author of 'Science and Belief,'" for thus it ran, "seems to have lost touch with humanity. His deductions might be correct if men were bloodless, merciless automatons. He regards them as might some reptile—let us say, a toad scientifically inclined." Across this criticism, which seemed to me unnecessarily severe, was written in German: "Infamous scoundrel! Would that I might crush you like a toad!"

"A curious wish," I said, pointing to the passage.

"And from Marnac a most dangerous one," he answered. "I can only hope we shall reach Lemsdorf in time."

"Lemsdorf again! And why Lemsdorf?"

"For the excellent reason, Cousin Robert, that Mechersky, who comes of land-owning Polish stock, is holiday-making at Castle Oster, a place he has in that neighbourhood. And as sure as I sit here, where Mechersky is, there will be that madman, Rudolf Marnac. If he means to murder the man, he will have had nigh on a month to bring it off. Heaven grant that we're in time!"

The tone in which he spoke thrilled me with a dreadful anxiety. The danger was

"There was no one visible."

indefinable; but fear draws its darkest terrors from the unknown.

"One thing more," I said. "How did you discover Mechersky's whereabouts?"

"I had thought him at St. Petersburg; but a wire to a friend there gave me the information I required."

I have neither the necessity nor the inclination to dwell on that journey. It was very late when we rolled into the station of the good town of Leipsic, where we spent the night at a convenient hotel. Yet it was at an early hour that Graden roused me from a tired sleep to catch the Posen express. The country through which we now journeyed was of a melancholy similitude, and the broad plains, though reasonably cultivated, affected me with a mental depression which the cheery efforts of my companion could not conquer. The day was drawing to its close as we reached Posen and passed through that fortress city into a land of desolation. Gloomy pine woods, great lakes on which the dying sun threw patches of ruddy gold, forlorn heaths and swamps that, as I imagined, could scarce be equalled for sheer dismalness of aspect, slid by us in a never-ending chain. Save for the Eastern sky, glorified by the fiery sunset, the heavens were obscured by ponderous clouds of muddy grey that foretell the first snow of winter. Darkness had fallen when we changed carriages at a junction; but it was close upon midnight before my cousin, who had been sitting with a Continental Bradshaw on his knees, thrust his head out of the window and cried that the lights of Lemsdorf were in sight. Our luggage was piled upon an antiquated cab, and in ten minutes more the host of the "Goldner Adler," a thin, handsome Pole, was bowing a stately welcome to his guests. Supper—and then to bed.

The room assigned me was an oak-panelled apartment of considerable size, and the single candle with which I was provided seemed only to deepen the lurking shadows round the walls. The huge china stove failed to warm a place so thoroughly ventilated by draughts. At another time the cause of our journey, combined with the uncanny nature of these surroundings, might have acted on my nerves. But I was too weary, too angry with my present discomfort, to give opportunity to fanciful terrors. The bed was small, and in all probability damp. I took off my coat, rolled myself in a thick travelling rug, heaped the clothes upon me, and blowing out the candle I had placed on a table at my elbow, lay down to sleep.

How long I may have slept I cannot say, but I was awakened by a sudden flash of light that struck like a blow through the darkness. For a score of seconds, it may have been, I lay motionless. The room was in utter darkness and silence. Then I heard a footfall, a creaking of a door. I sprang from my bed, only to trip and fall heavily over the rug which I had carried with me. I groped for the table, found it, and lit the candle, crouching, half expectant of some attack when I should reveal myself. I looked keenly about me—the room was empty.

But I had had a visitor, for the door was still ajar. I ran to it and, shading the light with my hand, peered down the passage. There was no one visible. I returned to the room, this time locking the door securely. Perhaps, after all, I reasoned, there had been no cause for my alarm. Some fellow-guest might have mistaken his chamber, retiring quickly on discovering his error. This argument heartened me, for, to be honest, I was shaken not a little. I examined the room carefully, without result; and then, after a composing cigarette, slipped back into bed, leaving the candle burning in the centre of the room.

It snowed that night, and to some effect, as the morning light showed me. The broad, slovenly street beneath my window was thickly coated; and though the fall had ceased, a dull sky, streaked as with muddy whitewash, threatened a further downfall. It was bitterly cold, and I flung on my clothes in a vile temper.

Graden was meditating before the stove when I entered our breakfast-room, with the strange book he had shown me during the journey in his hands.

"You look pale as a ghost. Are you quite fit?" he asked kindly.

"Oh, yes; though my night was not particularly peaceful."

"What do you mean?"

I told him briefly of my unknown visitor. He seemed greatly interested, questioning me minutely on various points.

"Your theory may be correct," he concluded. "Some guest may have mistaken his chamber and hurried off on discovering his mistake. Yet, if he had a light with him, how came he to make such an obvious error; whereas, if it was the striking of a match that roused you, what was the man doing wandering in the dark?"

"To tell the truth, when I first woke, I imagined it was Marnac himself."

"I have considered that point. I do not think it could have been he."

"And why?"

"Before you were down this morning I had a talk with our landlord. The guests at his house are of two classes—commercial travellers and those having business at the dye-works. They do not stay long—usually a week at most. Of the nine which he now has, none has exceeded that limit. He knows them all personally—six commercials, two dye-works men, and a rich Englishman, one George Wakefield, who has been staying with some magnate in the neighbourhood. But here is Herr Reski himself."

"Gentlemen," said the landlord, bowing low, "your sleigh is at the door."

"How far is it, then, to Castle Oster?" I asked him.

"Close on twenty miles; and with this fresh snow it will be heavy going."

Ten minutes later we slid on our silent runners, to the tinkle of the bells, out through

"'Gentlemen,' said the landlord, bowing low, 'your sleigh is at the door.'"

the squalid, sprawling town, out through the wooden hovels of the suburbs, out past the dye-works, with their tall, melancholy chimneys, out into the snow-clad levels beyond, and there from out of the east there sprang upon us a great and bitter wind, chilled by its long journey over the boundless steppes of frozen Russia. Here and there, across the plains, a whiff of powdery snow, like the smoke of heavy guns, would leap up before the fiercer blasts, only to burst and fall as they lulled once more. To the south and east the pine-woods ranged their formal ranks, black against the dazzling carpet at their feet. It was a scene of utter desolation.

We drove in silence. Graden sat in a huddled mass, his chin buried in the great woollen comforter he wore, staring out over the plain with fixed, introspective eyes. For myself, I sat amongst the rugs beside him in vague speculation. What could be this danger that threatened the scientist from St. Petersburg in his home at Castle Oster? After all, might not our whole journey be a folly born of Graden's imaginings, a blind guess that had dragged us half across Europe? I shivered, and shivering, muttered anathemas on the climate.

We entered the forest. On every hand stood the pines, stretching away in long, melancholy avenues floored with drifted snow. The laden branches bowed before us, now and again, at the whirl of a passing gust, flinging their burdens from them. Once a willow grouse, white as the snow beneath it, swept on steady wing through the trees. Once from the far, far distance, borne upon the eastern breeze, there came a cry, a weird, hopeless echo in the air, that set the horses snorting. I knew what it must be—a wolf who felt the first pangs of the winter's hunger gathering round him. But there was no sign of man nor marks of sleigh tracks on the newly fallen snow.

We did not travel fast, though our driver did his best. The snow had not hardened and settled into that enchanting surface on which the runners speed so swiftly. Midday was past before we saw, through a sudden gap in the forest, a rising mound crowned with a low, grey building. "Castle Oster!" cried our driver, turning in his seat to claim our attention. In ten minutes more we had halted at a gate set in a high stone wall.

Before we were clear of our rugs the driver had slipped from his perch and tugged at a rusty iron bell-pull. We waited without an answer. Again he rang; but Graden did not wait the result. The door was not bolted; it opened to his vigorous arm, and we followed him into the broad courtyard of the Castle.

Before us sprawled the main building, flanked by little towers, like the pepper-box turrets of an old Scotch mansion. The windows were shuttered; the chimneys were smokeless save for one above the central porch, from which a dark plume rose and trailed away to the westward—the solitary sign of habitation. To our right and left were ranged outbuildings, stables, coach-houses, and the like; but all in a condition of ruinous decay. Patches fallen from the roofs laid bare the rafters; from the broken gutters trailed long pendants of ice. Against the old doors the snow had piled itself in heavy drifts. No sound broke the brooding stillness. It was a picture distressingly forlorn.

"Has Professor Mechersky, then, no servants?" asked Graden of our driver. I noticed that he hushed his voice in speaking; he, too, felt the uncanny influence of the place.

"Two, mein Herr—a man and a woman. I cannot think where they can be."

"I had understood he was a man of means. Why does he allow this disrepair?"

"I do not think the Professor cares. He shuts himself up with his experiments, when he is here—which is not often now. His rooms look to the south on the other side. For the rest, the house is not furnished."

"Well, I suppose there is a servant who will—— Heavens! what is that?"

From somewhere within the house there came a shriek, a cry of supreme terror. Again and yet again it was repeated before it shrank away into silence. Graden ran across the court to the main door, and I was hard upon his heels. He pulled the bell and hammered fiercely upon the heavy oak panels; but no one answered.

"I don't believe the thing is bolted," said he. "Keep the handle turned, and let me try what I can do."

He stepped back a dozen paces, and then came running at the door like a bull. The giant caught it squarely with the point of his shoulder; there was a sharp crack; the next instant we were both sprawling on the floor within.

We found ourselves in a great and dusty hall, indifferently lighted. Against the wall on my right I could dimly discern the figure of a woman crouched on the floor, sobbing bitterly, her face buried in her hands. She did not move, despite our violent entrance. At the foot of the main staircase an old man was bending over a something that lay motionless. He looked up at us with a white, pitiful face.

"He is dead—the master is dead!" he whimpered.

Graden strode up to him, and I followed at his heels.

Professor Peter Mechersky—for such I knew it must be—lay huddled under an old grey cloak that spread wing-wise from his neck, a blot upon the polished oak of the floor. From his face, thin though it was and wasted with disease, he must have been a middle-aged man who had preserved a singular beauty. He had died as a child might fall asleep. Yet the horror that he had escaped he had left to the living; for his attitude was abnormal, impossible, and ghastly to behold.

It was not right that a body should resemble an egg that is broken.

My cousin swept aside the cloak for a moment, and replaced it reverently, though with a hand that trembled.

"He has not a sound bone in his body," he muttered, and then, turning to the old servant, "How did this happen?" said he.

"He had been ill for some weeks, mein Herr, and we begged him not to leave his room. But to-day he declared himself better; he insisted that he should descend to the library. Half way down the stairs he tripped and fell. I ran to his side and found him, as you see him, crouched—like—like——"

"Like a toad?"

"Yes, mein Herr, like a toad."

The man broke into hysterical weeping. Graden searched in his pocket, produced a flask of brandy, and prescribed a liberal dose. He seemed to revive under its influence.

"The Englishman, Herr Wakefield, was most anxious about my master's health," he stammered out. "The Herr Professor became indisposed some ten days after his arrival; since then he has been most kind, most considerate, sitting by the master's bed for hours. He would allow no other doctor to visit the master. He is a kind, good man, this doctor, the Herr Wakefield."

"So I believe. How came he to know your master?"

"I am not sure; but I think he brought a letter of introduction from a Professor Marnac, of Heidelberg, a gentleman of whom my master disapproved, yet admired for his learning."

"And this Englishman, did he prescribe for your master?"

"Of course. They loved each other, and sat late into the night in their discussions. When my poor master was taken ill, Herr Wakefield took complete charge of him. Ach! If he did but know what had happened!"

"Then he is not here?"

"No; he drove to Lemsdorf yesterday afternoon. He had to return to his own country. Ach! If he did but know!"

It was plain enough—Marnac the linguist was Wakefield the Englishman. It was he, new from this thing that he had done, who had come creeping to my room in the night, being suspicious of the strangers from the South. It was he that had brought about this mysterious horror. I turned from the poor monstrosity upon the floor and leant, shuddering, against the wall. As I did so, Graden strode past me to the open door.

"Driver, can your horses take us back?" I heard him say.

"Not without rest and feed, mein Herr. The snow was very bad, and they are tired."

"Would a hundred marks to the driver assist them?"

"It is impossible. They could not reach half-way. Wait, mein Herr, and it may be done."

My cousin came up to me and laid his great hand upon my shoulder.

"I'm afraid it's the truth," he said. And then turning to the dead man's servant, "Your master—had he horses?" he asked.

"Three, mein Herr, but they have not yet returned from Lemsdorf, where they went this morning with the big sleigh for provisions."

With a sharp order Graden sent our driver hurrying to the stables. Then, with his arm linked in mine, we followed the old servant into a low-roofed dining-hall. As I dropped upon an oak settle before the great china stove, he thrust his flask into my hands and, with a word of encouragement, slipped away. I knew that he was re-examining the body, but, doctor though I was, the spirit of investigation had gone out of me. I could no more have assisted him than a medical student can watch, unmoved, his first operation.

In about twenty minutes he returned, bearing a tray upon which was set bread and cheese, flanking a great ham. I turned from the food with disgust; but my cousin fell to diligently, complaining the while at my folly in not eating when I had the chance.

"You must pull yourself together," he protested, with his mouth full. "Try this ham now. It isn't half bad."

More to humour him than with any intention of following his advice, I drew my seat to the table.

"Come, now, that's better," he cried, carving away. "To tell the truth, I haven't the slightest idea what that devil Marnac has been up to. But what I do know is

"Graden sprang out of the sleigh and strode up to the angry farmer."

that we've got to catch him—dead or alive. Therefore I recommend you to stoke up your body with this excellent—hallo!"

Knife and fork in the air, he sat motionless, staring at the dish before him.

"What's the matter now?" I asked irritably; for, indeed, his hearty appetite annoyed me.

For answer he rose and pealed the bell. The old manservant, with the brandy flushing his white cheeks, tottered into the room.

"I am sorry to trouble you," said Graden courteously, "but we both set such store by your hams that we wish to know where they can be obtained. Do you cure them yourself?"

"No, mein Herr, but it is done near by," answered the man, with a look of blank surprise.

"Indeed. The Lemsdorf ham is a discovery; it should make a stir. I wonder I had not heard of its merits before."

"You see, mein Herr, the big curing station has not long been established."

"A new enterprise?"

"Yes, mein Herr. It belongs to Herr Drobin, a South German. Two years ago he took the big farm at Gran, which you passed on your way here. It is this side of the dye-works. He has many pigs in the forest. His hams are becoming famous from Warsaw to Königsberg. It is said he has some secret in the feeding or curing—no one knows which."

"Thank you—that is all."

The door was scarcely shut when I turned hotly upon Graden. "How dare you sit here in this house of murder and talk of the excellence of the food?" I cried furiously. "It is shameful, indecent!"

"Yet we will visit the farm of Gran on our way back. I have some little inquiries to make."

"We shall do nothing of the sort," I snarled.

"If you were a soldier or an explorer, Cousin Robert," he said, leaning across and tapping me kindly on the arm, "you would know that in any expedition one alone can be responsible. The rest obey, whether they be few or many. As it is, I beg you to recognise that fact and to obey."

He was right, and I knew it. But to save appearances I walked to the window and stood drumming upon it with my fingers for a while before I answered him.

"Well, do as you please," I said at length.

"I think the sleigh may be ready by now," he said. "Come, let us go out and inquire."

There is no need to dwell on this miserable drive. The tired horses dragged slowly forward, the driver, sullen and frightened, urging them on with blows and curses. Mile after mile of pine-woods marched past us, but we did not speak, crouching in the furs. At last, as night was falling, we reached the edge of the forest and swung aside from the main road into a track that skirted the edge of the pines. The ground sank away into a hollow like the palm of the hand. At the lowest point I could see a square, wooden building flanked by rows of outbuildings. It was, as I imagined, the farm of Gran. But before we reached it, our driver suddenly drew up his horses. A man was advancing towards us through the trees. Our driver turned, and with a wave of the whip explained the situation.

"It is Herr Drobin," said he.

I was not favourably impressed with this breeder of pigs. He was an elderly man, full bodied, with white hair, that stuck out stiffly from under his fur cap, a red, bulbous nose, and shifty, suspicious eyes. He saluted us with a touch of his cap in military fashion.

"And what is your business, gentlemen?" he asked.

"It is less business than gratitude," said Graden courteously. "We have made this little pilgrimage to thank the producer of the Lemsdorf hams."

"You are not dealers, then?"

"No, but I——"

"Then take yourself off!"

"Herr Drobin!"

"Go! clear out! Do I not make myself plain?" he cried, his flushed face nodding in time to his violent gesticulations. "I will have no spies about the place!"

Graden sprang out of the sleigh and strode up to the angry farmer. For a moment I thought there would be a scrimmage; but the huge bulk of his antagonist was not without its effect upon the German. I have often noticed that great stature has a curiously soothing influence on the bad temper of an opponent.

"Why did you call me a spy?" demanded my cousin.

"The people about here gossip of some secret I hold," he answered sulkily. "Perhaps they speak true; perhaps false. Who can say? At least, I am no longer a fool; my eyes have been opened. 'You have a good thing here, Herr Drobin. There is a great future before you, if only you keep your knowledge to yourself,' said the Englishman to me. 'If strangers come asking questions, they will be spies; send them away.' It was fine advice he gave me; anyone can see that. So be off with you!"

"I am an Englishman myself, Herr Drobin. May I ask my compatriot's name?"

"I do not remember."

"What, then, was he like?"

"I cannot describe him."

"You are discreet, Herr Drobin. Come, now, let us strike a bargain. I will make a guess at your secret; if I am right, you will tell me what you know of this Englishman."

The German started back, staring at Graden with little, bloodshot eyes, in which surprise and fury were oddly mingled. Then, side by side, they stepped into the shadow of the pines, whispering together.

"They are all liars, these Germans," said our driver confidentially, turning to me. "For myself, I am a Pole."

"You heard what was said. Do you know anything of this English visitor to Herr Drobin?"

"Most certainly, mein Herr. He was of the name of Wakefield. He has stayed several nights at the 'Goldner Adler.' For the rest, he has been the guest of him who lived out there," and he made a gesture down the road that we had come.

A nameless fear took me by the throat—a fear of unknown possibilities. I would have questioned the man more, but at that moment Graden and the farmer emerged from the shadow of the pines. The latter had abandoned his truculent manner. Indeed, he seemed oddly subservient. As Graden stepped into the sleigh, the man bowed low a curtsy, which my cousin answered with a curt nod of dismissal.

"Drive on!" he cried, and once more we were ploughing our way back to the Lemsdorf road.

"Did you ever study the properties of the root called madder, commonly known as a dye?" asked my cousin suddenly.

"No."

"Then I must explain from the beginning. It is right that you should hear."

He pulled the flaps of his deerstalker cap over his ears—indeed, it was bitter cold—and settled himself amongst the rugs. I caught the outline of his face—the jaws set, the cheeks drawn, the eye hard and keen, the whole purposeful and remorseless.

"When I was slicing the ham to-day," he continued, "an odd thing happened. My knife struck the bone and passed through it as if it had been putty. At a second glance I noticed that the interior of the section so divided was of a brownish red. It set me thinking. I began to remember certain facts. The talk of the old servant concerning a secret held by the owner of the pig-farm at Gran concentrated my suspicions, the proximity of the dye-works confirmed them. I was almost certain of Herr Drobin's secret before he charged me with coming to steal it.

"Let me explain. Madder is a dye, as you know. But administered to man or beast, it has the curious effect of colouring and pulping the bones to a gristle. It is used sparingly on a few South German pig-farms, that the hams may appear attractive when carved. Herr Drobin introduced it into German Poland. He obtained the root as he required it by arrangement with the dye-works. Perhaps their presence suggested the idea to him.

"Whether or no Marnac knew of the uses of madder before he came to Lemsdorf, I cannot tell. From my talk with Drobin it would seem that his visit to his farm was more or less of an accident. But, either way, the visit gave him the weapon by which he 'might make a toad' of his enemy. That bitter criticism, you may be sure, was for ever running in his diseased brain. The practical details he learnt at the farm would help him in—what he had undertaken. His advice to that old German was a sound move, designed to cover his visits to the farm and the suspicions they might afterwards have excited.

"His method of getting into touch with his victim was simple. He introduced himself as an Englishman by a letter which he himself wrote in his capacity of Heidelberg professor, well knowing that the police had not made public their suspicions of him. He assumed the name of Wakefield—the first that suggested itself to him — and the nationality of an Englishman, for, as we know, he spoke the language to perfection. He administered madder in some form until Mechersky grew ill; after which, in his position of medical attendant, the rest was easy. He fled when he knew that the end of the tragedy was at hand, that every bone of his victim was fragile as thin glass. Probably he caught a momentary glimpse of us in the 'Goldner Adler'; and his midnight visit was to assure himself of your identity. You were in great peril that night, Cousin Robert; I shudder to think how great.

"He has probably escaped to-day; there

is a fast train to the west at twelve o'clock he could catch. But I vow before Heaven, I vow before you as my witness, that I will pursue this fiend until I have run him down. Heaven knows I have no hatred towards him. I feel to him as a man might feel towards a mad dog which is a danger to the peaceful men, women, and children of his village. It is the duty of the citizen to risk his life in its capture."

"Where do we go now?" I asked.

"To the railway. We must gather what news we can."

The winter night was falling drear and cold when our tired horses staggered up to the station door. I scrambled out, hungry, cramped, exhausted in body and mind, and followed my cousin within. The station was empty at the moment save for a distant corner where a man sat huddled on a travelling valise. We advanced at once upon him. When we were a dozen feet away, he started up and faced us.

It was Mossel, the lieutenant of the Heidelberg police.

"Any luck, mein Herr?" said he to Graden.

"What in the world are you doing here?" was the astonished answer.

"Well, mein Herr, I thought you knew something, and followed you. When I arrived this morning, I said to myself: 'The great white English ferret will be at work to-day searching for the rat. I will wait at the station like a net into which Mr. Ferret may turn the rat.'"

Graden skipped up to him and shook him warmly by the hand.

"Capital, Mossel, capital! And you—had the net any luck?"

"The net was sitting upon the rat's luggage when you arrived this moment. The net has been here for five hours, and is cold and hungry. The net is of opinion that the rat must have seen him and abandoned his luggage. He has not left by train."

"But he can escape in no other way. We have him, Mossel, we have him."

"So it would seem," said the lieutenant calmly.

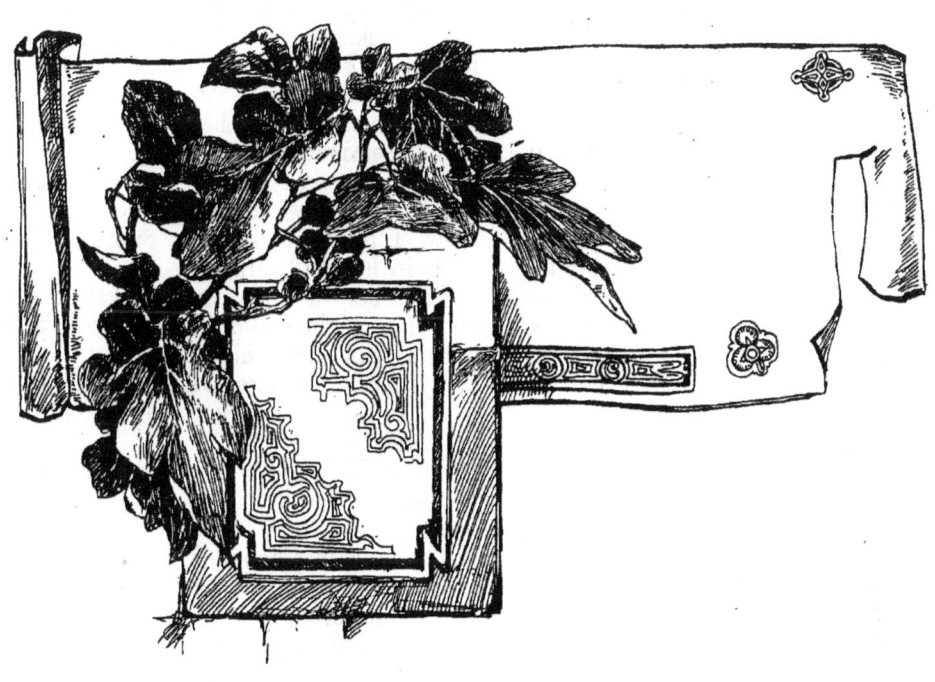

THE TRAIL OF THE DEAD:

THE STRANGE EXPERIENCE OF DR. ROBERT HARLAND.

By B. FLETCHER ROBINSON and J. MALCOLM FRASER.*

III.—THE CHASE IN THE SNOW.

I HAVE endeavoured to give the facts of my strange story without omission or exaggeration. If I have failed, it is not from forgetfulness; for I do not think there is a single detail that is not permanently fixed in my memory. Even now I have but to shut my eyes to see the face of Marnac peer into my old rooms at Heidelberg, to stand once more trembling with terror in the desolate courtyard of Castle Oster, to drive through the blinding snow to where the body—— But enough. I do not forget.

I have already told you of the murder of Professor von Stockmar by his rival, Professor Marnac of Heidelberg, and of the discovery of the crime by my cousin, Sir Henry Graden, the well-known scientist and explorer, who was then my guest at that University. I have described the steps that led to our following the murderer to Lemsdorf, in German Poland, and the means by which he compassed the death of the unfortunate Mechersky. I have, moreover, laid before you the evidence that led my cousin to believe that Marnac was suffering from delusions, and that his extraordinary crimes were in revenge for certain harsh criticisms of a book on which he had spent many years of labour. In my last statement I traced the pursuit down to the station of Lemsdorf, where the murderer, flying from the scene of his revenge upon the Russian Professor, had been turned back from the railway by Mossel the lieutenant of the Heidelberg police, who had followed us to render assistance. Mossel, indeed, had waited by Marnac's luggage for six hours, but the man himself had failed to appear.

The winter's sun, chilled to a dusky ball, was dipping behind the snow-clad ridges to the eastward when we scrambled back into the sleigh. As our tired horses stumbled through the outskirts of the straggling wooden town, the shadows rushed across the sky as if flying the pursuit of the gale that shrieked amongst the houses. Night had fallen.

Surely we had him in our hands.

He had not fled by rail. Somewhere in the town he must be lurking, this grey-haired figure with the heart of a hunted wolf. The thought of it drove away the aches and cramps of exhaustion, and I sat bolt upright in my seat, staring into the gloom ahead, half expecting to see him move across the snow before us like a slinking beast of prey. We had decided to drive straight to our own inn, the "Goldner Adler," where, as we had discovered, Marnac, under the name of Wakefield, an English traveller, had also passed the previous evening. Little had we thought that the being we pursued, fresh from the murder of the man we had come to save, was sharing the same roof-tree. Perhaps there might be news of him at the "Goldner Adler." Reski, the tall, handsome Pole, who had about him more of the feudal knight than a country innkeeper, met us in the porch, bowing a stately welcome.

"You have had a bad drive, gentlemen," said he. "The wind has been fierce, and the snow, I fear, was heavy. Supper will be ready in half-an-hour."

"I believe a Mr. George Wakefield slept here last night," said Graden, dusting the clinging flakes from his outer wraps. "It is always pleasant to meet a compatriot. If he is still in the house, perhaps he will join us at our meal."

"Herr Wakefield! No, mein Herr, he has not yet returned."

"So, he has gone out?"

The innkeeper hesitated, glancing uneasily at his questioner. He was evidently in some uncertainty of mind.

"He is a strange man, the Herr Wakefield; though, perhaps, for an Englishman——"

"He is not more mad than usual, eh, Mr. Landlord?" laughed Graden.

---

* Copyright, 1903, by B. Fletcher Robinson and J. Malcolm Fraser, in the United States of America.

"Mein Herr, it was not my intention to speak thus of your great people," apologised the man. "If he has surprised us, it is doubtless because we, being ignorant country-folk, do not understand his customs."

"Why, what has he been about?"

"Well, mein Herr, it is this way. After you had started for your drive to the house of the Professor Mechersky, Herr Wakefield came running down from his room with many questions concerning you. He seemed sorry that you had gone without seeing him. He then paid his bill with the liberality of the English, who are indeed a great and generous nation, and commanded that his luggage should be carried to the station for the midday train. At eleven he himself set out for the station upon foot. We were sorry to lose so good a guest. What, then, mein Herr, was our surprise when a little after twelve he reappeared, having ridden back upon the sleigh that had taken his luggage to the station! The man who drove it told me that Herr Wakefield had left his luggage upon the platform unregistered, and that he had seen a stranger standing by it as if in charge."

Graden glanced at Mossel, who grinned luminously.

"Proceed, Mr. Landlord," he said.

"He had only peeped into the station and left at once, the man said. He demanded of me a sleigh and good horses, but the best I had were with you, and it was necessary to send for others from a neighbour. He was very impatient of the delay, using angry words. At last he drove away, and he has not returned."

"Then, turning it slowly back, he drove a pin through the thin paper at the spots immediately above the indentations on the page below."

"Who went with him?"

"Ivan, my eldest son."

"Did he say where he was going?"

"No, mein Herr; only I heard him cry to Ivan to follow the eastern road which is towards the Russian frontier."

"And while he waited for the horses, what did he do?"

"As I have said, at first he abused me roundly for the delay. Indeed, mein Herr, I was surprised at his knowledge of German, for before he had spoken it very badly. For the rest, he sat by himself, reading, in the best room."

"Please to show us there."

We tramped in single file after the landlord through the ill-lit passages to the "best room," a parlour set aside for important guests. It seemed a peculiarly inartistic apartment, with green wall-paper and angular chairs covered with purple antimacassars. On the central table stood a lamp, and beside it lay a number of those dingy books that seem common to inns of all nations. Graden made for them at once, and as he sorted through the pile of time-tables, catalogues, and trade-papers, we stood watching him in surprise. Suddenly he stopped in his search with a little grunt of satisfaction, and drawing a chair to the table, sat down. I looked over his shoulder. He was actually reading a German Baedeker!

"Doubtless you are planning a picnic-party?" I suggested, with as much sarcasm as I could put into the question.

"I know you are tired and hungry, my good Robert," he answered; "but please keep quiet."

He had reached "Lemsdorf"—I could see the name at the top of the page—and now was turning the leaves very slowly. Suddenly he held up the Baedeker to me.

"Do you see that?" he asked sharply.

A jagged line of paper ran along the inner crease of the guide-book. The map of the district had been torn away!

Mossel thrust me gently aside and, bending over, examined the under page thus left exposed. He took the book from Graden's hands and, carrying it to the lamp, continued his scrutiny.

"You are quite right, Mossel," said my cousin. "His pencil had a sharp point."

"You have a keen eye, Herr Graden," grinned the policeman. "In our business you would have made some reputation."

"This is a new edition. How long have you had it?" asked my cousin of the innkeeper.

"But a few days, mein Herr."

"And have you been visited by any tourists in that time?"

"No, mein Herr."

"Then this should make it a certainty, for I have a Baedeker of my own upstairs. One moment, while I fetch it."

Graden's chair toppled to the ground as he rose. In three strides he was out of the door. I turned to Mossel with a demand for an explanation.

"Wait till Herr Graden returns," he grunted sulkily.

I have the strongest objection to those silly tricks of secrecy with which the professional police endeavour to magnify their most simple discoveries. I was speaking my mind strongly on the subject when my cousin reappeared.

"Hallo! what's the matter?" he asked. I explained the position, while the fat German chuckled in an oily, irritating manner.

"Is not the official always the same?" said Graden, with a grim smile. "Come to the light, Robert, and I'll explain."

It was certainly an ingenious discovery they had made. Upon the page upon which the map should have rested were several slight indentations, evidently the result of marks made upon the lost paper by a pencil with a fine point. With great care my cousin tore out the corresponding map from his guide-book and fitted it into the vacant place. Then, turning it slowly back, he drove a pin through the thin paper at the spots immediately above the indentations on the page below.

"The devil take him!" he cried. "Look, Mossel. This doesn't help us, after all."

It was true enough. The pin-pricks showed, first, Lemsdorf; then a cross-road some ten miles to the east; and then Bromberg, to the north, on the Berlin-Thorn, and Gnesen, to the south, on the Posen-Frankfurt railways. He had evidently been measuring and calculating indecisively.

"Do not trouble yourself, Herr Graden," said Mossel, with a wave of the hand that had more than a suggestion of patronage. "There are still telegraphs. I will have him detained at whichever place he reaches. I shall return in half an hour—to a good supper, I trust, Mr. Landlord."

We followed him to the outer door, which opened to a writhing wilderness of snow-flakes, for the fall had recommenced. The policeman turned up his collar with a grunt of disgust and melted into the darkness. We turned to meet the face of the

"'It is Ivan, my son!'"

landlord, white and drawn with a terrible anxiety.

"My son!" he gasped. "What of my son?"

"Heaven pardon me!" cried Graden, "I had forgotten him!"

"This man he drove, that is about to be arrested—is he a criminal? Do not spare me, mein Herr."

"Your servant—our driver to-day—will be telling the tale in your kitchen, of the death of the Professor Mechersky, of Castle Oster. This man, whose name is Marnac, killed him. That is why we pursue. Yet, my friend, I see no danger for your son, unless——"

"Unless what, mein Herr?"

"Unless he refused to assist in the escape of the murderer."

"He is an honest boy, a good boy, but very stubborn. His horses were borrowed; he had promised to return them to-night. He would never consent to drive this man to Bromberg or Gnesen, which is at least an eighteen hours' journey. Oh, mein Herr, mein Herr! what is happening—out there in the snow?"

"We are in the hands of Providence, my friend," said my cousin gravely, laying his hand on the landlord's arm. "You can do nothing but pray that it may be well with the boy."

I was very sorry for Reski. As I made my toilet in my room upstairs, the danger of his son grew upon me. Fate, accident, Providence—whatever you choose to call it—is a strange thing, for indeed it chooses its victim with a fine impartiality. When I entered our supper-room, I found my cousin equally disturbed.

"This is a bad business about the landlord's son," he said, "I've a good mind to follow the sleigh, though it's little good that would do."

"It's an awful night," I grumbled, for indeed the wind was shrieking in the roof like a lost soul.

"You're a queer chap, Robert, with your confounded mannerisms," he said. "Yet I'll wager you'd be the first to be off into the storm in a matter of life and death."

It was not exactly complimentary, but I let it pass.

Mossel was delayed. It was close upon twenty minutes more before he arrived, a snow-swathed, stamping bear of a man, whose curses preceded him as he rolled down the passage to our room.

"What's up, Mossel?" Graden demanded sharply.

"The wires, mein Herr Graden, the wires! *Potztausend!* but this storm has brought them down like clothes-lines."

"A special train, then."

"They have not an engine in the shed. I have been to see; it was that which delayed me."

Graden drew a sheet of paper from his pocket and glanced at it swiftly.

"There is not a train till ten in the morning," he said. "He will be at Bromberg, which is the nearer town, by eleven at latest. This is a branch line, and we could not get there under three hours. It is now seven. An old man as he is could hardly travel through such a night without stops for food. Again, this lad who drove him may have refused to proceed. We must chance it, my friends, and follow."

"I thought you had already so decided when I saw the sleighs at the door," said Mossel.

"Sleighs, Mossel? I ordered no sleighs!"

"Well, they're there. Two troikas with three good horses apiece. Come and see for yourself."

The policeman had spoken the truth. On the leeward side of the porch two sleighs were waiting. The light from the open door behind us shimmered on the drifting snow and flashed on the bells about the horses' necks. It was bitterly cold, and I was turning to retreat into the hall when a man wrapped in furs moved out of the darkness. It was the keeper of the inn, his face grey-white, like the underside of a sole.

"'Stop, or I fire!'"

"Whose sleighs are these?" asked Graden sharply.

"Mine, Mr. Englishman, mine. I follow to save my boy."

"And the horses?"

"The best in Lemsdorf. They are private teams, lent by those who had pity upon my sorrow."

"May we come with you?"

"I would ask for nothing better, mein Herr."

Inside of ten minutes I was ready to start, with a borrowed cloak flung over my thickest clothes, and a huge hunch of bread-and-meat in my hand. Quick as I had been, Mossel and my cousin were already dressed and in consultation. We were to drive to the cross-roads, they told me, and then separate, the one sleigh, with Graden, Mossel, and an experienced driver, taking the road to Bromberg, which, being the shorter, was more likely to be the one Marnac had chosen; the other, containing the innkeeper and myself, was to follow the Gnesen road. I was not particularly pleased at the prospect of parting with my friends, but I made no objection to this plan. We entered our sleighs, rolling ourselves in the rugs.

"Are you armed?" Graden called across to the innkeeper in his little seat before me.

"Yes, mein Herr. Do you go first, for you have the better team."

The chase was up indeed!

As we passed on to the plain outside the town, the gale that came charging out of frozen Russia leapt upon us with a howl of furious joy. The flakes that rose from beneath the curved runners and the beating hoofs fled spinning into the night. The sky hung low and black and starless above the white sheet of rolling snow. The little sleigh-bells grew silent in the heavier drifts, breaking out again where the track was harder. A hundred yards ahead the sparks of Graden's pipe flashed as they kindled in the wind. The fall had almost ceased.

My driver sat squarely before me, with a rein in each of his fur-gloved hands. I could not see his face, but from his projecting head and hunched shoulders I could imagine how he looked, peering over his horses into the night, with fear gripping at his soul.

I must admit that for myself I was in a condition of petulant discomfort. The slightest movement seemed to give entrance to some new draught that chilled my arm or ran trickling down my spine. Now and again a flake of snow lodged in my neck or ear and melted icily. Tired, cold, and hungry, I lay amid my rugs, cursing the folly that had led me to take a hand in a business that should have been left to the police. I had the keenest desire for a quarrel, but being to all conversational purposes alone, that relief was impossible.

Within two miles of Lemsdorf we had left the plain for the forest. The moon was obscured, yet a faint light filtered down from above, finding a reflection in the snow, and emphasising the black pillars of the pines that went sliding by. There was now no trace of our companions save the marks of their runners on the track; over the woods brooded an utter silence, broken only by the swish of our sleigh and the murmur of the bells rising and falling in a low, monotonous melody. It was as if we were passing through the waste places of a dying world. One of my feet began to grow numb, and when I turned about that I might shelter it, the snow that had gathered on my collar plunged down my neck, so that I shivered with cold. But on the whole I was reasonably warm amongst my wraps, and a feeling of drowsiness grew upon me.

It was Reski's voice that woke me. We had halted in a dim clearing in the woods. A score of yards away the second sleigh was waiting. Evidently we had reached the cross-roads, where we were to part.

"Any tracks?" shouted my driver.

"No," came Graden's answer. "The wind and the fresh fall have cleared them away. Are you all right, Robert?"

"I am exceeding uncomfortable, if that is what you want to know," I shouted back. Indeed, it was a silly question to ask me. My temper was not improved by a distant chuckle which I attributed to Mossel.

"Cheer up, Robert!" continued my cousin. "If you run across him, you must do your best. Reski will see you through, never fear; but I don't think there is much chance of your coming up with him, for he will have taken the shorter route which we follow. Anyhow, remember that the rendezvous is at the 'Drei Kronen,' at Thorn. If you catch him, telegraph there; if the wires are down, send a messenger. Do you understand?"

"You are perfectly lucid."

"Well, good-bye."

The snow spurted from under their horse's hoofs as they swung on to the north road. Then my driver shouted to his team, and we, too, rushed forward, but on the other track curving south and east. For a minute I could hear their bells tinkling an echo in the distance. Then they died away into silence.

My interest in the chase suddenly expanded. Now that my cousin had deserted me, it seemed an ugly, dangerous business. Marnac would stop at nothing, that was certain. Supposing we should chance upon this desperate maniac, what then? My driver was armed, and had the appearance of a bold, courageous man. Was he so in reality? I stared up at his back and wondered.

We had travelled the half of a mile, when from the black of the forest before us rose a cry, a fierce, chuckling bay that sent the horses plunging across the road. In the solitude of those ice-bound woods it sounded the more threatening, the more utterly malignant. I sprang to my feet, gripping Reski by the shoulder.

"What is that?" I cried.

"Wolves, mein Herr."

"Will they attack us?"

"Calm yourself, mein Herr," he answered gruffly, his eyes still set on the track before him. "The winter is young, and their bellies are not empty. There is no danger."

The pace of the horses had dropped to a slow trot. They advanced stiffly, with staring eyes and ears pricked forward. I remained standing, peering across the driver's seat at the white track that ran dimly away between the banks of pines.

Suddenly from a snow-powdered thicket before us there burst a chorus of low snarls that grew into the short, angry barks of dogs disturbed. With a jerk the horses stopped, trembling and squeezing themselves together with the fear that was on them.

"They have something there," cried Reski, and there was a shudder in his voice. "Otherwise they would not be so bold. Take the reins, mein Herr."

He thrust them into my hands and jumped from the seat. His pistol flashed, and I caught a glimpse of forms scurrying over the snow. Then the darkness fell again like a veil.

"What have you found?" I shouted.

"Under the trees it is hard to see," came back his answer. "Perhaps—I was mistaken. But wait."

He struck a match, and his tall, thin figure sprang out in silhouette as he moved slowly forward, shielding the light with his hands.

"Here are the footprints of the wolves... it was here that they were gathered. There is something by the tree.... It is not a log—*mein Gott!* but it is not a log, though it lies so still.... I fear to approach—how I fear! Have mercy! It is a man! It is Ivan, my son!"

We were on Marnac's trail—the trail of the dead.

* * * * *

At last it was all over. Alone, for I dared not leave my hold upon the frightened horses, Reski carried his son to the sleigh and laid him there beside me, with a rug across the face. He had been killed from behind, poor lad, with a revolver shot in the back of his head. He had refused to proceed, and Marnac had not hesitated. That was plain enough. I thanked God that we had been in time—to save him from the wolves.

Yet there had been but a short delay. For when Reski had seen his dead bestowed upon the sleigh, he had taken the reins and sent his horses forward. He did not speak, nor did I offer him consolation. But as I watched him sitting above me, peering ahead like some old teak figure on a vessel's bows, there was a grim intensity about the man, a fixed resolve that was strange to witness. So we fled through the night, down the interminable avenues of pines, bearing our dead with us.

It was one o'clock when we lit upon a wayside inn. Our clamour aroused the landlord, who directed us to where a kettle simmering on the stove gave a warm mash for the horses and hot brandy for ourselves. He was sleepily incurious, nor did he inquire what was the thing beneath the rugs which we carried with us. But he gave us news. Marnac had left there less than two hours before. He had been greatly delayed by a collision with a tree, and some rough repairs had been necessary. One of his horses, too, had been slightly lamed. Yet Reski showed no unusual interest in the tale we heard. He spent his time with his horses, grooming and soothing them. It was not till they had rested three-quarters of an hour that he called me out from my seat by the stove, and again we swept away upon the chase.

It was at dawn that we sighted him. He was climbing a long slope, a black speck in the white riband of a road. Above him, long flakes of orange cloud were slowly brightening and deepening in colour. As he topped the hill, the sun came peering up over a moorland heaped with tumbled drifts. The sky flushed and faded to a deep cobalt blue. So day came.

It almost seemed as if our horses understood. They increased their pace without a touch of the whip, tugging at the frozen, twisted reins. As they, too, rose the hill, Reski shouted to them, and they stepped briskly forward. The fresh snow had frozen, and we travelled well, the surface crackling as we crushed over it. We were less than a quarter of a mile from him when he turned and noticed us. We saw him spring to his feet and lash his team, but the off-side horse was running stiffly and his pace scarcely

"'There is the murderer, mein Herr!'"

increased. He leant down, fumbling and searching at his feet, while he held the reins in one hand. After that he did not hurry, but drove steadily forward, glancing at us now and again over his shoulder.

We drew up swiftly—four hundred yards, three hundred yards, one hundred—— And then, with a short, fierce bark of rage, the Pole dragged out his revolver and fired. As he did so, the sharp hum of a bullet, like the buzz of an angry bee, fled over us. I ducked my head at the sound; but I give myself the credit of saying that I poked it up again the next moment.

"May the Fiend grip him, but he has a Mauser pistol!" cried Reski, and I saw that the weapon in his own hand was of the common bull-dog make. "At this range I can do nothing against him."

He lashed his horses, and they plunged gallantly forward. I could see that Marnac had stopped his sleigh and was cuddling his weapon with a perfect coolness. Even at that distance I seemed to feel the goggling murder in his eyes.

Zip! zip! He had missed again!

Thung! I saw one of the galloping horses stagger, and then his head and shoulders seemed to fall away, as if he had dropped forward into a hole. There was a bumping and a twisting wrench, the snow by the roadside seemed to spring up at me, and the next instant I was struggling in cold, blinding darkness.

I wriggled out from the drift, gasping,

with the flakes in my mouth and eyes. The sleigh was twisted across the road, half covering the dead horse. The other two had scrambled to their feet and now stood shivering, with drooping heads. The fall had knocked the heart clean out of them. Reski lay beside them, huddled where he had fallen. Eighty yards away Marnac had stopped and was watching us. He seemed satisfied with what he saw, for presently he turned and, lashing his team, trotted on down the road.

I don't suppose it was more than a couple of minutes before Reski came round, though it seemed long enough to me. He had got a nasty thump on the head, but as a matter of fact his wrist turned out to be the more serious business, being very badly sprained indeed. I made a sling out of a neck-wrap and fixed him up as well as I was able. The man had a remarkable vitality, besides brute courage, for, the moment I had finished, he walked over and examined the sleigh.

It looked hopeless enough. One of the runners had been torn almost clean away, and the central part was badly cracked. The body of the poor lad Ivan lay on its back in the roadway, staring up at the sky. I threw a rug over it.

"Well, we can't go on, that's certain," I said.

"Not in the sleigh, mein Herr," he answered calmly.

"And how else?"

"There are the horses, one for each. When you have freed them of their harness, I will ask you to assist me to mount."

There was no good arguing with him, and I was ashamed to seem less eager than a man in his crippled condition. With his clasp knife I cut the twisted traces away and freed them of their collars. At his direction I dragged the body of Ivan into the sleigh and left him there decently covered.

Reski mounted from the stump of a tree, to which I led the stronger of the pair. I was a fairly good rider, but I was excessively stiff from my long drive, and not a little shaken by my fall. My beast seemed to have the sharpest knife-bone of a back that Nature ever gave to horseflesh. But, after all, there was nothing to be gained by grumbling. Perhaps I was growing wiser by painful experience.

A curious pair we must have looked that morning. Reski, with his arm in a sling, and the butt of his revolver peeping from his waist-belt, would have made as good a stage brigand as need be. For myself, I was in too much of immediate pain from the jolting trot of the brute I rode to carry a formidable appearance. I could never have imagined that a horse lived with such adamantine fetlocks as mine seemed to possess.

I have no exact record of the time, but I should imagine that it was about half an hour later that we sighted Marnac again. He was then a good three-quarters of a mile ahead, but travelling leisurely. Also, I was very glad to notice that we were free of the waste lands, and that the spire of a church was poking out amongst some poplars ahead of him. He would never dare to use his revolver a second time when men were about. Also, we might procure another sleigh and team.

Reski sent his heels into his horse, and we quickened our pace, though the poor brutes were getting very done and drove heavily along with hanging heads. It was about then that I noticed a man behind us.

We were topping a slight rise when I looked round. He was then some distance in our rear, but coming up fast. As far as I could make out, he was in a sort of uniform and well mounted. The possibility of official help was very pleasant.

We were gaining on Marnac, who had not yet noticed us.

With kicks and curses from Reski, and the application of a hazel branch from myself, we had squeezed a lumbering gallop out of our horses. The sleigh was not more than one hundred yards away. Reski gripped his reins in his teeth and drew his revolver.

"Stop, there! Stop, I say, in the name of the law!"

It was the man from behind who hailed us, but we rode on.

"Stop, or I fire!"

I pulled up. I don't think it was very cowardly when you think of it. Besides, I was anxious to explain.

Reski rode on.

The man who had shouted flashed by me, travelling at an easy gallop. He was dressed in a neat green uniform and carried a drawn revolver.

Reski rode on.

It was all over in a moment. The stranger cried another warning, to which the Pole answered with a snarl over his shoulder. The next instant there was a sharp report, and Reski's horse pitched forward, throwing his rider clear. He was then scarcely thirty yards from Marnac's sleigh.

The Pole was not hurt apparently, for despite his injured arm he scrambled to his feet in an instant. But he had lost his revolver in his fall and was helpless. He began a furious explanation in his national tongue, dropping the hated language of his Teuton conquerors.

"Speak in German, you Polish dog!" growled his captor, and then turning on me as I rode up—

"Here, you," he said, "dismount and stand by your accomplice. If you resist, I shoot!"

I obeyed. From his manner he was without doubt a policeman. Also I respect the law.

"Now, you," he said, addressing me, "explain, if you can, who is that man you shot and left in the broken sleigh down yonder. Remember, it is against you that you have already tried to escape and refused to surrender?"

"There is the murderer, mein Herr!" I cried, pointing to Marnac's sleigh now rapidly vanishing. "We were chasing him. Go after him at once, or he will get away."

The policeman laughed long and lond.

"A pretty tale!" said he. "This dog of a Pole here has been in mischief, without doubt; and you, you who are——"

"An Englishman," I said proudly.

"Aha! perhaps you thought you were once more murdering the helpless Boer. A Pole and an Englishman! *Mein Gott!* it is no wonder that together they hatched some devilish contrivance."

It was no use to make a further appeal. Reski had seen that already. Side by side we tramped through the snow, with our captor and his ready pistol behind us. In half an hour we had reached the village we had seen ahead, and were lodged in a cell infamously damp and cold. All communication with our friends was refused till the arrival of some local magistrate.

As eleven o'clock hammered from the steeple outside, Reski raised his head from his chest and glared across at me.

"He will have arrived at Gnesen," he said. "There is a great choice of trains."

It was true enough. Marnac had escaped us once again.

TRIUNITY.

THOU knowest how I loved the man I thought
    Thou wert, but who I learned to see
Had never been. Ah, lost dream-love who brought
    Such blissful hours and days to me!

I may not wholly love the man thou art,
    Whose being is my misery,
But dearer far than all the world my heart
    Doth hold that man thou yet couldst be!

URSULA ARNOLD.

THE TRAIL OF THE DEAD:

THE STRANGE EXPERIENCE OF DR. ROBERT HARLAND.

By B. FLETCHER ROBINSON and J. MALCOLM FRASER.*

IV.—THE ANONYMOUS ARTICLE.

IN my narrative of the pursuit of Professor Rudolf Marnac, it will have been observed that Fortune had been cold to us. In the incident which I now relate we were to some extent more favoured; for though our supreme object was not achieved, we were yet enabled to save the life of her who is dearest to me in all the world.

I have told you of the homicidal mania which fell upon the Professor, and of the series of events which caused my cousin, Sir Henry Graden, the eminent scientist and explorer, to be associated with a Heidelberg student, as I then was, in an effort to contrive his capture. How we failed to bring about the murderer's arrest in Poland, through the stupidity of a forest guard, I have already explained. By the time I had obtained my release, Marnac had again disappeared. A linguist well provided with money, and on all points but one perfectly sane, had no difficulty in finding refuge in the cities of Europe.

I have been in some doubt as to the best means of briefly describing the present incident. Miss Mary Weston, with whom I discussed the matter, at once offered to place her diary at my disposal. Upon its perusal I suggested that she should herself extract the necessary items, adding such introduction and explanatory notes as seemed necessary. To this she has very kindly consented; and the first portion of this remarkable story I therefore leave in her hands.

MISS MARY WESTON'S NARRATIVE.

It was in the winter of 1899 that my father's health began to fail. In the May of the following year I returned from my school near Paris, and instead of entering at Girton, as my father had previously arranged, I became his secretary. I was then just eighteen. I did the very best I could, and

---

* Copyright, 1903, by B. Fletcher Robinson and J. Malcolm Fraser, in the United States of America.

in his dear, kind way, he made me forget my miseries at the endless blunders I committed. You see, there were only we two; for my mother died shortly after I was born, and I was their only child. We saw few people at our little house, which was on the Trumpington Road, just outside Cambridge. Ladies I met would often pity me for the dull and lonely life I led, and that used to make me very angry. We were never dull or lonely, my dear father and I.

It may seem absurd that so distinguished a man as Dr. Weston, M.A., D.Sc., F.R.S., the Regius Professor of Physic at Cambridge, should have relied on the help of a half-educated schoolgirl. But he was always pleased to say that my love and sympathy were worth far more to him in his work than if he had been served by the cleverest woman that ever headed an Honours list.

I well remember the appearance of Professor Marnac's book, "Science and Religion," which was published simultaneously in German and English at the beginning of the June of that year. My father was violently opposed to it, but I was far more concerned over the state into which it threw him than I was about the book, which, as a matter of fact, I never read. He dictated to me a most severe criticism, which at his instructions I sent to the editor of the *University Review* at 102A, Henrietta Street, Covent Garden, London. The article was signed "CANTAB," a pseudonym that my father often used, as he had the greatest objection to publicity.

About ten days after the August *University* appeared—that being the number which contained his article—my father received an anonymous letter. It was my duty to open and sort his correspondence, and I was thus able to intercept it. It was addressed to "Cantab," and had been forwarded, unopened, by the editor of the review. The envelope bore a German stamp, but the post-mark had been smeared and was quite indistinguishable. The letter was neatly written in English. It consisted almost entirely of the most violent personal threats against my father. The writer declared that he would soon find out "Cantab's" real name, and would suitably repay him for his slanders against the greatest scientific work of the century. I was very frightened about it, but several friends to whom I showed the letter laughed away my fears, saying it was undoubtedly the work of some madman, and advising me to burn it. This I did. I never mentioned the affair to my father, whose health was giving me great anxiety at the time.

During September my father had taken a cottage on the Cornish coast, and when the end of the Long Vacation came, the doctors forbade his return to Cambridge. I had hard work to persuade him that it was best to obey their orders; but at last he gave in, and we settled down for the winter.

The cottage was built at the foot of a low hill strewn with boulders and torn by the autumn rains. Upon its summit the chimney of an abandoned tin-mine rose against the sky like a vast flag-pole, with roofless buildings grouped around it in melancholy decay. It was always a depressing spot to me, and I rarely visited it, though the view was splendid. About half a mile before the cottage the moorland ended abruptly in a line of glorious cliffs, two hundred and fifty feet of granite and shining porphyry from brow to breaker. This was my favourite walk. I loved to crawl to the edge, that I might peer over at the reefs that sprang out from the tumbled rocks at the cliff foot like the bones of a giant's hand. I have lain thus for hours watching the great rollers advancing in that stately, inexorable march of theirs, rank following rank, until they burst in thunderous green fountains of foam. Sometimes, when a fierce wind blew from the southwest, the spray they hurled into the air would wet my face, even where I lay so infinitely far above them.

Between the cottage and the cliff the ground dipped into a little glen, or goyal, as the country-folks called it, choked with storm-twisted trees and deep with gorse and ferns. Through it ran our cart-track, winding down to the fishing village of Polleven, where the tiny, stone-roofed houses clung to a gap in the cliff wall like barnacles on a rock.

Besides my father and myself, Marjory, our cook-housekeeper, who had been with us ever since I could remember, was the only other inhabitant of the cottage. On Tuesdays and Thursdays a red-cheeked maiden, who had quite remarkable powers of breaking crockery, came to help from Polleven.

So were we living on November 27. From that date I will chiefly rely upon my diary for the details of my terrible experience. Please do not laugh at the form in which I wrote it. Mr. Harland has asked me to make no alterations, and so here it is.

Friday, Nov. 27.—I have quite an important piece of news to-day, Mr. Diary. So no more grumbles, please, about your having sunk into a weather report. Yes, sir, I have met a stranger—fancy that—a visitor, in the winter, at Polleven!

Mr. Hermann—for that is his name—has been a dabbler in science, he tells me, all his life. I shall snare him before long and lay my spoil in triumph at father's feet. Since the weather has been so bad, it has been very lonely for him indoors, poor dear, with only ignorant me for company. I am certain Mr. Hermann will be just the man for him. A good stiff talk will brighten him up wonderfully.

I chanced upon him this afternoon. He was struggling along the cliff edge in the teeth of the wind. His age should be about sixty, but he is very well preserved. He is clean-shaved and close-cropped and is altogether very neat in his appearance. His eyes behind his glasses are absurdly young, if I can so describe them. They are so active and clear that if it were not for the wrinkles above them, I should have knocked ten years off his age. He asked me the way to Polleven, and as I was bound for the village, I took him in charge. On the way he told me that he had just taken a room at the inn there. He is writing a book, it seems, and wanted a quiet corner. He will find it at Polleven! He speaks with but a slight accent, having lived much in England, though his father was a German, as his name denotes. This was his first walk, and he seemed much impressed with the wildness of the scenery.

I told father about him at supper. He said he would be very pleased to meet him.

Saturday, Nov. 28.—I am filled with the triumph of success. Mr. Hermann and father are hard at it over their pipes in the study. They do not seem to be opposed on any big question, which is most lucky, for some very learned men get into dreadful tempers with each other when contradicted.

It is the butcher's day at Polleven, so I walked there this morning to give the orders.

I met Mr. Hermann coming up from the quay. He is very fond of sailing, he said, and had engaged a small trawler and two men, so that he can have a good blow when the weather permits. He kept on rubbing his hands and beaming upon me, as if he had struck upon some new idea which pleased him. I told him I thought he had done a very sensible thing, and that in my opinion a great many clever men would write the better for a dose of fresh air taken daily. He laughed a good deal at this and complimented me on my wit. My wit! Think of that! As I knew there were plenty of chops in the house, I asked him to lunch, saying that my father, who was an invalid and could not go out much, would be delighted to make his acquaintance. He accepted at once and we walked back together.

Later. — Father says that Mr. Hermann is unusually well read, and that he had had a most interesting talk with him. Yet he did not seem very enthusiastic about him. I hope they did not quarrel. It rather spoilt my triumph. Father did not seem to have anything definite against him— only a general impression that he was a queer fellow. I think this rather absurd.

Sunday, Nov. 29. — Mr. Hermann sat behind me at church this morning. He sang the hymns in a high voice that would have been amusing under ordinary circumstances. After church he walked with me some distance up the hill. He condoled with me on my lonely

"So we stood watching each other."

life, and that always annoys me. Indeed, I am afraid I was rather rude to him about it. To make amends, I invited him to tea on Tuesday.

Monday, Nov. 30.—Father is not so well to-day. He has had more trouble with his cough, I fear, though he tries to make light of it. I wish I had not asked Mr. Hermann. I must take care that he does not see father to-morrow. The doctors were most particular in their instructions that nothing should over-excite him; I fear that the two might get into some silly argument.

Tuesday, Dec. 1.—Under this head my diary is a blank. I will try to set out the events of that day as calmly as I can. May God in His mercy help me, in His good time, to forget them!

My father seemed no worse in the morning, though by my persuasion he kept to his bed. His own room was on the ground floor—for he had been forbidden to climb stairs—and looked out upon the little garden at the back of the cottage.

Marjory had begged off for the afternoon, and I agreed, though this would leave me alone to serve my visitor. However, tea-making is no very difficult matter, and to pacify me Marjory had cooked one of her best cakes. She left shortly after two; Mr. Hermann arrived half an hour later.

I had not expected to see him so early, and was copying out some letters which my father had dictated, when he knocked at the door. As I showed him into the room, he chanced to pass the table on which they lay.

"What a beautiful hand your father writes!" he said politely.

"Thank you for the compliment, Mr. Hermann," I answered.

"My dear young lady, I am too old for riddles."

"The writing is mine."

"Is that really so?" he exclaimed, with a quick, startled look at me. "I could have guaranteed that it was a man's hand. Is there nothing private here—may I examine?"

"Oh, certainly," I said. "They are letters to tradesmen."

He picked up the sheets, and moving to the window examined them closely.

"You are sure this is your writing—there is no mistake?" he said presently.

I was rather annoyed at his persistence, and, telling him curtly enough that the writing was mine, went out to get the tea. At the kitchen door was the small boy who brought us our letters and papers from Polleven. There was only one letter that afternoon, which I placed amongst the tea-cups on the tray which I was carrying to the sitting-room. As I entered, Mr. Hermann stepped forward to help me.

"I fear I am giving you a great deal of trouble," said he.

"Please don't apologise," I answered, laughing. "I always do it when our servant is out."

"As she is now?"

"Yes."

"Then you have no one in the house?"

"No one—save my father."

"Indeed! Is that so?"

He dropped into a chair by the fire and sat staring into the coals, his chin resting on his hand. Certainly his behaviour was extremely odd that afternoon. As he did not speak, I opened the envelope, which was addressed to my father. It contained a second letter, and a short note from the editor of the *University*, stating that a person of the name of Sir Henry Graden had called for "Cantab's" address, and inquiring whether he might have permission to disclose it. He forwarded, he added, a letter from Sir Henry, which, as he believed, contained an explanation of this request.

I have the original letter before me now. This is how it runs:—

"Jerrold's Hotel,
"To 'Cantab.' "Strand, London, W.C.

"MY DEAR SIR,—As Mr. Rolles, the editor of the *University Review*, has not seen fit to inform me of your name and present address, I have written this letter on the understanding that it will be forwarded to you immediately. I should much have preferred to explain the matter personally, but as I may not receive your answer for several days, I dare not delay. It is my duty to inform you that Professor Rudolf Marnac, of the University of Heidelberg, is now a fugitive from the police. The charge against him is one of murder. I know that the man is guilty; I believe him to be the victim of a homicidal mania.

"His mania is of an unusual type, being directed solely against his scientific opponents. In the *University Review* of August last you criticised his book with extreme severity. He saw that number, for I have in my possession a copy of the article covered with the most dangerous threats against you in his own handwriting. Two distinguished scientists, Von Stockmar of Heidelberg, and Mechersky of St. Petersburg, who similarly attacked him in the papers, have already fallen victims to his extraordinary cunning.

You will observe, sir, the logical conclusion. Until he is captured you will be in danger.

"For your personal information I may tell you that he is a man of over sixty years of age. When last seen he had a long beard which was of a silky white. He wears glasses, but his eyes are unusually keen and intelligent. His hands are small and beautifully made, his finger-nails being apparently manicured. In whatever disguise he may assume, he will probably continue to keep them in good condition. He may change his appearance in many ways; but if you are in doubt of any pleasant stranger, I beg you to note his hands.

"On the receipt of your answer I am prepared to come to you at once. I shall then be able to give you further particulars.

"I beg you not to disregard this warning, and until you see me to be most careful in your movements. Of course, if your pseudonym is an absolute secret, you will be safe enough. But there are always chances.

"Sincerely yours,
"HENRY GRADEN (Bart.)."

I glanced up cautiously. Mr. Hermann still sat huddled in his seat by the fire. One of his hands I could see clearly, for it lay upon the arm of his chair. It was small as a woman's, and the nails had received so fine a polish that they shone pinkly in the firelight!

A wild terror clutched at my throat, so that for a space I sat dumb and motionless, gasping for breath. But then there came to me the realisation of the purpose for which this man had come, and at the thought of it my blood came surging back into alert activity. There may be many an English girl who loves her father as dearly as I do mine, but there is never one of them that loves him more. I can say honestly that after that first great shock of fear my mind was swept clean of my own danger. For my father I was ready to meet Death on his own ground, at his own terms, and try the issue.

And yet my first act was one of such folly that I can hardly bring myself to set it down. Perhaps it was that the words of the letter were rioting in my head; perhaps that my whole will was centred in an effort to control the tones of my voice.

"Do you take sugar in your tea, Professor Marnac?"

That was what I said to him.

It was out, and I could not recall it. As he rose, I sprang back, placing the table between us. A cup, caught by my skirt, smashed loudly on the floor. So we stood watching each other.

He showed no sign of anger. Only the expression of his eyes had changed to a cold, sneering insolence that was a most dreadful thing to see in so old a man.

"I observe, dear lady, that you hold a letter in your hand," said he, without a harsh note in his musical voice. "May I suggest that it contained the discovery which you so very incautiously have announced?"

"I shall answer no questions."

"If you will consider, dear lady, you will perceive that you merely waste time. Tell me—do you know the object of my visit?"

I hesitated a moment. Was there anything to be gained by pretending ignorance? None, so far as I could see.

"So I imagine," I replied.

"You relieve me of a load of explanations. There is, however, one point on which I myself desire information. Through the courtesy of the editor—or assistant editor—of that admirable periodical, the *University Review*, I was allowed a glimpse of the manuscript of an article signed 'Cantab.' It was a scurrilous effort, dictated by the meanest jealousy. It was designed to destroy my book—my book which is my life's work—do you understand?—my whole life's work."

His voice rose to his last words till it ended in a shriek of passion.

"Well, and what of that article?" I answered boldly.

My question calmed him in an instant. There was a crafty leer in his eyes as he spoke again.

"Of course, it was your father's. No sentence it contained was unworthy of so scholarly a pen. But why, dear lady, why was the original MSS. in your hand?"

"My father had nothing whatever to do with it," I said, speaking very slowly and distinctly. "I wrote it myself."

"You!" he cried, staring at me. "You wrote it?"

"Certainly. Do you think me incapable? If so, I direct your attention to the record of the Honours that I took at Cambridge."

If ever a lie be pardoned, may I not claim mercy for this of mine?

"Will you swear this to me?"

"Why not? I am not ashamed of my work."

He stood staring at the table in front of him for some moments, his hands pressed to his head.

"She must suffer, then," he muttered.

"But if I had known! A girl—it was hardly worth the trouble."

"Don't you think you had better go back to your inn?" I suggested.

"Not until we have settled our little account together, dear lady. You are young, yet young vipers can sting. Is it not better at once to put an end to their powers of mischief?"

"Yet the young can run where the old cannot follow. I am nearer the door than you. At your first movement I shall be clear of the house."

"And leave your father as a hostage?"

His words struck me like a blow. I swayed forward, gripping the table with both hands. He could have seized me then if he had wished; but he knew I was in his power, and held away.

"Do not forget that, dear lady," he continued; "it must be either you or him. There is no way of escape for both, I am afraid."

I am writing down the facts as they occurred. I desire no credit for following my duty. What I did then, many thousands of girls would do to-day. For there remained no way out of the pit into which we had fallen—my father and I—save one, and that I accepted gladly, readily.

"Then take me," I said to him.

"You have sadly upset my little arrangements. I had not thought of so fair an offender. Let me see." He paused, softly rubbing his chin.

There was a cat-like gratification about the creature as he stood glancing at me from time to time, with a smile flickering on his thin lips; and all the while my soul was searching, searching for the way of escape that I could not find.

"On the whole, it is the happiest plan," he said suddenly, with a little sigh of relief. "Let us make a move to the front door."

The sun was dropping to the western sea in angry banks of cloud. His rays shone so strongly in our faces that I had to shade my eyes as he pointed out the manner in which death should come to me.

"You are a strong, brave girl," he said with a little bow, "or I would not suggest so novel a scheme. I shall sit here in the porch and watch you as you walk over the moor, down into the little valley, up again, and so to the cliff edge. After a time for suitable meditation—let us say two minutes —you will step off into eternity. Do not fear, it is an easy method of putting an end to an infinity of troubles.... Keep back! keep back, I say!"

He was an old man, and it was worth the

"I shrank away from the black ring pointed at my chest."

effort. But as I sprang towards him, he whipped out a revolver from his pocket, and I shrank away from the black ring pointed at my chest.

"Such folly is not what I should have expected from Miss Weston," he continued. "Should you cause me to kill you, I shall certainly not spare your father. And why should two suffer for the fault of one?"

"How am I to know that even if I accept

this that you offer, you will let him go unharmed?" I cried.

"On my word of honour, I will not hurt a hair of his head."

"Your word of honour!"

"Do you doubt me, mademoiselle?" he shouted, flaring up into another burst of passion. "I come of an honourable house, a house that served its kings in many wars before the Revolution destroyed us. I am no pig of a German; I am a Marnac of Toulouse, mademoiselle, and we hold to our word though we are torn in pieces."

"But how can you, a gentleman, drive an innocent girl to so frightful a death?" I pleaded with him.

"Innocent? Did you not write that article?" He spoke eagerly, with a glance of keen suspicion.

"Yes. I wrote it."

"Then go. Remember, I wait and I watch. If you fear to do this thing, yes, even if you hesitate too long over there upon the cliff edge, I shall kill your father."

Without another word I began to walk down the sloping moor towards the sea.

* * * * *

I have asked Miss Mary Weston to end her narrative at this point. I think it better that I should now take up the threads of the story.

After Marnac's escape from Poland, Sir Henry Graden and I travelled to Berlin. There we carefully examined the book of extracts which had come into our hands, and sent warning letters to those writers who from the marginal notes seemed to have especially roused this madman's anger against them. The extreme animosity which was evinced against "Cantab's" article in the *University Review* especially alarmed us for the author's safety. Finally we determined to proceed to London, discover his identity, and take the necessary steps for his safety. Distasteful as was this detective business to a man of my studious habits, I nevertheless felt that it was my duty to assist my cousin in hunting down the murderer.

It was on the evening of Sunday, November 29th, that we arrived at Charing Cross Station, from which we removed to the morose respectability of Jerrold's Hotel. At eleven on the following morning we were ushered by a buttony boy into the editorial sanctum of the *University Review*.

Mr. Rolles—for such we had discovered was the name of the editor—remained seated before his American roller-top desk. He was a very large and sleek young man, with plump cheeks of a dingy colour, and *pince-nez* glasses which he wore half-way down his nose. His general appearance was suggestive of a capacity for plum-duff and sugar-water, and he oozed self-appreciation from every pore.

"And what can I do for you?" he inquired, with a sedate patronage.

"In the month of August," said my cousin, declining the chair that Mr. Rolles suggested, "you published an article signed 'Cantab,' dealing with a book written by Professor Marnac, of Heidelberg."

"Most certainly. Pray proceed."

"For the most urgent private reasons I desire 'Cantab's' name and address."

"Which I cannot give you," said Mr. Rolles, lighting a gold-tipped cigarette.

My cousin walked up to the editorial desk and spoke down upon him.

"From my card, sir, which I perceive you have before you, you can judge that I am a respectable person."

"Perhaps, perhaps," smiled Mr. Rolles; "but nowadays even baronets, you know, are—well, not always worthy of such implicit confidence as you demand."

I saw the right hand of my cousin steal out towards the editorial collar, but he restrained himself.

"You reduce me, sir, to speak of myself with less good taste than modesty," he said. "Have you never heard of my name as an explorer or a scientist?"

"Very often, my dear Sir Henry; though even for so distinguished a light I cannot break my most sacred rule. If you choose to write to 'Cantab,' I will forward the letter. Further I cannot go."

I don't think that Mr. Rolles will ever realise how near he came to a thorough trouncing. For a moment my cousin, so to speak, hung in the wind. Then he drew up a chair and sat down at the corner of the desk.

"I will accept your offer, sir," said he. "Give me a blank sheet of paper."

The letter written, it was handed over to Mr. Rolles, who gave us his word that it should go by the next post. Then we retired into the street.

My cousin was simply unbearable that day. He was always impatient of delay; but in all our wanderings together I have never suffered from him more acutely. He dragged me aimlessly about the streets, set me down to lunch at a comfortable restaurant, and then swept me off before the coffee arrived. I endeavoured to escape him, but the attempt was a hopeless failure. Five o'clock was striking when he turned his face eastward—he had been inquiring for letters at the Travellers', in Pall Mall—and, with his most unwilling companion trotting beside him, again advanced on Covent Garden, near which the office of the *University* was situated.

"I'm hanged if I can stand this suspense!" he explained. "Marnac has had five or six days' start of us, and anything may be happening. If that idiot Rolles still refuses the address, I will thrash him till he gives it up, and take the consequences."

He meant what he said—he always did—and I followed him, with unpleasant visions of a summons at Bow Street and caustic paragraphs in the evening papers.

But we were in luck. Mr. Rolles had retired to the Athenæum for his tea, and in the assistant editor, who received us, I recognised an old acquaintance. He was a clever young Scot named Raeburn, who had lived on my staircase at Cambridge, and rowed bow to my two in the college eight. He appeared delighted to see me, and became duly impressed when I introduced him to my distinguished cousin.

"Is there anything I can do for you?" he asked me, after a few minutes of the conversation usual in such circumstances.

Evidently he had no knowledge of our previous visit.

"Sir Henry here is anxious for the name and address of 'Cantab.' You will recollect the man I mean; he contributed an article to your August number."

"Well, it's against all the rules; but, of course, with you it doesn't matter. He is Dr. Weston, the Regius Professor of Physic at Cambridge. The old gentleman has been very seedy, I hear, and is down at Polleven, on the Cornish coast, for the winter. That article seems to have attracted a lot of attention. I had an old fellow here kicking up a fuss about it less than a week ago."

"What did he want to know?" broke in Graden sharply.

"It was a long rigmarole of a story, but it boiled down to this: that we were charged with hopelessly misprinting Dr. Weston's MSS. To get rid of the old boy, I sent up for the original copy of the article and showed it to him. He went away quite satisfied after that."

"Did he mention Dr. Weston's name?"

"No. That is—I——"

"Did you?"

"Yes, I believe I did. But I took it that he knew it already. Hallo! Anything wrong?"

Raeburn has since admitted his doubts as to our sanity; for without another word my cousin rushed from the room, and I followed at his heels.

From the *Review* office to our hotel was no great distance, and this we ran, regardless of the indignation of jostled wayfarers. My cousin plunged into the smoking-room and seized a Bradshaw. I looked over his shoulder with an equal excitement. The next express from Paddington was at midnight, and it was timed to arrive at the nearest station to Polleven that the map showed us by twelve-thirty the following morning. But that village itself was distant by road a good fifteen miles from the station. With Cornish hills we should be lucky if we arrived there by three in the afternoon. The Postal Guide informed us that our letter of warning would be delivered about twelve o'clock next day. A telegram—for there was no wire to Polleven—would scarcely arrive earlier. There was nothing more to be done.

It was, indeed, shortly before three o'clock that our carriage groaned and screeched its way down the steep descent into Polleven village. At the inn we soon discovered the direction of Dr. Weston's cottage, and taking the advice of the landlord as to the roughness of the track thither, we left our carriage and started off on foot. After a stiff climb of three-quarters of a mile between rugged cart-ruts running with water from the winter springs, we emerged into a little glen, sparsely wooded. At the further end, built on the higher ground, we caught a momentary glimpse of a building which we took to be the place we sought. From our right, low, booming reverberations told of distant breakers on a rock-bound coast.

It was I who first saw her, a glimpse of white amongst the bare skeletons of the stunted trees. Then at the turn of the path we met her. Her face was pale as fine linen, her eyes fixed and glassy, her arms with her clenched hands rigid by her sides. She might have been the ghost of some great lady who had died by cruel wrong. So blindly did she walk that I believe she would have passed us if Graden had not sprung forward and barred her way.

She woke as a sleep-walker wakes, with a shuddering surprise. "Who are you?" she asked faintly. If she had not grasped the branch of a tree, I think she would have fallen.

"'Who are you?' she asked faintly."

"Are you a relation of Dr. Weston's?" asked Graden very softly and kindly.

"His daughter."

"And you go?"

"To kill myself. Oh, no!" she burst out as we sprang forward. "It is no good! You cannot help me. The devil sits in the porch, waiting and watching. If I delay, he will kill—my father—my poor old father, who is so ill! Let me go—to the cliff—let me go, I say!"

Graden slipped his arm round her waist, and from his great height looked down at her with those honest blue eyes of his that made every child his friend at once.

"I am old enough to be your father, dear," he said. "You can trust me, can't you? Yes, yes, I knew it. Now tell me—what have you to do?"

"He is waiting in the porch," she answered him. "If he doesn't see me throw myself over the cliffs, he will kill father."

"Could he see us coming by the path which brought you here?"

"Oh, yes; above this glen it is open moor right up to the cottage."

"Is there a way to the back of the house?"

"Yes; but there is no time."

"That is foolish talk. Come, tell me."

"About two hundred yards back on the track you followed here there is a little spring amongst the rushes. There is a path, a short cut which the boys from the village sometimes take that leads into the clump of firs by the garden wall. The wall is quite low—and then—oh! then—you could get straight into father's room. It is on the ground floor; the room on the left as you open the back door. You could lock the door and defy the other man."

"Now listen to me, dear," said Graden. "You must walk on very, very slowly. Take all the time you can. At the cliff top make several starts as if you would jump, but feared. Mind that you do not go too near the edge. And so in ten minutes come home. We will meet you, and all will be well—at least, for your father," he added grimly.

"I understand," she answered simply, and walked on.

It was a wild rush that we made. We found the spring, and turning to our right crashed into the thicket—for the "path" was a courtesy title. The hanging scrub brushed our faces, in the open patches the dead gorse dug its spines into our knees. We quickened our pace in the more open fir-wood, vaulted the four-foot wall of the little garden, and, panting like exhausted hounds, ran furiously upon the house. There was no time for dodging and crawling. It was a forlorn hope we led.

And Dr. Weston was alive.

He sat amongst his pillows, a great book upon his knees, gazing over his spectacles with the most profound amazement on his kindly old face at the two dishevelled strangers who burst in upon him. Leaving me to guard and quiet him—for, indeed, the shock might prove most dangerous—Graden dashed out on his errand of vengeance. Two minutes later I heard him call, and breaking off the excuses that I was inventing, I ran through the house to join him.

Miss Weston and he were standing before the porch—alone. She was leaning on his arm, panting from great exertion.

"Think of it, Robert!" cried my cousin. "He chased her—the devil followed and chased her!"

"How is my father?" she faltered. "Is he —as this gentleman says—quite unharmed?"

"Quite safe, I assure you," I answered.

"I must go to him."

"One moment, Miss Weston," said my cousin. "We have yet a duty to the public safety. Which way has the man run?"

She told her story quickly. After she had left us and gained the cliff turf above the glen, she glanced back. To her surprise, she caught a glimpse of him standing amongst the trees on the opposite slope. Her delay had aroused his suspicions, and he had followed her. She walked slowly forward and, as we had directed, moved uneasily about on the verge of the precipice. Presently she again glanced over her shoulder. He had now crossed the glen and was standing in the open watching her. The distance between them was about two hundred yards. She knew that we must have nearly reached the cottage, and that if he had not already attacked her father, there was no further danger. So she started to run along the coast. He shouted and drew his revolver; but either he thought the distance too great, or he feared the noise of the report, for he did not fire. But her action evidently puzzled him, seeing that it left her father completely at his mercy. He did not pursue her far, but instead turned and gazed in-tently at the cottage. On her part, she also stopped running to watch him. From where they stood the garden was fully exposed, and at that moment our forms appeared as we vaulted the low wall. At which sight, Miss Weston said, he gave a most horrible scream, shaking his fists towards us and filling the air with imprecations. Then, without further noticing her, he set off towards the town. For herself, she came back as fast as she could run, meeting Graden before the door. She added some useful particulars as to his alias and his residence at the inn.

And so, her story ended, the brave girl passed into the house, while we dashed away in pursuit. My cousin stuck to his work most manfully; but age will tell, and I was a minute to the good when I stumbled into the parlour of the inn. They had not seen Mr. Hermann, they told me, since lunch-time; perhaps he was down at his boat.

"Boat—what boat?" I gasped.

"Why, zur," said the landlord's wife, grinning at my eagerness, "the guid gentleman be mighty vond o' zailing, an' he hath hired Mark Pennyfold's noo trawler, the *Agnes Jane*, for a matter o' two months. And now I comes to think on it, I did hear Mark zay as how he an' his zun were going out with Maister Hermann betwixt dree an' vour o'clock."

I ran down the narrow street towards the quay, between the quaint old cottages, with their fish stretched out to dry, and their nets, fishing-boots, and gear tumbled before the door-sills. As I reached the little breakwater, the sun, low on the west horizon, was throwing great golden streamers through gaps in the purple clouds that were piled as high as if a cataclysm of Nature had set the Andes on the Himalayas. From their feet came gusts of wind, fierce and icy cold. Even to my shore-going eyes it threatened dirty weather.

But I had no time for cloud effects. There, fair in the glittering path that the sun had daubed upon the waters, a red-sailed fishing-boat was running close-hauled to the sou'-westward.

"What boat is that?" I asked a lad who lounged against a mooring-post at my elbow.

"That, maister—whoi, it be Mark Pennyfold's *Agnes Jane*, 'er as was 'ired by the stranger from Lunnon, 'Ermann by name."

A hand fell on my shoulder. It was Graden's. He had heard and understood. And so we two stood together watching the red sails fade slowly into the gathering haze of the night and the storm.

THE TRAIL OF THE DEAD:

THE STRANGE EXPERIENCE OF DR. ROBERT HARLAND.

By B. FLETCHER ROBINSON and J. MALCOLM FRASER.*

V.—THE AMMONIA CYLINDER.

THE sail crept forward down the river of sunset gold that streamed in wild splendour from a crevass in the ranges of cloudland. The light that burnished the sea glowed upon the Polleven cliffs, tinging with fire the breakers at their feet; it threw fierce shadows amongst the clustered cottages of the Cornish fisherfolk, and painted a richer scarlet on the sails of the trawlers huddled beneath the sheltering arm of the little quay. It was a scene that rises before me, as I write, with a curious detail, though, indeed, at the time I took no pains to observe it. For on that departing vessel was he whom we had chased across Europe, madman as we supposed, murderer as we knew him to be. We had saved an innocent girl from his vendetta, and in my heart I thanked Providence for that mercy; but Rudolf Marnac, the Heidelberg professor, was still free, free with fresh schemes of vengeance against his scientific opponents hatching in his twisted brain, and with all the wisdom of his great learning to help him in his deadly purposes.

"So this is the end of your clever plans!" I cried, turning savagely on my burly cousin. "He has escaped again, got clear away. What are you going to do? Shall we follow him?"

"In the face of the storm?"

"Why not—if that is the best you can suggest?"

"You have changed, my little cousin," said he, regarding me with a kindly look, though, indeed, my words had been unmannerly. "The Fates have played the very deuce with the sedate student that I dragged out of his pleasant rooms at Heidelberg just twelve days ago. How that youngster grumbled at prospective discomforts! How he shrank from the thought of being mixed up in a business that was 'better left to the police'! Do you remember?"

"Don't we waste time?" said I.

"Perhaps. Ah! here she comes—just the thing for which I was hoping."

Running down the village street came Miss Weston, with three or four men behind her. We met her at the entrance to the quay.

"Well! have you caught him?" she panted.

"No; there he goes." My cousin pointed an arm at the distant sail.

"Oh, thank God!" she exclaimed earnestly. "I knew he was armed, and I was so afraid for the brave men who had saved my father and me."

She looked from one to the other of us with an honest gratitude in her eyes that to me seemed worth the risk of all the dangers in the world.

"And Dr. Weston?" asked my cousin.

"My father is no worse; but of course I did not tell him all. He imagines that I was annoyed by some tramp, and declares he will have a man about the cottage in future. You and your friend must come back with me, Sir Henry. I want to introduce you to him."

"Some other time, I hope. At present this young firebrand here insists that we should follow Marnac by sea."

"That is quite impossible, sir," she said, turning upon me with an anxious look. "I have enough experience of the weather to know that a storm is coming. I am certain that Sir Henry Graden will help me to dissuade you."

"I am afraid not, Miss Weston," broke in my cousin before I could reply. "We have been like over-eager hounds, losing the scent by flashing forward too quickly. It must be sheer, dogged hunting now, and no more cutting off corners. By the way, there is a fact which perhaps one of you can tell me," he said, turning to the little group that hung behind her skirts watching us with a bucolic interest. "Did the *Agnes Jane* yonder carry provisions on board?"

---

* Copyright, 1903, by B. Fletcher Robinson and J. Malcolm Fraser, in the United States of America.

"Surely, zur," said one who stood a little forward of the rest—a stout, bearded man with a face as brown and seamed as a withered cider-apple. "Mark Pennyfold, as is owner, was telling about this furrin gent only last night down tu the 'Plough Inn.' 'E allowed 'im to be a funny zort of toad, vur 'e 'ad 'is orders to keep a week's vittles on board, though the reason was passin' his onderstanding."

"Would Pennyfold take a trip to France if he were asked?"

"Surely, zur, ef 'e be paid accordin'. 'E be most mazed on the colour of a bit of gold is Mark."

"That settles it, Miss Weston," continued Graden in his short, businesslike way. "Now please to remember my instructions. You have the facts concerning Professor Marnac in my letter. Lay an information against him for an attempt on your life, and see that the county authorities circulate his description along the coast. I don't think there is the slightest chance that he will return to trouble you, but be on your guard, and have a man to sleep in the house. Now, my lads, who has the swiftest boat in the harbour?"

"Now you be askin' a question," said their spokesman gloomily. "You zee, it be this wise. At the regatty, as my *Pride o' Cornwall* was reaching for the west buoy, there comes, all of a sudden like, a girt wind from over the eastern beacon which——"

"He means, Sir Henry, that his boat is reckoned the fastest, but at the regatta she was disabled by a squall," broke in Miss Weston, interrupting a story which was evidently familiar in its length and detail. "This is Sir Henry Graden, Isaac Treherne, and he is trying to capture the wicked man in the *Agnes Jane* yonder, the man who, as I told you, tried to kill me. Will you take him in the *Pride of Cornwall*?"

Isaac was a study of indecision. He twisted up his mouth, scratched his head, regarded the sunset attentively, and kicked a pebble over the edge of the quay.

"I du wish, miss, as I 'ad been nigh you when 'e tried it," he said at last. "I would 'ave set about the hugly toad proper, that I would. But, beggin' your pardin, and seein' he be got away, 'twould seem a matter for the perlice mor'n for we uns. Moreover, there be the fish contract, and the *Pride* is only waiting her crew to zail."

"It means a hundred pound in your pocket, my man," snapped Graden.

"A 'undred pounds is a 'undred pounds," replied Isaac with a sententious inconsequence.

"But, Isaac," broke in Miss Weston, "when the story gets round to Mark Pennyfold, he will say that you refused because you knew that the *Pride* could never catch the *Agnes Jane*."

"Zo he wull—the liard!" cried Isaac, with a sudden burst of indignation. "I never thought on that, miss. A pretty tale he will be telling in every public from Bude to Penzance! Come along, gentlemen, come along. I'll show 'e a thing, and Mark, tu, the liard!"

We ran to where the little trawler lay moored to the quay, and tumbled on board. One man was sitting in her stern mending some tackle, and Isaac apparently considered his services sufficient, for he cast off the ropes at once. Miss Weston was waiting on the head of the quay as our boat crept by. I shall always remember that picture of my darling as she stood on those old grey stones, with their seaweed beard dropping to the swirl of the tide below. The fire of the sunset lit her tall, graceful figure leaning to the breeze. One hand was to her hair, the other waving us adieu. No fairer figure of encouragement could men desire who started on a perilous adventure.

"Good-bye! God keep you both!" So she cried to us.

We shouted a reply, but I doubt if she heard it, for at that moment the wind caught the great red sail on our foremast, swinging it across with a thunderous flapping that shook the little vessel from stem to stern. In another moment we were rushing forward in pursuit, with the spray from the bows in our faces and a white trail of foam marking our path from the land.

I do not think that more than ten minutes had passed from the moment of our arrival on the quay, though by my writing it may seem that I have underestimated the time. The *Agnes Jane* was, as far as I could judge, about a mile away to the southward, a distance which we decreased to barely a thousand yards before the full strength of the growing wind we brought had reached her. After that, however, we gained very slowly, if at all.

I was never a good sailor, a fact which the long rollers soon recalled to my remembrance. The occasional bursts of spray which flew over us added greatly to my discomfort, for my clothes, though warm, were not waterproof. I have always been susceptible to chills, and the prospect of passing the night in dripping garments seriously alarmed me. It was, therefore, with a sense of great relief that I observed Isaac produce some spare oilskins, and boots happily lined with flannel.

The seafaring appearance which I assumed did not, however, allay my internal sufferings, which soon became acute. Huddled on the leeward side of the boat, I watched the chase with an appearance of interest which was mere hypocrisy. To be sincere, I regarded my cousin, who was enjoying a pipe

"'Good-bye! God keep you both!' So she cried to us."

of strong-smelling tobacco on the windward side of me, with a more immediate enmity than I felt towards Marnac himself.

The sun sank amidst a cloud conflagration of sullen and thunderous magnificence. The coastline behind us darkened and faded until the crests of the breaking waves rose ghastly white against the gloom of the shrouded land. But fortunately the sky above us was still clear, and a silver crescent of the moon, swinging at an angle as if the wind had tilted her, showed us the chase heading southward. It was evidently some port in France for which she pointed. My cousin had joined Isaac, who was at the tiller, and the pair conversed in low tones, glancing frequently to the north-west, from which the wind blew strong and cold.

It was, according to my remembrance, past nine o'clock that the steady pressure of the wind failed. In its place came gusts, fierce and uncertain, spaced with lulls of restless calm. Ignorant as I was of sea weather, I began to grow uneasy. There seemed a menace in the dark, mysterious wall of cloud to windward, a rampart edged with silver from the moon. Motionless it hung like a heavy curtain that at its rising would reveal some monstrous spectacle. For the first time I realised the insignificance of our boat, its loneliness amidst the hurrying wastes of the sea, and my anxiety passed into alarm. It was about this time that my nausea suddenly left me. This was a great relief to me, for I was well aware that an excess of sea-sickness may result in a serious prostration.

It was in one of the lulls I have mentioned that Isaac gave my cousin the helm and with his man's assistance lowered the sail on the smaller mast at the stern which, I believe, is known nautically as the jigger. They also reefed the larger canvas on the foremast. The *Agnes Jane*, which was now not more than four hundred yards away, showed no sign of following our example.

"Mark Pennyfold must be mazed," said Isaac, on his return aft. "'E must have zeen us were chasin' 'e, yet 'e gives we no chance o' speaking 'im; and now 'e be chancing his boat by carrying on with that press o' zail. Plaze to keep thy hand on the tiller, zur."

The little Cornishman rolled forward to where I sat, and stood, making a hollow of his hands. A great stillness held the sea and air, save for the whisper of the gliding waves.

"The *Agnes Jane*, ahoy!"

He drove the words over the black waters like the blast of a trumpet.

"The *Agnes Jane*, ahoy!"

Again he called, and this time there came an answering voice.

"Help!" it cried—the one word—and was silent. We waited, but that was all.

"It is no good, Treherne," said my cousin. "They have an ugly customer on board who does not mean to be taken. He has his pistol at their heads as like as not. They must take their chance of——"

His words were lost in a stirring note

like the throbbing of a giant harp-string, a note that rose to a shriek and then melted into a rattling, drumming roar, the uttermost diapason of the storm-wind. For some seconds we heeled over, so that I could have dipped my face in the bubbling waters; and then, slowly gathering way, we shot forward through the flying spray, with Treherne yelling to his man in tones that even out-sounded the squall itself.

We were upon her almost before I realised the disaster that had befallen her. I caught a glimpse of the level lines of timbers about the keel, the red sails awash in streaks of hissing foam; and then I saw my cousin lean out and grip a something in the water. For a moment I thought he would be dragged from the boat, but Isaac, letting go the tiller, circled his legs with a pair of muscular arms and held on like the little bulldog he was. With three great heaves Graden lugged the dripping thing he held to the boat's edge; with a fourth he landed it fairly on board. The *Agnes Jane* had gone, and with her the unfortunate men she carried—save Marnac only.

Thus Fate in its own strange manner had given him to us at last!

Shouting like a madman, I started towards the stern, where my cousin was bending over the huddled body he had saved. But even as I did so I saw a black mass, crested and streaked with hissing white, rush up from the obscurity to windward. For a space it seemed to hang above us, while Isaac yelled as he tugged wildly at the tiller. Then, with a wild roar that drummed in my ears like the explosion of a mine, it threw itself upon us, hurling me into the bottom of the boat, choked, deafened, and blinded.

I do not know how we lived through that first furious hour. Isaac Treherne made no second mistake, but crouched at the tiller, tricking the succession of great seas that swung upon us out of the throbbing blackness. Stung by passing hailstorms, drenched to the skin, and aching with cold, I toiled with a tin pannikin, baling, baling until my back creaked with stiffness and my hands could scarce feel the handle. Graden and the sailor worked beside me, so that we managed to keep the water under. Now and again a slit in the rushing dark above us showed me Marnac lying by the steersman's side. Was he alive or dead? I did not know, nor did I stay my labour to make inquiry.

The daylight came at last, the God-given light for which all poor mariners must pray in their hours of danger. With it came a lessening of the wind and a falling sea. Yet there had been an angry menace in the brilliant colours that lit the eastern sky, and I stared eagerly over the muddy green of the hurrying surges. Indeed, I was the first to see a steamer's smudge of smoke on the western skyline.

"Her be making for we, gentlemen," remarked our steersman, after a long stare at the distant vessel. "Happen her would take 'e aboard, if you be so minded. The weather be blowing up again, and it's a long reach back to Polleven."

"I don't like deserting the ship, Isaac," said Graden; "though, to tell the truth, I don't relish another day in the chops of the Channel."

"Bain't no desartion, sir. Me and Jake can take her whoam; and, to tell 'e the truth, her'll ride the lighter for the want of him!"

He pointed to where Marnac sat crouching under an oilskin coat. Save for occasional shivers, the old man seemed to be no worse for his handshake with Death. He received the sailor's remark with a benevolent smile.

"Doan't 'e go grinning at me, you wicked-minded old toad!" cried Isaac. "'Twas only through special mercies that Providence forgot you was on board. We'd ha' been sunk for zarten, else."

Within half an hour we could see the steamer clearly, an ancient tramp of the seas, bluff in the bows, square in the flank, with a colouring of soot and rusty iron. She answered our signals with a melancholy toot and stood towards us. Graden, who had been watching her approach at my side, turned and walked aft.

"I have already dropped your revolver overboard, Professor Marnac," he said; "but I must trouble you to hand me your pocket-book. Money, you know, is often the most valuable of weapons."

The Professor obeyed with a gentle cluck of amusement.

"I trust, Sir Henry, that the notes are not damaged," he said in the low, musical tones with which I was so familiar. "Indeed, I was assured that the case was waterproof."

"Now your loose gold, if you please."

"Here it is, Sir Henry, with my watch and chain. Observe that my pockets are now completely empty. Ah, Mr. Harland! forgive me if I did not notice you before. I fear that these nautical adventures will interrupt your course of studies. Did you hear whom the University have appointed in my place? I should be sorry if my students, amongst whom I always held you to be the most studious, if not the most able, should be long without a lecturer—like sheep that have lost their shepherd, Mr. Harland."

I turned from him with a feeling of nausea. Mad or sane, he had done such

"I saw my cousin lean out and grip a something in the water."

deeds as placed him beyond the intercourse of humanity.

The steamer was close upon us now, and as she came rolling down the heave of the swell we were hailed from the bridge in a tongue that was strange to me. Before we could reply, a seaman had sprung to the bulwarks and sent the coils of a line spinning over us. This Isaac made fast, allowing a fair space to intervene between his little craft and the rusty metal fabric that towered above us.

"Good-bye, Isaac," said Graden, shaking the little Cornishman warmly by the hand. "I will see to your cheque the moment I get to London."

"Doan't 'e mention it, zur. I was right proud to take 'e. Nor do 'e trouble about we uns. Jake and I will be making Polleven by midnight at latest—please be."

It was an anxious scramble—they had to swing out a chair for Marnac—but the trawler was as handy as a row-boat, and at last the three of us stood on the deck of the stranger. A more ill-assorted trio of bedraggled voyagers never ranged in line.

But if we were strange to look upon, so were the group of men who confronted us. They were of the degenerate Latin breed, dark, small, uncertain in temper, and dirty by nature and training. Their seafaring dress seemed as ill-suited to them as a sash and a coloured cloak would be to a British shellback.

"Eengleshe?" asked one whom I took to be the mate. "Eengleshe? What say?"

"We are Englishmen who were driven out to sea by last night's storm. If I may see the captain, I will explain," said my cousin.

The man grinned his lack of comprehension. Plainly his vocabulary was of the smallest.

"These men are Portuguese, Sir Henry," said Marnac, stepping quickly forward. "I know their language. Allow me to explain the situation."

But he got no further. My cousin's long arm shot out, gripping his collar firmly from behind. With a gentle heave, he swung the Professor from his feet and dropped him behind us.

"Please to keep silence, Professor Marnac. Your explanations might be somewhat biassed," said he, with a grim smile. And then turning to the sailors, who had been watching the little scene with evident surprise—

"Do none of you speak English?" he asked.

They seemed to understand the question, for some talk, eked out by much gesticulation, ended in one of their number trotting up the ladder to the bridge, where he disappeared into the wheel-house. An instant later a long, red-headed man emerged and came running towards us.

"And shure wud Oi not have greeted yer honours before now," he exclaimed in the most strenuous of brogues; "but 'twas me trick at the wheel, and niver a wan of these spalpeens wud relieve me. An' what can Oi do fer ye now at all?"

"What boat is this?"

"The Portugaise ship, San Joseph, fr'm Buenos Ayres to Hamburg wid a mixed cargo, and a darned mixed crew, sorr. If it hadn't been fer a back answer whin the wine was in me, faith! it's not on this greasy flat-ir-ron that Tim Blake wud be after serving."

"Do you speak the language, my man?"

"Indade an' Oi do, sorr; an' good raison, seeing that 'tis fower years come Christmas that Oi've been steward on th' yacht iv wan iv tha' Portugaise nobility."

"That's good news. And now where is the captain?"

"Faith! but 'twas a jool iv a toime we were after havin' in the Bay last night, sorr, an' the old man's turned in. The second mate has gone aft, gatherin' his courage in both hands fer to wake him. Indade, sorr, 'tis a r-resolution that wud put the fear iv the Lord into a better man than him."

"Rather a Tartar, eh?"

"A strong man, sorr, an' a good seaman fer a greaser, though his temper is most pro-digious. But see, here he comes, like a dook out iv a theatre."

He was indeed a fine figure of a man, fully six feet in height and proportionately broad. His skin was very dark, and his eyes of the deep blackness that I have since observed in Indian races, but very soft and glowing. His hair, which he wore at a greater length than is customary amongst sailors, showed under his cap in glossy curls; and his moustache was twisted back almost to his ears.

He bowed to us with a deliberate courtesy, muttering a greeting in his own tongue. He spoke no English, and it was through the medium of Tim Blake that he offered us hospitality. It was no time for explanations, so, guarding Marnac between us, we hurried down to a large cabin where warm garments and steaming glasses of hot brandy-and-water were brought by the worthy Irishman, to whose care we had been assigned. As far as could be judged, I had not contracted so much as a cold in the head, despite my long exposure. When we had completed our change of clothes, my cousin beckoned me outside the cabin, closing the door on our prisoner.

"I have asked Blake to take me to the captain, for it is right that he should know the true position of affairs," he whispered. "While I am gone, you must sit with Marnac. Remember, do not let him out of your sight for a moment."

"Very well," I said, and he strode off down the dark alley of the passage-way.

When I re-entered the cabin, I found Marnac muffled to the chin, under the blankets of a bunk. He gave me one of his quick, evil glances, that was unpleasantly reminiscent of an aged rat surprised in an iron gin. I had so great a horror and detestation of the man that his mere presence was a source of physical discomfort to me; and when, sitting up amongst his wraps, he commenced to pester me with questions, I could endure it no longer. I retired outside the cabin, seating myself with my back to the door. I was as well there, I argued, as in the interior, and in a position infinitely more satisfactory to myself.

The garments they had lent me were thick and warm; the dose of brandy had been considerable. I was weary from the toil of a sleepless night. Those are my excuses for the fact that in the course of the next five minutes I fell soundly asleep.

It was Graden who woke me, a very angry and exasperated Graden who shook my senses into me with unnecessary violence. I started up, protesting against his treatment.

"I thought better of you than this," he said, with his hand still fixed in my collar.

"My back was against the door. He could not pass without waking me. What does it matter?" I grumbled, with every sign of irritation.

"I told you to watch him, to stay inside the cabin, and I find you snoring here. No more excuses, please. You know the ability of the man. Let us hope he has not taken advantage of any chances you gave him."

He opened the door cautiously, peeped in, and then flung it wide with a great oath. The cabin was empty!

Yet there was no doubt as to his manner

"'Tis fower years come Christmas that Oi've been steward on th' yacht.'"

of escape. In the middle of the flooring there gaped a hole, with a heavy square of wood lying beside it. On examination, we found that this entrance had also been barred by a grating, which now swung downwards on its hinges, disclosing a wooden ladder, the foot of which was indistinguishable in the gloom below.

"He is in the hold!" I cried. "He is hiding somewhere amongst the cargo! We shall never find him without the help of the crew."

Amongst the excellent points in my cousin's character was that of perfect self-control. There was no anger in his voice to remind me of my blunder when he spoke again.

"It's not the hold, cousin Robert," he said. "This is the ship's *lazarette*, where the food is stored. There are usually two entrances, each similar to this. If he has escaped by the second, it's a bad business. It will mean he has found a friend, for these gratings should be secured. But it may be that he is lurking amongst the pork and the biscuits. If so, we ought to find him easily enough. I don't want to bring the crew into this affair if I can help it. It will be enough if the captain knows."

"But he does—you have told him."

"That's the blackest part of the luck. The ship caught it pretty badly last night; they were right in the thick of it. I found the captain on deck superintending three or four sailors who were clearing away the wreckage of one of the boats. He was in an amazing temper, and Blake advised me that if I had a favour to ask him, I had best let him cool off a bit. So I dismissed the Irishman and climbed up to the bridge. I should think I'd been there about twenty minutes watching the work, when I saw a sharp-looking lad pop out from the companion and go over to where the captain was standing. They had a fine pow-wow together, looking up at me from time to time. It rather puzzled me, and presently I dropped down the stairs and walked over to where they were. The captain seemed decidedly chilly, and I soon saw by his manner that he was not wanting a talk just then. Whereupon I came below. So kindly light the lamp I see in the bracket yonder, cousin Robert, and we'll go hunting again."

We descended the ladder, Graden going first, and I following with the lamp, the light of which I endeavoured to throw over his shoulder.

It seems a cowardly thing to confess, writing as I am in the broad daylight, with the bees amongst the flower-beds singing their song through the open window, but though we were two to one, and our quarry an old man, my cousin had twice to rate me for the deliberation of my movements. We peered about amongst the lurking shadows, with the thunder of the seas hammering on the iron sides without. Now and again a heave of the ship would send us staggering apart, to bring up amongst unexpected barrels. Perhaps it was the want of sleep that had jangled my nerves, but I knew in my heart that if I were suddenly to catch a sight of those wicked eyes staring out from the gloom before us, I should shriek and run like a hysterical schoolgirl.

But Marnac was not there. The grate of the second stairway was closed and locked, and yet he had disappeared. Someone had helped him—that was plain enough. We stood disconsolate amongst the details of the ship's larder.

"Well, he's gone right enough," said my cousin. "Hallo! what the deuce is this?"

He took the light from my hand and stooped to examine something at his feet. It was a steel cylinder, about eight feet in length; a second lay beside it.

"Ammonia! So they run a cold storage on board."

"How do you know that?" I asked.

"My dear cousin, if you can't remember the part that ammonia plays in the manufacture of ice, I shall not attempt to—hallo! stop that—stop that, I say!"

He sprang forward, caught his foot in an empty sack, and fell heavily, extinguishing the lamp. As he did so, I saw an arm reach down and draw up the grating through which we had descended. A key clicked in the padlock. Graden was on his feet in an instant, and together we rushed to the foot of the ladder.

In the patch of grey daylight above us we could see the face of the captain looking through the bars, and peeping down beside him, with the sweetest dimple of an old man's smile upon his lips, was Professor Marnac!

There was a pause, filled with much whispered talk from above. Then the red head of our friend Tim Blake came thrusting into the picture. He seemed much distressed at the situation.

"Faith! but 'tis not Oi that knows fwhat to belaive," said he; "but the skipper here will have it that yer-re a pair iv desprite and revolting characters. Oi am also to tell ye, gintlemen, that ye've the very divil's own choice of ut. Eyther ye will let me r-run through yere pockuts wid me practised hand, upon which ye may come up an' make us acquainted wid yere gineral defence, or, if ye refuse, be jabbers! but they'll clap on the hatches an' lave ye in the dark."

"Tell the skipper, Blake," said my cousin, "that he has been grossly deceived, for we are law-abiding English gentlemen. Nevertheless, if he will keep to his terms and hear our case out, we consent to being searched."

The Irishman vanished, and again came the murmur of voices. Then he reappeared, unlocking the grating and descending the ladder. At the edge of the hole I could see the faces of several members of the crew, and caught the gleam of drawn knives. Evidently they did not trust us.

When it was over, we followed Blake up the ladder and waited quietly while he laid out Graden's revolver and our few belongings on the flap of a central table behind which the captain was standing. A short speech by that worthy, and the Irishman began again.

"The skipper wud have ye know," he said, addressing Graden with a growing dignity that would have been comic enough at a less unfortunate moment, "that ye stand accused iv carrying off the ould gint yonder and committin' burglary on his person. Fwhat do ye say to that, sorr?"

"It is absolutely untrue."

"Wan for him, thin. But Oi'm to ask ye how ye account fer th' possession iv that pocket-book the skipper is holding so loving in his hand. He says that there's close on five hundred pounds in ut. Is ut yours?"

"No—it belongs to the old gentleman."

"The divil it does! Then how did ye come by ut?"

I feel certain that if my cousin could have told his story directly to the captain, the honesty of his manner and the simplicity of his narration would have had effect. But this pleading at second-hand was a sorry business. From his long pauses and facial contortions I soon gathered that Blake was not the linguist that he claimed to be. Indeed, the version which the captain received from him must have been something astounding. The tale was scarcely concluded when the captain raised his hand, and the flounderings of the interpreter ceased abruptly.

Thus was his decision translated. He would touch at Southampton, where the case could be fought out in the English courts. In the meanwhile, as the evidence was overwhelmingly against us, we should be placed in irons and confined in the cabin where we then were.

He was a just man. Angry though I was at the time, I have come to think he did the right thing. The harmless appearance of Marnac, his ability to plead his cause, our obvious endeavour to keep him from communicating with the crew, our possession of so valuable a pocket-book belonging to him —no, we cannot blame the captain if he decided in his favour.

To attempt resistance would have been absurd. The men about us carried knives, and the butt of a heavy revolver showed warningly from the captain's pocket. For the first time in either of our lives the handcuffs snapped at our wrists. They moved out one by one; the door was closed and barred upon us. In another three minutes we were both sound asleep. Our ill-fortune, the doings of our most dangerous enemy, the irons at our wrists—we forgot them all in the dead, still sleep that Nature grants to the very weary.

It was Blake who woke us with our midday meal. He was in his most talkative mood. Guilty or innocent, it made small difference to him, after he had decided upon the fact of our gentility. He was agog with the manner of Marnac's escape from us. The lad who was servant to the captain had been down in the *lazarette*, and from pure curiosity had poked up the trap in the cabin floor. With promises of money, Marnac had persuaded the youngster to guide him to the captain. In their haste they had forgotten to close the trap and grating behind them, though they had secured those at the head of the second ladder. Marnac had waited in the captain's room while the lad went forward to find his master. It was doubtless their interview that Graden had observed from the bridge. When the supposed victim of our plot had told his story, they had armed themselves and come to arrest us, calling the Irishman and two more of the crew in case of resistance. They had found us below—a source of delight to the Portuguese sailors, who had a healthy terror of Englishmen; and the rest we already knew.

"Come, my man," said my cousin after he had concluded, "for yourself, now—do you believe us guilty?"

"Faith, sorr, 'tis a quare business entoirely," he answered, scratching his red pole indecisively. "For whether 'tis you or the ould gintleman that they'll lay by the heels in Southampton Water, it's not fer me to be after saying. Sure 'tis wan of the two—which is all Oi knows."

"Now listen to me, Tim Blake," said my cousin. "My name is, as I told you, Sir Henry Graden, and I am a rich man. I am not asking you to neglect your duty, which is to keep us in; but if you will have an eye to the door so as to keep that old gentleman out, there'll be five-and-twenty pounds in your pocket."

Whatever the Irishman may have thought of our characters, there was no doubt as to his belief in the genuine nature of the offer. He beamed upon us with a childlike jubilation that was quite comic in its enthusiasm.

"Indade, sorr, indade, and I will!" he cried.

"Have you the key?"

"I have, sorr. Wud your honour like to kape it! You can turn the lock whin I knock fower times."

"That will hardly do," said my cousin, laughing. "We might have the captain visiting us, which would mean a change of gaolers. Now as to the trap-door—is that also secured?"

"The lad we spoke of—he has the kay, sorr. May the divil seize him!"

"We can't leave it like that. See if you can fix it up to better advantage."

Blake raised the outer block of wood which fitted level with the flooring, and inspected the grating below. It was secured by a padlock—a precaution necessary enough, for honesty is not the prevailing characteristic of a Portuguese crew. After a moment's thought, he drew from his pocket a handful of assorted rubbish from which he extracted a large nail. Graden's boot served as a hammer, and with this he drove it into the key-hole.

"'Twill hould it foine!" cried he, regarding his work with exultation.

And so, with fresh assurances of watchfulness, he left us.

The wind rose again that afternoon, and by four o'clock it was blowing very hard. The seas drove against the sides of the old ship in thunderous murmurs; now and again they sprang the bulwarks, crashing down upon the deck above us and shaking the iron fabric in convulsive tremors. In the confined cabin my nausea again visited me. Enough that I was supremely miserable.

At six, Blake had brought us a supper. His presence irritated me; and when he pressed food upon me, I spoke my mind strongly on the lamentable want of tact general amongst sailors. He gave us the comfortable news, however, that we were expected to reach Southampton by three next morning.

The night crawled on. Blake had helped us into bunks and covered us with rugs. I found the handcuffs of small inconvenience. I could hear Graden snoring. For myself, I could not get to sleep, but lay in the lowest misery, staring at the opposite partition, that rose and fell at the ship's rollings with a sickening regularity. Just before midnight, the lamp—that had probably been injured when Graden fell in the *lazarette*—smoked, stank, and expired. I was too unwell to care, except for the smell.

Yet it was the darkness which saved our lives.

It was about half an hour later that I first noticed it—a faint ray of illumination winking in the centre of the cabin floor. At first I imagined that the nausea had affected my eyes, and so peered into the black of the night, rubbing them impatiently. But the rays steadied and, if anything, increased in volume. It was a ghostly thing to witness, this white knife-edge of light stabbing up from the solid planking without cause or explanation. I was about to shout to Graden when I remembered the trap-door. Someone was below in the *lazarette*!

For some moments I remained staring at the crevice through which the rays passed up to me. After all, it might be some member of the crew; but if not—if it were Marnac! What then? He was an old man; he could not force the grating, even if he had obtained the key. We had seen to that.

I do not pretend to say that I was unafraid. There were devilish possibilities in a hatred such as that in which the mad Professor held us. Yet after a while my curiosity overcame my fear, just as my fear had put aside my sickness. I rolled from my bunk—noisily enough, I dare say, but all sound was dulled by the turmoil without. The pitching of the vessel made it impossible for me to stand, so I crawled forward to where the edge of the trap was outlined. I felt for and found the ring, gripped it with my teeth, and slowly, for the irons hampered my balance, raised the edge. Then with my hands I thrust the edge of the boot, which I had removed for that purpose, into the crack. Flat on my face, I peeped below.

It was indeed Marnac. The light of a

ship's lantern, jammed between two barrels, drew streaks of silver from his white hair as he bent to his labour. Seated astride one of the steel cylinders that we had noticed, he was unscrewing the last of the nuts which secured its iron cap. What he intended I had no idea.

He was fingering the nut which the

"Marnac spun round with a scream of the most violent passion."

spanner had loosened, when I saw a face creep out of the shadow behind him. It was the captain's boy. With infinite caution he moved forward, with a blending of alarm and curiosity in his manner that showed he was no party to what was proceeding. Probably the key to the *lazarette* had been purloined from him, and he had discovered its loss. When scarcely two yards from Marnac, the lurch of the ship threw him from his balance. As he stumbled forward, Marnac spun round with a scream of the most violent passion. Swinging the heavy spanner, he brought it down upon the bent head with a scrunching blow. The lad dropped upon the floor face downwards; nor did he try to rise again.

"Murderer!" I cried down upon him, in horror at so fearful a spectacle.

Marnac dropped his weapon and started back, his fingers twitching, his eyes searching wildly round for a sight of his accuser. Yet when, at last, he saw my face above him, he drew himself together without a sign of trepidation for his discovered crime—save that the hand with which he gripped the stairs still shook slightly.

"Ach! but it is you," he whispered up. "For a moment I thought—but it was the folly of a child. And so, Mr. Harland, you come again to trouble me. Well, it is for the last time—mark you that—for the very last time."

He sat himself across the cylinder. As he did so, I felt a hand upon my shoulder and knew that Graden was awake.

"You might have spared the lad," he said very quietly.

Marnac looked up with one of the beast-like glances that showed the disordered brain.

"It was a necessity," he said. "He would have prevented my act of justice upon you—upon you who have tried so hard to hinder me in my revenge upon my enemies who are also the enemies of science. Do you understand what I am about?"

"Perhaps," answered my cousin grimly, and at the word he jerked away my boot, letting the trap fall into its place.

"To the door, Robert," he whispered. "To the door and shout for help, or it is all over with us. He must have noticed the ammonia cylinder this afternoon. If he turns the tap, that stuff will choke the life out of us. The gas is under immense pressure and will pour up into this den like water from a fire-hose. Run, man, run!"

I staggered across the heaving cabin to the door and dropped upon my knees, hammering with my irons and screaming for aid. It seemed to me that the thunders of the storm redoubled in violence, as if Nature was conspiring to shout me down. Once I looked round and saw that the light about the trap had gone. Graden had smothered the spot with blankets. Presently he came groping to me, raising his great voice in hoarse bellowings.

And then it happened.

There came an acrid, piercing scent to my nostrils, that grew and grew until my lungs seemed to contract, so that I fought for very breath. My cries ceased. I struggled to my feet, with my head raised like a bird shot through the lungs. Brilliant lights flashed in my eyes; there were hollow drummings in my ears. And then it seemed that the air left me in a vacuum. I fell, and forgot it all.

* * * * *

It was daylight when I remember facts again. The motion of the ship had ceased, and there was an English stranger by my side. My chest felt bruised and battered, and my eyes still watered freely. Also I was very weak and ill.

"My cousin?" I faltered.

"We have got your friend round," said the doctor—for so I felt that he must be, "also the other man."

"What man?"

"The man who pulled you out after the cylinder exploded. A red-headed fellow—Blake, I think his name is. You owe your lives to him. You had both fainted when he opened the door."

"Then he heard us, after all! Tell me—what became of Marnac?"

"I really don't know about him. I don't think he was injured. Oh! perhaps you mean the old gentleman who bolted?"

"Bolted?"

"Yes; of course, there was great excitement over the accident. The captain was dreadfully cut up over the death of his servant. He could not imagine how it came about. When the ship arrived here, Mr. Marnac, or whatever his name was, slipped away by a shore-boat, while everyone was fussing over you. Your friend has gone to inquire about him, I fancy. The old man had something against you both, hadn't he? Or was it you against him?"

"Both, doctor, both," I whispered, shutting my eyes.

TO A FRIEND.

WHEN work for you is ended,
    And, scorning your poor soul,
You leave it undefended
    And say—"It missed the goal"—

The Judge will just ignore you,
    But heed, as it ascends
In loving triumph for you,
    The verdict of your friends.

                JESSIE POPE.

THE TRAIL OF THE DEAD:

THE STRANGE EXPERIENCE OF DR. ROBERT HARLAND.

By B. FLETCHER ROBINSON AND J. MALCOLM FRASER.*

VI.—THE END OF THE TRAIL.

IN my narrative, now drawing to its conclusion, I have endeavoured to avoid emotion or exaggeration. Yet as I glance over its pages, I cannot proclaim myself as satisfied. On such an evening as this, with the summer woodlands beneath the cottage basking in the tender glory of the sun's farewell, with the silence of the day that is ending holding the quiet fields—on such an evening, I say, my story, even to myself, appears impossible, a nightmare born in the land of evil dreams. Yet I have but to turn my eyes to where my dearest wife sits at her work, to know that it is true; for it was in that time of danger that Providence gave to me the most generous of the gifts that can be bestowed upon man.

Two days after Marnac escaped from our pursuit at Southampton, a little council was gathered in the parlour of Dr. Weston's cottage at Cornish Polleven. In his great arm-chair by the fire sat the old scholar, with the lamplight exposing the delicate fragility of a face whereon consumption had set its warning. In odd contrast was my cousin, Sir Henry Graden, who confronted him. Great-statured, stern, keen-eyed, he was of that type that can fearlessly execute, as well as intelligently conceive, a plan. Mary Weston was on a cushion at her father's knee, his hand in hers; and it was more often to that noble girl that my glance wandered than to my cousin, though, indeed, it was he who now set before us the position of affairs.

It was right, he said, that Dr. Weston should know, even as his daughter knew, the danger that hung over us. And so, from its commencement, he told that terrible story: how Marnac, the celebrated Heidelberg professor, had been seized with a partial mania born of heredity, nurtured by overwork, brought suddenly to the light by the violent attacks delivered against a book on which he had spent half his life; how he had planned to destroy his more bitter adversaries, and how, by his insane cunning, he had brought about the deaths of Von Stockmar and Mechersky; how, in his desperate flight from our pursuit, he had killed the son of Reski, the Polish innkeeper; how he had come to England to end his vengeance upon Dr. Weston; and how he had been led to believe that Mary was the writer of the attack which had incensed him. All this he explained; and while he spoke, the shadow of the terror seemed to creep over our very souls, so that we drew together like sheep that hear the cry of the wolves in the snow-clad hills beyond.

It was Dr. Weston who first broke the silence that followed Graden's conclusion.

"You have referred to a certain book or diary belonging to this Marnac," said he, for, indeed, my cousin had mentioned that discovery at Heidelberg. "And I gather that from it you first learnt the names of the scientific enemies against whom an attack might be directed. Did this madman include in his butcher's list any persons besides Von Stockmar, Mechersky, and myself?"

"There were several other names," replied my cousin; "but I do not think their criticisms were sufficiently severe to place them in serious danger. I have, however, communicated with them all. On the least suspicion they will inform the police and also telegraph to me at my London house. My servant there is kept informed of my address from day to day."

"And the police?"

"In international matters they move slowly. It has been a chase across Europe, remember. Months have often elapsed before very ordinary criminals have been arrested. But this man is a remarkable linguist; he has some five hundred pounds yet in his possession, and he has the cunning common to the partially insane. The English police have full information, but by this time he may be in France or Belgium."

---

* Copyright, 1903, by B. Fletcher Robinson and J. Malcolm Fraser, in the United States of America.

"What, then, do you propose, Sir Henry?"

"For the moment we have no definite objective. It would be useless for us to start for the Continent without further information. Until it reaches us, we shall stay in this country."

"I quite understand. I trust that for the ten days that we still have at Polleven, you will consider yourselves my guests—though I fear that the size of my cottage forbids me asking you to leave your quarters at the inn."

"Are you, then, returning to Cambridge, Dr. Weston? I thought you had settled here for the winter?" asked my cousin.

"It was so intended, but my doctors have ordered me to the Engadine. They say—it is my only chance, Sir Henry."

Mary Weston's eyes rose to her father's face in one brief, pitiful glance, and then her head drooped forward. Poor girl! she knew that he had spoken truly.

"The Engadine?"

Graden rose in his ponderous fashion and stood with his back to the fire. I could see that the intelligence concerned him—concerned him, indeed, too nearly for immediate comment. It was some moments before he spoke again.

"Forgive me, Dr. Weston," he said; "but is this a sudden resolution?"

"We decided yesterday."

"Is it common property? Do the villagers know?"

"Really, Sir Henry, I have no idea. I should not think they know."

"I will be quite plain with you, Dr. Weston, for that is always the best. Until this madman is secured, you and your daughter go in some danger. You should be safe enough in Switzerland, if you keep your address a secret. But even then we must arrange that you have a travelling companion that can be trusted."

"I shall be very glad to go," I interjected.

"No, Robert, that will never do," he said. "To divide our forces would be the worst generalship. Our duty is plain. We must be prepared to strike at the enemy wherever he may be found. Otherwise, there will be

"'No explanatory letters to old friends, Miss Mary.'"

weeks of anxiety for us all, and Heaven knows what devilish work going forward! Whom can we send? That we must first decide."

"There is Mossel?" I suggested, recalling the aid that stubborn German policeman had already rendered us.

"He would come, gladly enough. But I do not think the Heidelberg authorities would sanction his departure on so vague a journey. No! I am afraid Mossel is out of the question."

"What of Reski? I saw him find the body of his son; he would travel to the world's end if it brought a chance to meet the murderer."

"The very man! I thank you, Cousin Robert."

And so it was settled. We were to send a telegram to the Polish innkeeper next morning. If he agreed to our request, money could be forwarded in time for him to meet us in London, where he would take up his duty as escort to Dr. Weston and his daughter.

"Remember, please, that your destination is a secret," said Graden, as we made our adieus. "There must be no leaving of indiscreet addresses, Dr. Watson; no explanatory letters to old friends, Miss Mary."

"My father and I—we understand," she said, looking him gravely in the eyes. And so we passed out into the starlight.

They were pleasant days that followed—days that seemed to me the happiest in my life. Was it the contrast with the events of that terrible pursuit which gave them their perfection? So I argued at the time. Yet each hour I knew more clearly that it was Mary's bright eyes that warmed the winter sunshine, and Mary's presence that gave the beauty to that wild, inhospitable coast. Of mornings we walked together on the cliffs; and as night drew in, blotting out the grey wastes of the Channel seas, we joined Graden and her father in the little parlour, listening to the talk of those two great-hearted, simple men. On the second day, Reski's answer came, accepting the trust we offered. Then for a week there was no news from the outside world to trouble us, and no incident at Polleven to remind us of our danger save one, which, insignificant though it seemed, I do right to set before you.

As I have mentioned, a narrow dell or "goyle," as the West-country folk would have it, ran between the cottage and the sea. It was a ruinous place in the winter-time, sprinkled with trees knotted and bent under years of conflict with the winds, and floored with dead bracken and patches of gorse. In the summer it was, doubtless, pleasing enough; but in that December weather it seemed shrivelled and forlorn. Indeed, it was not a spot we greatly favoured.

It was about four o'clock on a Saturday afternoon, the fifth day of our visit, that Miss Weston and I entered it from the seaward side. We had taken a sharp walk to Bredairs Strand, where the famous caves are situated, and were returning for tea. We came upon them at an angle of the thicket —a man and a woman seated on a fallen log in eager conversation. Miss Weston held up a warning hand to me, with amusement twinkling in her eyes.

"Oh, Mr. Harland!" she whispered, "and at her age, too!"

"Why, who was it?" I asked, for their backs were turned towards us.

"Don't you see? It is Martha, our housekeeper. She is five-and-forty if she is a day. Fancy Martha with a young man of her own! I wonder who it can be?"

Whereupon she fairly gave way to her merriment in a low ripple of laughter. It was loud enough to reach the ears of the pair before us, for they started to their feet, the woman facing round boldly with flaming cheeks, while the man, after one swift glance, dropped back a step and stood shamefacedly, with downcast eyes. Miss Weston nodded to Martha, and we passed on up the track.

"Oh! I am so very, very sorry!" she cried to me when we were out of earshot. "I am certain that wretched man is only after her savings. What a silly old dear she is!"

"He seemed about the average in bashful rustics," I answered her.

"He is one of the worst men in the village —a drunken loafer, who never leaves the inn bar until he is almost starving. I wonder at Martha, for, besides his reputation, she knows——"

"What?" I asked, for she had stopped with a little shiver.

"They say in the village that Penruman— for that is his name—acted as a sort of servant to Professor Marnac while he was at Polleven. At least, I know that Penruman brought us messages from him twice, and once he came with a book that had been lent to father."

"Was Penruman courting Martha then?"

"I don't know, Mr. Harland; but this is the first time I've seen them together. Please don't say anything more about it. I will have a talk to Martha privately, and see if I can put some sense into her silly head."

As I was walking back to the inn before dinner, I caught sight of Penruman coming out of the village post-office. He slouched

"As I was walking back to the inn before dinner, I caught sight of Penruman coming out of the village post-office."

away up a side-street at sight of me. You may think me dull enough, but I had no suspicion of the truth.

If I had only known!

We all travelled to London together, taking rooms for the night at the Charing Cross Hotel; for though Graden had chambers in the Albany, he preferred that we should not be separated. It was here that Reski joined us. Sorrow had burnt its mark upon the Polish innkeeper. His thin, handsome features were yet more drawn; and though his courtly manner was unchanged, an alien ferocity lurked in his dark, reflective eyes. It would not go well with the murderer of his only son if he should meet him face to face. So I thought as he stood before us, his hat raised, bowing us a welcome.

At nine-forty on the following morning, we were gathered in a little group on the departure platform. Graden, who had talked with Reski far into the night, repeated his orders. To preserve the secret of Dr. Weston's residence was of the first importance. He would register himself and his daughter in the name of Jackson. All letters, whether from or to the travellers, were to be forwarded under cover to Graden's chambers, where a servant in whom he had absolute trust would despatch them to their respective addresses. On the slightest suspicion of danger, a telegram would bring our assistance from whatever spot our quest had drawn us. Neither Dr. Weston nor his daughter were to leave their hotel at Pontresina, even for a walk, without the escort of the Pole.

"I do not wish to alarm you with absurd rules, Miss Mary," concluded my cousin; "but it is well to be cautious. Besides, it should be only for a few days. I have found means of awakening the Continental police to interest in his capture, and we may hear of his arrest at any moment. Ah! there goes the whistle. Good-bye, Dr. Weston. Good-bye, my dear girl. God keep you!"

He was old enough to be her father; yet I did not consider his age was sufficient excuse for the kiss that he touched on her forehead.

We saw her handkerchief fluttering from

the carriage window as the train drew out of the station. I watched it fade into the muddy grey of the morning; and as it disappeared, the love I had hidden from myself rushed over me, so that I stood with staring eyes, perhaps as foolish and woe-begone a figure as humanity has ever smiled to witness. And for this I shall always thank my cousin, Harry Graden, that he slipped his arm in mine, leading me down the platform as if he had noticed nothing out of the ordinary in my manner.

"We shall soon have news," he said quietly. "For information that will lead to his arrest, I have offered the police, here and on the Continent, a reward of five thousand pounds."

He spoke the truth. News came soon, indeed.

We were lunching together in Graden's chambers on the fourth day after their departure, when the telegram arrived. My cousin opened it. As he read, I saw the line of his jaw set and harden. Then he handed it across the table. This was the message:—

"*Fear we are in great peril. Come at once.*—WESTON."

The realisation of those words must have come to me slowly, for it was Graden's hand on my arm that woke me from the stupor into which I had fallen. Even then I could hardly understand. "There is a train at two-twenty," said he. "Can you be ready in five minutes?"

"But how can the man—how can Marnac have discovered where they are?" I stammered.

"In five minutes, I said!" he barked out. "You have no time to waste."

We had still a quarter of an hour to spare when our cab rattled over the cobbles of the station-yard. While my cousin took the tickets, I stood at the bookstall, staring at the backs of the novels, with that call for help twisting in a devil's chant through my head. "In great peril. Come at once," so it ran, over and over again. Several passing strangers turned and regarded me curiously over their shoulders.

I do not think we spoke more than once before reaching Dover. I asked if he had telegraphed a reply. He had done so, he said, at Charing Cross.

There was a brisk sea running in the Channel, but I felt no sickness. Indeed, the passage did me good; for I behaved quite sanely as we passed our bags through the Calais customs.

Into the train again, and on into the night that had fallen. I had a sleeping-berth reserved in the *wagon-lit*, but I did not visit it. Sometimes a fury of impatience seized me, so that I paced the corridor, peering out into moonlit country that went sliding by, in its never-varying sequence of plain and woodland and steeple-crowned village; but, for the most part, I sat huddled in my chair—thinking. Heaven help us!

"Sometimes a fury of impatience seized me, so that I paced the corridor, peering out into moonlit country."

What torture an active mind inflicts upon poor humanity! Grant a man the imagination of an ox, and many are the woes he will be spared!

Dawn stole out on us at Basle, and we stood upon the platform, our faces showing pale in the tinted curtain of the sky that hung above the snow-clad ridges to the westward. The air was very cold, but not with the English bitterness in its breath.

We had half an hour to wait. Graden despatched a second telegram to Pontresina, marking the progress of our journey. He also wired to Thusis, ordering a carriage to meet our train.

The sun was up, very red and bold, as we passed through Zurich; and where it touched the great lake, the waters shone scarlet as blood under the slanting rays. Before us the Alps were heaving upward, growing mightier every hour, with the pinnacles of their strange frost kingdoms blushing in the early sunshine. By eleven o'clock we had left the open country, passing into a labyrinth of valleys, crowned with pines, waiting black and silent on their snow carpets, scored with torrents and patched with frozen tarns. Coire was reached by half-past one, and the narrow gauge of the Thusis line carried us through meadows and brushwood morasses until we crossed the upper Rhine and drew into the station which is set under the cliff bastions, outworks of the Alp citadels beyond.

It was then three of the clock. There were still forty miles left of our journey—a ten hours' drive over the passes to the distant Engadine.

A carriage with three horses was waiting to our order without the station. We entered it at once, and the driver swung his team into the Tiefenkastell road. Fifty francs from Graden had impressed him with the necessity for haste. Yet our progress was insufferably tedious. Once across the bridge, we dropped into a walk, while our straining team tugged heavily up the pass of Schyn. To our left, the ridge barred the view; but on the right, narrow valleys sliced deep into the glittering heights above gave us sight of the stately peaks that sentinelled the eastern sky. In an hour we had entered the forest of Versasca—for such, I have learnt, is its name—and so climbed on through the dismal avenues of pines till we passed through galleries and tunnels, hewn deep in the cliff-side, out into the barren snow-fields once again.

The sun was setting as we rattled over the pavement of the hill village of Tiefenkastell, that crouched in the shadows of the Albula Gorge. The dying rays struck fiercely on the distant peaks, until those pale ice maidens found rosy blushes for such reckless gallantry. It was a spectacle of infinite grandeur, and, despite my impatience, I leant from the window watching the light fade and whiten into the opals of the after-glow.

"We can thank our luck that there's a moon," said my cousin, as I drew back into my corner. "These drivers know the road like a book, but I should like our fellow to see where he's going in the Berguner Stein."

"Is it dangerous?"

"A ledge for a carriage-way, and a precipice for a ditch on the near side, is not particularly pleasant for the nerves when you can't see your hand before you."

"You have been here before, then?"

"Oh, yes!" he said, and so we fell into silence.

It was past six o'clock when we left Filisur, a tiny group of deep-eaved houses, and dropped down the hillside to the stream. As we rose the further slope through a wood of scattered pines, the moon came peering out from behind two bare and lofty peaks that towered above us into the southern night, lighting their icy summits so that they glittered like blades of polished steel. It was a scene of such melancholy desolation that as our horses halted on the crest of the hill, I lowered the window, thrusting out my head for a better view.

In front of us the white road curled down into a gorge, an ink-black wedge of shadow that drove into the distance between silver cliffs bright with the moonlight.

"Is this the place you spoke of?" I asked.

"It's the Berguner Stein, if it's that you want to know," growled my cousin from amongst his wraps. "Also, I wish you would have the goodness to shut that window."

But the remembrance of what he had told me about the dangers of the place sent my eyes to the driver's box. As I was leaning from the left-hand window, I did not expect to see more than the fellow's hat; but, to my surprise, there he was well in view, his coat huddled about his ears. As we moved forward, the mystery explained itself. The man I saw was not driving.

"We've taken up a passenger, Cousin Graden," said I, pulling in my head.

"What's that?" he asked sharply, for my voice had been lost in the loud complaining of the brakes as we trotted down the decline.

"The driver's giving a friend a lift," I cried, leaning towards him. "I suppose he picked him up at the last village, where——"

I reached no further, for at that instant there rose from without a cry of such utter terror that I sank back into my place as if struck in the face by a crushing blow. I saw a falling body flash by the right-hand window; the outcry of the brakes ceased with a grating clang. And then, with a bound like that of a leaping horse, the

3 D

great post-carriage rushed roaring down the hill.

I thrust out my head, clinging to the sills of the open window.

The man upon the box-seat was lashing the horses so that they sprang forward in furious bounds. Even as I watched, he cast away his whip with a peal of wild laughter that sounded high above the turmoil of the flying hoofs and the heavy wheels. He turned his head, bending sideways, the reins held loosely in his right hand. It was the face of Marnac that stared down upon me.

His hat had gone, his white hair streamed backward in the wind. And he was mad —mad with an open insanity of which I had observed no trace before. He shrieked at me in triumph, waving his hand now to the horses, now to the chasm beyond the four-foot wall that guarded the road. He cursed me with furious gesticulations. Even as I write, I seem to see those eyes staring at me out of the white paper—eyes goggling with the lust of murder. Heaven send that time will wipe that remembrance from my brain!

I shrank back into the carriage, that rocked and swung and danced beneath me. Graden's huge shoulders almost blocked the other window; but I caught sight of the glint of his revolver in the moonlight. Was it to be man or horse? One or the other, if we were not to leap the precipice at the first sharp turn. Suddenly he shouted, and again I struggled to my post. In the darkness down the road was the glimmer of lights. Nearer and nearer they drew, and I, too, raised my voice in a scream of warning. The last fifty yards we took in one bound—or so it seemed. I saw a carriage grow out of the shadow that the cliffs above us drew across the road; I saw our leading horse swing to the left and leap blindly at the low wall that hid Heaven knew what frightful depths below; and then, with a tottering slide that seemed to wrench the heart out of me, we curled, as a motor skids, into one thunderous crash that blotted out the world.

MRS. HARLAND'S NARRATIVE.

I have been asked by my dear husband to conclude the story of which he has placed the greater part before you. I should have preferred that he had not tried to recall details which I know he cannot remember without suffering; but having once yielded to the persuasion of his friends, I am ready to take every share of the burden that he will yield to me.

My father and I, with Reski, the man that Sir Henry had summoned from Poland, arrived in the Engadine without any incident that is worthy of description. We had engaged rooms in the principal hotel under the name of Jackson, as had been suggested. My father stood the journey very well. But this necessity for giving a false name annoyed him extremely. It was the first time in his life that he had done so, he said, and I had some difficulty in persuading him not to confess the whole circumstances to the manager on the day after our arrival.

It was on the fourth day of our visit, about five in the evening, that we received a telegram from London. It read:—

"*We are coming at once.*—GRADEN."

As can be imagined, we were very puzzled about it. We had sent no message, and we could not think what was the reason for their sudden determination. Reski behaved in a most curious fashion when I told him. It might have been the news of some great good fortune that had reached him.

"It is very well, very well," he kept on repeating in German — a language which, fortunately, I can speak, though not very correctly.

"What do you mean?" I asked him.

"Ach, Fräulein! if the two Englishmen are coming, does it not mean that Marnac is here?"

I suppose I turned rather pale, for the fear of that dreadful man was always in my heart, though, indeed, I pretended to father that I had forgotten he existed. But the next instant Reski had dropped down on one knee, taking my hand and kissing it.

"I am a dog, Fräulein!" he said simply. "I did not think of what I spoke. But it is the thing for which I forget all else—to meet this man who killed my son. For your father and yourself, have no fear. It is I that will ever watch. You trust me, Fräulein?"

"Indeed, Reski, I do," I answered him; and so we parted.

I was nervous that night, and about one in the morning I thought I heard a noise in the passage outside. Very cautiously I opened my door and peeped out. My father's door was the next to mine, and between the two lay Reski in a great fur rug that he had. He waved his hand to me with a little smile, as if I were a child he was bidding to be of good courage. I slept undisturbed after that.

It was as we took our place for a twelve

o'clock *déjeuner* that we received the second telegram. This is how it read:—

"*If danger presses, communicate fully police. We started on receipt of your message, and will be at Thusis by three. Should be at Pontresina at one o'clock to-night. Order rooms.*—GRADEN."

I called in Reski at once; for he had refused to have his meals with us, though my father had invited him. He looked very grave, indeed, when I translated the message.

"You sent no telegram, Fräulein?"

"No, Herr Reski."

"Nor you, mein Herr?"

"No, Reski, no," said my father.

"Then someone has sent it in your name. I do not like it. It would seem a trap."

"A trap?"

I stared at him with fear gathering about my heart. Who had done this thing? And why?

"It would seem, Fräulein, some scheme of the old grey devil. What he intends, I cannot guess; nor can I think how he discovered that we are here. But there is a thing plainly to do. I will start for Thusis, to warn those who are hastening to us."

"I will come with you, Reski," said my father.

"You know that cannot be. I have no fear, with Reski to protect me. I will go."

Love gives great strength to woman, and I spoke as one who expects to be obeyed. It was much trouble to persuade them; yet from the first I did not mean to yield. My dear father had barely recovered from the fatigues of his long journey; to let him take this drive of forty miles would be the gravest folly. Yet it was not right that we both should leave our duty to a man of whom we had no real knowledge. Mr. Harland and his cousin had endangered their lives to save us; now that peril seemed to be closing round those gallant gentlemen, we could not both sit idle. Plainly it was I who should go.

And so at last it was agreed between us.

It was shortly after one o'clock when Reski and I rumbled off in our post-carriage across the snow-bound slopes of the valley to Ponte. Then began a climb of dreary monotony. Up and up we dragged, turn after turn through forests of larch and pine, with the Engadine growing wider, and its houses sinking into specks beneath us. At last we reached the crest of the Albula Pass, and trotted forward over the snow levels till we plunged down the steep descent of the rock-strewn Devil's Hall—as the mountaineers named it of old. The sun had set ere we rattled into Breda, and the moon had swung out from the southward when Bergun was reached. Half an hour later we had passed through the forests into the shadows of that black and dangerous gorge—the Berguner Stein.

Fresh snow had clogged the road on the Albula, and we had made slow progress, to our increasing anxiety. It was now impossible that we should reach Thusis before they started; but we had calculated that near Tiefenkastell we might meet them. That the snow had not fallen so deeply on the lower slopes, and that

"He shrieked at me in triumph."

they had moved more quickly, we could not know.

We had passed the last bend that turned upward, leading in a long slope to the entrance of the gorge, when we stopped suddenly. Reski sprang out; clambering after, I found him by the driver, who was pointing with his whip up the road. The man had been warned to give us notice of any approaching vehicle.

"It is a post-carriage," he said. "They have stopped to breathe their team."

The road had been carved and joisted along the cliff side, and where we stood, under the mighty wall of rock, the shadows were gathered darkly. To our left the rugged barrier rose dimly into the night, clear only where its battlements broke the pearl of the sky at some great height above us; to our right, a low stone coping hid the grim uncertainties of the precipice. But fifty yards up the slope the cliffs fell back, and the road stepped out into the silver moonlight, mounting the hill, through a border of stunted trees, in a simple curve, as white and well defined as a chalk mark on a blackboard. On its crest I could see the patch on the snow carpet that marked the waiting carriage. It was, perhaps, the half of a mile away.

The patch of shadow moved slowly forward.

Suddenly, though distance hid the suggestion of the cause, the pace increased. Faster and yet faster it swept down the road; in the white silence of the night the muffled hoof-beats came thumping to our ears. The carriage grew clearer. We could see how it rocked; it might have been some great ball that flew bounding towards us.

For some moments we had stood motionless, helpless, before this amazing apparition. It was Reski who first understood; it was he who seized me by the arm, screaming in his excitement to run—to run down the way we had come. And in my panic I obeyed, flying wildly towards the sharp bend in our rear. I had almost reached it when there came a thought to me that jostled out the remembrance of my own safety, turning me back, with Heaven knows what anxiety in my heart. Robert and Sir Henry—could they be the travellers that came galloping to almost certain death?

The runaways had but one chance—to hug the cliff, thereby giving space to clear the turn without charging the low wall that guarded the unknown depths of the gorge. But to my horror, I saw that this was a chance our driver was preventing, for it was he who had edged his team against the cliff. They would have to pass him on the outer side.

I started up the road, shouting to him; but as I did so, I saw Reski spring upon the box. I heard cries of furious altercation, and then the driver was thrown from his place. He dropped on hands and knees; then rose and came running past me round the bend.

The whip cracked, and our team swung across the road, drawing up on the edge of the precipice. If the man who drove the runaways were not struck with terror, they had yet a hope of safety.

They were not one hundred yards away. I could see in the bright moonlight how the horses bounded forward, the traces now slackening, now tightening to the desperate plunges. Seventy yards—and the driver had gone mad. He was waving his arms and shrieking, not in terror, but rather in whoops of joyous exultation. It was a fearful thing to see those gestures and to hear those wild imprecations when death was so very near. Another second, and they were in the shadows, close upon us.

And Reski? I had almost forgotten him. Stiff as a soldier upon duty he sat, the reins tight in his hand, looking neither to right nor left, waiting the fate that might come to him. It was only thus that he could hold his team in their place—only thus, at the risk of instant annihilation. Did he dare this for the simple love of his neighbour? Did instinct tell him that they were indeed our friends? God rest him, whether or no! for by whatever rank men knew him, he was a most honourable gentleman.

Like a flash of light striking through darkness, I realised that the runaways were still holding the outer edge of the road; that it must happen—that there was no escape. And as I did so, there came a crushing, rending shriek that filled the whole air like the falling of a thunderbolt. Dimly I saw the great carriages collide, rebound—and then but one remained.

The spirit went out of me. I covered my face with my hands, crouching against the cliff, praying to Heaven that at least the screaming of the horses might soon be ended.

How long I stayed there, I do not know, but I was roused by footsteps passing before me. I started up with a cry.

"I beg your pardon, madam," said a well-known voice. "By Gad! if it isn't Mary Weston!"

It was Sir Henry; but what was that he carried in his arms?

"Who is it?" I asked, pointing.

"It is Robert," he answered gravely. "He has had a nasty tap on his head, I'm afraid. If you will look to him, Miss Mary, I will go back and shoot those poor beasts of horses."

* * * * *

They found them next morning, lying close together at the foot of the precipice. They told me that their faces were curious to see, for Marnac still grinned with the vacancy of his insanity, and Reski wore also a happy smile, yet one most different, for it was such as those carry who die in a noble effort, covering their memory with honour. For as Sir Henry has explained, it was Reski who saved their lives. They could never else have cleared the bend of the road. As it was, when their leading horse jumped the wall, his weight swung their carriage round, striking the other on the side, so that while they were left, battered, on the edge, with one horse dangling—until the harness broke—Reski, his carriage and his team, were hurled over the cliff.

Marnac had already been flung to destruction at the first impact.

We learnt in time the details of his insane scheme. A heavy bribe had won the help of the Cornish loafer—though, to be honest with him, the man had no suspicion of the evil purpose to which his telegrams would be placed. From poor Martha, love-lorn and middle-aged, he had gathered his news. It was Marnac who had sent the further telegrams to Sir Henry, calculating well the time at which they could arrive. He had stayed at the village of Alvaneu, and when the carriage passed it, had begged a lift as far as Bergun, a request granted readily enough by their driver. The poor fellow had been struck on the head at the entrance of the gorge, and so thrown from his place. He had not been seriously injured, and, indeed, was of much assistance to us all later in that evening.

I must add that Sir Henry despatched the whole of the great reward he had offered to Reski's next-of-kin. They were but distant relatives, as his wife was dead, and it had been his only son that Marnac murdered.

So ended the story that Robert, rightly enough, has named "The Trail of the Dead," for indeed it was a blood-stained path. I would have had Robert himself to conclude it, but that he insists that there is no necessity. One thing only does he ask that I should add —though, indeed, it is a matter that will have been already guessed. To please him, I will write it down.

Robert and I were married in June.

THE MAGIC FLUTE.

A THRUSH is singing on the walnut tree,
   The leafless walnut tree with silver boughs;
He sings old dreams long distant back to me,
   He sings me back to childhood's happy house.

O, to be you, triumphant Voice-of-Gold!
   Red rose of song above the empty bowers,
Turning the withered leaves, the hopes grown cold,
   To Springtide's good green world of growing flowers.

Might the great change that turns the old to new
   Remould this clay to better blossoming,
I would be you, Great-Heart, I would be you,
   And sing like you of Love and Death and Spring.

ROSAMUND MARRIOTT WATSON.

The Battle of Fingle's Bridge

How the Ferns and the Rushes Fought the Gorse and the Heather, and What Came of the Battle.

By B. Fletcher Robinson.

The little boy walked across the wooden bridge, and curled himself up amongst the ferns. He was very unhappy—he was indeed. And you will say he had good reason when I tell you about it. He knew, just as you and I know, that every year from July to September there is a dreadful battle going forward on the moorlands; for the rushes down by the streams and the great bracken ferns on the lower slopes have to fight for their lives against those fierce people the heather and the gorse, who come marching down from the heights above to seize the valleys where they dwell.

He had asked daddy about it, daddy who understood all about wars and soldier men; and daddy had told the little boy how the rushes were troopers armed with lances, and the bracken were the splendid British infantry, while their foes were wild tribesmen from the hills. Those were great days indeed when daddy and he walked together, the long legs and the short ones, watching the progress of the fight that changed with every turn of the cliff path; there had been none like them since daddy sailed away to join his redcoats at the back of the sunrise.

For when the little boy had asked other little boys to come out and see the battle on the moors they had laughed at him quite rudely, so that he was obliged to hit them hard on the nose to prove how stupid they were. It was different with Marjory, his old nurse—Marjory who was wise in the doings of the fairies, and who knew what happens when you pick a ragged robin, or make faces when the wind changes, and why the jays' talk annoys the thrushes. Yet it was only an hour ago that Marjory had failed him; for meeting her in the hall she had said very quickly:

"Now, don't come bothering me, Master Frank, with your silly old nonsense. I can't think what your poor dear father was about stuffing your head with stories about ferns and such like being alive and pitching into each other. Run away like a good boy."

How was he to know that the washing was late, and that aunt had been speaking quite crossly to Marjory about it? How was he to know that in the evening Marjory would come and beg his pardon? How, indeed?

And this is the reason why he was crouched sadly amongst the bracken ferns that afternoon feeling that people were blind and hard and unbelieving. Under the warm sunlight he sat blinking down the valley, and nodding, nodding, nodding.

* * * * *

He was not the least afraid when it happened. It seemed quite natural for the rushes to be moving out of the gloomy marsh of Orme, which lay down the valley below the wooden bridge; for it was a damp and miserable place at the best. They made a pretty sight as they came trotting forward up the strip of grassland between the stream and the moors, their thin green lances flickering in the sunbeams and their fairy bugles sounding like song birds at dawn. Their horses, too, were dears, all fire and sinew, and quite six inches high; while as for their general, he was the most perfect little gentleman ever seen.

He rode a good four feet before the rest clad from head to heel in dark green armour. He had a fierce white moustache, a neat pointed

Copyright, 1903, by C. Arthur Pearson Ltd., in the United States of America.

The general drew rein, and seemed to make a speech to his men.

beard, and the sharpest grey eyes that ever stared defiance at an enemy from under a helmet. Below the bridge he drew rein and seemed to make a speech to his soldiers, though the little boy was too far away to hear what he said; and they, leaving but four trumpeters and a score of men as a bodyguard to their general, turned their horses and trotted back down the way that they had come. The knight himself rode forward, with a squire bearing a white flag of truce beside him, to where an ant-hill rose amongst the daisies. There he dismounted and stood leaning easily upon his lance.

An honest-seeming fellow was the Baron of the Bracken Ferns, who came striding towards him from amongst the willows by the stream. Across his broad back—for he was a good four inches round the chest, this giant —swung a great battle-axe fit for the dealing of mighty blows. The yellow hair that fell to his shoulders was crowned with a curling coronet of golden fronds. Behind him, ten abreast, tramped his escort, one hundred strong, clad in tunics of Lincoln green. They also bore stout axes in their hands. In the distance the river's banks were covered by tens of thousands of the bracken infantry, who had, without doubt, been ordered to approach no nearer.

"Well met, good brother," cried he to the Knight of the Rushes; "we are here at the spot and hour arranged with a flag of truce above us and but few men at our backs. Where, then, are these, our enemies, who were to meet us? Do they not mean to keep their tryst?"

"They are even approaching, fair sir," answered the little cavalier, with a courteous bow of welcome, "and gathered on the hill I do observe many of their companies, men whom, if I mistake not, it will be great honour to meet in gentle warfare, for they do seem both well armed and valiant."

The little boy glanced up the slope of the moor, and, behold, it was all in motion, moving downward in great squares of gold and purple. It was a very strange and wondrous spectacle. Indeed, it reminded the little boy of something which he had spelt out that morning, something which, if he remembered rightly, Mr. First Reader described as:

> The Assyrian came down like the wolf on the fold,
> And his cohorts were gleaming in purple and gold.

He did not know what an Assyrian was, and he was rather uncertain about cohorts; but he felt that, whatever they were, they must have looked then very much as that hillside did now.

It was the coming of the invaders, the golden gorse and the purple heather, and even as he watched them, their generals swung out on to the plot of grassland, and came striding towards the ant-hill. A strange pair they made, those two, the King of the Gorse and the Chieftain of the Heather. For the first was of a rare and pompous beauty, clad in armour of pure gold that flashed and shimmered in the sunlight; and the second was a little gnarled and withered man dressed in a short coat of purple tartan shot with grey.

The King bore a great spiked club which he swung valorously as he came; the Chief stole softly beside him with a naked dagger in one hand and a sword of rusty steel in the other. A score of feet from the ant-hill they halted amid a clamour of sounds; for the pibrochs of the heather screamed and the great trumpets of the gorse challenged the echoes, while in answer the bugles of the rushes shrilled, and from the bracken bodyguard rose the sullen murmur of the drums.

One thing the little boy noticed with an uneasy feeling: the bodyguards of the new-comers were very many. For, though the Baron of the Bracken had but one hundred, and the Knight but a score of men, yet with the King were close upon a thousand gold-clad warriors, while gathered behind the Heather Chieftain a wild array of tribesmen stood with drawn weapons as if expecting some sudden order. Yet they, too, bore white flags of truce; and the little boy could not imagine that a soldier lived who would break the peace beneath it.

"Greeting, good people!" cried the King of the Gorse. He spoke as a monarch to his subjects, but the Baron of the Bracken and he of the Rushes made no obeisance. Instead they took a step forward with the stride and glance of free men.

"Your Majesty has summoned us and we are here," said the former boldly, "though for what purpose we do not know. Indeed, we had imagined that by the last treaty our lands were well-defined, and that there could be no cause of quarrel between us."

The King was about to make an angry answer when the Chieftain plucked him by the sleeve and spoke in his stead.

"Good sirs," said he, in a thin, quavering voice, "if there be no cause of quarrel between us why have you gathered armies which wait, as I can see, amongst the willows and upon the edge of the marshes? Also, you well know that the King has reason for his anger, seeing that many of the people of the bracken and the rushes have crossed the border, settling upon his territories on the hill. It is for you to explain and to humbly ask his pardon."

"Well met, good brother," cried the Baron of the Bracken to the Knight of the Rushes.

"Chieftain of the Heather, you speak with cunning as is your custom," answered the Baron of the Bracken, "yet you do wrong to blame us. Where our people have settled they have the plain right to live. It is you who year by year alter the landmarks, thus striving to prove us in the wrong; it is you and the men of the gorse who, by enlarging your claims, push us ever back into the valley, and now, even at the last, we have resolved to make a stand knowing that your desire is to see us diminished and blotted out. Am I not right, Brother of the Rushes?"

The little knight stepped lightly forward.

Upon his face was a smile of great contentment.

"My friend has spoken with a gift of pleasant words that is denied to me," said he, "and if you are not satisfied, my worthy chieftain, I hereby offer to make good his claim and mine against you, man for man, at any time or place and with any weapons that it may please you to name."

Now even as he was speaking a very wicked thing was happening which the little boy watched with anger and shame in his heart; for the chieftain had beckoned with his hand and his mob of tribesmen had begun to move, creeping forwards slyly a step at a time. They were scarce half the size of the bracken or the gorse; but if they were small they were broad and strong with fierce, evil-looking faces and eyes that glowed as red as those of an angry rat; also they were very many.

The little boy felt quite certain that they meant to play some low and cowardly trick, and he tried ever so hard to prevent it by shouting a warning to the Knight of the Rushes just as we try to escape from something dreadful that we meet in dreamland. But he could not utter a sound.

"Worthy knight," said the chieftain with a smile of such real badness that you could have told at once that he was not at all a nice person to meet, "you have challenged me to fight, but I am a feeble old fellow, and perforce must leave the dealing of hard knocks to younger men. Still, my good sir, I should be sorry if you were disappointed of a little sword exercise. Perhaps some of my tribe may be less peaceful than their chief."

He turned and raised a low cry like the

A strange pair they made, those two, the King of the Gorse and the Chieftain of the Heather.

rustle of dry leaves in the autumn gale, and at the sound of it the heather men rushed screaming forward.

The little boy knew all about a white flag of truce, how it is a sign of peace, how all fighting must cease where it is carried, how those who meet beneath it must never come to blows unless they would forfeit their honour, how it protects even heralds who come to declare war. So when he saw this wicked thing happen, this attack on men who had come trusting in the honour of their enemies, he put his hands over his face for very shame. And when he looked up again this is what he saw:

The hundred bracken yeomen who had come with their lord had gathered round him in a dark green square, on the edge of which the little axes flashed like diamonds in the sunlight as they struck swift and hard at the men of the heather, who buzzed about them like a great swarm of angry bees. But at every fresh charge the tribesmen with knife and sword cut a patch out of the square, just as you might bite a mouthful out of a piece of bread and butter. The good yeomen always drew together again, filling the places of their dead comrades; but each minute they grew fewer and fewer. As for the Knight of the Rushes, he had got to his horse, and the little boy could see him galloping away towards the marsh, which, considering the danger of his friend, seemed a very cowardly thing to do.

All over the meadow and the moor wild deeds were happening; for down the hill were rushing the armies of the gorse and the heather to join in the fight below, while from amongst the distant willows the regiments of the bracken were running forward in dark green lines to aid their lord. And it was this that saved those in the square from being all killed at once, for the fresh troops from the hill had to turn aside to check the bracken regiments from coming to the help of their comrades, and so could not lend a hand in destroying the square.

"Oh, it's a wicked thing, a wicked, wicked thing," said a voice in the little boy's ear.

She was the daintiest of fairies, as bright and blue as the sea itself. She was sitting on a chip of rock at his elbow watching the battle; and now and again a tear like a tiny seed pearl rolled down her cheeks and splashed on the stone below. He was usually afraid of girls, was the little boy, chiefly because he could never understand them. But she looked so sorry that he forgot all about his bashfulness, and spoke to her just as if she had been a boy too.

"What is your name?" said he.

"Forget-me-not," she answered, dabbing her eyes with a tiny leaf. "I'm a flower, you know."

let no one live near them even if they are ever so small. They crush and destroy all of us flowers, the selfish wretches. And now they are going to kill our good Lord of the Bracken, who came, trusting in their honour."

"And the Knight of the Rushes has run away," said the little boy.

"Run away? How dare you say that? *He* run away—the bravest, truest, gentlest, soldier of all the plains. But hark—do you hear that? He is coming, the rushes are coming to the rescue," and she sprang to her feet, clapping her tiny hands.

Carried by the breeze from down the valley

"Oh, it's a wicked thing, a wicked, wicked thing," said a voice in the little boy's ear.

"And did you see it all from the beginning?"

"Of course—and I knew what would come of trusting those horrid hillmen. We all hate them and fear them."

"Why is that, Forget-me-not?"

"If you don't know that," she cried, glancing up at him, "you must be like one of those silly babies of flowers that grow in pots and glasshouses—you must be a town boy."

"But I'm not," he answered crossly, "I'm a country boy."

"More shame to you, then, for not noticing things. The bracken are always kind and careful of us. We live where they live side by side, and as for the rushes they don't trouble us at all. But with the others it is so different. The heather and the gorse will

there arose the notes of the bugles, hard, fierce and shrill like the scream of an angry hawk. Turning he saw them come, these dashing troopers, line following in line, thousand after thousand. Before them trotted their general, his face set, stern, revengeful. They were within fifty feet of the hard pressed square when again their bugles shrieked to the echoes; and at the sound the points of the lances dropped, and with a pattering like the first raindrops of a thunderstorm, the rushes loosed their horses and flung themselves upon the foe.

The little boy stood up and cheered, it was so splendid, so glorious. The tribesmen fled just as the chickens in the yard always did when Snap, the wicked terrier, ran barking among them. But fast as they ran the tiny horses galloped yet faster, and every time a lance dipped and rose a tartan body lay motionless. It was a rout, utter and complete. Seeing their allies beaten, the golden soldiers of the gorse also began to run backwards, shouting to each other as they climbed the hill.

"They have won, our friends have won," cried Forget-me-not. "Oh, if they will only stay content and not pursue the tribesmen, then all will indeed be well."

The little boy did not ask why this was; for just beneath him the Baron and the Knight were meeting, and he was watching them open-eyed. They did not shout or embrace or do anything foolish of that sort, but just shook hands like the two brave men they were.

"And what now, brother?" asked he of the Bracken.

"Can you be in doubt?" answered the fiery little knight; "they are scattered, defeated—it is our chance to wipe away the memory of a hundred insults, to teach them a lesson they will not soon forget. On, on —up the hill."

"We have them at a disadvantage in the valley, but on the moors——" the Baron of the Bracken hesitated and shook his head.

"Surely my brother is not afraid?"

"Sir Knight, I know that you speak in a temper heated by the battle? yet you might have spared me that word."

The Knight bent his head and fumbled with his waistbelt.

"Friend, I crave your pardon," he muttered. "But indeed time presses."

"Enough, worthy Knight. Where the rushes go, you will not find the bracken far behind. And now to our plan. See you that little streamlet that has dug a furrow in the shoulder of the hill? Let that be your road and remember, as you love me, that if you leave the water you are lost, you and all your men. For myself, I and mine will follow after our enemies and fight them where we find them. Goodbye, brave Knight—if we do not meet again."

The two friends shook hands staring each other in the eyes and then moved off to the head of their armies. Forget-me-not burst out sobbing so miserably that the little boy felt quite cross with her.

"What is the matter now?" he asked her.

"You great big goose, don't you understand? Down in the valley the gorse and the heather never can fight well, but on the top of the hill which is their home they are far stronger than the bracken, and they will beat them ever so badly. The rushes cannot help their friends much, for, of course, they must not leave the streamlet."

"But why not?" cried the little boy.

"You silly! Did you ever see rushes anywhere where there was not water?"

"Oh," said the little boy, feeling snubbed.

But despite what Forget-me-not said, her friends pushed their way most bravely at first. The rushes galloped up the bed of the water-course scattering the gorse who had gathered there to left and right; while marching forward in their great green squares the bracken drove the heather from the lower slopes of the moor.

But as they climbed higher and higher up the hill the battle changed. The wild tribesmen rallied, and came rushing down upon the square in purple masses. At each charge hundreds of the bracken were killed, so that the leading squares became broken up, and the yeomen fought without order in little clumps of desperate men. And when the rushes, forgetting their warning, left the stream to come to the aid of their friends, the golden regiments of the gorse sprang upon them, knocking the riders from their saddles and laming the horses, so that the few who got back to the water again came riding down the hill with broken lances and hanging heads.

So now it was the bracken alone that bore the whole fury of the gorse and the heather. Nobly they fought, those splendid foot soldiers; but square after square melted away like lumps of sugar dropped into a teacup until all scattered and beaten they came running back into the valley with their shouting enemies hard upon their heels. It was a very dreadful thing to see.

The little boy and Forget-me-not sat very still, holding each other's hands for help and comfort in their sorrow. Not twenty yards away the Baron and the Knight, their armour bent and their helmets dented with sword stabs, had gathered a few of their bravest to fight a last fight with the conquerors. But

He could see through the veil of smoke how the heather and gorse were flying wildly back.

stoutly as they bore themselves, it was plain that in a few more moments all would be over with them.

"It shall not be," cried Forget-me-not, suddenly looking up at the little boy with a white strained face. "It is very dreadful, but it is the only way—the only way. Have you those things about you that will light a fire?"

"I have some matches if that's what you mean."

"Then throw one amongst the heather—it is the one thing the tribesmen fear."

"But daddy told me it was shameful and wicked for anyone to set the moors on fire."

"If your father saw what you see now he would order you to do it. And now I, Forget-me-not, the kindest of the flowers, beg this favour of you."

Somehow he knew that she was right. He drew out the brass box which he always had about him and struck a match. The flame burnt thin and clear, for the breeze had died away.

"Where?" he whispered nervously.

She pointed with her hand to a knot of tribesmen just below, and he stooped and placed it amongst them.

A single puff of flame, and the smoke was rolling thick and fast up the hill. For a moment he could see through the veil of it how the heather and gorse were flying wildly back screaming a warning to each other; for a moment he caught sight of the bracken and the rushes standing safely in the damp grass by the stream, and it seemed to him that the Knight and the Baron were waving him thanks and goodbye. Then the smoke swirled down thicker, denser than before, and all was blotted out. It poured up into his face, blinding his eyes and stinging in his nose. He could almost feel the burning breath of the flame below. And now Forget-me-not, grown very strong and tall, was pulling and tugging at his shoulder, shaking him into—what—he —hello—"Marjory, is that you?"

* * * *

Marjory it was, Marjory tugging him through the smoke across the bridge and never letting go till she plumped him down on the other side.

"Good sakes, Master Frank," she cried, giving him an extra shake. "But what a fright you gave me, you wicked boy. The hill all afire and you sitting in the middle of it as sound asleep as ever was known. If your dear aunt hadn't sent me to fetch you just by chance like, you'd have been burnt into a coal, sure as life."

"Then who set the hill on fire?" asked the little boy, rubbing the sleep out of his eyes.

"One of they silly picnic parties from Chawley way, I'm thinking. Though, bless you, it's hard to tell with the moor as dry as touchwood. Won't Keeper Webber be talking—oh, my word! But come along and have your tea, there's a dear."

FOGBOUND

He raised the collar of his fur coat. In three steps the fog had him in its grasp.

A POWERFUL SHORT STORY.

By
B. FLETCHER ROBINSON & J. MALCOLM FRASER.

Illustrated by A. J. GOUGH.

CAPTAIN FRANCIS DELANEY came of good Galway stock. His breed was displayed in a caustic wit, to which a trace of brogue gave an added piquancy, and, on suitable occasions, in a very desperate and uncompromising valour. These qualities he supplemented with a modesty, partly natural, partly the result of soldierly etiquette. For the rest, he was tall and thin, with a big nose, black hair, and a pair of grave brown eyes set in a hollow, sun-dried face.

In a more normal period London would have welcomed Captain Delaney as a celebrity, if of a minor lustre. His defence of an isolated post in a tribal rising on the Afghan border had received considerable notice in the Press. It was rumoured that his V.C. had been deserved on four separate occasions. But the gloom of South Africa was upon the land, and his arrival at Southampton had passed unnoticed. His relatives were in Ireland or abroad; his acquaintances in the great city were few; and when the hotel at which he had ordered rooms engulfed him, he became nothing more than "the gentleman in No. 95 on the third floor."

During the comic opera to which on the night following his arrival he had turned for light recreation, he had noticed a growing density of the atmosphere, a phenomenon which, on his leaving the theatre, was at once explained. A November fog had fallen on the midnight city. From its depths came shouts and imprecations as the broughams moved up to carry off their owners. Agitated fathers of families plunged into the misty darkness in a vain effort to secure four-wheelers, link boys carrying torches ran hither and thither, the heads of horses came

(47)

thrusting on to the pavements to be seized and turned back by the theatre commissionaires.

In short, the scene was one of uncomfortable confusion, which Captain Delaney, drawing his fur coat more tightly about him, watched with an amused interest. He had been born and reared in the south of France —for his mother had suffered from lung troubles; afterwards he had passed from Sandhurst into the Indian Staff Corps; his leave had been mainly devoted to sport; he knew little of London, and of the possibilities of a November fog nothing at all.

He was amongst the last to leave the shelter of the porch. It was a good mile to his hotel, which was situated in a respectable square off Regent Street, but he was in no way dismayed by the prospect of a walk which offered so unusual an experience. He lit a cigar, raised the collar of his fur coat, and turned westward. In three steps the fog had him in its grasp.

It possessed nothing in common with any mist with which he was acquainted. It hung motionless in a stagnant solidity; it was dry, leaving no trace of moisture; and the scent of it came in choking waves like the down-draught of an ancient chimney on a windy evening. The very pavement on which he trod was indistinct, and he found himself walking with the high, slow step of a man who explores an unknown and dangerous pathway. The gas lamps had melted into patches of glowing haze, and even the electric lights had narrowed to pin points of useless illumination.

All sound had ceased. Occasional cabs moved slowly along the roadway; a few belated men groped their way upon the footpaths; but neither the rumble of wheels nor the echo of footsteps warned him of their approach. The silence seemed the strangest freak in surroundings which even to his unimaginative mind appeared abnormal and mysterious.

It has been mentioned that Captain Delaney was ignorant of his London. That he should have kept in the right track would have been surprising. As it was he soon found himself utterly astray. The occasional directions he received from those of whom he enquired but further confused him. Once out of the main thoroughfares he continued to wander aimlessly through a labyrinth of minor streets.

It is an eerie feeling to be submerged in a fog-bound city. Bold though he was, Delaney's imagination began to play him odd tricks. The touch of cold railings to his exploring hand startled him like the sudden grasping of a reptile; the misty houses assumed desolate and bewildering shapes; the curb once left behind, a crossing became a trackless expanse, suggestive of sudden dangers and ambuscades. In short, before half-an-hour had passed, Captain Delaney was wishing himself well out of a position that every moment was becoming more and more unpleasant.

He had been for some little time groping his path along a terrace of large houses that might have been fashionable among the *beau monde* of the Georges, when the street expanded into what he took to be a small square. He had halted, uncertain whether to retrace his steps or to explore a place which as like as not possessed no other issue, when he observed from the glow in the haze immediately before him that someone carrying a light was advancing in his direction. He awaited his arrival, intending to ask for further information.

The footman, for such, indeed, was the apparent rank of the new-comer, halted before Captain Delaney and raised the stable lantern that he carried with a nervous movement.

"You are punctual, sir," he said.

He was a sallow-faced young man, wrapped in an ill-fitting livery coat of grey and purple. His beard was close-cropped, and his voice, which seemed curiously smooth and courteous for a man in so inferior a position, was marked by a slight foreign intonation. Captain Delaney regarded him with a humorous surprise.

"You were expecting me, then?" said he.

"I merely obey the orders I received."

"Which were?"

"To conduct you to the house of my mistress. In this fog you could scarcely be expected to find it for yourself."

Captain Delaney was still of an age to appreciate adventure. Caution, indeed, suggested a further explanation. He remembered tales of strangers suffering ill in London. Might not this fellow be acting as a lure for some criminal association? But the thought of personal danger was no bar to a man of his temperament—indeed it inclined him to an immediate decision.

"Very well, I will follow you," said he.

The footman turned, and, holding the lantern that its light might fall on the roadway, preceded Delaney. In this order they crossed the street, skirted a small, railed garden that marked the centre of the square, and finally halted at a door which, from its massive mouldings and the florid ornamentation above the portico, evidently belonged to a mansion of some size. It opened to a discreet knocking, and they passed within. His guide assisted in relieving him of his hat and coat. In another moment he was being ushered into a room on the ground floor, the door of which

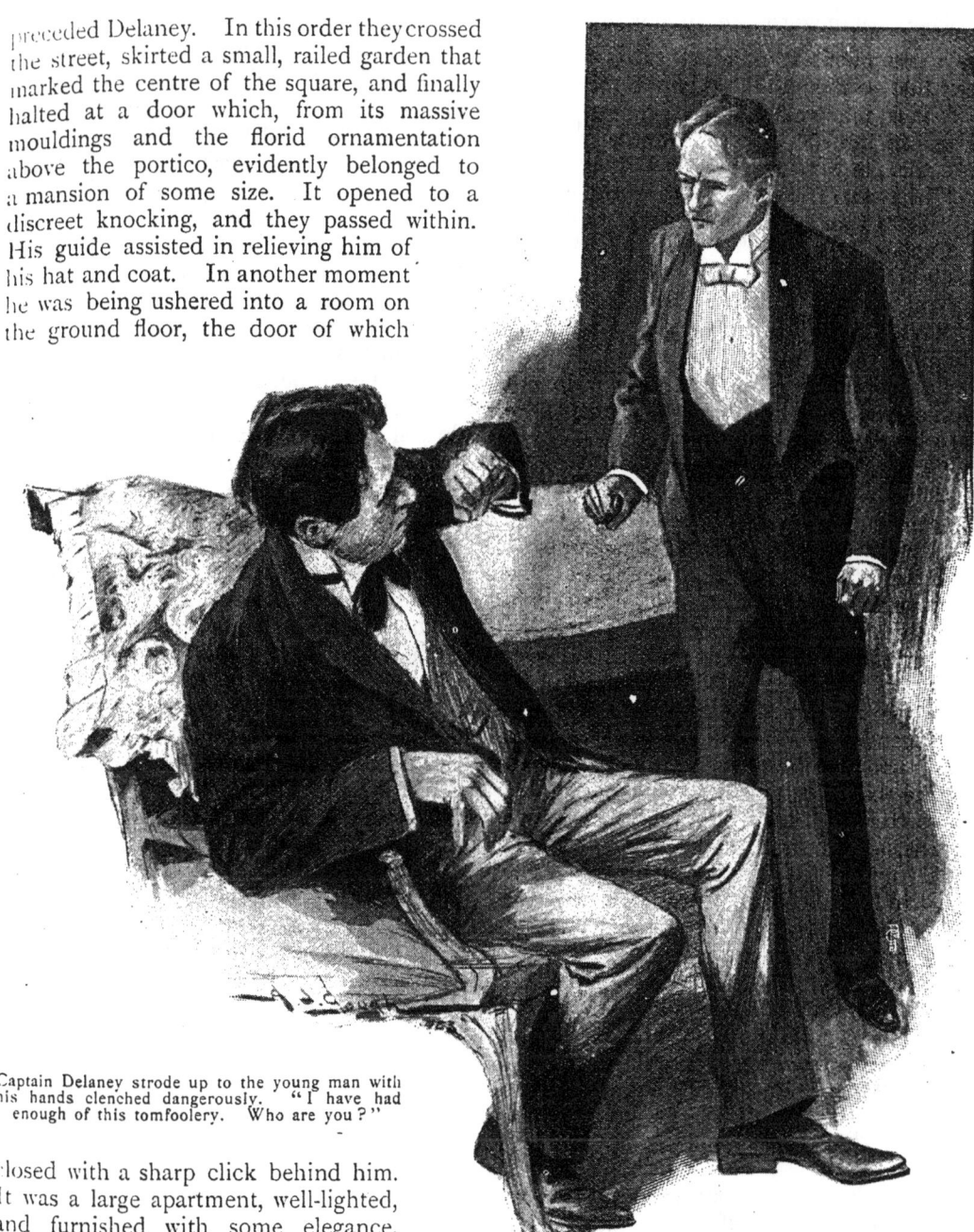

Captain Delaney strode up to the young man with his hands clenched dangerously. "I have had enough of this tomfoolery. Who are you?"

closed with a sharp click behind him. It was a large apartment, well-lighted, and furnished with some elegance. The further side was occupied by two windows, which were shuttered and barred. Under an overmantel, heavy with oak carvings, a wood fire burned cheerily in the open grate. Before the hearth a young man was seated in a deep, well-cushioned chair. His length of hair, his extravagance of tie, and the loose fit of the velvet coat, into the pockets of which his hands were thrust, suggested a foreign student or artist. He remained for some moments gazing into the fire, as if unconscious of his visitor.

When he raised his eyes Delaney was astonished at their expression. So cold, so remorseless were they, that the soldier found it difficult to repress an exclamation of surprise.

"Your excellency expected more agreeable company," said the young man, using the French tongue—a language with which his visitor was perfectly acquainted.

Captain Delaney was in no mood for explanation. He saw in the affair a servant's mistake that might place an unknown lady in a compromising position. It was necessary that he should do his best to shield her.

"This intolerable fog is my excuse for a foolish mistake," he apologised. "I am not, then, in No. 104, Hamildon Square?"

"I have no knowledge of that address."

"Then I must wish you good evening."

Captain Delaney, rather pleased with his ready excuse, turned and tried the door behind him. It was bolted from the outside.

"What is the meaning of this?" he asked sharply.

"Merely, your excellency, that I do not desire to lose a friend upon whose hospitality I so long imposed myself."

"I do not recollect the occasion."

"Possibly not. Your guests were very numerous. Won't you sit down?"

Captain Delaney hesitated for a moment and then obeyed, choosing a position that commanded both the door and his companion. For the latter he had no fear; even if he were a dangerous lunatic he was no very formidable opponent. But for the unknown accomplices without he owned to a vague apprehension. He could imagine no explanation for their conduct.

The young man seemed to have forgotten his presence. He had fallen again into a reverie, his elbows upon his knees, his eyes fixed upon the glowing embers. The position was becoming farcical, or so the soldier held it.

"I have apologised for the accident which brought me here," said he, rising. "To be frank, I have no desire for your further acquaintance. If you do not cause that door to be opened I will break it down."

"Your excellency must be aware that men do not trap wolves in wicker cages. You will merely damage your fists on the iron panels."

Captain Delaney was an even-tempered man, but there was an end to his endurance. He strode up to the young man with his hands clenched dangerously.

"I have had enough of this tomfoolery. Who are you?"

"That does not matter. It is enough that I know you, Prince Michael Pavaloff."

"You have made a mistake, monsieur. My name is Francis Delaney, a captain in the regiment of Guides."

The young man threw back his head and laughed in a subdued, mirthless fashion. Bending forward he touched a bell by his side.

"Then you must be identified," he said.

There was a creaking of wood on wood from the further end of the room; as the panel slid back a hole gaped in the wainscot. From out of it there came thrusting a face, wasted, hollow-cheeked, with deep-set, fiery eyes. Then the man himself, long, lean, with stooping shoulders, shuffled from the opening, and two others followed after him. They were foreigners plainly, and, in their dress and bearing, gentlemen. They gathered in a silent group, watching Delaney with a curious, cat-like gratification.

"Tell me, Count Nicolas," asked the young man of him who had entered first, "do you know this person?"

"I do, brother. He is Michael Pavaloff."

"Where have you seen him?"

"At the salt mines of Van."

"Many times?"

"Very many—perhaps every month during my five years of torment in a living hell."

"And you, my comrades?"

"There is no mistake. Nicolas speaks truly," they answered him together.

"I thank you, comrades; it is sufficient. Perhaps your excellency will now realise that to lie to us is useless. Moreover, I was myself in the salt mines for three years—for three years, I say to you, Michael Pavaloff, Prince of Little Russia, one time Governor of Van and for ever slave-driver and assassin!"

The whole body of the young man throbbed to the passionate rush of his words. From the rest came the guttural murmur of a jury, equal to his own.

Captain Delaney faced them with an outward calm though his eyes were very bright and watchful.

"Gentlemen," said he, "I am, as I told you, an English officer. I have never been in Russia in my life. The sooner you realise your mistake and let me go the better for you."

"Michael Pavaloff," replied the young man, "we thought you a clever man, but you are behaving like a fool and a coward. Perhaps an explanation will make you wiser. Amongst the political prisoners at Van—men as well born and reared as yourself—whose lives you cursed with every cruelty, every insult, a society was formed. The members were twelve in number, eleven men and one a woman; their object your death—should they ever be freed. Of the twelve four died—you best know how—two escaped, three were released and three are

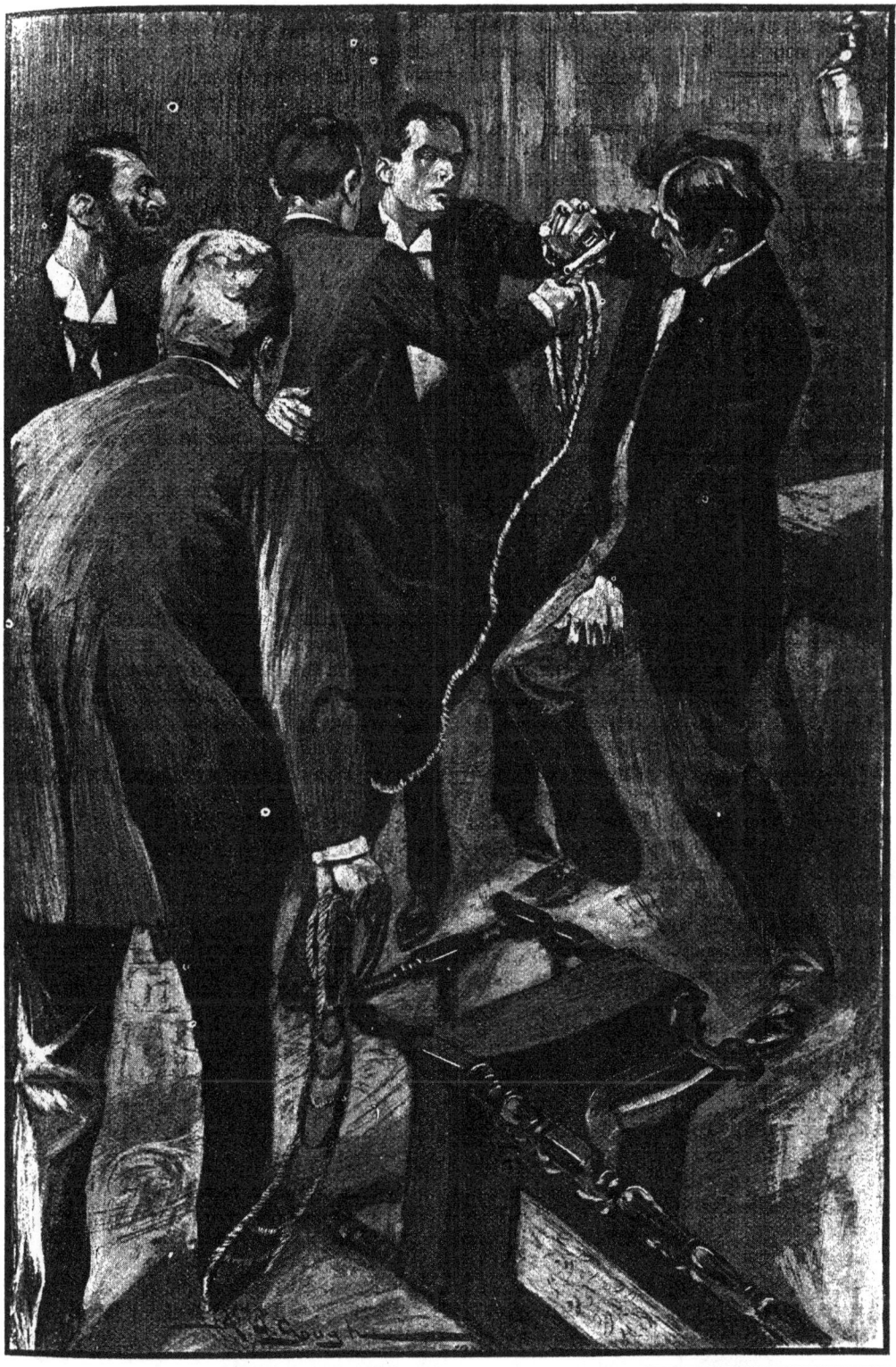

With a sudden spring he caught the man Nicolas round the waist, and using his body as a shield, rushed upon Ivan's revolver. The three went down in a shrieking heap.

still suffering in Siberia under your successor. The five who had come to freedom found you were travelling abroad. They followed you, being well provided with money. We were near you at Naples; we failed in our attempt to entrap you at Paris; here in London—at last we meet you face to face. What have you to say?"

"Nothing that I have not told you already. I am an English soldier—if you choose to question me you will find I tell the truth."

The spokesman of the Russians turned and whispered with his friends. Delaney's eyes glanced swiftly to the door—the window—the fanatics before him. He could see no way of escape, but it was not in his breed to despair. Leaning against the wall, he thrust his hands into his pockets; the next instant he was looking down the barrel of a revolver.

"Raise your hands," cried the young man. Delaney obeyed with an irritating yawn. To the outward eye the whole affair bored him intensely.

"We offer you a certain concession," continued the Russian. "Though it is not without danger to ourselves. You may communicate to any friend you choose the fact that you are at the point of death——"

"I beg your pardon?"

"Of death, Michael Pavaloff—on the condition that you tell us what you have done with Madame Paula. She was to have brought you herself or to have preceded you, having named the rendezvous—in which case there was one appointed to conduct you here. If you have brought about some foul play——?"

He stopped suddenly, with a look of furious suspicion.

"My good fellow," said Delaney, "I do not know the lady. As she seems to have been in doubtful company, I am equally concerned as to her welfare."

"You waste your time, Ivan," cried the man called Nicolas. "He has a heart of stone."

The young man Ivan waved his hand, and at the sign two of the group sprang to a tall cupboard by the fire. From this they drew a rope and a jointed ladder. Glancing at the roof, Delaney noticed for the first time that an iron ring had been screwed into the central rafter. The conclusion was obvious.

"You Paul and you Nicolas—bind him."

The revolver again covered Delaney as the pair advanced. They were within a yard when he made his effort.

With a sudden spring he caught the man Nicolas round the waist, and using his body as a shield, rushed upon Ivan's revolver. The three went down in a shrieking heap, and the weapon flew on to the hearth. Delaney was first on his feet and sprang towards it. He crushed the nose of a face that barred his way, and a man dropped groaning. But a leg tripped him. He fell, and as his fingers closed upon the butt, the rest flew at his prostrate body like wolves worrying and screaming with a horrible rage. A vicious blow behind the ear half stunned him; there was a knee in his back and hot hands at his throat. He held on grimly to the weapon, but a man was stamping on his fingers. He could hear faintly—a long way off it seemed—the voice of Nicolas crying for a knife, a knife for the bear's throat. And then, as it appeared to him, the tumult was blotted out by a clap of thunder. Again and again it sounded, filling the universe with its roar. The pressure of the knees, the grip of the strangling hands, relapsed. A body fell heavily across his face. There was warm blood in his eyes and mouth, his own or another's he could not tell. And then came silence.

He was dazed and weak, but still conscious. The weight of the body which lay across his head was suffocating. If he could only get air! When someone dragged it from him he was very grateful. He sat up, rubbing the blood from his eyes that he might see who his friend could be, and there, bending over him, line for line, and feature for feature, was the image of himself!

"Who the devil are you?" asked Captain Delaney.

The image laughed, and with the laugh the strange resemblance melted. For it was no honest burst of merriment, but a hideous dragging of the lips, suggestive of the snarl of an animal.

"I understand and I apologise," cried the stranger in excellent English. "To be the double of a Russian official is not without its danger. I am Prince Michael Pavaloff."

"Then for heaven's sake be careful; these fanatics will return and —— "

"If you will look round you will notice that I am already out of danger."

Delaney staggered to his feet and stood supporting himself against the wall. It was a gruesome spectacle even for a man who had seen the horrors of barbaric warfare. Three bodies sprawled upon the floor, two being face downwards and the third upon its back with one thin arm raised stiffly as if in appeal against an unjust fate. They seemed stone dead—shot in their tracks through heart or brain. The young man who had acted as spokesman lay huddled across a chair coughing out his life in shivering tremors. There was the scent of a battle in the air.

"Did you—did you do it all yourself?" asked Delaney.

Prince Michael Pavaloff laughed again in his unpleasant fashion.

"When I was sixteen," he said, "I had the honour to be known as the best pistol shot in St. Petersburg. I took them by surprise—it was quite easy. Indeed, I have two cartridges left in my revolver; with one I will finish the game."

He moved across the room, avoiding the bodies, and shot the dying man behind the ear. With a thud like the falling of a sack of wheat the body rolled from the chair to the floor.

"I am sorry to see you have lost your nerve," said Delaney coldly.

"You are pleased to be sarcastic. Perhaps you forget that three minutes ago that man was about to have you hung by the neck."

"Not at all. I am grateful for an opportune rescue. Yet, I am still of opinion that the killing of the wounded is best left to savages."

"My good fellow," cried the Russian, with a malignant flash of his dark eyes, "if you were in a country wherein gentlemen were more careful of their honour and less concerned for their skins I should know how to answer you. As it is I will condescend to explain. I had been warned by our police—the good police—that I was being followed. Indeed, so close a description of these men had been given me, some three weeks ago, that I recognised them the moment I entered the room. They were political prisoners in the salt mines of Van when I had the honour to be Governor of that tedious locality. Apparently they had some cause of grievance against me— though, indeed, I do not recall treating them differently to the other dogs with whom they were herded. But these politicals, who have met with so sudden a conclusion to their plotting, acquired from somewhere a dangerous ally—an ally unknown to our police. It was a woman, my dear fellow, and, what is more, a beautiful woman. Who can resist beauty? Not I, at any rate. She brought me in to supper to-night. My promise of secrecy preceded the pretty indiscretion. While I was taking off my coat in that dark hall outside I heard the devil's own clamour that you and our friends there were raising. The bolts of the door were drawn, but I slipped them back, and stepped in revolver in hand as I have said. I recognised them, and, luckily for you, I caught sight of your face and understood. That is all I know—if you are curious as to details, ask madame, here."

He turned laughing, pointing with his finger; and Delaney saw her for the first time.

She was crouched in the corner to the left of the door. Beautiful she might be, but horror had twisted her face into a white mask of suffering. Her great black eyes stared wildly at the bodies where they lay. So she remained motionless, clasping her cloak of silk and fur about her.

"Come, bestir yourself, madame," cried the Russian. Stooping, he grasped her arm, and jerked her roughly to her feet. She gave a little cry like a child awakened.

"Here, stop that!" said Delaney.

The Prince let go his grasp so suddenly that she staggered and fell heavily to the ground.

"Now, mark what I say, Mr. Englishman," he cried. "This is the second occasion that you have seen fit to quarrel with my behaviour. Those who know him will tell you that Michael Pavaloff does not receive suggestions for the bettering of his conduct from his inferiors."

Delaney walked past him, and raised the lady to her feet. Her eyes were still upon her dead comrades, and she shrank away from him, shivering.

"You will be pleased to observe that this lady is under my protection," said he. "You have had great provocation; but, to be frank with you, your present behaviour suggests the ill-conditioned bully."

For answer the Prince struck him across the lips, and Delaney promptly knocked him down. As he fell, his revolver dropped from his hand, and the soldier put his foot upon

The Prince struck him across the lips, and Delaney promptly knocked him down. As he fell, his revolver dropped from his hand.

marksman; the odds must at least be made even. It was not fear, but love of fair play.

"I have the right to name the conditions, Prince Michael Pavaloff, and they shall be as follows. Of the two revolvers one only shall be loaded. Also we will fire across a table. How does that please you?"

"It is the suggestion of a lunatic."

"Rather that of a practical man. For believe me, my skill with the pistol is very indifferent."

The veneer of the Russian's civilisation was wearing perilously thin. His colour had faded to a muddy grey, from which his dark eyes shone with a beast-like ferocity; his lip bled where he had bitten it; his hands clawed and plucked at his clothing. It was not a pleasant sight for a lover of humanity. But Captain Delaney seemed to notice nothing unusual.

"Well, Prince, and what is your answer?" he enquired politely.

it. It was a wise precaution; there was sudden death in the Russian's face as he gathered himself up from the floor and leant panting against the wall.

"You will fight me," he stammered out.

The wild Irish blood caught hold and carried Delaney away in a reckless pugnacity.

"With all the pleasure in the world," said he.

"There are two pistols here—does that please you?"

British common sense bridled the Irish enthusiasm. This man was a notorious

"It shall be as you suggest. I gladly stake my life upon a chance that may lead to my scattering your brains upon the floor."

The soldier picked up the Prince's revolver and stepped across to where the second weapon lay. They were of similar appearance and calibre. From both he extracted the cartridges empty and full. Then he paused, hesitating.

"I am a sad bungler not to have thought of it," said he. "But one revolver must be secretly loaded—and how shall we manage that, you and I?"

"I am at your disposal, gentlemen."

It was the lady who had spoken. Save for her deathlike pallor there was no sign of her agony as she stood, tall and defiant, with the lights sparkling on the diamonds at her neck and shimmering on the beautiful cloak she held about her.

"She can be trusted for the work," sneered the Prince. "With all weapons suited to assassination she is, without doubt, familiar."

"Then we accept your offer, madame," said Delaney. "Observe; I place the revolvers and cartridges upon this chair. Stand with your back to us, and place a cartridge in which you choose."

"And be also pleased to observe, madame," added the Russian, "that I take this knife from your dead comrade, and at a sign of treachery I drive it between your shoulders."

The lady bowed and moved to the chair. A yard behind her the two men stood side by side, the Prince with the bared knife in his hand.

"Have you finished?" asked Delaney, after a minute's pause.

"The work is done, sir."

"Then kindly step away from the chair."

She had covered the weapons with her handkerchief, leaving the butts protruding.

"Honour me by choosing first," said Delaney. He was quite cool, but his throat seemed strangely dry.

The Prince stepped forward and raised the revolver nearest to him. The soldier took the other. Turning about, they moved to opposite ends of the table. A body lay huddled in the way of the Prince, and he pushed it aside with his foot.

"Even in death these carrion can annoy us," he said. "Shall we ask madame here to give the signal?"

"At the dropping of her handkerchief."

They were facing each other over the six feet of tablecloth. Delaney found himself following the intricacies of the woven pattern and hating the colour combinations. He raised his eyes and met those of his antagonist goggling with the lust of murder. What horrors had this passionate brute not perpetrated on those over whom he had ruled? There had been women amongst them, and men of culture and breeding open the more to subtle insults. His victims, who had tracked him across a continent, had been seeking, perhaps, a revenge that was just, if ever revenge so could be. He had had the luck on his side again—and now—would it continue?

"Perhaps it will be better if madame counts three before dropping her handkerchief," suggested the Prince.

"It is a good idea," said Captain Delaney.

She took her stand at the side of the table, the bundle of silk and fluffy lace held high. Then she began to count very slowly and distinctly. At "one," the two men raised their weapons; at "two" they took steady aim, eye to eye, motionless, as if frozen in their places; at "three" the fingers crooked lovingly upon the triggers.

And then happened a most amazing thing.

The handkerchief was falling from the lady's fingers when from the Prince burst forth a hideous cry. It was the scream of a man in the extremest agony of pain and terror. His eyes still stared into the soldier's face, but the fury had left them like a flame suddenly extinguished. The room still echoed to the sound when it shook with an explosion which in those narrow quarters reverberated like the report of a cannon. At the same instant it seemed to Delaney that someone struck him a heavy blow full and square upon the top of his head. He dropped forward, grasping the edge of the table to save himself from falling.

It was perhaps a minute before Delaney so far recovered his senses as to realise that the Prince's bullet was not really in his brain, and that the blood which blinded him was from a scalp wound only. He peered into the smoke which still clouded the room in sluggish eddies. His antagonist he could not see, but the lady still stood beside him.

"It's a very extraordinary thing," stammered the Captain, still clutching the table and feeling very ill. "Most extraordinary, for I could have sworn I fired, too."

"You have killed him."

"What, I? Why, that's impossible. Only one revolver was loaded; and just look what he did to my head."

"Nevertheless it is true, for I loaded them *both*."

"Oh! Did you? And why, madame?"

"You might have chosen the empty weapon—then he would have escaped."

"Egad, that's logic," continued Delaney, dabbing the blood that trickled freely down his forehead. "But how the deuce did he come to miss me? Didn't he shout out something just before we fired? My head aches so confoundedly I can hardly remember. Perhaps that put him off. Let's have a look at him, anyhow."

Very slowly and painfully the Captain worked his way round the table and peered over the further edge.

If ever a man died in the terror of this world and the next it was Michael Pavaloff, Prince of Little Russia and sometime Governor of Van, who lay flat upon his back with the blue-ringed bullet-kiss showing clearly in the centre of his forehead. Fixed upon the tendons of his leg, just above the heel, were the teeth of the man called Nicolas. It had been his body, wounded unto death, that the Prince had spurned aside, rousing thereby the last flickering spark of understanding in one who had lived only for revenge. Death had not loosened that last grim grip of the jaws. The dead still hung to the dead. It was a very dreadful spectacle.

"He thought the devil had him by the heel. No wonder he shot wide," cried Captain Delaney, staggering back in horror. The dead men seemed to move in twists and curves. Lights flashed in his eyes. The floor rose up towards him with a rush, and then he passed into the silence of the outer dark.

He was alone when he awoke. Yet he had not been uncared for. A flask of brandy was by his side, and his head, which was swathed in bandages, rested on a comfortable pillow. A sheet had been placed over the bodies that had been drawn together in the middle of the room. He thanked God for it. He got to his feet feeling jumpy, but quite capable of walking. The door of the room was open, the light in the deserted hall burning. He found his coat, slipped the catch of the entrance door, and closing it carefully behind him, passed out into the grey of a misty morning. Seven was striking from a church clock over the way. There was no one about.

* * *

The murder of that fashionable and well-known Russian, Prince Michael Pavaloff, by Nihilists, thrilled all London. The papers devoted columns to the inquest. According to the best information, he had been decoyed into a house rented by the gang, and after a desperate resistance, in which he had killed no less than four of his opponents, he had been shot down. There was no mention of a lady or of a certain captain of Native Cavalry. Nor did they come forward to offer their evidence.

THE END.

FLEUR-DE-LYS.

Adown the village street she went,
Upon her task of mercy bent,
With such a smile of sweet content,
    So fair to see;
The kiss of child, the prayer of dame,
Fell on her as she went and came,
As pure and peaceful as her name—
    Fleur-de-Lys!

Oh, lily-flower, you do not know
That one who saw you loved you so—
In those dear days of long ago
    How sad was he;
So sad, so lone, because you were
For his heart's peace too passing fair—
Far out of reach, beyond compare—
    Fleur-de-Lys!

Amid this world of toil and ill,
Old thoughts of you his dreaming fill,
For you are his good angel still,
    And still shall be;
Though lone the path that he must take,
His empty heart, though fain to break,
Dwells nearer Heav'n for your dear sake,
    Fleur-de-Lys!

CLIFTON BINGHAM.

THE DEBT OF HEINRICH HERMANN

By B. Fletcher Robinson.

Hermann & Sons lay tucked away in a narrow tributary to that rattling, roaring river the Commercial Road, E. It was old as firms go nowadays, dating back to the German outlander, Heinrich Hermann the First, who dealt in monkeys and parrots, and strange sea-shells that he bought from the sailormen who manned the fleets of the great East India Company. It was Heinrich Hermann the Second who added the wine vaults next door to the premises, and had to do with larger beasts that were swung off ships' decks by derricks, snarling their rage and fear behind the canvas of their iron cages. With Heinrich Hermann the Third the firm grew mightily in reputation till there was scarcely a menagerie or a wild beast show in the country but in their time had had dealings with it. It held to its name though Hermann the Third had no sons, being, indeed, a bachelor of five-and-forty.

He was a tall, bony man, with a face so thin and drawn that it seemed misplaced on such shoulders as he carried. His eyes, deep set under scanty tufts of red-brown hair, stared out upon the world with an unwinking decision. His chin was prominent, and harshly moulded. But the dogged set of his countenance was spoiled by his mouth, which was afflicted by a nervous twitching at the corners as if the man were suppressing an ever-recurring grin. It was a deceptive infirmity, for there was nothing of the humorist about Heinrich Hermann the Third.

A gaunt, unsociable figure he made as he waited at his shop door on that blustering November evening. Now and again, as a keener blast blew whirlpools in the straw litter that trailed from under his warehouse doors, he hugged the heavy seaman's cloak he wore more closely about him. From the distant thoroughfare came the low droning thunder of waggon wheels on cobbled pavements. Beyond it the naked yards of the dock shipping hung above the clustering roofs, each rope showing clear against the glow of the angry sunset. There was the raw strong smell of stagnant salt water in the air.

"Good evening. Have I kept you waiting?"

He had not heard the young man's step, and he swung round on him with an agility that was remarkable in one of his heavy build.

"Sorry if I startled you, Mr. Hermann, but an electrician has to scramble into odd places sometimes, and I find rubber soles to my shoes are safest."

He was a bright, well-built fellow of six-and-twenty, and he meant the apology he offered.

"It is noding, Mr. Ransome," said Hermann, speaking with the broad Teutonic accent that was his inherited custom. "You are bunctual, und as for startling me—well, in my piziness we cannot afford nerfes. And how is Miss Fane?"

"Very well, thank you, Mr. Hermann. But what is the special work you mentioned in your letter? I am quite curious."

"Der wedding day—is it fixed?"

"Of course. I thought you knew. It is just six weeks to-morrow. But what is it that——"

"You are imbatient, my young friend. Surely der talk of lofe should be sweeter to you than your jargon of esdimates, und batteries und fuses. Dare, dare, you grow angry. Bardon me, if I hof offended. Come inside, und I will explain—what I meant by der letter."

He led the way down a dusky passage that ended in a small room comfortably furnished. A spirit decanter stood upon the table, and a box of cigars lay hospitably open. Ransome refused neither.

"And where do you keep these beasts of yours—these lions and tigers, and the rest?" he asked, settling himself in a rocking-chair.

"Dey are all around you, Mr. Ransome. In der warehouse, in der covered yards behind, und in der vaults below. Ach! But listen!" and he held up a warning hand.

From some spot—whether near or far away Ransome could not tell—came a long, low mutter that grew and grew till the room throbbed to its reverberations. Then it sunk into an echo, a silence.

"He came to-day. It is new to him und he is uneasy."

"What is it?"

"A tiger, und a fine sbecimen; he is alreaty sold."

"You must have stout nerves," said the young man laughing uneasily. "I don't think I could sleep in comfort with such noises in my ears."

"A man who liv' by der railway does not wake to ebery bassing train. But, inteed, dere is one cry dot when it come in der deep of der night——"

He stopped, watching his companion, his mouth twitching with his odd affliction.

"One cry—and what is that?"

"It is from der pride of my collegtion, Mr. Ransome, a West African gorilla. In his capture he kill dree natives. On der voyage a sailor—who come too near his cage—died quickly. If he were now in dis room he could tear us as a woman tears a linen sheet, for he has der strength of seven men. Sometimes at night he remember his forest, he recall der indignity dot he has suffer, und he drum upon his breast und roar his anger to der stars. *Mein Gott!* It is not a goot thing to hear—in der darkness."

"Well, I suppose it is your business to keep such creatures though I would as soon harbour a murderer. But it grows late, Mr. Hermann, and I am due at an eight o'clock supper."

"At der Fanes?"

"Yes," said the young man shortly. "Come. What do you want of me?"

"Haf you bring my letter mid you, as I asked?"

"Yes, there it is," said the electrician, drawing the envelope from his pocket. "Moreover, I have told no one of our appointment."

"I tank you. It is goot. Und now let me exblain dese brecautions. You must understand dot I loan certain of my vaults to drainers who desire to make from me purchases dot are suitable to deir trade. Dey are in dis way able to study der moods and der manners of beasts I haf to sell. One of my best customers ask me to haf electrig lights fix in two of der vaults in a manner concerning which he demand great secrecy, for it is a drick of his piziness which is most jealous breserved. It is for dis reason I sent for you—a junior bartner. I desire an esdimate from your firm which will include sbecial workmen dot you can guarantee as silent, trustworthy men. I am brepared to bay dem well, Mr. Ransome."

"So that is all, is it? Indeed, you puzzled me by your letter. If you will show me the vaults and describe what it is you want I will post you a rough estimate to-morrow."

Hermann rose and opening a corner cupboard drew out a lantern which he lit from a spill thrust into the fire.

"Is gas then quite excluded from the premises?" asked the young man.

"No, he is laid in der oder buildings. But my man he has gone home, und my lodgers, though, indeed, dey are many, do not sit oop after sunset. Will you be bleased to come mid me?"

Ransome followed the tall figure bearing its swinging patch of yellow light into the dusky yard without. They halted at an iron-barred gate in the further wall. This opened to a key, and they descended a short flight of stone steps that ended in a passage faced and paved with ancient bricks. Whisps and mounds of straw were littered on the floor, and the warm air was sickly with heavy, pungent odours. Before the third door on the right the dealer stopped, throwing the light upon it as he drew the bolts. Passing within, he put a match to a rusty gas bracket on the wall, and set his lantern on the stones below.

It was a large vault some thirty feet by twelve in measurement. About two-thirds of it was cut off by a row of substantial iron bars set in the floors and ceiling. In the middle of this barrier was a little gate fastened by a bolt and padlock. A row of hot water pipes against the wall explained the tropical atmosphere.

"Dere is der first blace, Mr. Ransome," said Hermann in his dull monotone, though, indeed, his lips were twitching as if in an excess of merriment. "Der main light will be midin der cage—a great cluster of lamps set in der ceiling, and shielded by thick glass. Berhaps you would like to examine der spot?"

He unfastened the padlock as he spoke, and pulled open the iron gate. So low was it that Ransome had to drop on his hands and knees to enter.

"Pah! How this den smells! It's like a ferret-house," said he, peering about in the shadows.

"Berhaps. He was here to-day."

"He? And who is 'he'? Hello, there, Hermann! Stop that! Stop that, I say!"

He was back at the iron gate with a nervous spring. But before he reached it the key had turned in the padlock. The dealer stepped back from the bars. He was too late.

"I have no time for practical jokes, Mr. Hermann," said the young man angrily. "You will be pleased to open that gate at once."

The dealer leant against the wall watching his prisoner. His hands were clenched together before him as if he were repressing a violent emotion. His forehead dripped with perspiration.

"I haf someding to dell you," said he, speaking in short guttural throbs. "It is a liddle story, berhaps a very old und common story; but to me dot can hardly be exbected to make a difference. Der was a man who grow old. He had money enough, but he was much alone. He lofe a young girl. She had sixteen years, und he wait. He saw her very often, und she did not dislike him, dis man. So he say to himself dot on her eighteenth birthday he would do dot for which he had long und suffer und pray. He would ask her to be his wife. And when der day come for which he had wait for two years he go to her, und show her all dot was in his heart. But she was change. He press her hard for a reason. Mein Gott! But she shrink from him mid fear! And den—she tell him—she lofe some oder.

"Dot night he pass in der deepest pit of hell. Und der next day und der next. Many days. It was der same. So dot he would gladly haf welcomed death; so dot he grew so strange to look upon dot he fear to see his own eyes in der glass. He would haf kill himself, but dot from his pain come a hope that put out der fire in his brain, a hope dot grew and grew until it fill the whole world. It was der hope of revenge."

For the first time the young man's courage failed him, for the face that gloated at him through the bars was not that of a sane man. He stepped further back into the cage, shivering.

"So he form a liddle plan, a cunning liddle plan—und his plan it has succeeded. Dis rival, so fortunate, who creep und whisper und steal, shall suffer as he suffer. For an hour, a day, a week, maybe, he shall life in such bain of mind dot he too will pray dot the end it may come quick. Look, Cecil Ransome, look what it is which will do dis for me, which will pay der debt Heinrich

Hermann owes to der man dot steal from him Mary Fane."

He sprang to a small iron wheel fixed in the wall. As he swung the handle a rusty chain grated in its pulleys overhead. Inch by inch there grew a faint grey light patching the gloom that lay upon the further end of the vault. It was a sliding panel that was slowly rising. A shadow darkened the glimmering square, for a moment hanging there irresolute. Then with a shambling rush *it* came—a rush that carried it to the iron barrier where it clung. And from it broke a cry first choked and broken, but quickly swelling into a loud continuous scream, utterly inhuman—a howl half of fury and half of despair, such as might arise from the throats of the legions of the lost. It tore at the bars, saliva dripped from its jaws as its great head, pitted, coarse-haired, grotesque as a mask in a winter's pantomime, wagged slowly to and fro, while its long arms flickered out like the lunges of a striking snake to where its master stood beyond their reach.

Ransome was a brave man, but his danger was too horrible. Crouching against the wall he shut out the sight of the raving beast with his fingers, and so waited for the end.

He heard the creak of the sliding panel behind him as Hermann let it fall, the slam of the vault door, and the shooting of the outer bolts that told him he was left alone—with this thing of terror. He peered between his fingers.

The gorilla still clung to the bars, gazing after its master with a hatred that was inhumanly human. At last, with a grunt of useless fury, it dropped to the ground, and turned its staring eyes upon him. It moved towards him—very slowly.

* * * * *

"I think he must be mad, Sir Richard," said the young house surgeon. "If not, it's a matter for the police. But, anyhow, it's such a remarkable document that, as you happened to be in the hospital, I should like you to see it."

He laid a little book on the table in the circle of the lamp. The great doctor opened it, and glanced at its contents.

"Seems nothing but calculations and business appointments," he grunted.

"It's at the end that you'll find it."

"How came he to be admitted, Mr. Thompson?" he asked, fluttering over the leaves.

"An accident case. He was scooting across the Commercial Road when a van caught him, and rolled him into the gutter. Police thought him badly hurt, and brought him in; but I can find nothing much the matter with him. It seems more like sheer starvation and nervous shock than anything else. I gave him a dose, and he's sleeping it off. I came across the book inside his shirt when I was examining him. It seemed such a deuced odd place to keep it that I glanced into it, and lit on this diary business. I think you've got it now. It begins just there."

"Very well, I'll read it. You needn't wait."

The great man turned his chair to a comfortable angle, and so began:

Wednesday, one o'clock a.m.—If this should ever come into human hands, being saved from apes and devils, let it be taken to the police. If they will go into the main cellar of Heinrich Hermann's Repository, off the Commercial Road, and open the third vault to the right, they will discover the cage wherein I was done to death. Where my body will be hidden, if, indeed, any trace of it remains, I cannot say.

At seven o'clock this evening I, Cecil Ransome, of the firm of Williams & Ransome, electrical engineers, Victoria Street, was enticed by the man Hermann into a cage containing an ape beast. God preserve my reason till the end.

This he did for purposes of revenge. It is moving this way. I must——

It is quiet again. Hermann, through his ape, is my murderer, for he well knew, when he shut me up with it, that sooner or later it would tear me in pieces—"as a woman tears a linen sheet" were his words. This statement is enough to hang him; but that I may ease my brain from the dread of death, which is ever before me, I shall continue to write whatever may happen in this book—so far as it allows me—until the end.

When Hermann left me this evening his ape advanced upon me so that in my great terror I gave myself up for lost. But, as I discovered, it was for the time simply curious. It plucked continually at my clothes, tearing away several of the buttons, besides bruising the flesh beneath; indeed, one snatch ripped the sleeve of my jacket clean away. I had the sense to lie silent through it all, and after a while it left me for its lair of straw in the further corner of the cage.

The stone flags have bruised and cramped my limbs, but I dare not alter my position.

I have no hope of rescue for no one is aware of my appointment, and even the letter that made it I brought with me. Strangers have been lost before now in this district. I have no doubt that the river police will be warned; the docks also may be dragged for my body.

I should like Mr. Fane, of Marlow Villa, Abbey Road, N.W., to be told that my last thoughts were of his daughter. God comfort her.

It is a restless sleeper, moaning continuously. I can just distinguish it as it lies in the darkest part of the cage. I think that I should have gone mad if Hermann had not left that gas jet burning—though its light is very small.

It was only when it pressed into my leg as I lay that I remembered my knife. It has a stout blade. I have hidden it in my remaining sleeve. Perhaps a thrust at its eye —but even in its death throes it would kill me. I shall wait till the last struggle before I use it.

Five o'clock.—When it took to wandering about the cage I dropped back into childhood. I thrust my handkerchief into my mouth that I might not babble aloud. It is quiet again now; but for an hour it has been shambling to and fro before the bars. Its strength must be stupendous. I could see its shoulder muscles swell and sink against the gas outside. Then it fell into a fit of melancholy, crouching on the floor, its whole body shaken with sobs; but just as suddenly it rushed into a flurry of savage ferocity. It sprang at the bars shaking them till they rattled in their sockets, and its screams filled the cage with sound. I was so cowed that if it had attacked me I should have made no resistance. But I think it had forgotten that I was there. If it had remembered I am sure—but what does it matter. It is quiet now in the straw.

Thursday evening—A dreadful day. Torment of mind and body. In such way madness comes. And yet—no, it is not hope, for it opens no path of escape—and yet it may be that Hermann will have to find another way of killing me. But even this is foolish imagining. The beast is a thing of moods. This minute he may again change —this minute as I write. Oh, Lord! I am in Thy hands!

When I had finished the diary last night I dozed. Its cries awoke me. The ape was struggling at the bars, and there was Hermann, his lantern above his head, peering into the cage. He started when I moved, and his lips twitched into that caricature of a grin of his, the coldest nightmare of merriment that I can imagine.

"You lay still," he said. "For der moment I thought you slep' der sleep dot does not waken. Berhaps by der evening you will do so. Who can tell? For der present here is breakfast for two."

With an iron staff he unfastened a small grating near the floor to the right of the cage, through which he thrust a great bowl of rice and fruit that he had brought with him. As the ape seized it he walked across and tossed a packet between the bars almost into my lap.

"Bread and meat," he said. "Water you will find in der trough at der top of der cage."

And then, though it is not necessary that I should write his words, he spoke coarsely of some one who is very dear to me. So that I fell into a rage, of which I am even now ashamed. It must, indeed, have been a great joy to him. For forgetting my peril I sprang to the bars and clung there cursing him like a fool.

"It is a well-matched couple," he said. "Can it be two apes or two men? It is hard to tell der beast from der human."

I glanced sideways. Not a yard from my elbow it was hanging to the bars, and watching us. It almost seemed that it understood.

It must have been for over two hours that the ape squatted on the ground before me. All that time it was watching me with a sullen curiosity; it seemed like some monstrosity of a man sitting in judgment upon me, trying to solve a difficult puzzle. My slightest movement angered it. I grew stiff and numb; I had not drunk since the previous night and my throat was like dust. At last I grew reckless, sooner or later—what did it matter. I rose to my feet as coolly as I could and moved in the direction of the tank at the top of the cage. The next instant I was flung against the wall, with my jacket ripped from neck to waist. It shook the heart clean out of me. I burst into angry tears and sobbed like a school-boy, rubbing my bruised arm and shoulder. But it did not attack me again. Instead, it shambled off to the bars where it began again its prisoner's march —up and down, up and down.

The next instant I was flung against the wall, with my jacket ripped from neck to waist.

It was an hour later that I reached the tank, and drank. Then I crawled back to my place, which is on the left hand wall, a third of the way between the bars and the top of the cage. All this I did without molestation. I ate my sandwiches, and felt stronger to meet my death, though loving life yet more.

It was at five that Hermann came again with our evening meal.

I cannot say how it occurred to me. I have made endeavours to remember, but still I cannot explain. It was when Hermann had turned to go, and the ape was raging at the bars, that I rose and ran to his side imitating it, gesture for gesture, scream for scream. And when silence fell the beast and I looked each other in the eyes as might two enemies who had met on neutral ground. Nor was I afraid. So hope came to me. Hope? Can I call it by that name?

Friday, noon.—I slept last night for four hours. Hermann came with the food at nine o'clock. I could see that he was puzzled about me, but he said nothing. As he left I again rushed at the bars, though this time I was alone, for the ape sat quiet, watching me. When I had finished, I walked back to my place. It began to eat its food with its eyes upon me. But I was not molested.

Afterwards as it dozed on the straw I had the courage to examine the bars. They are solidly built. The grate in the centre is secured by a padlock, which is very strong.

Eight o'clock.—The ape beast has struck me and taken my food. And I am so hungry. It destroyed it before my eyes, and the other devil looked through the bars and saw and laughed at me. It had plenty of its own. Why should it take the little I had? Very well. Wait till you sleep. I know the risk. But it took my food, all I had, and rubbed it in the mud. That is enough. My strong, sharp, clever knife—my friend, I kiss you. Also Hermann laughed at me.

Saturday, 11 a.m.—I cannot explain my folly of the night. It was the act of a child, sulky and vindictive. If my attempt had succeeded how should I have been better? It is the man and not the beast that I have to fear. Let me set it down, nevertheless.

About midnight it slept. Very slowly, with great care, lest I should make the slightest noise, I crawled towards the straw where it lay. My knife open in my right hand, my thumb over the top of the hilt that I might drive it the deeper.

The ape was in a sort of nest. Slowly I raised myself and peered over the edge of the straw.

It lay upon its back, the legs drawn up, its breast heaving to great sobs. Tears were hanging on the hairs beneath the closed lids. It might have been a man fallen asleep in some extremity of sorrow. Chance could not have granted me a better opportunity.

But I could not strike. It was a caricature of humanity. To stab it would be murder—or so it seemed to me. Was not the poor brute a prisoner like myself without the possibility of escape? And he must have been a chief in his own land, a free ranger of the forest before whom all other beasts crept away. It was more likely to have been curiosity than malice that had made him take my food. My anger left me at that thought. I sank back to the floor. But I was too late. With a sudden grunt it raised its head above the rampart of straw. An arm shot out, and gripped me by the shoulder. With a gentle heave he lifted me to him. My knife slipped from my fingers, and was lost.

He regarded me curiously for a moment, while I waited for death almost with relief. But there was no anger in his eyes. Presently he nestled back into the straw, with his arm still gripped around me. I made no effort to escape. And so it came about that we two miserable beings fell asleep side by side in the place of our imprisonment.

Saturday, 8 p.m.—Hermann is growing angry. He carried a whip this evening, with which he struck at the ape. This drove it into a most dreadful fury; but I do not fear it now. Hermann cursed us terribly through the bars. The madness grows upon him, and we are in his power. How will it end?

Sunday, mid-day.—I could hear church bells this morning, muffled, but still easily distinguishable. I wonder if she prayed for me. Heaven knows I need her prayers! What does she imagine has become of me? Has she given up hope? But it is folly to dwell on these things.

Monday, 5 a.m.—I have abandoned my dancing before the bars. It knows what is in my mind without a further pantomime.

Monday, mid-day.—I have no time to write. Shall I ever bring it to understand?

Tuesday.—The scheme goes well. It is taking notice. But Hermann has much reduced our food. There was but a scrap of bread for me to-day. I am so very, very tired. It may be too late—after all.

Wednesday, noon.—I will set it down. Whatever happens there must remain a record.

On Monday I was examining the padlock of the grate that holds us here. It is of a new and complicated design. I soon saw it would be useless to attempt to pick it. Also Hermann examines it twice a day when he comes. He is cunning enough to suspect me of improvising a file. A strong bar runs through the staple, but the staple itself is of old iron bitten deep with rust. As I was examining it the ape shuffled to my side. Ah, my friend, I thought, if I had but your strength, or you had but my knowledge.

That was how the idea came to me.

I have gained some influence over it now. It is especially fond of imitating all I do.

I hear Hermann's step outside. The ape has gathered itself like an arched bow. Its eyes burn like glowing coals. Hermann is coming in! Oh, my——!

By Tuesday night it began to understand that it was a fine brave thing to pull at the padlock. This morning I went further, using all the force I had—though that was little enough—in a great display of tugging and straining. It seemed very interested. In a funny ape fashion I think it was laughing at my feebleness. Presently it may try, and then——

Later.—We are free, free, free! Brave ape, we are free!

Wait, my friend, wait. We have our master Hermann to reckon with. The outer door cannot be forced. If he finds that we have passed the bars he will leave us to starve, you and I. In your hunger you will soon forget. Then you will kill me. Have patience, then, brother ape.

I have been lightheaded with the joy of it, and have written foolish things. About four o'clock the ape began to pluck hard at the padlock, so that it nipped its fingers. And then in sudden anger it put forth the strength that Nature gave it. The great hairy muscles swelled. The very bar which it gripped for leverage bent like a reed. I yelled aloud, half in joy half in fear, at the spectacle, and it answered me with such a scream that I staggered as from a blow. Mingling with it came the dull snap of parting iron. The staple had broken. It waved the padlock above its head, and then dashed it to the floor.

In a few minutes Hermann will be here. We are crouching against the wall. I have no difficulty with it now. It squats patiently by my side watching the door. There is death in its eyes. Unless I warn Hermann I know that it will—— But what can I do? Consider, what can I do?

I hear Hermann's step outside. He has stopped, and is fumbling at the bolts. The ape has gathered itself like an arched bow. Its eyes burn like glowing coals. Its great teeth are bare like the jaws of a skull. Hermann is coming in. Oh, my——!

* * * * *

"I am sorry I kept you so long, Sir Richard," said the house surgeon apologetically.

The great man was stalking up and down the room with his head sunk forward, and his hands clasped behind him. The strange diary lay upon the table.

"It's no matter," he replied, without looking up.

"I sent a cab to that address in the diary, and the girl and her father came back in it. I thought it right they should know—that is to say, if it were true."

"Well?"

"It's true enough as far as their part of the story goes. They have been searching all London for him, and had pretty well given him up for lost."

"And how is he progressing?"

"Still very weak, but nothing serious. He'll be all right in a few days. The girl behaved like a brick. No fuss or tears—nothing to excite the patient. By Jove! But they do love each other!"

"I will see him myself presently."

"Very well, Sir Richard. Is there anything else?"

"You had better send to Scotland Yard, and give them the address of that place in the Commercial Road. Tell them to take a stretcher with them for the man's body. It will be an ugly business. That beast must be loose, too, and mad with blood. They had better go armed."

"Yes, Sir Richard. And the diary?"

"I will keep it for him. He can tell the police his own story when he is strong enough. I'm not sure if that diary would not bring him within our muddle-headed murder law. But, mark you, it was his only way, Mr. Thompson, his only way."

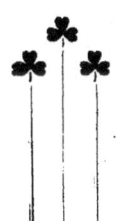 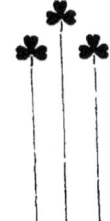

This is to Give

... PRELIMINARY NOTICE OF ...

PEARSON'S XMAS XTRA.

The extra Christmas Number of all Pearson's publications. It will be brighter and better than ever, and will contain 16 pages in colour, and many splendid stories.

ON SALE NOV. 17th. **1/-.**

THE CHRONICLES OF ADDINGTON PEACE

By B. FLETCHER ROBINSON.

Joint Author with Sir A. Conan Doyle in his best Sherlock Holmes Story, "The Hound of the Baskervilles."

THIS IS THE FIRST OF THE STRANGE AND STARTLING EXPERIENCES WHICH BEFEL THAT FAMOUS DETECTIVE, ADDINGTON PEACE. THEY ARE TOLD IN A MOST CONVINCING MANNER, AND SHOULD ON NO ACCOUNT BE MISSED.

I.—THE TERROR IN THE SNOW.

"Toot, toot, toot," quavered the flute.

"Bother the fellow," said I, ringing the bell violently. "This is absolutely unbearable."

I, James Phillips, had taken the ground floor rooms for the charm of their seclusion. The stream of westward-moving traffic split upon the grey front of Westminster Abbey and parted north and south, leaving Keble Street as undisturbed behind that venerable bulwark as a canoe in a backwater.

The studio which opened from my sitting-room was the single modern incongruity in a house designed to the taste of an earlier day. As a lodging, it had seemed an artist's ideal; yet for my first two nights of residence I had been condemned to listen to the faint pipings of an amateur musician on the floor above. It was an intolerable outrage on my privacy; that is just how I felt about it.

"Did you ring, sir?" asked Hendry, poking in his head. A perfect servant was old Jacob Hendry, once sergeant of infantry, and now a combination of cook, valet, and housemaid, who kept my clothes in spotless order, grilled a steak to a turn, and spent his spare time in producing the most inartistic wood-carving I have ever seen.

"Who is responsible for that diabolic noise upstairs?" I asked him.

"You mean the flute, sir?"

"You have guessed it, Hendry."

"It's a person from the Yard."

"Yard—what yard?"

"Scotland Yard, sir," he said, with that mystery in his voice that some people think proper to assume when referring to the police. "His name is Peace, Inspector Addington Peace. You will 'ave read about 'im in the papers."

"Nothing of the kind."

Copyright, 1904, by B. Fletcher Robinson in the United States of America.

"When you was in the Paris studio, as likewise in Rome, I 'ad my *Lloyd's* sent out regular," said Jacob confidentially, "and it was full of 'im and 'is games. My word, but he's a sly one, by all accounts."

"He will have to stop that noise, whoever he is," I answered. "And what is more, Hendry, I am going up to tell him so."

There was a look of sincere alarm on the old fellow's face as I pushed by him. I think he imagined that it was my intention to assault the police and retire for a month to the nearest gaol with a ruined reputation.

I ran up the dark stairway with the haste of a man who wishes to do a bold deed while his temper is hot within him. Inspector Addington Peace might be as omnipotent a detective as ever a novelist created, but he was not going to play the flute of an evening as long as James Phillips occupied the floor beneath him. The notes ceased as I knocked at the door.

"Come in," said a pleasant voice.

Inspector Addington Peace was seated in a comfortable chair before a fire that glowed hostility to the December cold without. He was a little man, clean shaved, fresh-coloured, and plump as an October partridge. For his age, you might have guessed any year between thirty and forty. He did not rise, but his small blue eyes watched me over the top of gold-rimmed glasses with a mild and benevolent expression that smoothed the creases out of my temper like a flat-iron. It is impossible to abuse even a flute-player when he regards you as a welcome guest, and I remained in uneasy silence by the door.

"Your protest is quite justifiable, Mr. Phillips," he said, smiling down at the flute he still held in his chubby fist. "My progress is most disappointing."

"But how did you know—?" I began.

"Tut, tut, sir," he interrupted. "You pealed your bell, banged your door, and rushed up the stairs. Is it difficult to guess who you are and why you came?"

I laughed, too; the humour of this odd little man was catching. At his suggestion I lit an excellent cigar, dropped into a chair, and soon forgot my injuries in his easy conversation. An hour quickly slipped by, and when I rose to go I asked him if he would dine with me on my return from Cloudsham in Norfolk, where I was spending Christmas. He would be pleased, he told me; and then as he stooped to light a spill in the coals:

"You stay with the Baron Steen, I suppose?" he asked.

"Yes."

"And why?"

"Why?" I echoed in some surprise.

"You have relatives or other friends?"

"My nearest relative is a sour old uncle near Carlisle, who calls me hard names for using the gifts Providence gave me instead of adding up figures in a smoky office. As for friends—well, I am a fairly rich man, Inspector, and, as such, have many friends. What is there against the Baron Steen?"

"Oh nothing," he said, puffing at his pipe, so that he spoke as from a cloud, mistily.

"I know that he has played a bold game on the Stock Exchange," I continued, "and there may be a few outwitted financiers growling at his heels. But it would be hard to find a more thoughtful host. Yes, I am going to Cloudsham to-morrow."

We shook hands warmly on parting, and as I descended the stairs he leant over the rail smiling down upon me.

"Remember your dinner engagement," I called up to him. "I shall see you after the New Year."

"Yes, if not before," he said, with a faint bubble of laughter as I turned the corner.

It was on the afternoon of December 24th that I stepped from the train at the little station of Cloudsham. Fresh snow had fallen, and the wind came bitterly over the frozen levels of the fen country. A distant clock was striking four as the carriage passed into the crested entrance-gates and tugged up a rising slope of park land dotted with ragged oaks and storm-bowed spinnies, which showed as black stains upon its snow-clad undulations. At the summit the road bent sharply, and I saw below me the old manor of Cloudsham, beyond which—a sombre plain, losing itself in the evening mists that swathed the horizon—stretched the restless waters of the North Sea.

The house lay in a broad depression, in shape as the hollow of a hand, save only on the seaward side, where the line of cliff bit into it like the marks of a giant's teeth. The grey front looked up, across a slope of grass land, to a semi-circle of forest that swept away in dark shadings of fir and oak. From the long oblong of the main buildings were thrust back two wings, flanked on the nearer side by a chapel.

From the back of the house to the edge of the sea cliffs, a distance of some quarter of a mile, ran an irregular avenue of firs with clipped yew walks and laurel-edged flower gardens on either hand.

A dozen men sweeping the paths and a telegraph boy on a pony mounting the hill towards me showed as black pigmies against the drifts of snow.

My bachelor host was absent when I was ushered into the great central hall where the house party were met together for their tea. I am by nature shy of strangers, taken in large doses, and it was with relief that I recognised Jack Talman, the grizzled cynic of an Academician, sitting in a corner seat well out of reach of draughts and female conversation.

"Hello, Phillips," he welcomed me. "And what financial gale brings you here?"

"What do you mean?"

"Don't put on frills with me. I've come to paint old Steen's picture, if he will give me the fifteen hundred that I'm asking for it. Lord Tommy Retford yonder is here to unload some of his old furniture—you know Tommy's rooms in Piccadilly, don't you? Furnished by a dealer in Bond Street, and twenty-five per cent. commission to Tommy on everything he can sell out of them. That's Mrs. Talbot Slingsly talking to him. Pretty woman, got into trouble in New York, was cut by all America, and captured Slingsly and London Society at one blow. Scandal never does cross the Atlantic somehow—all the dirty linen gets washed in the herring-pond. That's old Lord Blane by the fire; very respectable, and lends money on the sly. 'Private gentleman will make advances on note of hand'—you know. Fine woman Mrs. Billy Blades—that's she on the sofa. She's been making desperate love to Steen, but no go. The gay old dog's too clever for her. That long chap's her husband. Watch him prowling round, looking to see if he can pouch a silver ashtray or something, I expect. By Jove, Phillips, but it's as good as a play, ain't it?"

"And this is London Society!" I exclaimed.

"No," he cackled, shaking with vast amusement. "No, man, no. It's the Smart Set, that advertised, criticised, glorious, needy brigade of rogues and vagabonds—the Smart Set. Bless 'em all, say I; they're the best of company, but it's as well to lock up your valuables before you become too intimate with them."

I finished off my tea while old Talman sucked at his cigarette in great entertainment.

"You'd like to see the house," he commenced again. "Come along, I'll show you round—I want a walk before dinner."

It was a most interesting ramble. We passed from room to room admiring the carved oak, the splendid pictures, the Sheraton furniture, the cabinets of old china, the armour, and the tapestry. For the manor was filled with the heirlooms of the de Launes, from whom the Baron Steen rented it. And though the present peer, a broken-down old drunkard, was living in a little villa at Eastbourne on eight hundred pounds a year, the family had been a great and glorious one, finding mention on many a page in English history.

At the end of the great dining-room, set in the black oak wainscot above the fire, was the portrait of a boy. It was a Reynolds, and a worthy effort of that master hand. The lad could have been no more than fifteen years of age, but in his eyes was that grave, distracted expression that usually comes with the painful wisdom of later years. In more closely examining the picture, I noticed that a large portion of it at the bottom right-hand corner had been repaired or painted out. I called Talman's attention to this misfortune, asking if he knew the cause.

"They painted out the wolf," he said, "and with good enough reason, too."

"A wolf?" I said.

"If old de Laune were to hear me gossipping about it he'd kick me out of the place—he would, by Jove. But with Steen in possession it's safe enough. Mind you, though, you mustn't mention it to the ladies—on your word, now."

"Yes, yes," I said eagerly; "go on."

"Such things frighten the women," he explained. "Well, it was in this way. Phillip, and he was the sixth earl, was our ambassador at St. Petersburg somewhere about the year 1790. Once when he was out hunting, he shot an old she-wolf that was peering from the mouth of a cave, and inside they found a thriving family of four cubs. One of them was white, an albino, I suspect. He saved it from the dogs and took it home. When he came back to Cloudsham the next year he brought it along with his wife and his boy—an only son. They say it was a great pet at first, but it grew sulky with age, and finally was kept chained in the stables.

"One Christmas Eve, just as dusk was closing in, de Laune was trotting down the drive—he had been hunting at a distant meeting—when he heard a fearful screaming from the lower gardens towards the cliff. He put spurs to his horse, and in two minutes was galloping through the shadows of the fir avenue towards the sea. All of a sudden his horse pulled up dead, threw him, and bolted. When he got to his feet—he wasn't hurt luckily—what did he see but the body of his son, lying with his throat torn out, and the white wolf standing over him, the broken chain dangling at its neck.

"They say he was a giant, this Phillip de Laune, and of a very wild and passionate temper. Anyway, he went straight for the beast, and, though he was dreadfully mauled, he killed it—Heaven knows how—with his bare hands. That's why the present branch of the family came by the place. Pretty gruesome, isn't it?"

"A strange story," I told him; "but why must it be kept a secret from the ladies?"

"Because the beast walks, man. There's not a labourer in Norfolk who would go into the lower gardens on any night of the year, much less on Christmas Eve."

"My good Talman, do you mean to say you believe this?"

"I don't know—but I wouldn't go into the lower gardens to-night, if I could get round. Think of it, Phillips, the white shape with the bloody jaws lurking in the shadows—ugh—let's go and get a cocktail before——"

"I beg your pardon, sir, but the Baron is looking for you. He asked me to find you, sir," he continued, addressing himself to me with a slight bow. "He is waiting in his room."

As he preceded us thither, Talman whispered that Henderson — meaning thereby our conductor—was Steen's valet and a very clever fellow by all accounts.

The Baron, fat, high-coloured, and hearty, welcomed me with an open sincerity of pleasure well calculated to place a guest at his ease. A remarkable old boy was the Baron Steen. He always seemed to carry with him a jovial atmosphere of his own, in which those to whom he spoke were lost and blinded out of their better judgment.

He was kind enough to pay me some compliments upon my water-colour work. Whatever else can be brought against him, no one can deny that he was a sound judge of art.

The dinner passed pleasantly enough that night, with free and witty conversation. Our bachelor host was in his most humorous mood, keeping those about him in shouts of laughter. Facing him, at the extremity of the long table, was his secretary, a thin, melancholy youth of about four-and-twenty. My fair neighbour told me that Terry, as he was named, had been intended for the Church, but that his father, having ruined himself on the Stock Exchange, had persuaded the Baron to give him work. He was devoted to his patron, which, she smiled, was not surprising, seeing that he must be well on his way to rebuilding the fortune his father had lost.

I am not an ardent gambler, and when I do play I admit a preference for games in which brains are of some account. The roulette table soon bored me, and after I had seen the last of a few pounds, I contented myself by watching the changing fortunes of the rest of the party. Just before eleven the Baron, who had parted with considerable sums of money in perfect good humour, excused himself, and before the rest had settled down to the table again, I slipped away to my bedroom, where a selection of novels and a favourite pipe offered more congenial attractions.

The room was of considerable size and majestically furnished. It was on the first floor at the extremity of the right-hand wing, and looked out over the gardens on the cliff. A branch road from the main drive ran beneath the windows to an entrance at the back of the house.

They had steam heat on the upper floors, and the high temperature of my room had drawn stale and heavy odours from the tapestry on the walls and the ancient hangings that fringed the huge four-post bedstead. It was the atmosphere of an old clothes shop on a July day. I pulled back the curtains, opened the window and thrust out my head for a mouthful of fresh air.

It was a quiet, moonless night, lit by the stars that blinked in their thousand constellations. Though the snow lay deep, the air struck mildly. Indeed, if it were freezing, it could not have been by more than two degrees. Upon the edge of the distant cliffs robes of confusing mist curled in veils as thin as moonlight; but in the foreground the yew walks and aisles of ancient laurel showed clearly upon the white carpet. About the central avenue of firs which carved the gardens into two the darkness lay in impenetrable pools of shadow. As I waited, the silence was startled by a bell. It rang the four quarters in a tinkling measure, followed by eleven musical strokes. I knew that the sound must come from the little church that lay to my right; but, though I leant from my window, the angle of the wing in which I was hid the building from me.

I feel that the story which I have now to tell may well turn me into an object for ridicule. I can only describe that which I saw; as for the conclusions at which I arrived there are many more practical people in the world than myself who would have judged no differently. At best it was a ghastly business.

I had returned to the dressing-table and was changing my dress coat for a comfortable smoking-jacket when I heard it—a faint and distant cry, yet a cry which was crowded with such terror that I clung to a chair with my white face and goggling eyes staring back at me from the mirror on the table. Again it sounded, and again; then silence fell like the shutter of a camera. I rushed to the window, peering out into the night.

The great gardens lay sleeping in the dusky shadows. There was nothing to be heard; nothing moved save the curling wreaths of mist that came creeping up over the cliffs like the ghosts of drowned sailormen from their burial sands below. Could it have been some trick of the imagination? Could it — and the suggestion which I despised thrust itself upon me—could it bear reference to that grim tragedy that had been played in the old fir avenue so many years ago?

And then I first saw the THING that came towards me.

It was moving up a narrow path, hedged with yew, that led from the gardens and passed to the right of the wing in which I stood. The yew had been clipped into walls some five feet high, but the eastern gales had beaten out gaps and ragged indentations in the lines of greenery, so that in my sideways view of it the path itself was here and there exposed. It was through one of these breaches in the walls that I noticed a sign of movement. I waited, straining my eyes. Yes, there it showed again, a something, moving swiftly towards the house with a clumsy rolling stride.

It was never nearer to me than fifty yards, and the stars gave a shifty light. Yet it left me with an impression that it was about four feet in height and of a dull white colour. I remember that its body contrasted plainly with the dark hedges, but melted into uncertainty against a patch of snow. Once it stopped and half raised itself on its hind legs as if listening. Then again it tumbled forward in its shambling, ungainly fashion—now hidden by the yew wall, now thrust into momentary sight by a ragged gap until it disappeared round the angle of the house. Doubtless it would turn to the left, round the old chapel, across the snow-bound park, and so to the woods—where a wolf should be!

I was still staring from the window in the blank fear of the unknown, when I heard the swift tap of feet upon the road beneath me. Round the corner of the wing came a man, running with a patter of little strides, while a dozen yards behind him were a pair of followers. What they wanted I did not consider; for at that moment the sight of my own kind was joy enough for me. The electric lamps in the room behind me threw a broad golden patch upon the snow, and as the leader reached it he stopped, glancing up at where I stood. The light struck him fairly in the face. It was Addington Peace!"

"Did you hear that cry?" he panted; and then with a sudden nod of recognition: "I see who it is, Mr. Phillips—well, and did you hear it?"

"It came from over there—in the fir avenue," said I, pointing with a trembling finger. "I don't understand it, Inspector; I don't indeed. There was something that came up the yew walk behind you about a minute afterwards. I should have thought it would have passed you."

"No, I saw nothing. What was it like?"

"A sort of a dog." I hesitated; for under his steady eye I had not nerve enough to tell him of my private imaginings.

"A dog—that's curious. Are all the rest of you in bed?"

"No; they're gambling."

"Very good. I see there is a door at the back there. Will you come down and let me in after I've had a look round the gardens?"

"Certainly."

"If you meet any of your friends you need not mention that I have arrived. Do you understand?"

I nodded, and he waddled off across the lawn with his two companions at his heels.

And then I first saw the THING that came towards me.

I slipped on an overcoat and made my way quietly down the stairs. From the roulette room, as I passed it, came the chink of money and the murmur of merry voices. They would not disturb us, that was certain. I reached the garden doors in the centre of the main building, turned the key, and walked out into the gloom of a great square porch.

As I have said, the temperature was scarcely below freezing point, and if I shivered in my fur-lined overcoat it was more from excitement than any great chill in the air. For a good twenty minutes I waited listening and peering into the night. It was not a pleasant time, for my nerves were jangled, and I searched the shadows with timorous eyes, half fearing, half expecting, Heaven knows what hideous apparition. It was with a start which set my heart thumping that I saw Peace turn the corner of the right-hand wing and come trotting down the drive towards me. There was something in his aspect that told a story of calamity.

"What is it?" I asked him as he panted up.

"I want you—come along," he whispered, and started back by the way he had come.

We passed round the right-hand wing, under my bedroom window, and stopped where the yew walk ended. To right and left of the entrance two stone fauns leered upon us under the starlight.

"This thing you call a dog—could you see it as far as this?"

"No; the angle of the wing prevented me."

"You saw it pass in this direction. Are you certain it did not go back the way it came?"

"Yes. I am quite certain."

"Then it must either have turned up the road, in which case I should have met it; or down the road, where you would have seen it as it passed under your windows; or else have run straight on. If we take these facts as proved, it must have run straight on."

"That is so."

We had our backs to the laughing fauns. Before us lay a broad triangle of even snow, with the chapel and wing of the house for its sides, and for its base the carriage drive on which we stood. There was no shrub or tree in any part of it that might conceal a fugitive. Close to the wall of the house ran a path ending in a small side door. The chapel, which was joined to the mansion, had no entrance on the garden side.

"If it entered this triangle and disappeared—for I am certain it was not here when I ran by—we may conclude that it found its way into the house. It had no other method of escape. Kindly stay here, Mr. Phillips. This snow is fortunate, but I wish the sweepers had not been so conscientious about their work on the paths."

He drew a little electric lantern from his coat, touched the spring, and with an eye of light moving before him, turned into the path under the wall. He walked slowly, bending double as he swept the brilliant circle now on the exposed ground, now on the snow ridges to right and left. The sills of the ground floor windows were carefully examined, and when he reached the door he searched the single step before it with minute attention. A curious spectacle he made, this little porpoise of a man, as he peeped and peered his way like some slow-hunting beast on a cold scent.

It was not until he left the path for the snow-covered grass plot that I saw him give any sign of success. He dropped on his knees with a little chirrup of satisfaction like the note of a bird. Then he rose again, shaking his head and staring up at the windows above him in a cautious, suspicious manner. Finally he came slowly back to me with his head on one side, staring at the ground before him.

"You thought it was a dog?" he asked. "Why a dog?"

"It looked to me like a big dog—or a wolf," I told him boldly.

"Whether it be beast or man, or both, I believe the thing that killed him is in the house now."

I jumped back, staring at him with a sudden exclamation.

"Who has been killed?" I stammered out.

"Baron Steen. We found him on the cliffs yonder. He was badly cut about."

"It's impossible, Inspector," I cried. "He left the roulette table not a quarter of an hour before you came."

"Ah—he was a cool hand, Mr. Phillips. It was like him to put off bolting till the last minute. The warrant against him for company frauds is in my pocket now. But someone gave the game away to him, for his yacht is lying off the beach there with a boat from her waiting at the foot of the cliff. But we've no time to lose—come along."

Before the big garden porch the Inspector's two companions were waiting. He drew them aside for a minute's whispered conversation before they separated, and disappeared into the night. What had they done with the body? I had not the courage to inquire.

We entered the house, moving very softly. In the hall Peace took me by the arm.

"You're a bit shaken, Mr. Phillips, and I'm not surprised. But I want your assistance badly. Can you pull yourself together and help me to see this through?"

"I'll do what I can."

The Chronicles of Addington Peace.

"Take me up to your room, then."

We were in luck, for we tip-toed up the great stairs and down the long passages without meeting a guest or servant. Once in my room, the Inspector walked across and pushed the electric bell. Three, four minutes went by before the summons was answered, and then it was by a flushed and disordered footman who bounced into the room and halted, staring open-mouthed from me to my companion.

"Sorry to disturb your dance," said Peace, beaming upon him from over his glasses.

"Beg pardon, sir, but you startled me—yes, we was 'aving a little dance in the servants' 'all; but it's of no consequence, sir."

"A slippery floor, eh, with so much French chalk on it?"

The young man glanced at the powder on his shoes and grinned.

"So you are all dancing in the servants' hall, are you?"

"I believe so, sir, barring Edward, who is waiting on the party, and Mr. Henderson."

"And where is Mr. Henderson?"

"He is the Baron's man, sir. I should not presume to inquire where he was. Beg pardon, sir, but are you staying here to-night?"

"This is a friend of mine," I interposed. "He will stay the night, but you need not trouble about that now."

"A smart fellow like you can keep his mouth shut," continued the Inspector sweetly. "You wouldn't go shouting all over the house if you were let into a secret—now, would you?"

"Oh no, sir; on my word I wouldn't."

"This thing you call a dog—could you see it as far as this?"

And so Peace told him of the projected arrest, of the murder, and of his own identity. The colour faded from the young man's cheeks, but he stood very stiff and grim, never taking his eyes from the little detective's face.

"And what can I do, sir?" he asked, when the tale was over. "He was a good master to us, sir; whatever there was against him, he was good to us. You can trust me to help catch the scoundrel who killed him if I can."

"I see this room is warmed by steam heat. Is that the case with all the bed rooms and passages?"

"Yes, sir. The only open fires are in the reception-rooms. When the Baron made the alterations last year they left the grates for the sake of appearance; but they are never lighted, save on the ground floor."

"And in what reception-rooms are there fires at the present moment?"

"The dining-room fire has died out by now," said the young man, ticking off the numbers on his fingers. "But there is one in the big hall, one in the library where the party is playing, one in the little drawing-room, and one in the Baron's room."

"And the kitchen?"

"Of course, sir, one in the kitchen and one in the servants' hall."

"That is all. Are you certain?"

"Quite certain, sir."

Addington Peace breathed a contented little sigh, glancing up at the ceiling with a half smile.

"Good; and now for the bath-rooms."

"The bath-rooms, sir?"

"Exactly."

"There are two bath-rooms in each wing; some of the gentlemen have tubs in their own rooms besides."

"Now, I think we know where we are," said the inspector briskly. "No chance of the roulette party breaking up, is there?"

"Oh, no, sir; not for another two hours, at least."

"I want you to return, Mr. Phillips, and try your luck at the tables for a spell," he said, with a quick glance at me. "It is now eleven thirty; be back in this room at twelve fifteen. I am going to take a walk round the house with our young friend here in the meanwhile. The Baron had a secretary, I believe?"

"Yes, a man called Terry."

"Bring him up with you when you come. I shall want a talk with him. Is all quite plain?"

"Yes," I told him, and so we parted.

When I stepped into the roulette room I stood for a moment blinking at the players like a yokel at a pantomime. The scene was to me something unreal, a clever piece of stage effect, with its flushed and covetous faces, its frocks and its diamonds, its piles of sparkling gold, and the cry of the banker as he twirled the wheel. How could they be doing this with that bloodstained patch on the cliff edge, with that unknown horror slinking through the snow—how could they be doing this if they were not acting a part! An odd figure I must have looked, if there had been anyone to notice me. But they were too eager in the game to hear the opening of the door or to see who went and came. I walked over to the fireplace, lit a cigarette, and watched them, my nerves growing steadier in the merry chatter of tongues. They were all there, the men and women of that careless house party, all there —save one who lay silent wherever they had laid him.

Half-an-hour had slipped by, until, at last, with an effort, I walked to the table and threw down two sovereigns on the red.

It won, and I laughed at the melancholy omen; not, perhaps, without an odd note in my voice, for the man over whose shoulder I leaned to gather my winnings glanced up with a startled expression. It was young Terry, the secretary; the very person I wanted to see.

"Anything the matter, Mr. Phillips?" he asked. "You're not looking very well."

"Don't worry about me," I told him. "But I want a word with you in private."

"Certainly—just one moment."

He had been winning heavily, and it took him some time to crowd the bank notes into his pockets. A sovereign slipped from his fingers and rolled under the table as he rose; but he paid no attention to it.

"I have something to tell you. Can you come up to my room?" I asked him.

He hesitated, looking regretfully at the table, where Fortune had been so kind to him.

"It happens to be rather important," I said.

He followed me without another word. I did not attempt to explain until we had passed up the stairs and through the corridors to my room. He seated himself on the great bed with a shiver of cold, drawing the heavy curtains about his shoulders. And there I told him the story from the beginning to the end, hiding nothing, not even my belief in the supernatural nature of the thing which I had seen.

He never moved, but his face grew so pale and drawn that towards the end it seemed as if it were a powdered mask that stared at me from the shadows of the curtains.

"My God," he cried, and fell back upon the bed in a passion of hysterical tears.

I tried to help him, but he thrust me fiercely away, so I thought it best to let him get over it himself. He was still lying on the thick quilt, sobbing and shivering, when the door opened and Peace stepped into the room. I explained the situation in a hurried whisper; but when I turned again Terry had got to his feet, and was watching us, clinging to the bed-post.

"This is Inspector Addington Peace," I told him. "Perhaps you can give him some information?"

"Not to-night," he cried. "Don't ask me to-night, gentlemen. You cannot tell what this means to me; to-morrow, perhaps——"

He dropped down upon the bed, covering his face with his hands. He seemed a helpless sort of creature, and my heart went out to him in his calamity.

"A night's rest is what you want," I said, patting him on the shoulder. "Come, let me give you an arm."

He took it at once, with a grateful glance, and I led him down the corridor, with Peace in sympathetic attendance. Fortunately, his room was in the same wing, so we had not far to go. When we reached it he thanked us for our care of him. And so we left him, returning to my bedroom in silence, for, indeed, the scene had been a painful one.

"But I want a word with you in private."

"Peace," I said, when the door had closed behind us. "What was the thing I saw in the yew walk?"

He had seated himself in an easy chair, and was polishing his glasses with a large silk pocket-handkerchief.

"I think you already have an explanation," he answered cheerfully.

"If it amuses you to sneer at my superstition——"

"You refer to the legend of the de Laune's. I have heard the story before, Mr. Phillips; nor am I surprised that you believed it to be the ghost wolf."

"I did—but now I want you to disprove it."

"On the contrary, all my evidence supports your theory."

I stared at him, with a creeping horror in my blood. I was beginning to be afraid—

lamentably afraid. Peace leant back in his chair, with his eyes, vacant in expression, fixed on the wall. He seemed rather to be arguing with himself than addressing a listener.

"Baron Steen," he said, "met with his death on an open path between a shallow duck-pond and a little pavilion. He had fought hard for life, had rolled and struggled with his enemy. There were four or five punctured wounds in his throat and neck, from which he had bled profusely. And now for the thing that killed him—whatever it was. It could not have fled down the cliff path, for the boat's crew waiting below had heard the screams and had come running up by that way. They were with him when we arrived, and assured me they had seen nothing. It could not have turned to the right or left, for, though the paths had been swept clean—doubtless by the Baron's orders, for he would not desire his way of escape to be easily traced—the snow on either side lay in unbroken levels. It could only have retired by the yew avenue, and it did not break through the hedge. That, again, the snow proved clearly. So, we may take it, that whatever the thing may have been which you saw—it killed Baron Steen; further, it escaped into the house—this, you will remember, we decided in the garden.

"Let us imagine it was a man—that you were deceived by the uncertain light. His clothes must of necessity have been drenched in blood. He could not have struggled so fiercely with his victim and escaped those fatal signs. Yet, he cannot have burned his clothes, for the fires are downstairs where people were passing. Nor can he have washed them, for neither the bath-rooms nor the bedroom basins have been recently used. I have spent some time in searching boxes and wardrobes with no result. Stranger still, as far as my limited information goes, everyone in the house can prove an *alibi*—save two."

"And who are they?" I asked eagerly.

"Mr. Henderson, the Baron's valet—and yourself."

"Inspector Peace——" I began angrily.

"Tut, tut, my dear Mr. Phillips. I was merely stating the facts. Mr. Henderson's case, however, presents an interesting feature, for he has run away."

"Run away," I said. "Then that settles it."

"Not altogether, I'm afraid. I think it is more a matter of theft than murder with Mr. Henderson."

I stared at him in silence as he sat there, with his chubby hands clasped upon his lap, a picture of irritating composure.

"Peace," I said, struggling to control my voice. "What are you hiding from me? It is something inhuman, unnatural that has done this dreadful thing."

The little detective stretched himself, yawned, and then rose to his feet. "I have no opinion except that I think you had better get to bed. Don't lock your door, for I may find time for an hour's sleep on your sofa before morning."

* * * * *

The news was out after breakfast—the news that led to mild hysterics and scurrying ladies' maids to the packing of boxes, and the chastened sorrow of those gentlemen who owed the Baron money. Through all the turmoil of the morning moved the little detective, the most sympathetic of men. It was he who apologised so humbly for the locked doors of the bath-rooms; he who superintended the lighting of fires, and the making of the beds, and the packing of trunks for the station so closely that the housemaids were convinced that he entertained a secret passion for each one of them; it was he who announced Henderson's robbery of the gold plate, following it by information as to the culprit's arrest. The establishment had by this time become convinced that Henderson was the murderer, and breathed relief at the news.

They had brought the body of Baron Steen to the house early in the morning—it had been laid in the garden pavilion on its first discovery.

With death in so strange a form present amongst us, I was disgusted by the noise and bustle, the gossip and chatter amongst the guests of the dead man. I wandered off in search of the one person who had seemed sincerely affected by the news, the young secretary, Maurice Terry. He was nowhere to be found. A servant of whom I inquired told me that the secretary had kept to his bed, being greatly unnerved by the tragedy, and I strolled up the stairs again on an errand of consolation. The door was locked, and there came no answer to my continued tapping.

"Terry," I called through the keyhole. "It is I, Phillips; won't you let me in?"

"I have a key that will fit, if you will kindly stand aside," suggested a modest voice. I rose from my knees to find the Inspector at my elbow.

"It would be a gross intrusion," I told him. "If he wishes to be alone with his sorrow, we have no right to disturb him."

"He is seriously ill."

"How did you discover that?"

"By borrowing a gardener's ladder and looking through his window. He is unconscious, or was ten minutes ago."

A skilful twist or two with a bit of wire and the key was pushed from the lock. The duplicate opened the door. Peace walked into the room and I followed at his heels.

On his bed, fully dressed, lay poor Terry, with a face paler than his pillows. His breath came and went in short, painful gasps. One hand strayed continuously about his throat, groping and plucking at his collar with feverish unrest. It was a very painful spectacle.

"I will send for a doctor at once," I whispered, stepping to the bell. But Peace held up a warning hand.

"Come here," he said, "I have something to show you."

With movements as tender as a woman's he unfastened the man's collar and slipped out the stud. Then he paused. The eyes that watched me from behind the gold-rimmed glasses had turned cold and hard.

"If it is as I suspect, you may be called as a witness. Do you object?"

"Yes; but I shall not leave you on that account."

"Very well," he said as he opened the shirt and the vest beneath it.

Smeared and patched in dark etching upon the white skin was a broad stain of blood, of dried and clotted blood, the life's blood of a man.

"He is wounded, Peace," I cried. "Poor fellow, he must have nearly bled to death."

"Do not alarm yourself," said the Inspector drily. "It is the blood of Baron Steen."

* * * * *

A week had gone by, and I was sitting alone in my Keble Street rooms, when Peace walked in, with a heavy travelling coat over his arm.

"Thank Heaven, you have come at last," I cried. "How is Maurice Terry?"

"Dead—poor fellow," he said, with an honest sorrow in his voice. "Yet, after all, Mr. Phillips, it was the best that could have happened to him."

"And his story — the causes — the method?" I demanded.

"It has taken some hard work, but the bits of the puzzle are fitted together at last. You wish to hear it, I suppose?"

"According to your promise," I reminded him.

"It is a case of unusual interest," he said. "Though it bears a certain similarity to the Gottstein trial at Kiel in '89."

He paused to light his big pipe, and then sat back in his chair, with his eyes fixed in abstract contemplation.

"I was convinced that the murderer was in the house; and that he had entered by the side door, towards which you had seen him pass. When studying the spot I made a discovery of some importance. Steen had left by the same exit. Also he had reason to fear some person in that wing, for he had turned from the path and made a circuit over the grass. I had already noted his broad-toed boots when examining his body—and the footprints in the snow were unmistakable. Who was his enemy in that wing? It was a problem to be solved.

"I discovered no stained clothing, and no signs of its cleansing or destruction. From what information I could gather, all the house party had been in the roulette room save you yourself; and all the servants had been at the dance save Henderson and a man waiting on the guests. But in the course of my search the footman who

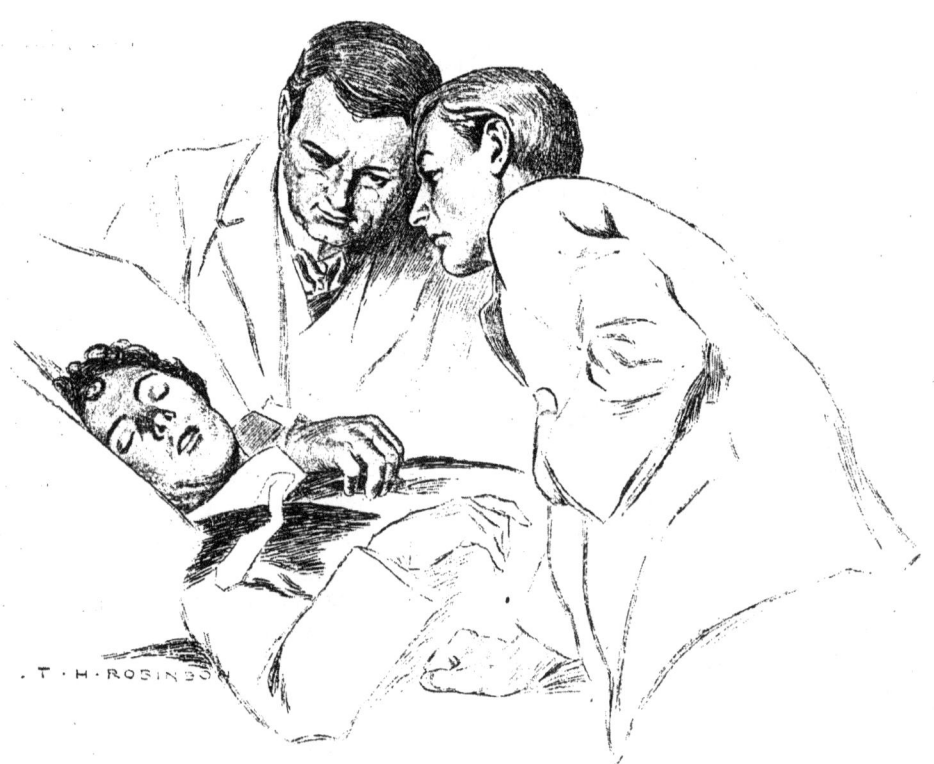

"It is the blood of Baron Steen."

accompanied me discovered that a quantity of gold plate was missing. It was reasonable to imagine that Henderson was the thief. Probably the confidential valet had learnt of the Baron's projected flight and of the warrant for his arrest. It was a moment for judicious robbery, the traces of which would be covered by the confusion of the news. But was Henderson also a murderer? I did not think so. The death of his master was the one thing which would wreck his scheme. In the early morning I interviewed the farmer on whose cart he had driven into Norbridge. He told me that, acting on orders he had received from Henderson, he met that person at the corner of the stables at eleven o'clock precisely—five minutes before the murder occurred. That finally eliminated the valet from the list.

"On my return from the farm I examined the gardens again with great minuteness. At the corner of the little pavilion, about fifteen feet from where the body had lain, there was a patch of bloody snow. This puzzled me a good deal, until the solution offered itself that the murderer had tried to wash his hands in the snow, the water of the pond being frozen hard. Yet, his clothing would also bear the stain. What had he worn that showed so white to you in the starlight? Could it have been that he wore no clothes at all?

"A naked man—the suggestion was full of possibilities.

"It was fortunate that I had brought assistants to help me in Steen's capture. Their presence gave me a wider scope, for they were both good men. I left them to search the pavilion and laurels for the clothing, which the murderer might have concealed when he realised how fatal was its evidence. As I walked back to the house I began to understand the situation more clearly. The main drive, curving down the slope of the park, was in view of a tall man coming up by the yew walk. The murderer might have noticed our approach. What more natural than that he should have bent double as he ran, thus obtaining the cover of the left-hand hedge, which was not more than four to five feet high? Did not this answer to your description of the thing you had seen? It would have been cold work for him. I made a note to be on the look out for chills.

"For a couple of hours I devoted myself to speeding those guests who caught the eleven thirty train. I do not think a trunk left for the station of which I have not a complete inventory. Indeed, the Baron's creditors have to thank me for the return of several trifles of value, which were included, accidently, no doubt, in the ladies' dressing bags.

"After the carriages had started I went in search of Terry, and discovered that he had not left his room. Equally to the point, his windows looked down upon the spot where the Baron made his détour over the grass while escaping. I became interested in this young man. The score was creeping up against him. A ladder from an obliging gardener allowed me to observe him from the window. A visit to the housekeeper gave me a duplicate key to his door. What happened in the room you know, Mr. Phillips."

"But, the motive—why did he kill his patron?" I asked him eagerly.

"I doubt if we shall ever learn the truth on that point," he said. "As far as I can make out, Steen was directly responsible for the ruin and disgrace of Terry's father. Probably the son did not fully realise this when the Baron, with a pity most unusual in the man, gave him the secretaryship. But of all participation in the flight he was certainly innocent, for he was in bed at the time."

"In bed!" I cried.

"Don't interrupt, if you please. What happened I take to be as follows: Terry was in bed when the old man tried to creep past his window. Somehow he heard him, and, looking out, understood what was up. Perhaps that rascal Henderson had told him the truth about his father; perhaps Steen had promised him compensation—he had a mother and sister dependent on him—which promise the financier meant to avoid, along with many more serious obligations, by running away. At any rate, passion, revenge, the sense of injustice—call it what you like—took hold of the lad. He caught up the first handy weapon; it chanced to be a dagger paperknife—dangerous things, I hate them—and rushed down a back staircase and through the side door in pursuit of his enemy.

"When that had happened, which happened, the fear that comes to all amateurs in crime took him by the throat. He wiped his hands in the snow; he tore off his sleeping-suit—that is how I know he had been in bed—and thrust it, with its terrible evidences of murder, into the thatch of the little pavilion. We found it there next day. Then he started back to the house as naked as a baby.

"He saw us running down the hill, and made for the side door, bending double behind the hedge. Who were we? Had we noticed him? Believe me, Mr. Phillips, whether he had held the murder righteous or no, it was only the rope he saw dangling before him. Might not the alarm be given at any moment? He dared not wash himself, and the stains had dried upon him. He hurried on his clothes, shivering in the chill that had struck home, and so to the safest place he could find—the roulette table."

"It is well that he died," I said simply.

"It saved time," remarked the Inspector, with a grim, little nod at the wall.

Next month the story of "Mr. Tauberry's Diamond" will be told.

The Chronicles of Addington Peace.

By B. FLETCHER ROBINSON.

Joint Author with Sir A. Conan Doyle in his best Sherlock Holmes story, "The Hound of the Baskervilles."

THESE ARE THE STRANGE AND STARTLING EXPERIENCES WHICH BEFEL THAT FAMOUS DETECTIVE, ADDINGTON PEACE. THEY ARE TOLD IN A MOST CONVINCING MANNER, AND SHOULD ON NO ACCOUNT BE MISSED. THE FIRST WAS ENTITLED "THE TERROR IN THE SNOW."

II.—MR. TAUBERY'S DIAMOND.

"HI, young fellow! Does Inspector Peace live here?"

He spoke roughly enough, and I returned his stare with an equal irritation. When a man may not indulge in day dreams on his own doorstep, the state of society wants mending. He was a big bully of a fellow, with a red face, a curled, white moustache, and a single eye-glass, through which he regarded me with an air of extreme ill-temper.

"The Inspector lodges on the second floor," I told him coldly.

"Do you live here too?"

I had a mind not to answer him, but, after all, it was not worth while making trouble over an impudent question.

"Yes," I said; "I rent the ground-floor and the studio behind. My name is Phillips. I am an artist. For the past four years I have studied abroad. If you would like to see my birth certificate I will go and fetch it for you."

To my surprise, he burst into a shout of laughter, swaying his body from side to side. It was quite a time before he recovered himself.

"Good, lad, good, lad," he chuckled; "gad, but I deserved it. Allow me to introduce myself. My name is Gunton, sir; Colonel Theophilus Gunton, and I'm very pleased to meet you."

He held out his hand, which I shook, without any great degree of enthusiasm. "Is this Addington Peace at home, do you think?" he continued.

"I don't know," I told him. "I should walk upstairs and find out, if I were you."

"There I recognise the practical head. You know him?"

"Yes."

"Then, we will go together. You can introduce me."

I was offended at the noise and bluster of the man, but he had grabbed my arm, and I didn't want a scene at my own door. I led him up the stairs, his voice growing silent as his lung capacity weakened. The Inspector's voice cried an invitation to my knock, and I entered, with the Colonel puffing at my heels like a locomotive on a stiff incline.

"Sorry to disturb you, Peace," I said; "but this is a gentleman of the name of Gunton, and he appears anxious to make your acquaintance."

The plump, little man rose from his easy chair and stood looking at the stranger through his gold-rimmed spectacles with an expression of great good humour.

For myself, I was about to withdraw when the Colonel's hand dropped heavily upon my shoulder.

Copyright, 1904, by B. Fletcher Robinson, in the United States of America.

"Don't you go," he said. "A cosmopolitan, a detective, and a man of the world as I am, form a unique combination. And, by gad, gentlemen, we shall want all our brains over this affair."

I glanced at Peace, who smiled and nodded. So I stayed.

The Colonel kindly consented to take the most comfortable chair, sighed, stretched out his legs, lit a cheroot, and then, without further introduction, plunged into his story.

"Perhaps you have heard of Julius Taubery? No? Well, it's a name as well known throughout India as the Viceroy's. He is the head of one of the richest firms in Calcutta. Went out there as a young man, worked well, married well, and ended well in all things, save his constitution, with which he played the very devil. In 1900 he returned and took a fine London house in Portland Place, together with an old hall down in Devonshire. A month ago the doctors ordered him out of England for life. Rough on him, wasn't it, seeing that he had spent two-thirds of his time out of it already? But the south of France is his only chance, they tell him; so, like a wise man, he is selling off his sticks, and settling down at Mentone, without squealing to show how much it hurts him.

"Julius and his wife—she's one of the kindest-hearted women—have been giving some farewell parties to their old friends. They had a lunch to-day, one-thirty sharp, and a lot of people turned up. After the ladies had left us, the talk, as luck would have it, fell on precious stones; and Julius Taubery is a crank on them if there ever was one. His wife wears the finest jewels in London, and the old man is supposed to have many thousand pounds' worth more locked away, which he won't trust even her with the handling.

"'Gentlemen,' says he, 'I will show you something that may interest you. It is a new purchase of mine, and it happens to be a remarkable stone!'

"He pulled a green case from an inside pocket, flipped it open, and there the thing was as big as a walnut. The lights were on, it being dull weather, and the stone blinked and sparkled like the sun on dancing water.

"'My word, Julius,' I said. 'But that's a risky bit of stuff to carry about with you.'

"'It's going to the bank this afternoon,' he answered. 'So if you want to examine the pretty pebble, gentlemen, this is your last chance.'

"And with that he took it from its case, as proud as a young husband of his first baby, and sent it round the table.

"I was sitting on Julius' left. Between us was a fat old boy, who was a stranger to me. He took a long stare at the stone, whistling softly between his teeth, before he passed it on. It went from hand to hand, never out of sight, so far as I could notice, until it came to Sir Andrew Carillon, who fancies himself an expert on gems. They say that when Lady Carillon is in the stalls, the play is finished to the women sitting behind her, for they can't keep their eyes off her pearls. Sir Andrew pulled out a magnifying glass, and began examining the diamond.

"'I congratulate you, Taubery,' he said after about a minute. 'You have acquired a historical stone!'

"Old Julius leant back, with a smile half-way round his head, but he didn't say a word.

He was a big bully of a fellow.

"'This stone,' said Sir Andrew in the heavy, pompous way that he has, tapping it with his magnifying glass to attract attention. 'This stone is the celebrated Hyderapore diamond, to which first historical reference is made in the year 1584. It was captured by the Rajah of Hyderapore from a ruling chief in the Deccan after a battle, in which four thousand men lost their lives. In 1680 it was stolen from the Rajah's palace by a Spaniard, who escaped to Bombay, where he was robbed and murdered. The stone disappeared for about sixty years.

"'It subsequently came into the possession of one of the East India Company's agents, who was stabbed to death in his bungalow near Calcutta about 1760. The diamond, which is held to have inspired the attack, was saved from the robbers by the appearance of his guests and servants. The widow brought it to Europe and sold it to the Duc d'Alembert, who lost his diamond and incidentally his life in the French Revolution. It turned up again at the Court of Napoleon III., being then in the possession of Henri Marvin, the well-known financier. Until to-day I thought it was still in his family.

"'It is one of the very few large diamonds that is absolutely without flaw, and its value in the open market to-day would be approaching thirty thousand pounds. Anyone who takes an interest in historical stones might be tempted to give even a higher price; for there has been enough blood spilt over it, gentlemen, to fill the bath of its fortunate possessor.'

"He laid down the diamond on the table and looked at his host with a malicious grin. But all connoisseurs are alike; they are as covetous of each other's pet treasures as so many cats.

"All the time that Sir Andrew had been speaking, the fat fellow next to me had been snorting and swelling until, 'pon my soul, I thought he was in for a stroke of apoplexy. I am the best-tempered of men, but I have my limits, and the old grampus was one of them.

"'Are you in pain, sir?' I asked him.

"'Yes, I am, sir,' he said in such a high, squeaky voice that all the table could hear him. 'I object to listening to the definitions of so-called experts, who cannot tell a diamond from a glass marble. Experts? Humbugs, that's what I call them!'

"'Do you refer to me, Professor Endicott?' began Sir Andrew, leaning forward, with a very red face.

"'Most certainly I do.'

"'Then I must ask you for an explanation or an immediate apology.'

"'A man who can make so ludicrous an error deserves neither the one nor the other,' cried the professor in great excitement. 'That stone has been in the possession of the Princes of Pavaloff for three hundred years. Prince Peter, the present head of the family, kindly allowed me to examine it when I was at Moscow in 1894. I was not aware that he had sold it. I trust, Mr. Taubery, that you obtained it from a respectable source; if not, I should be no true friend did I hide from you my belief that it has been stolen.'

"If a man had said such a deucedly insulting thing to me I should have knocked him down there and then. I would, 'pon my soul, without thinking more about it. But Julius lay back in his chair, smiling all over his face. I suppose those collectors get accustomed to each other's little ways; they're a queer lot, anyway.

"'You can be quite easy on that point, Professor Endicott,' he said. 'Prince Peter was, unfortunately, involved in the late Dolorouski conspiracy, but had time to slip across the Russian frontier before the police could arrest him. I bought the diamond from his agent in Paris.'

"'You interest me deeply, Mr. Taubery,' struck in Sir Andrew, speaking very softly, though we could all see he was in a devil of a rage. 'Even I was not unaware of the existence of the Pavaloff diamond. If my memory does not fail me, it is slightly disfigured by a flaw on the eighth facet?'

"'Certainly, Sir Andrew,' said our host; 'if you examine the stone you will see that such is the case.'

"'There is no such blemish on the diamond I have before me. Therefore I humbly suggest that you have been deceived by this Parisian agent as to its origin.'

'This thing is a fake, a clumsy imitation. Taubery, you have been robbed!'

"Professor Endicott climbed to his feet, with a grunt of dissatisfaction, and leant over the table, thrusting out his podgy fist to receive the jewel. He remained standing, with his body swayed forward, so that the electric lights above the silver centre-piece might shine the brighter upon what he held. Presently he dropped his hands to his sides and stood staring about him like a ploughman lost in Piccadilly.

"'This is not the stone I examined five minutes ago,' he stuttered.

"'Nonsense,' said old Julius, with a shadow of fear in his eyes. 'Nonsense, Endicott; look again.'

"'Can it be that two such famous experts have made a mistake?' sneered Sir Andrew. 'Can it be that a humble amateur like myself is right and that they are wrong? As I told you, gentlemen, the Hyderapore diamond——'

"'Hyderapore diamond be blowed,' squealed the fat man. 'This thing is a fake, a clumsy imitation. Taubery, you have been robbed!'

"We were all on our feet in an instant amid a clamour of tongues. But there was one man amongst us that kept his head; one man who realised that his honour was in peril; that immediate action was necessary. His name—if I am not too egotistical —is Theophilus Gunton.

"Fortunately, I have a voice of some power, and a manner that, when my feelings are strongly moved, is, perhaps, not unimpressive. I commanded and obtained silence. I begged them to resume their seats; they obeyed.

"'Julius Taubery,' I said. 'Has your diamond disappeared?'

"He answered that it had, looking at the imitation stone, which they had returned to him, in a silly, scared way.

"'Julius Taubery,' I continued, 'we, your guests, lie under a stigma, an imputation. We cannot leave the house under such circumstances. Someone must have brought the imitation stone with him for a purpose that it is needless to define. The real jewel must be in his pocket at this moment. Let us, therefore, be searched.'

"They all sat silent as mice under my eye,

save the Professor, who grunted as if in dissent.

"'Do I understand that you object to my plan, sir?' I asked him. 'Do you refuse to be searched? And if so, may I ask why?'"

"He gave me an angry look, but he had not the courage to contest the point.

"'Then, I may take it that we are all agreed. Taubery, you have a library upon this floor. As I passed the door before lunch I noticed that there was an excellent fire there. Professor Endicott and myself will retire to that room. I will search the Professor; the Professor shall search me. After that the rest of the guests will come, one by one, into the room, where we will search them in turn. Let us have no delay. Professor Endicott, I am very much at your service.'

"I went through that party, gentlemen, as our Transatlantic cousins would express it, with a fine-tooth comb. And I feel it my duty to say that not one of them raised the smallest objection to the severity of my methods. They were like lambs, gentlemen, they were, by thunder! But I obtained no result. The Taubery diamond had disappeared.

"Poor old Julius was quite broken down about it. He placed the whole matter in my hands. On my way to Scotland Yard I remembered what an old friend of mine had told me about you. 'If you are ever in a hole, Gunton,' he said, 'get Addington Peace—he is the man.' You were off duty. I inquired your address; I am here. And, now, what are you going to do?"

"Can you remember who it was that introduced the subject of precious stones at your luncheon party?" asked Inspector Peace.

"'Pon my life, I don't know," said the Colonel, polishing his eye-glass with a red silk pocket-handkerchief. "It was one of the fellows at the other end of the table, but I can't say which of them."

"Yet, it is presumable that the guest who came with an imitation diamond in his pocket is the man who started a discussion which resulted in Mr. Taubery producing his latest treasure."

"So it is, by Jove," cried the Colonel;

"I never thought of it. Clever work, Inspector, eh?"

"Exactly," said Peace blandly. "And, now, as regards the place in which the robbery was committed."

"I locked the door," answered the Colonel, smacking his trousers pocket.

"Please let me have the key. Thank you. And now as to the windows. Were they closed and fastened?"

"I saw to it myself."

"After the search in the library, did any of the guests return to the dining-room?"

"I am no fool, Inspector. I left old Julius there to see to that. No one went back. When I had finished searching I joined Julius and we locked up together. The butler had called in the policeman on the beat, and I left him sitting in the passage watching the door and drinking beer."

"I must go to Portland Place. What is the number?"

"I will drive you there with all the pleasure in the world, Inspector," said the Colonel cheerfully. "Come along."

I left them at the foot of the stairs, obtaining a whispered promise from the detective that he would give me a call that night if it was not too late when he returned.

I spent a disconsolate evening at the club. Never did I play a more degraded hand at bridge, though I should certainly have taken exception to the remarks of my partner under more ordinary circumstances. There is a point at which fair criticism ends and deliberate insult begins.

By ten o'clock I was back again in my rooms, where I loitered, amongst my books and pictures, in restless expectation. It was chiming midnight when there came a discreet tap at my outer door, and Addington Peace walked in. He sat himself down in the easy chair I offered, and permitted me to mix him a whisky and soda.

"Tell me, have you found the diamond?" I said eagerly.

"No."

"Nor the thief?"

"I know him to be one of five men—that is all."

"Five? And how do you make that out?"

"It is very simple. The real diamond was examined by Professor Endicott; it was an imitation that reached Sir Andrew Carillon. Therefore it is reasonable that one of the five who sat between them changed the one for the other."

"So you strike out the Professor and Sir Andrew?"

"If either of them had been implicated they would hardly have raised the quarrel that resulted in the discovery of the theft."

"And this suspected five—who are they?"

"Our friend Colonel Gunton, Mr. Thomas Craddock, a clerk in the War Office, the Hon. George Carstairs, Lord Wintone's brother; Mr. Abel Field, of Grey and Field, car manufacturers; and the Rev. Aubrey Power, a minor canon of Westminster Abbey. I have made some slight inquiries and find nothing against them. Carstairs, Craddock, and Power are men of moderate income, the other two are rich.

"Yet this gives us one important conclusion. The actual thief is an amateur in crime. So far as anyone knows, this is his first offence. But it was not a sudden temptation to which he yielded. On the contrary, he was carrying out his share in a plot that had been long and carefully prepared. He substituted an imitation diamond for the original as it passed through his hands—an easy matter; but who thought out the scheme, who had this admirable imitation made, who knew that Taubery was leaving the country and that the diamond was to be sent immediately to the strong room of a bank, where the substitution that had taken place might not be discovered for months, perhaps years?

"Who, in short, had the clever brain, the far-sighted judgment, the familiarity with jewels and those who deal in them, all of which would be required in the originator of such a fraud? Not Gunton, nor Craddock, nor Carstairs, nor Field, nor the Rev. Aubrey Power. There is someone who has influence over one of these men, someone pulling the strings behind the curtain. I shall consider it an honour to make that person's arrest. I shall, really, Mr. Phillips."

Inspector Addington Peace beamed upon me as he concluded with an expression of hopeful enthusiasm, and lit a cigarette at my reading-lamp.

"This unknown criminal genius has got the diamond, anyway," I said.

"I am not so sure of that. Consider the position of the actual thief on the discovery that the stone was false. He must have been in a state of blind terror. If we may suppose that Colonel Gunton is innocent, the bellowing of that worthy gentleman must have frightened him the more. To be searched, discovered, and actually disgraced—a pleasant prospect, surely! We may take it that he was heartily sorry for the part he had played; that he wished the diamond a thousand miles away. To get rid of it previous to the ordeal before the Colonel and Professor Endicott in the library—that would be his object."

"Yet here I am met by the simple difficulty that I cannot find the diamond. I have made the closest investigation without result. As Colonel Gunton told us, Mr. Taubery remained in the dining-room to see that none of the guests returned after they had been searched. The door was subsequently locked and a policeman stationed in the passage outside; the windows were fastened. Therefore the thief could not come back to recover what he had temporarily hidden. All which might seem to prove that, though Colonel Gunton affirms that he went through the guests with an expert hand, one of them managed to keep the diamond about him and carry it away. Yet such an achievement suggests rather the professional than the amateur criminal. And, if for that reason alone, I believe that the stone is still in the house. However, we ought to be able to decide that point within a week."

"I can't see why, Peace," I said.

"No? Then, pray don't trouble about it. And really, Mr. Phillips, as I have a long day's work before me, it is time I was off to bed. Do you know it is one o'clock?"

I knew how useless it was to question the smiling little man when he thought he had told enough. So I bade him good-night with the best grace that disappointment would permit. It had been kind of him to trouble about me, anyway.

Three days went by, and I had not had the chance of asking Peace for news. For two nights, as I discovered by inquiry, he slept out, only appearing for an hour about noon to change his linen; for he was most careful of his appearance and as cleanly as a cat. Indeed, I had a secret belief that his nails were regularly manicured in Bond Street. When I did see him it was by accident, and, to be frank, nothing he had done gave me a greater surprise.

I was walking through Kensington Gardens about eleven o'clock on a visit to a friend whose studio lay to the north of the park. It was charming weather. The fresh leaves on the smoke-black boughs, the flower beds rich in variegated colouring, the deep-throated coo of the pigeons, the chatter of innumerable sparrows, all told that winter was passed and spring was calling a welcome to summer. I had just turned from a long shrub-walled walk into an open space when I came upon the amazing spectacle of Addington Peace flirting with a very pretty nursemaid.

Whatever the little Inspector had been, whatever he was, there was nothing of the Don Juan in his composition. I had already noticed that he took pains to avoid the opposite sex, with that uneasy consciousness of their presence which marks the bachelor with principles. Yet there he sat sharing the same bench and talking earnestly into her ear, while before them a little boy pedalled industriously up and down upon a tricycle-horse, a long-maned, long-tailed toy set on three wheels, and propelled by indifferent pedals. It was idyllic, domestic, but distinctly surprising.

As I passed the bench Peace turned his spectacles upon me without a glimmer of recognition in his mild blue eyes.

I had just finished my breakfast next morning, when in walked the Inspector. I laughed, indeed I could not help it, and he answered me with a quick glance, half annoyance, half reproach.

"Something is going to happen to-day in the matter of the diamond," he said. 'But, I warn you, Mr. Phillips, that if you intend to make fun of me you shan't know a word about it."

"You entirely misjudge me," I said, sticking my nose into my coffee cup to hide a grin.

"Very well. There is a sale of furniture to-day, at the house of Mr. Julius Taubery, No. 204 Portland Place, the 'property of a gentleman going abroad for the benefit of his health,' as the catalogue has it. I should advise you to be here a little before four o'clock this afternoon."

"I am very much obliged to you, Peace," I said, making a note of the number on my shirt-cuff.

He nodded with a faint shadow of a smile at the corners of his mouth, shook a plump finger of warning, and trotted out of the room.

I was punctual at my appointment and shouldered my way through the crowd of chattering dealers, into the big dining-room of number 204. A private auction to me always seems a melancholy business. True, I knew that in this case the owner was a rich man, that his furniture and carpets and fittings had been bought only a year or two before, and were not the loved collection of years. But the tumbled disorder, the mud of many feet upon the floor, the noise of the bidders answering the raucous voice of the auctioneer, were all an insult to the peace, the privacy, and the hospitable memories of a stately home. It was with relief that I saw Colonel Gunton's eyeglass shining near the window, and elbowed my way towards him. He had a little boy with him, whom he carried perched on his shoulder, well out of the way of the crowd.

"Hello, Phillips," he shouted, in a tone that successfully competed with the auctioneer's. "Come to see the last of old Taubery's household gods, eh? Confound those dealers, what a noise they make bidding for that table. 'Pon my soul, when I think how many good dinners I've had with my toes underneath it, I feel quite sentimental, I do, Phillips, strike me."

To emphasise his sensations he glared ferociously at a weak individual who was pressed against him by a swirl in the crowd, and asked him what in thunder he thought he was doing.

The great table was bought, the last of the heavy furniture; and there only remained a few details that were auctioned, some separately, some in oddly-assorted lots. It was during their sale that my talk with the Colonel was interrupted by the little boy upon his shoulder.

"Oh, father," he cried, "there's George's bicycle-horse. Won't you buy me George's bicycle-horse?"

A long-tailed, long-maned toy was raised by one of the auctioneer's men, who grinned under a running fire of chaff. I had an idea that I had seen that gallant charger before, though where I could not remember.

"Who is George?" I asked the Colonel.

"It's Taubery's grandson. His daughter's a widow, you know; she and the boy live with the old people. Hi, there, ten shillings."

A grey-haired man in an overcoat who stood near by nodded his head at the auctioneer.

"Eleven shillings — going at eleven shillings."

"Fifteen," bawled the Colonel.

"One pound," said the grey-haired man.

I had no idea what the cost of such toys might be; but the price, second-hand, seemed high. Several of the dealers gathered about the chair on which the auctioneer was standing looked back at us over their shoulders.

"Confound those dealers," cried the Colonel. "If an outside buyer wants anything they try to squeeze him out. They're all in league. It ought to be stopped. It's a monstrous shame. It's iniquitous. Twenty-five shillings to you, sir."

"Thirty," said the grey-haired man.

"Two pounds."

As the bids increased the temper of the Colonel grew worse and worse. Those who were well out of his reach began to chuckle, and finally to laugh outright. At four pounds ten he hesitated. With a supreme effort he made it five.

"Guineas," said the grey-haired man.

I am sorry to say that the Colonel swore. In one stupendous oath he denounced all who dealt in second-hand goods of any description whatsoever. Then, with the little boy sobbing on his shoulder, he surged through the crowd like a battleship in a head sea, and disappeared amid a chorus of disrespectful laughter. It was before the auctioneer had sufficiently recovered from his surprise that I felt a gentle touch on my arm. It was Addington Peace.

"There is a four-wheeled cab waiting about thirty yards up the street," he whispered. "Go and get into it. I will join you presently."

Quite half-an-hour had dragged by when the cab door was swung open and the detective sprang in. At the same time I noticed a covered cart with a grey pony in the shafts pass the other window at a leisurely pace. Our driver must have had his orders, for he turned his horse and followed in the same direction.

Peace sat in a contented heap, so I left him alone and contented myself with staring out of the window. We were going northward towards Hampstead. The lines of houses broke up into separate villas. Lilac and laburnum bushes peeped over the garden walls. The throng of traffic grew thinner, the pavement less crowded. It was past five when we drew up at a little public-house standing back from the road. Peace toddled out and I followed at his heels.

"He is unloading his cart in Ashley Street, yonder," said the driver, leaning from the box, as he pointed with his whip to a side road. "Do you want me to wait, sir?"

The inspector nodded and disappeared through the inn door, leaving me on the pavement. As he had given me no orders, I strolled back to the corner and peeped down the road, which ran at right angles to the one in which I was.

About forty yards away stood the little covered cart with the grey-haired old dealer of the auction-room talking to a lad beside it. Presently the lad crawled under the canvas hood and handed down the identical long-tailed horse that had brought about the public discomfiture of the gallant Colonel Gunton. The dealer pushed it across the stone pavement into a little furniture shop, and the boy, whipping up the grey pony, drove quickly away.

I turned back to find the detective at my elbow.

A street lamp showed him to me clearly— a white-faced youth with a straggling, brown moustache and an indecisive chin.

"Peace," I said, "what is your interest in that bicycle-horse?"

"It happens to play the comedy part in our little mystery."

"What do you mean?"

"Only that it has a hole in the saddle for a pommel should a little girl ride it, and the hole leads down to a hollow inside. Do you guess what it was that dropped into the hollow inside?"

"Not Mr. Taubery's diamond?"

"Exactly. Yet we have still to find out the man who put it there."

"But in the meantime the old dealer may——"

"Tut, tut, Mr. Phillips. The old dealer has nothing to do with it. He is only obeying an order to buy the toy whatever it cost, and to keep it until called for. We may have to waste some time, so I have ordered a steak and fried potatoes in an upper room that conveniently overlooks the door of his shop. Let me show you the way."

We passed through a long bar at which a dingy assemblage lounged and smoked, and so upstairs into a private room, the windows of which commanded Ashley Street. We ate our meal in relays, one watching at the window while the other disposed of his section of stringy steak and heavy beer. The daylight softly faded, the gas jets sprang out along the street, the tramp of home-coming fathers dropped into silence— but there was still no caller at the furniture-shop. The shutters had been put up for the night. It seemed plain to me that nothing would happen for that evening at least, though Peace did not seem to despond.

Nine o'clock—ten o'clock—ten thirty, and the customer arrived.

I had watched his cab come rattling down the street with a casual interest, for many had come and gone since we first mounted guard. It had passed the little shop and was almost beneath us when a head was thrust out of the window and a voice cried irritably to the cabman. A street lamp showed him to me clearly—a white-faced youth with a straggly brown moustache and an indecisive chin.

The cab turned about, and pulled up opposite the shop door. The inspector touched my arm, and we walked down the stairs, picked up our driver, who was smoking in the bar, and so bundled into our own vehicle. A few whispered instructions and we drove slowly round the corner into Ashley Street.

The customer had been expected. As we passed the shop at a walking pace I could see that the dealer and his assistant were hoisting the bicycle-horse to the roof of the waiting cab. Fifty yards more and we drew up by the pavement.

Peace kept the windows closed, so that I could not look back along the road; but through the glass in front I could see that our driver was quietly taking note of affairs. It was not the first time that the inspector had employed him, as I learnt afterwards, and the man knew his business.

Suddenly our cab whisked round and set off at a rapid pace. The stranger had selected a fast horse, that was evident. We swung through a maze of narrow streets, tugged up a long hill, skirted a stretch of open common—a part of Hampstead Heath, I believe—and finally stopped in the shade of some tall trees. As I got out I saw the lights of the chaise stationary at some distance up the road.

"There may be trouble, Mr. Phillips," whispered the little detective. "I'm not certain I ought to bring you along. If anything——"

"Nonsense!" I interrupted, glancing down at him with some amusement.

"Well, take this, anyway. I had it from a German burglar."

He thrust a strip of hardened rubber into my hand, about eighteen inches in length by two in thickness.

"It will stun a man without leaving a mark," he said gently.

The four-wheeler that we had followed was waiting before a green door set in a high brick wall. Without any attempt at concealment, Peace walked to the door and tried the handle. It was not locked, and we passed into a fair-sized garden set about with flower beds and clumps of laurel. In the middle I could see the outline of a square grey house. Two of the ground floor rooms glowed behind their curtains, the rest was darkness.

We crossed a corner of the lawn and stopped behind a patch of bushes directly in front of the entrance porch. The night was very still and silent. What desperate men were gathered in that quiet place? How could we hope to arrest them flushed with the triumph of so splendid a prize. To be truthful, I began to feel a certain anxiety in our position; though upon Peace's face, showing white in the gloom, was a look of perfect serenity—a look that I could not understand.

"Mercy, oh, mercy!"

It was a trembling wail of terror, a wail that was suddenly blotted out by a roar like the challenge of a bull. From within the house came the crash of overturned chairs and the jingle of breaking glass. And all the time the shrieks and hoarse ravings drew nearer and louder, until with a loud bang the hall door was flung open and a man tumbled down the steps as if thrown from a catapult. His assailant, in black silhouette against the hall lights, hesitated for a moment, stick in hand. Then with a shout of rage, he sprang forward and struck at the moaning wretch who squirmed on the gravel at his feet.

"Now, Jack Steadman, that is quite enough," said the inspector, pushing his way through the laurels.

I was amazed at the sudden, bulldog decision of the amiable little man.

"And who may you be?" cried the other, with a furious oath.

"My name is Addington Peace, of the Criminal Investigation Department of Scotland Yard, and I arrest you both for being concerned in the robbery of a valuable diamond, the property of Mr. Julius Taubery."

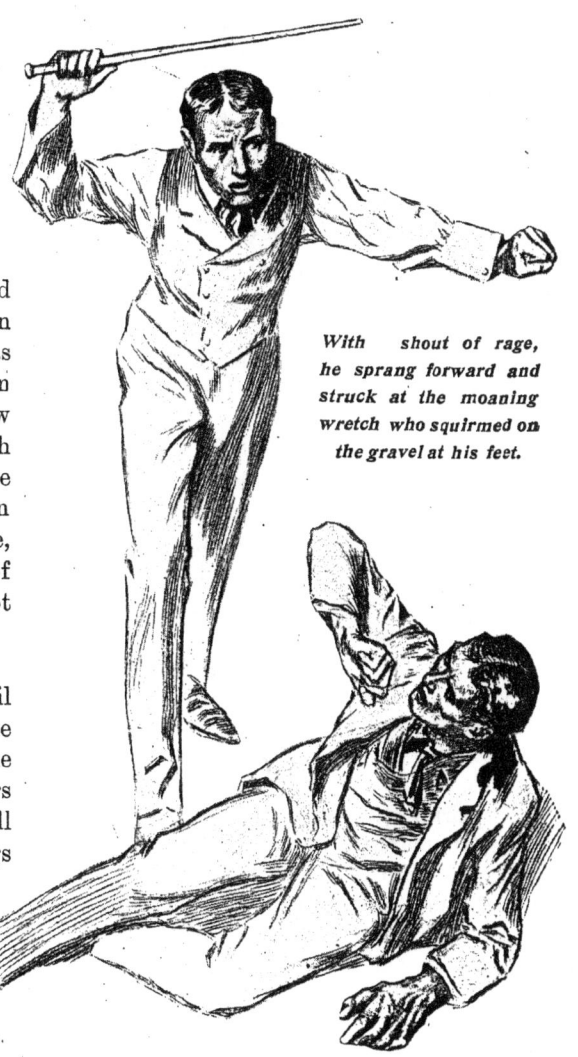

With shout of rage, he sprang forward and struck at the moaning wretch who squirmed on the gravel at his feet.

"Stolen a diamond!" he bellowed. "Do you call that a diamond?"

He flung down a stone that sparkled in the lights behind him, and stamped it into the gravel with his heel.

"I am aware that it is the imitation," said the inspector. "But it was not your fault that you missed the real thing. I have a cab waiting. You had better come with me quietly. And I warn you, Steadman, that anything you say will be used in evidence against you."

* * * * *

It was after two in the morning before the inspector tapped at the door of my rooms. I had made the fourth of that odd cab load to the nearest police-station; for, though Mr. Jack Steadman had blustered, and the Hon. George Carstairs had grovelled and whined thither, they had consented to go at last. And there I had left the detective and his prisoners, driving to my rooms to await his return.

"The case was not quite so difficult as you suppose, Mr. Phillips," he said, in answer to my question. "You remember that I believed the diamond to be still in the house?"

"Certainly."

"It would be hard to imagine a more useful bait. It was certain that the thieves would have another bite at it; it was also certain that I ought to be able to hook them when they did. Yet I very nearly lost the diamond after all. Taubery, Gunton, and the servants had all declared that, since the robbery, nothing had been moved from the dining-room, passage, or library. There they made a mistake.

"Taubery's little grandson, George, happened to leave his toy horse in the passage from the dining-room, and into the hole made for the pommel that poor creature, Carstairs, had dropped the diamond with a last despairing effort to get rid of it before Colonel Gunton searched him. Ten minutes afterwards the little boy went out for a walk with his nurse, taking the horse with him. When he returned it was left, as usual, in the servants' quarters at the back. I never set eyes on it until a day later. Even then I should not have suspected what it contained had not the nurse complained to me of a man who followed her when she took George for his daily airing in the Park. That was the sign for which I had been looking. I accompanied the pair on the following morning. I saw the man, but did not recognise him.

"Neither the nurse nor the boy could well be carrying the diamond about with them. There remained the horse. That night I extracted the real diamond, and not wishing to spoil my bait for the shy fish, I dropped the imitation stone into its place.

"The toy was watched by night and day. It was through a hint from me that it was included in the sale. Poor Colonel Gunton! I admit that his eccentric bidding startled me for a moment.

"You can understand Steadman's fury when, after all his plots and risks and expenditure, his silly dupe brought him back the identical imitation stone that had been made to deceive old Taubery. I don't believe that the Trojans could have been more astonished when the Greeks emerged from the wooden horse, than was Steadman when he took out the diamond from the toy and found it to be the imitation!"

"And who is Steadman?"

"A very dangerous fellow, Mr. Phillips. I recognised him the moment he appeared at the door. For years he was a bookmaker in Paris, but left when the place got too hot for him. As a card-player he is well known and avoided. He has been in low water lately. So has his dupe, Carstairs, as I now discover. Lord Wintone, the young man's brother, set him up as a coffee planter in Ceylon, but he spent all the money given him and returned six months ago. He must have heard of the new diamond and mentioned it to Steadman; for Steadman hatched the plot—there is no doubt about that. Carstairs was merely a dupe and a foolish, vicious dupe at that—he never had the ability to rise higher in crime. How the two became acquainted I do not know; but they have been seen together several times lately. You may take my word for it, that the public will be well rid of them for a year or two."

Next month the story of "Mr. Coran's Election" will be told.

The Chronicles of Addington Peace.

By B. FLETCHER ROBINSON.

Joint Author with Sir A. Conan Doyle in his best Sherlock Holmes story, "The Hound of the Baskervilles."

THE STRANGE AND STARTLING EXPERIENCES OF THAT FAMOUS DETECTIVE, ADDINGTON PEACE.

EACH STORY IS COMPLETE IN ITSELF.

III.—MR. CORAN'S ELECTION.

TEN o'clock! Big Ben left no doubt about it; for the giant clock in the tower of the British Houses of Parliament is a noisy neighbour. The last stroke thundered out as I climbed the stairs that led to the modest lodging of Inspector Addington Peace, and silence had fallen as I knocked at his door. I was alone that night and in the mood when a man escapes from himself to seek a friend.

I found the little detective at his open window staring across the tumbled roofs to where the Abbey towers rose under the summer moon. The evening breeze that came with the tide up the Thames blew gratefully after the heat of the July day. He glanced at me over his shoulder with a short nod of welcome.

"Even the police grow sentimental on such a night," I suggested.

"Or philosophic."

"'The reflections of Diogenes the detective, or the Aristotle of Scotland Yard,'" I laughed. "May I inquire as to the cause of such profound thought?"

He held out a slip of paper, which I carried to the central lamp. It was an old newspaper clipping, stained and greyed, relating in six lines how James Coran, described as a student, had been charged at the Bow Street Police-court with drunkenness, followed by an aggravated assault on the constable who arrested him. He was fined three pounds or seven days. That was all.

"Not a subject of earth-shaking importance," I said.

"No; but it has proved a sufficient excuse for blackmail."

"Then the victim is a fool," I answered hotly. "Why, from the age of the paper, the affair must have taken place at least twenty years ago."

"Thirty-two years this month."

"Which means that the riotous student is now a man of over fifty. If James Coran has gone down the hill, the past can't hurt him now; if he has led a respectable life surely he can afford to neglect the scamp who threatens to rake up so mild a scandal. Blackmail for a spree back in the seventies—it's ridiculous, Inspector."

The plump little man stood with his hands behind him and his head on one side, watching me, over his glasses, with benevolent amusement. When he spoke it was in the ponderous manner which he sometimes assumed, a manner that always reminded me of a university professor explaining their deplorable errors to his class.

"Mr. James Coran is a respectable middle-class widower who lives with his

Copyright, 1904, by B. Fletcher Robinson in the United States of America.

sister Rebecca and two daughters in the little town of Brendon, thirty-five miles from London. He arrives at the 'Fashionable Clothing Company'—his London establishment in Oxford Street—at ten o'clock in the morning, leaving for home by the 5.18. In his spare time he performs a variety of public duties at Brendon. He is a recognised authority on drains, and has produced a pamphlet on dust-carts. As a temperance orator his local reputation is great, and his labours in the cause of various benevolent associations have been suitably commemorated by a presentation clock, three inkstands, and a silver salver. His interests are limited to Brendon and Oxford Street; of world movements he thinks no more than the caterpillar on a leaf considers the general welfare of the cabbage patch. Please remember these facts, Mr. Phillips, in consideration of his case.

"Six months ago an envelope arrived at his house with two inclosures. One was the newspaper clipping you hold; the other a letter denouncing him as a hypocrite, and warning him that unless the sum of twenty pounds was placed in the locker of a little summer-house at the end of his garden, the writer would expose him to all Brendon in his true character as a convicted drunkard.

"Coran was in despair. He had imagined his unfortunate spree long forgotten. Not even his own relatives were aware of it. He was trying for a seat on the County Council; the election was due in a month, and he relied for his success on the support of the temperance party. As an election weapon the old scandal could be used with striking effect. So he paid—as many a better man has been fool enough to do under like circumstances.

"In three days—on Saturday that is—the election takes place. This morning he received a letter similar to the first, save that the demand was for a hundred pounds. He had just sense enough to see that if he allowed himself to be blackmailed again it would merely encourage further attempt at extortion. So when he arrived in town, he took a cab to Scotland Yard. I heard his

A long, grey-whiskered man in the lead, and the Inspector trotting behind.

story, and caught the next train down to Brendon. I did not call at the house, but gathered a few details concerning him and his family. In all particulars he seems to have spoken the truth."

"Must the hundred pounds be placed in the summer-house to-night?"

"No. The blackmailer gave him a day to collect the money. It must be in the locker to-morrow night by eleven o'clock."

"Which means that you will watch the place and pull out the fish as he takes the bait. It seems simple enough, anyhow."

"Oh yes," he said. "But it is the faulty sense of proportion in Coran which provides the interest in the case. Even at the time the scandal was no very serious matter. What must be his frame of mind that it should terrorise him after all these years?"

When I left him half-an-hour later it was with the promise that I should have first news of the comedy's conclusion—for a tragedy it certainly was not, save for the blackmailer, if Peace should catch him.

The following afternoon I was sitting in my studio with the cigarette—that comes so pleasantly after tea and buttered toast—between my lips, when my old servant, Jacob Hendry, thrust in his head to announce visitors. They came hard upon his heels—a long, grey-whiskered man in the lead, and the Inspector, with a quaint smile of apology, trotting behind. As they cleared the door, the little detective twisted round his companion and waived an introductory hand.

"This is Mr. James Coran," he said. "We want your assistance, Mr. Phillips."

The long man stood staring at me and screwing his hands together in evident agitation. He had a hollow, melancholy face, a weak mouth, and eyes of an indecisive grey. From his square-toed shoes to the bald patch on the top of his head, he was extremely, almost flagrantly, respectable.

"I am taking a great liberty, sir," he said humbly, "but you are, as it were, a straw to one who is sinking beneath the waters of affliction. Do you, by chance, know the town of Brendon?"

"I have never been so fortunate as to visit it," I told him.

"I understand from the police officer here that you have travelled abroad. Accustomed, therefore, to the corruption that taints the municipal life of other cities, you can scarcely comprehend the whole-souled enthusiasm with which we of Brendon approach the duties, may I say the sacred trust, of administering to the sanitary and moral welfare of our county. Those whom we select must be of unstained reputation. From a place on the sports committee of the flower show I myself have risen through successive grades until even the Houses of Parliament seemed within the limit of legitimate ambition. But, now, sir, now it seems that, through a boyish indiscretion when a student at the Regent's Street Polytechnic, I may be denounced in my advancing years as a roysterer, a tippler, almost a convicted criminal. They would not hesitate. Mark my words, sir, if Horledge and Panton—my opponent's chief supporters in Saturday's election, are informed of these facts, they will mention them on platforms, they may even display them on hoardings."

He paused, sighed deeply, and wiped his face with a large silk pocket-handkerchief. The situation was ridiculous enough, yet not without a certain pathos underlying the humour; for the man was sincerely in earnest.

"If I can help you, Mr. Coran, I am at your disposal," I told him.

"It is matter of considerable delicacy," he said. "My younger daughter, Emily, has formed an attachment which is most disagreeable to me."

"Indeed," I murmured.

"The young man, Thomas Appleton by name, is of more than doubtful character. Miss Rebecca, my sister, has seen him boating on the Thames in the company of ladies whose appearance was—er—distinctly theatrical."

"You surprise me."

"He has been known to visit music-halls."

"Did Miss Rebecca see him there, too?"

"Certainly not, sir; but she has it from a sure source. It was obviously my duty to forbid him the house. I performed that duty, and extorted a promise from my daughter that she would cease to communicate with him. In my belief, it is he who has discovered the scandal to which I need not again refer, and, in revenge, is levying this blackmail. The law shall strike him, if there is justice left in England."

"And where do I come in?" I asked, for he had paused in a flurry of indignation.

"Perhaps I had better explain," Addington Peace interposed. "Owing to this unfortunate love affair, it is plain that no member of Mr. Coran's family must learn that this young man is suspected or that steps are being taken for his arrest. It would not be unreasonable to fear that he might be warned. I am staying with Mr. Coran to-night, but I do not want to go alone. I might take an assistant from the Yard, but it is hard to pick a man who has not 'Criminal Investigation Department' stamped upon him. You look innocent enough, Mr. Phillips. Will you come with us and lend me a hand?"

I agreed at once. It could not fail to be an amusing adventure. After some discussion, it was arranged that Peace and I should be introduced as business friends of Mr. Coran, who had asked us down to Brendon on a sudden invitation. A telegram was sent off to that effect.

For the first fifteen minutes of the train we shared a crowded compartment. Gradually, however, our companions dropped away until we were left to ourselves. Mr. Coran was in evident hesitation of mind. He shifted about, screwing his hands together with a most doleful countenance. When he commenced to speak he leant forward as if afraid that the very cushions might overhear him.

"I have mentioned my sister Rebecca," he said. "She is a woman of remarkable character."

"Indeed," I murmured, for he chose to address me more directly.

"We have differed lately on several points of—er—local interest. It is very important that she should not learn the cause of my appeal to the police. Anything that aroused her suspicions might lead to consequences very disagreeable to myself."

"I will be discreet."

"My daughters will—er—benefit largely under her will. She would cut them out of it without hesitation if she learnt that their father had been connected with so—er—disgraceful a scandal. You understand the situation?"

"Perfectly. It must render your position additionally unpleasant."

He sighed, and relapsed into a melancholy silence, in which the train drew up at Brendon Station. A cab was in waiting, into which we climbed. A couple of turns, a short descent, and we drew up at a gate in a long wall of flaming brick.

As we walked up the drive I looked carefully about me. The house was also of red brick and of mixed architecture. I believe the architect had intended it for the Tudor period, with improvements suggested by modern sanitary requirements. The garden before the windows was of considerable size, with laurels and quick-growing shrubs lining the edge of a lawn and various winding walks. At the farther end a thatched roof rising amongst the young trees showed the position of the summer-house which played so important a part in the story we had heard.

It was striking half-past six as we entered the hall. Our host led us straight to our rooms on the first floor. We had been told not to bring dress clothes, so that ten minutes later we were ready to descend to the drawing-room.

Mr. Coran's daughters, a pair of pretty, bright-faced girls, were seated in those careless attitudes which denote the expected appearance of strangers. Miss Rebecca, a tall, spectacled female, whose sixty years had changed curves for acute angles, reposed in the window reading a volume of majestic size. She laid it down with a thump, removed her glasses, and received us with great modesty and decorum. The Inspector and a fox terrier, that set up a barking as we entered, were the only members of the party that seemed natural and at ease.

I found the dinner pass pleasantly enough, despite the gloom that radiated from the brother and sister.

Emily, the victim of the "unfortunate attachment," quite captured my fancy, though I am not a ladies' man. Twice we dared to laugh, though the reproving eyes of the elders were constantly upon us. In the intervals of my talk with her I obtained the keenest enjoyment from listening to the conversation of Peace and Miss Rebecca. The lady cross-examined him very much as if he were a prisoner accused of various grave and monstrous offences. Upon the question of anti-vivisection she was especially urgent.

"My brother refuses the movement his support," she said in a loud, firm voice. "My reply to him is torturer, inquisitor. What are your views on the subject?"

"The same, my dear madam, as your own," said the disgraceful little hypocrite. "How does the cause progress in Brendon?"

"I trust that in a few weeks our local branch will have been placed on such a basis as to be a model to the whole society."

"Aunt is rather a crank on anti-vivisection," whispered Miss Emily in my ear. "Do be careful if she tackles you about it."

I laughed, and the subject changed between us.

After the ladies left, Coran began a gloomy autobiography. His family, he said, had been living in the North of England at the time of his London escapade. No account of the affair, which appeared in only one paper, had reached them. He had left for Sheffield shortly afterwards, and it was not until ten years later that the death of his father had given him a couple of thousand pounds, with which he bought a share in his present business, which had greatly prospered.

Concerning Thomas Appleton, the young man whom he suspected, he spoke most bitterly. He was, indeed, in the middle of his denunciations when Peace slipped from his chair and moved softly to the window.

With a swift jerk he drew the blind aside and stared out. From where I sat I could see an empty stretch of lawn with shrubs beyond showing darkly in the summer twilight.

"A lovely evening," he said over his shoulder.

We both watched him in surprise as he dropped the blind and walked back to his seat, stopping on his way to pat the terrier that lay on a mat by the window.

"Is there anything the matter?" asked Coran.

"If we are to keep our business here a secret you must not talk too loud—that is all."

"I don't understand you."

"One of your household was listening at the window."

"Do you mean to tell me that I am spied upon by my own people?" cried Coran, angrily. "What gave you such an idea?"

"The dog there."

"Absurd!"

"Not at all, Mr. Coran. From where he lay he could look under the lower edge of the blind, which was not drawn completely down. He raised his ears; someone approached; he wagged his tail, it was a friend with whom he was well acquainted. If it had been a stranger he would have run barking to the window. It is simple enough, surely."

"Did you see who it was?" asked our host, with a sudden change of manner.

"No," said the little man. "But I think this conversation unwise. Shall we join the ladies in the drawing-room?"

Peace was in his most entertaining mood that night. Poor Emily, who was sitting by the French windows, staring sadly out into the gathering shadows, was led to the piano, where she recalled her forbidden lover in sentimental ditties. He engaged Miss Rebecca in an argument on the local control of licensed premises, which gave that worthy old lady an opportunity for genuine oratory. Even our melancholy host was drawn out of his miseries by a reference to the water supply.

When ten o'clock came, and the ladies were led away under Miss Rebecca's wing—they keep early hours in Brendon—I shook the Inspector by the hand in sincere admiration. It had been a really smart performance, and I told him so.

The little man did not respond. Instead he drew us together in a corner and issued his orders with sharp precision.

"Mr. Coran, at fifteen minutes to eleven you will leave the house by the drawing-room windows and place the envelope you have prepared in the locker of the summer-house. When you return do not fasten the catch, for I may wish to enter during the night. Walk upstairs to your bed and get to sleep if you can. Mr. Phillips, you will go to your room and stay there. The window overlooks the garden. If you want to keep watch—for I do not suppose you can resist that temptation—see that your head is well out of sight. When Mr. Coran leaves the house listen at your door. If your hear anyone moving, go and find out who it may be. You understand?"

"Yes," I answered. "But what are you going to do?"

"Discover a suitable place from which I can keep an eye on the summer-house. Good-night to you."

When I reached my room, I took off my coat, placed a chair some six feet back from the open window, so that the rising moon should not show my face to any watchers in the laurels, and so waited events. It was a soft summer night, such as only temperate England knows. There was not a breath of wind; a perfume of flowers crept in from the garden; every leaf stood black and still in the silvery light.

I heard a clock chime three-quarters of an hour in some room beneath me. The last stroke had barely shivered into silence when I saw Coran appear upon the lawn, walking towards the summer-house, the outlines of which I could distinguish amongst the heavier shadows of the trees by which it was surrounded. I remembered my orders, and crept softly to the door which I had left ajar.

The minutes slid by without a sound, and presently I began to wonder why Coran had not returned. His room was not far from mine. I must have heard his foot upon the stairs. He had disobeyed his orders, that was evident. However, it was not my affair, and I crept back to my point of observation.

Twelve! I heard the clock tap out the news from the room below. I was nodding in my chair barely awake. After all, it was a trivial matter this trumpery blackmail. Half-an-hour more, thought I, pulling out watch, and I will get to bed.

The affair was becoming extremely monotonous. I dared not light a cigarette, for I felt certain that Peace would notice the glow from outside and that I should hear of it in

They were a good thirty yards apart, the one following the other with stealthy strides.

the morning. Ten minutes, a quarter-of-an-hour—what was that moving under the trees by the edge of the drive? It was a man—two men. I crouched forward with every nerve in me suddenly awakened.

They were a good thirty yards apart, the one following the other with stealthy strides—not the sort of walk with which honest men go about honest business.

When the leader came to the path which led towards the summer-house, he turned down it, leaving the drive to his right. He avoided the gravel, keeping to the silent turf which fringed it. His companion followed him step by step.

It was a curious spectacle, these slow-moving shadows that drifted forward through the night, now almost obscured beneath the branches, now showing in black silhouette against a patch of moonlight.

As the first man melted amongst the trees about the summer-house, the other moved forward swiftly for a score of steps and then halted for a moment, crouching behind a clump of laurel. Suddenly he sprang up again and ran straight forward, cutting a corner across the lower edge of the lawn.

There was no shouting, but I could hear

the faint tramping of a scuffle and the thud of falling bodies. Then all was still again.

Peace had told me to remain in the house. But Peace had never expected two men; I was sure of that. I crept down the stairs, out through the French windows of the drawing-room, and so across the lawn to the trees about the summer-house.

As I passed through them I saw a little group standing in whispered conversation. They turned sharply upon me. One was a stranger, but his companions were Peace and, to my vast surprise, old Coran himself.

"Well, Mr. Phillips," asked the detective, "and what do you want?"

"I thought"—I began.

"Oh, you've been thinking, too, have you," he snapped. "Here is a young man who was thinking he would like to look at this extremely commonplace summer-house; here is Mr. Coran who was thinking he might help me by lurking about his garden instead of going to bed; and here are you with Heaven knows what ideas in your head. Perhaps you and Mr. Coran will do what you are told another time."

"I saw two men," I explained humbly. "I was afraid they might get the better of you. How was I to know that it was Mr. Coran who had disobeyed orders?"

"You are both pleased to be funny," said our host, and I could see he was trembling with rage. "But the fact remains that I caught this young man entering the summer-house for a purpose we can well imagine. Inspector Addington Peace, I charge this person, Thomas Appleton, with blackmail."

"Can you explain your presence, Mr. Appleton?" asked the detective kindly.

He did not look a criminal, for he stood very straight and square, regarding the three of us with an amused smile.

"Of course, I had no right to be here," he said. "Though why I should find a detective waiting to arrest me for blackmail, or why Mr. Coran should spring upon my back and roll me over I cannot imagine."

"This is much as I expected," snarled his accuser. "Effrontery and impudence are ever the associates of crime. Inspector, you will oblige me by producing the handcuffs."

"I should like a word in private, Mr. Coran."

They walked off together, leaving me alone with Mr. Thomas Appleton, who offered a cigarette.

"Has there been an epidemic of lunacy in the neighbourhood?" he inquired politely.

"No," I said, laughing in spite of myself. "But how, in Heaven's name, do you explain your visit to the summer-house at this hour of the night?"

"I am afraid I must decline to answer you," he said, and quietly turned the subject.

Coran returned, with a face of vindictive indecision. Under his veil of austerity there had smouldered a dangerous temper, which was close upon bursting into flame. But, after all, he had excuse enough. Heaven alone knew what baulked ambition, what treacherous insults he had come to associate with this young man. The same passions actuate humanity whether they view the world from one end of the telescope or the other.

"I have decided to waive your arrest for the present," he growled.

"It would certainly create a great scandal in Brendon," said Appleton firmly.

"You count on that, do you?" cried the elder man. "You think you have a hold upon me, that I am afraid of you. Take care, sir, take care."

"You choose to be mysterious, Mr. Coran. I have no hold upon you. But I should think twice if I were you before arresting an innocent man."

"Innocent! What were you doing here?"

"That is my business."

Coran turned away, wringing his hands together in his odd manner when greatly excited.

"Go," he snarled over his shoulder. "Go, before I strangle you."

As I dropped off to sleep half-an-hour later I was still wondering why Peace had refused a bed, remaining for the night in the garden. Could he expect more visits to the summer-house? Why had young Appleton come sneaking up at so late an hour if he were not guilty? The problem that had seemed so simple was changed into a maze of strange complications. I was too sleepy to trace them further.

I was awakened by a touch on my shoulder. It was Coran who stood by my bedside.

"We breakfast in half-an-hour," he said uneasily.

"I will be punctual."

"Forgive my importunity, Mr. Phillips; but promise me that you will be careful before Miss Rebecca. She is so very acute. I never knew a woman with a keener instinct for scandal. And, as a father, I cannot forget the future of my poor girls. If she knew the truth she would not leave them a penny; also her heart is affected."

"I am sorry to hear it."

"Thank you. It is very necessary that you should be discreet."

He stalked out of the room and left me wondering at him with an amused cynicism.

I started for London with my host by the 8.45. To avoid suspicion, Peace accompanied us to the station; but there he left us. He had, he said, work to do in the town.

Coran was cheerful with the limited cheerfulness that Nature allowed him. Doubtless he felt that he had his enemy in his power. He was very talkative concerning the final address which he was advertised to deliver that evening at eight o'clock. It was to be the completion, the coping stone to his campaign, and was calculated to insure his election next day. I expressed regret that I should not be privileged to hear it.

I lunched at my club, and, shortly after three, returned to my rooms. There, in my easiest chair, reading an evening paper, who should I discover but Inspector Peace.

"Hello," I said. "I didn't expect you back so soon."

"This is a very comfortable chair of yours, Mr. Phillips," he smiled. "I was glad of a rest."

"And how goes Brendon?"

"So well that I am going to take you down there by the 4.10 train."

I tried to draw his discoveries out of him, but he would tell me nothing. Something was going to happen which might interest me if I came along—that was the beginning and end of his news. It was sufficient to make me promise to join him, however, as he very well knew.

The local was just steaming into the station when a fat, red-faced man came panting out of the booking-office. Peace gave my arm a squeeze as he passed.

"That is Horledge, the supporter of Coran's chief opponent in to-morrow's election," he whispered.

"So you have been making some new friends since I saw you last?"

"One or two," he said, stepping into a carriage.

When we arrived at Brendon, the Inspector led me off to an inn in the centre of the town. It was a pleasant, old-fashioned place, with black rafters peering through the plaster of the ceiling and oak panelling high on the walls. The modern Brendon had wrapped it about, but it had not changed for three centuries. You may find many such ancient inns about London, which watch the march of the red brick suburbs with a dignified surprise, until one day the builder steps in, and the old Coach and Horses or White Hart comes tumbling down, and the Palace Hotel reigns in its stead. We dined early. At half-past seven, by the grandfather's clock in the corner, Peace rose.

"Mr. Coran's meeting does not begin until eight; but I want to be there early—come along."

The platform was empty when we arrived, but a score of people were already on the front benches. We did not join them, seating ourselves near the door. Brendon, or the graver part of it, moved by us in a tiny stream. A few elders walked up to the platform with the air of those who realise that they are something in the world. The clock above them was pointing to the hour when, with a thumping of feet and a clapping of hands, Coran appeared, and shook hands with the white-whiskered old chairman.

It was while the chairman was introducing "the popular and venerated townsman who had come to address them," that the red face of Mr. Horledge came peering in at the

"Mr. Chairman," he shouted. "I have a question to ask the candidate!"

door. He stood there for a minute, and then modestly sat down on the bench before us. Peace touched my arm and we moved along until we were just behind him. The whole affair was a deeper mystery to me than ever, but it was useless to question the Inspector.

The chairman ended at last, and, amid fresh applause, Coran rose and stood gazing down at the little crowd with a benevolent satisfaction. Their respect and admiration was the breath of life to the man. You could see it in his eyes, in his gesture as he begged for silence.

"My friends."

He had got no further when Horledge sprang to his feet with a raised hand.

"Mr. Chairman," he shouted. "I have a question to ask the candidate."

There was a slight outcry, a few hisses and groans; but the tide of local politics did not run strongly in Brendon. Besides, everyone knew Horledge. He had the largest grocer's shop in the town.

"It would be better to question him after his speech, Mr. Horledge," protested the old chairman.

"I should prefer to answer this gentleman at once," Coran interposed.

He stood with his hands, clasping and unclasping, before him, but never moved his eyes from his opponent. There was grit in the fellow after all.

"It would be simpler if you withdrew," said the red-faced man, shuffling his feet uneasily.

"That your party's candidate might be returned unopposed?"

"Don't force me to explain," cried Horledge. "Why not withdraw?"

"You waste the time of the meeting."

"Very well, gentlemen, I say that Mr. Coran there is no fit candidate, because——"

There is something unsettling in the official tap on the shoulder which the police of all countries cultivate, something which it does not take previous experience to recognise. Horledge's face turned a shade paler as he glanced over his shoulder at the little man who had thus called his attention.

"And what do you want?" he growled.

"I am Inspector Addington Peace, of the Criminal Investigation Department. I warn you, Mr. Horledge, that you are lending yourself to an attempt at blackmail."

The detective spoke in so low a voice that I, who was standing by his side, could barely catch the words.

"Bless my soul, you don't say so?" cried the other.

"I should like a five minutes' talk with Mr. Coran and yourself. After that you may take your own course. Will you suggest it?"

Mr. Horledge did not take long to make up his mind. He told the meeting that he might have been misinformed. If they would permit it, he asked for a five minutes' private conversation with the candidate.

The meeting received the suggestion with cheers. It was something unusual in the monotony of such functions. We walked up the central aisle between a couple of hundred pairs of curious eyes, mounted the platform, and followed Coran into a small ante-room, the door of which Peace closed behind him.

"On June 15th the Brendon Anti-Vivisection Society, of which you, Mr. Horledge, are president, received the sum of twenty pounds from an anonymous source," said the little detective.

"Certainly."

"That sum was extorted from Mr. Coran by the threat of revealing the secret which Miss Rebecca Coran told you this morning, and which you verified this afternoon by a reference to the old newspaper files in the British Museum."

"I had no idea—this is most surprising. I—is it illegal?" he stuttered.

"Blackmail for whatever purpose is illegal. Further attempts have been made to extort money. It is because they failed that they were placed in possession of the facts to-day."

"It seemed a low down trick, anyway," said Horledge penitently. "I wish I had never listened to the old cat. But Squaretoes—I beg your pardon, Mr. Coran—I mean our friend here has always been so virtuous that I thought it rather fun. On my word, his secret is safe with me. He can win the election, and welcome, after this."

"That is all, then. I want a word in private with these two gentlemen. Goodnight to you, and many thanks."

"Great Scott, Inspector, but you gave me a fright. I hope, Mr. Coran, you don't bear malice? That's all right, then. Goodnight all."

As he disappeared through the door the elder man dropped into a chair, covering his face with his hands.

"This is shocking!" he groaned. "Oh, Mr. Peace, are you sure it was my sister?"

"There is no doubt at all."

"But, what am I to do now?" he asked, looking from one to the other of us, with a pitiable expression. "Shall I withdraw?"

"Nonsense," said the little detective firmly. "Fight your election and win it, sir; and the best way to begin is to go back and tell them all about it."

"Go and tell them? Go and tell the meeting?" he cried.

"Yes. They'll like you all the better for it. Do you suppose there is no human nature in Brendon? Are you going to keep this miserable scandal hanging over your head all your life? If you stick to politics someone is sure to rake it up. Be a man, Mr. Coran, and get it over now."

"I will."

He had got to his feet, his eyes set with a sudden determination. He stretched out his hand to each of us, turned about, and marched out of the room like a soldier leading a forlorn hope against a fortress. As the door slammed behind him, Peace looked at me with an expression in which sympathy and humour were oddly mingled.

"Take my word for it, Mr. Phillips," he said, "many a reputation for desperate valour has been won by a less sacrifice."

* * * *

It was not until after two days that I heard the arguments by which the Inspector had worked his way to a conclusion. They form a good example of his methods.

"It was evident," he said, "that the blackmailer knew Coran's character, his position as regards the election, and the details of his house and grounds. Those facts suggested a relative or close personal friend. The theory that it was a relative was strengthened by the newspaper cutting. It was not a thing a casual acquaintance would be likely to keep by him all these years.

"From Coran I learnt that he had had differences of opinion with Miss Rebecca. In my conversation with her she spoke bitterly of his refusal to subscribe to her society for the prevention of vivisection. She returned to the subject several times,

"*They remained for some time together, and then Horledge took a train to London.*"

mentioning the financial difficulties in which the local branch of which she is the secretary was placed. Those facts impressed me.

"Before Appleton arrived last night I had carefully searched the summer-house. In a corner of the wood-work I discovered a note from Miss Emily. The place was the lover's letter-box. Indeed, I had been expecting that young gentleman's appearance long before he came. I did not, however, tell this to Mr. Coran when he pressed for an arrest. It would have been hardly fair on the girl. I do not imagine that they will find the old gentleman so stony-hearted after to-night. As for the young man, in the inquiries I made concerning him, I found nothing that was not straight and honest. I put him out of the list at an early date. Who the person may have been listening at the window I cannot say; but I conclude it was Miss Rebecca. She certainly did not attempt to carry off the parcel.

"This morning I discovered that an anonymous donation of twenty pounds was sent to Miss Rebecca's society the day after the first successful attempt at blackmail. I kept an eye on the house, and shortly after midday she walked down to Horledge's shop. He is the president of her society. They remained for some time together, and then Horledge took a train to London. I followed him to the newspaper room in the British Museum. Things were becoming plainer.

"I have now no doubt that Miss Rebecca guessed who we were from the first. She told the secret to Horledge, who was, you remember, one of her brother's chief opponents in the election, out of sheer feminine spite. I suspected the man would attempt something at the meeting on Friday night. My suspicion was correct, as you saw."

"And the election?"

"He won his seat on the Council. I think he deserved it, Mr. Phillips."

Next month will be told " The Mystery of the Causeway."

The Chronicles of Addington Peace.

By B. FLETCHER ROBINSON.

Joint Author with Sir A. Conan Doyle in his best Sherlock Holmes story, "The Hound of the Baskervilles."

The strange and startling experiences of that famous detective, Addington Peace,

Each story is complete in itself.

IV.—THE MYSTERY OF THE CAUSEWAY.

It was on Thursday, May 18th, 1899, that young Sir Andrew Cheyne was found dead of a gunshot wound in the grounds of Airlie Hall, his house in Surrey.

I was myself especially interested in the case, both because I was staying at a house within three miles of the Hall at the time, and because I thought that it was a case after Addington Peace's own heart. All the gossip came to us first hand. By breakfast we learned of the death. An hour later came the rumour of murder, and the fact that an arrest had been made. A man had been caught running from the spot where the body lay.

My host was a bachelor and a brother artist. His little cottage was bound by no conventions. Go or come, but don't trouble to explain—such was the custom. He was busy that morning, as I knew, so I appropriated his bicycle and set off through the lanes to visit the scene of the tragedy.

Airlie Hall lay some two hundred yards back from the main road. The drive, framed in white stretches of turf, and flanked by a triple avenue of chesnuts, ran in a straight line from the great porch to the entrance gates of twisted iron. Peering through the bars were a dozen villagers. Within, his hand upon the lock, stood a policeman, massive, red-faced, pompous with his present importance.

"May I come in?" I said politely.

"You may not," he said quite briefly.

I put my hand in my pocket, hesitated, and drew it out empty. It was too public a place for corruption. If Addington Peace had only been with me I thought—and so thinking came by an idea. Even a rural policeman would know the famous detective's name.

"My friend, Inspector Peace—" I began.

"Inspector who?" he interrupted.

"Addington Peace, of the Criminal Investigation Department. I hoped he would be here."

His manner changed with a celerity which was the greatest compliment he could have paid to the little detective.

"I beg your pardon, sir," he said. "The Inspector drove up from the station not ten minutes ago. If you will inquire at the Hall you will be sure to find him."

The servant who answered my modest ring led me through a dark passage of pannelled oak and out upon the terrace that lay on the farther side of the house. Below it a sloping lawn ran down to a broad lake fringed with heavy reeds. Beyond the lake a great park stretched away dotted with single oaks now struggling into foliage. It was a lovely view, unmolested by the centuries. As it was so it had been three hundred years before when some courtier of Elizabeth in tightly-fitting hose and immaculate ruffles chose it as the outlook from the windows of his dining-room.

Copyright, 1904, in U.S.A., by the Transatlantic Alliance Ltd.

"Sir Andrew's been shot—shot dead—on the causeway to the island."

In the middle of the terrace, Addington Peace stood, smoking a cigarette and talking to a tall and stately person in a black coat, who looked every inch the man he was—the butler of a British country house.

The little Inspector turned as he heard my footsteps on the gravel and nodded a benevolent welcome.

"A fine morning, Mr. Phillips," he said. "I did not know you were staying in the neighbourhood."

"I cycled over after hearing the news. Your name opened the gates, Inspector."

"Well, I am pleased to see you anyhow. Mr. Roberts here was giving me his view of this unfortunate affair. You may continue, Mr. Roberts."

The butler had been staring at me with great suspicion; but apparently he concluded that as a friend of a detective I was a respectable person.

"Well, gentlemen," he said in a soft, oily voice, as from confirmed overeating, "my mind is, so to speak, a blank. But what I know I will say without fear or favour. Sir Andrew had not previously honoured us with his presence, he having remained abroad from the death of Sir William, which was his uncle, some six months ago. Yesterday—that is, Thursday morning—he wired from London for a carriage to meet the 12.32 train. We were all in a flutter of excitement, as you can well imagine. But when he arrived, it was, he said, with no intention of staying the night. During the afternoon he saw his agent on business, and afterwards went for a walk, returning about six. He dined at eight, and had his coffee served in the small library.

"The last train to London was at 11.25, and we had our orders for a carriage to be ready for him at five minutes to the hour. At eleven o'clock precisely I took the liberty of entering the small library to inform Sir Andrew that the carriage was waiting, and that there was only just time to catch the train. He was not there, and, the windows on to the terrace being open, I walked through to see if he was sitting outside, the evening being salubrious for the time of the year. It was while I was there that I heard the footsteps of someone running on the gravel, and, first thing I knew, who should appear but Jake Warner, the keeper. 'Hello, Mr. Warner,' I says, 'and where may you be going in such a hurry? Is it poachers?' I says. 'No,' says he, in a sad taking, 'but Sir Andrew's been shot—shot dead, Mr. Roberts, on the causeway to the island.' 'Heaven defend us,' I says, 'but do——'"

"Quite so, Mr. Roberts," said Peace.

"We understand you were much upset. So you have no idea when it was that Sir Andrew left the little library?"

"No, sir, save that it was between 9.30 and 11.0."

"Thank you. And now, Mr. Phillips, I think we will go down and have a look at the causeway walk."

At the end of the terrace we found a policeman waiting. He touched his helmet to the Inspector, and, after a few words with him, led the way down some moss-grown steps and over a sloping lawn towards the lake. We skirted the righthand edge for perhaps two hundred yards, until we came to where a short causeway of stone had been built out into the water, joining the lawns to a shrub-grown island. The roof of a gabled cottage peeped out from the heart of its yews and laurels. The causeway, paved with great slabs of slate, was never more than five feet broad. On either side of it was a dense growth of feathery reeds, hiding the lake behind their rustling walls.

"What cottage is that?" asked Peace, pointing a finger.

"When he was a young man, Sir William, that was Sir Andrew's uncle, used to give lunches and teas there in the summer months," said the policeman. "But the place has been shut up for a long time now, sir. No one goes to the island barring the ducks, and they nest there by the hundred."

"Where did you catch the prisoner?"

"About this very place, sir. It was about half-past ten, and I was walking down the public footpath, which passes the east corner of the lake when I heard the shot. It seemed a strange time of the year for night poaching, but there are rascals in the village who wouldn't hesitate about the seasons so long as they had a duck for dinner.

"Off I raced as hard as I could put legs to the ground. When I came to the causeway head I pulled up and looked about me. There was a slip of a moon over the island, and a plenty of stars, so that the night was fairly bright. No one was in sight, but presently I heard the thump, thump, of a man running over turf, and who should come panting down the slope but Jake Warner, the keeper. He was in such a hurry that he was nigh as close as I am to you, sir, before he saw me.

"'Good Lord,' he cried, jumping back; 'and what are you doing here?'

"'Didn't you hear a shot fired?' I asked.

"'Not a sound of it,' he said, with a sulky face on him.

"It surprised me more than a bit. Indeed, I had begun to wonder if I could have been mistaken, when there came a clatter on the slabs of the causeway, and a man rushed out from the reeds like a mad thing. He gave a scream like a frightened rabbit when he caught sight of us, and tried to twist away, but his feet slipped from under him, and down he fell. Before he could recover I was sitting on his chest.

"'I had no hand in it,' he shouted. 'I swear to you it was not me. I was to meet him on the island. He was dead when I came to him.'

"'Dead—who is dead?' asked Jake, very anxious.

"'Sir Andrew Cheyne,' said the man, with a shiver.

"I was that taken aback that if he had made a run for it he might have done so for all I could have stopped him. As for Jake, he gave a yelp and disappeared down the causeway, like a rat into a hole. 'Sir Andrew is in France,' I said, for so Mr. Roberts had told me not a week before. 'You're crazy, man.'

"'Shut your mouth, you fool'—those were his very words, sir—'I tell you Cheyne is dead. Go and look for yourself.'

"'I must trouble you to come with me, then,' said I, taking him by the collar.

"We walked down the causeway between the reeds, he in front and me behind with my hand in his neck. About halfway down we came upon Jake, who was kneeling by the body, which lay flat on its back. I had never seen Sir Andrew and no more had Jake, so we had to take the stranger's word for it. When we found there was no sign of life left in him, I sent Jake to get assistance. He came back with Mr. Roberts and two of the men, who carried away the body up to the house, while I arrested my prisoner and walked him off to the lock-up. We found a loaded revolver upon him. He refused to say who he was or to make any explanation."

"And afterwards?" asked Addington Peace.

"I searched the causeway as soon as it was light. There was nothing to be found. But the evidence against the prisoner seems clear enough, saving the fact that the shotgun he used has disappeared. He must have thrown it into the water. They will drag the lake for it this afternoon. We've got the real murderer all right, don't you think, sir?"

"Did you search the island before you left last night?"

"No, sir."

"Might not another man have been concealed there?"

The policeman did not reply, save by colouring a deeper red and staring hard at his boots.

"Well, well, no one can think of everything," said Peace, with a flicker of a smile. "Come and show me where you found him."

The dark stain upon the slabs between the nodding reeds was sign-post sufficient. The little detective took one look at the spot, and then stood with his hands behind his back, peering about him.

"Were the prisoner's clothes wet?" he asked quietly.

"No, sir, quite dry."

"And how deep is the lake?"

"From three to six feet or so, I've always heard."

"Is there a boat on it?"

"Jake keeps an old punt, I believe, but the pleasure craft are under lock and key in the boathouse. They've not been in the water for years, and would leak like sieves."

"That is all. Go up to the house and wait for me there. I shall be back in an hour or so."

The policeman saluted and retired down the causeway, his heavy boots clattering upon the stones.

"Now we can get to work, Mr. Phillips," said the little man cheerfully, his eyes behind the gold-rimmed glasses dancing with a pleasant expectation. "While I am making a little examination of the causeway, I should be obliged if you will wait for me at the cottage on the island yonder."

The last thing I saw of him was a neat boot sticking out from the reeds into which he was crawling on hands and knees.

The cottage was an old-fashioned, one-storeyed building. The red tiles of its gabled roof had been delicately toned by age until they had sunk to a colour very restful to an artist's eye. Wooden shutters blocked the windows; its door of stained and worm-eaten oak was firmly secured. A path led through straggling laurel bushes from the door to the lake, and I walked down it to the loud outcry of the nesting ducks that rose with flapping wings about me and circled round to splash into the water at a safe distance. By a dilapidated wooden landing-stage I stopped to light a cigarette. As I threw away the match a ragged tear in the deep moss that covered the planking caught my eye. I stooped to examine it. Under the moss the wood itself was seared with a deep, fresh scar! I studied the rest of the landing-stage without result. Neither the moss nor the exposed patches of woodwork showed any similar signs. The one fresh scar—that was all.

I was still considering the problem when Peace joined me. He was in high good humour. For a time he stared at the mark with his head on one side like a meditative sparrow, and then, seizing me by the arm, led me back by the way we had come.

"Picturesque, eh?" he said, pointing to the old pavilion. "It catches your artistic eye. Perhaps you will have time to make a sketch of it this afternoon."

"Nonsense," I said, irritably enough. "Who shot this poor fellow?"

"No one."

"What—suicide?"

"Nothing so simple, I'm afraid. Now, don't lose your temper. You will understand within the hour. Come along."

"Where are we going?"

"To visit our esteemed friend Jake Warner. There is just a chance he may show temper. Shall we risk it, Mr. Phillips, or shall we call the policeman from the house yonder?"

I told him quite briefly that I would see the policeman condemned first.

Warner's cottage was a straw-thatched, ivy-covered little place, built on the slope of the park. Beneath it a brook that carried the overflow from the lake gurgled monotonously by. A thin, long-legged man, who was digging in a patch of garden, stopped his work at sight of us and waited.

"Jake Warner, isn't it?" Peace inquired over the low fence of split pine.

"Yes, sir."

"I am Inspector Addington Peace, of the Criminal Investigation Department."

Warner said nothing, but I saw his fingers clench upon his spade, as he gave the detective stare for stare.

"A fairly good breeding season for the ducks, I should imagine." continued the little man with a benevolent interest.

There was still no reply.

"I understand the foxes are very troublesome."

Warner threw down his spade and strode up to where we stood. His eyes had in them the dumb agony of a wild thing in a trap.

"I am a married man, sir," he said. "For my wife's sake take me away quietly."

"I have not come to arrest you, Jake Warner," said Peace. "If you are responsible for your master's death, it was by sheer accident. But the question is, are you responsible?"

"No, sir, I am not. But I can never prove it."

"Perhaps it would be best if you explained.

We remained where we were, with the fence between us, while he told his story.

"It was on Monday afternoon, sir," he said, addressing the detective. "I was crossing the public footpath that runs near

Warner said nothing, but I saw his fingers clench upon his spade.

the other end of the lake, when I fell in with a middle-aged, spectacled gentleman, who was strolling along with a tin collecting-case on his back, such as botanists use. We fell to talking, and one thing led to another, until, when I turned off down to the lake to see after my ducks, he came with me. He never meant no harm as I know of, but I would give all I have never to have seen him."

"What was he like?" asked the Inspector.

"A short fellow with a brown full beard and a slight stutter. Very pleasant he was to talk to; but this is outside the point, sir, as you will see. We walked down the causeway, and just before the pavilion what should we come across but three dead birds, all with their heads bitten clean off. It made me wild, for the foxes have been plaguing me cruel this spring. Sir William never would have one shot, though he had given up hunting many years. As for the young master, I couldn't say as to his views, for I had never set eyes upon him.

"The stranger, he sympathised very kindly with me and I told him my troubles. 'How can they expect a keeper to rear a decent lot of wild duck with a plague of foxes in his midst, I'm dashed if I know,' I said. He allowed that a fox who would kill ducks like that was as bad as a man-eating tiger. 'She's a cunning old vixen as won't let me get within shot of her,' I told him, 'but I've half a mind to set a spring gun for her on the causeway here.'

"Bless my soul, how that fellow laughed. He threw back his head and crowed with joy at my idea. 'A spring gun for a fox,' he says; 'why, keeper, it's the very thing. Think of the simplicity of it and the certainty of it and the security of it.' Those were his words. After that he sobered down and began talking more serious. Did I understand how to set a spring gun? I told him no; and then he explained how he had a friend from India who had often used them to kill jackals. Whether I did right or wrong, the fact is that I agreed to set the gun when he sent me the instructions.

"Well, sir, his letter arrived yesterday morning with careful little plans and all. I loaded my gun with buckshot and carried it down to the causeway shortly after dusk. I had lost several more ducks each day, and my mind was made up to have that old vixen. I fixed the gun with a thread of strong cotton across the path and round the trigger. You may think I took a wicked risk, but I had hardly ever known anyone to pass along the causeway in the daytime, far less at night. Yet, for safety's sake, I meant to take it up again at dawn.

"I walked home and sat smoking my pipe for a while. But I was worried and disturbed. I couldn't get it from my mind that there was danger in that spring gun left to itself as it were. Even if I bagged the old vixen someone might hear the shot and find the body. A dead fox would make me a marked man amongst all the hunting people about. I didn't like that thought neither. At last I couldn't stand it no longer, and set off back to the causeway. I was more than half way when I heard the shot and that set me running."

"I know the rest, Warner," said Peace; "but I want a few details. Did you see any sign of another man?"

"No, sir."

"Where was Sir Andrew hit?"

"The chest, sir; he got it full in the chest.

"So I understood. A curious elevation of the muzzle, eh? Did you expect a fox over five feet high?"

Peace brought out the words with a snap, but the under-keeper answered him without hesitation.

"That is the point, sir," he said. "That is why I am not responsible for the master's death. I set the gun at a level of one foot two inches from the ground, which I reckoned would take the fox about the shoulder. Someone altered the elevation of the muzzle after I had gone."

"The second forked stick that supported the gun was in the mud. Might it not have sunk under the weight, and thus raised the muzzle?"

"No, sir. I had pushed it through the mud down to the gravel. It was a good foot deeper when I went to look at it. A man must have used great force to get it so far through the gravel."

"What became of the gun?"

"After they carried Sir Andrew away, I must have gone off my head for awhile. What would they say to me for setting such a trap for my master? That was the only thing I could think about. I ran back and pulled up the sticks, and carried away the gun to the cottage here."

"But you saw the policeman arrest the man whom we may presume to be the murderer?"

"Yes, sir; but I was too wild to reason it out. I made up my mind this morning to tell them all about it at the inquest. That is the truth."

"Did you use the punt last night?"

"No, sir, it must have been the man that was caught. I missed her this morning, and after a search found her in the reeds near the island where she had drifted. Though I don't see how you could have known anything about the punt, sir."

"The iron shod pole had chipped the landing-stage. Please fetch me the plans and the gun."

When Warner returned, Peace slipped the envelope into his pocket, and examined the weapon with great care, snapping the lock twice.

"You had eased the trigger, eh?"

"Yes, sir; I thought a light pull would be best, so I oiled and loosened the screws."

The little man handed it back to him and turned away, staring over the lake towards the distant woodlands, with his podgy hands clasped behind his back.

"That fellow, sir—he must have done it, don't you think?" asked the under-keeper.

"So it would seem, Warner," said Addington Peace over his shoulder.

* * * * *

It was eleven o'clock on the following day when Peace was announced. I was sitting in the garden of my friend's cottage smoking my pipe and reading the paper. From within the villa came the sound of whistling that told of my host working at his Academy picture.

"Why, Peace," I said, "what brings you here?"

He seated himself on a corner of the garden bench and lit a cigarette.

"I went back to London last night," he told me. "And as I had to pass the cottage on the way from the station to Airlie Hall, I thought I would call in and see you."

"Any further news?"

"I have had an interesting visit. The botanist with the beard has stepped into a leading part in our little tragedy, Mr. Phillips."

"Do you mean——"

"Yes, I believe him to be the murderer of Sir Andrew Cheyne."

"Then the man under arrest is innocent."

"That scarcely describes him—but he had no hand in this crime."

"Confound you and your riddles," I said. "Where is the murderer? Have you caught him?"

"There is a carriage at the door. If you care to come along perhaps I may be able to show him to you."

It was a swift horse from the stables of Airlie Hall, and we covered the ground quickly. There was little talk between us. Twelve had struck when we stepped out at the overhanging porch of the old grey mansion and walked through into the library that overlooked the terrace and the lake. By the window, twisting his cap in his nervous fingers, stood Jake Warner. Peace nodded him a good-morning, and then slipped away with a word of apology.

"The detective gentleman wired that he wanted to see me," said Warner anxiously. "Do you know why, sir?"

I told him no, and he dropped into an uneasy silence. I amused myself by walking from picture to picture, for the walls were hung with splendid portraits — Gainsborough, Lely, and Romney—it was a veritable exhibition of those great masters. At last the door opened and the little man appeared, glancing from one to the other of us with his shrewd, observant eyes.

"Will you follow me, if you please?" he said.

We tramped up the great staircase, a wide sweep of polished oak, where a dozen men could have walked abreast, and so down a high-roofed passage into a majestic bedroom. In the centre stood a venerable four-post bedstead. The columns that supported the canopy were finely carved, and over the head was a faded coat of arms pictured in the needlework of two hundred years ago. The lattice windows were open. From without came the faint piping of the nesting birds.

Upon the bed lay something covered with white sheeting.

Peace walked up to it and paused, staring hard at the keeper, who stood beside me. Then with a gentle hand he lifted the sheet. On the pillows lay the head of an elderly man, dark, and full bearded.

Warner stepped back, clutching my arm.

"It's the botanist," he stammered. "What is he doing here? Was it him as killed the master, sir?"

"Yes," said the little detective; "he killed Sir Andrew Cheyne."

For a moment he stooped, busying himself about the head. With a gentle pull he lifted the heavy beard away. It was a face younger by a score of years that lay upon the pillows, a face handsome, after its fashion, though deep lined with evil days and ways.

"Sir Andrew, himself," cried Warner, with a sob of terror.

"That is also true," said Inspector Addington Peace, reverently replacing the white sheet.

* * * * *

It was an hour afterwards that Peace gave me the details. We were leaning against the stone balustrade of the terrace looking over the lake to the pleasant park land beyond. The breeze-swept rushes that marked the line of the causeway, the gables of the island pavilion that peeped above the foliage, lay to our right, framed in the rippling blue of the mere.

"My first important discovery," he said, "was a strand of pack thread tied to a young sapling at the spot where the body of Sir Andrew was found. On the other side of the path was a narrow hole between the slabs of granite, where a peg had lately been driven in. The rushes about it were broken here and there. The conclusion of a spring gun was obvious, and the reason suggested by the track of foxes along the edge of the reeds. Was the death an accident after all? If so, what business had the stranger under arrest—Fenton, I now find, is his name—upon the island at so late an hour?

"My conversation with the keeper gave some interesting results. It was plainly murder, and no accident. Someone had raised the muzzle of the gun so that it might kill a man and not a fox. Someone had expected a visitor to the island that night against whom he desired to revenge himself. Was Fenton guilty? The evidence against him seemed almost conclusive. He had admitted, you will remember, that he had an appointment with Sir Andrew. Yet, after he had set the trap, why had he continued to risk discovery by loitering about the causeway? How had he known that the spring gun was there at all? Why had he brought a loaded revolver? Why had he borrowed the punt and reached the island by so unexpected a manner? Was he also afraid of someone or some thing? My mind began to turn from him to the second stranger, the botanist with the collecting case. He at least had information about the setting of the gun.

"If you go there before settling with me, I communicate with the police at once."

"There was still a further point. Sir Andrew had been shot full in the chest. If he had been walking down the causeway he would have been hit in the side. How was that?

"Yesterday morning after I sent you away I walked into the village to make inquiries. They have few visitors, and the landlord of the inn remembered the bearded naturalist. He had only once visited the place, driving over from the station, and disappearing for several hours. A hot-tempered man, nervous and excitable—so he described him. When the cab was late he had broken out in a foreign tongue. That was all he knew of him.

"I caught the 3.15 to London and found Scotland Yard in the possession of some additional details. Sir Andrew had been in town for a fortnight living very quietly at a small private hotel off Piccadilly. He had no servant with him. He had been a wild, extravagant lad, they told me, and when his uncle had tired of paying his bills he had tried the stage, got deeper into debt, and finally fled to the Continent, where he lived on a small allowance that the old man made him. All this struck me as curious. The rake had indeed reformed if he heralded his accession to great wealth by dropping a servant and living quietly in a small hotel. Had he other reasons than economy?

"I visited the hotel that night. Sir Andrew had received few callers, the porter told me. I described the botanist, but without success. Then I tried Fenton. The porter recognised my description at once. He had called twice, the first time shortly after Sir Andrew's arrival, the second time on Tuesday evening. The waiter who had taken him up to the baronet's sitting-room told me that the first interview had been long, and that they had quarrelled violently on the stairs.

"'You shall never so much as see the place. If you go there before settling with me I communicate with the police at once.' He remembered some such threat shouted by Fenton on leaving. The second interview had been short, and, so far as he knew, friendly.

"I made a careful search of Sir Andrew's room. It was there that I solved the problem of the mystery; for in his dressing-case was an old 'make-up' box, no doubt a survival from his days upon the stage; and in the box was a full brown beard!"

"And so he was the botanist?" I said with a shiver.

"Yes, Mr. Phillips, he was the botanist."

There was silence between us for a while. I looked up at the splendid front of the ancient hall, and then across the lawns, over the sparkling mere to the park and the forest lands beyond.

"Was it for this?" I asked with a wave of the hand.

"Yes," said Peace, "I believe it to have been for Airlie Hall that he tried to kill Fenton. Heaven knows what dismal scandal the man held over him; but it was probably sufficient to drive Sir Andrew from England for ever. From inquiries made by the police, it appears that Fenton had been living on Sir Andrew for over two years. It was undoubtedly a bad case of blackmail. The young man, on hearing of his uncle's death, gave his persecutor the slip, and crossed to London. Fenton followed, and discovered him at his hotel. Probably he demanded a large sum, which was refused him. Whereupon he declared that the baronet should never so much as see Airlie Hall unless he paid, and left the young man with that threat upon him.

"For a time Sir Andrew stayed sulking in his rooms. He was a man of violent temper and unscrupulous past. Heaven knows what schemes of revenge he hatched in his rage and despair. Finally, on Monday last, he risked discovery, disguised himself in the beard, and went down to see the old place again. His meeting with the keeper was a chance, and their talk of spring-guns an equal accident. But the suggestion gave the baronet an idea. 'A spring-gun for a fox'—you remember his words as Warner told us. He laughed with hysterical joy at a means that would rid him of his enemy so simply and certainly. He made the excuse of the Indian friend, and saw Fenton again on Tuesday, giving him an appointment on the island at twelve o'clock on the following Thursday night, and at the same time promising to pay him what he asked at the meeting. By the last post on Wednesday he sent the plans to Warner in disguised handwriting and under a false name and address.

"Fenton suspected this sudden acquiescence. The scamp knew to what a state of impotent fury he had brought his victim. He took a revolver with him, and, having spied out the ground, crossed by the punt, instead of approaching the rendezvous by the causeway. Also, he came an hour and more before he was expected.

"Perhaps you now understand the plan. Sir Andrew would alter the gun and leave for the station before eleven. Fenton would be killed at twelve, and the blame rest on Warner. No one could suspect the young baronet, who would be in the train at the time of the accident.

"Sir Andrew found the trap, lifted the gun off the supporting props, and drove the outer one a foot deeper into the ground. I could see the marks of his feet, where he had stood while he pushed and twisted the stick through the clay. He replaced the gun, which would now be at an angle to hit a man in the chest or neck. He stepped back, looking to see if there was any sign of the lurking death to alarm a passer-by.

"What happened I can only guess. He may have slipped on the old slabs. But it was enough that he touched the thread, and the trigger, oiled and eased by Warner, jarred off at once. It was in a manner suicide."

"So that is the explanation," I said, when he had ended.

"It is partly guess work, of course," Peace told me; "but I think you will find that I am not far wrong when Fenton's trial comes on and, to save his neck, he makes a clean breast of his share in the business."

The trigger, oiled and eased by Warner, jarred off at once. It was in a manner suicide.

Next month the story of " The Vanished Millionaire " will be told.

The Chronicles of Addington Peace.

By B. FLETCHER ROBINSON.

Joint Author with Sir A. Conan Doyle in his best Sherlock Holmes story, "The Hound of the Baskervilles."

THE STRANGE AND STARTLING EXPERIENCES OF THAT FAMOUS DETECTIVE, ADDINGTON PEACE.

EACH STORY IS COMPLETE IN ITSELF.

V.—THE VANISHED MILLIONAIRE.

I, JAMES PHILLIPS, stood with my back to the fire, smoking and puzzling over it. It was worth all the headlines the newspapers had given it; there was no loophole to the mystery.

Both sides of the Atlantic knew Silas J. Ford. He had established a business reputation in America that had made him a celebrity in England from the day he stepped off the liner. Once in London his syndicates and companies and consolidations had startled the slow-moving British mind. The commercial sky of the United Kingdom was overshadowed by him and his schemes. The papers were full of praise and blame, of puffs and denunciations. He was a millionaire; he was on the verge of a smash that would paralyse the markets of the world. He was an abstainer, a drunkard, a gambler, a most religious man. He was a confirmed bachelor, a woman hater; his engagement was to be announced shortly. So was the gossip kept rolling with the limelight always centred upon the spot where Silas J. Ford happened to be standing.

And now he had disappeared, vanished, evaporated.

On the night of December 18th, a Thursday, he had left London for Meudon Hall, the fine old Hampshire mansion that he had rented from Lord Beverley. The two most trusted men in his office accompanied him. Friday morning he had spent with them; but at three o'clock the pair had returned to London, leaving their chief behind.

From four to seven he had been shut up with his secretary. It was a hard time for everyone, a time verging upon panic, and at such times Silas J. Ford was not an idle man.

At eight o'clock he had dined. His one recreation was music, and after the meal he had played the organ in the picture gallery for an hour. At a quarter past eleven he retired to his bedroom, dismissing Jackson, his body servant, for the night. Three quarters-of-an-hour later, however, Harbord, his secretary, had been called to the private telephone, for Mr. Ford had brought an extension wire from the neighbouring town of Camdon. It was a London message, and so urgent that he decided to wake his chief. There was no answer to his knock, and on entering the room he found that Mr. Ford was not in bed. He was surprised, but in no way suspicious, and started to search the house. He was joined by a footman, and, a little later, by Jackson and the butler. Astonishment changed to alarm. Other servants were roused to aid in the quest. Finally, a party, provided with lanterns from the stables, commenced to examine the grounds.

Snow had fallen early in the day, covering the great lawns in front of the entrance porch with a soft white blanket, about an inch in thickness. It was the head groom who struck the trail. Apparently Mr. Ford had walked out of the porch, and so over the

Copyright, 1904, in U S.A., by the Transatlantic Press Alliance, Ltd.

drive and across the lawn towards the wall that bounded the public road. This road, which led from Meudon village to the town of Camdon, crossed the front of Meudon Hall at a distance of some quarter of a mile.

There was no doubt as to the identity of the footprints, for Silas Ford affected a broad, square-toed boot, easily recognisable from its unusual impression.

They tracked him by their lanterns to the park wall, and there all trace of him disappeared. The wall was of rough stone, easily surmountable by an active man. The snow that covered the road outside had been churned into muddy paste by the traffic of the day; there were no further footprints observable.

The party returned to the house in great bewilderment. The telephone to London brought no explanation, and the following morning Mr. Harbord caught the first train to town to make inquiries. For private reasons his friends did not desire publicity for the affair, and it was not until the late afternoon, when all their investigations had proved fruitless, that they communicated with Scotland Yard. When the papers went to press the whereabouts of the great Mr. Ford still remained a mystery.

In keen curiosity I set off up the stairs to Inspector Peace's room. Perhaps the little detective had later news to give me.

I found him standing with his back to the fire puffing at his cigarette with a plump solemnity. A bag, neatly shaped, lay on the rug at his feet. He nodded a welcome, watching me over his glasses.

"I expected you, Mr. Phillips," he said. "And how do you explain it?"

"A love affair or temporary insanity," I suggested vaguely.

"Surely we can combine those solutions," he smiled. "Anything else?"

"No. I came to ask your opinion."

"My mind is void of theories, Mr. Phillips, and I shall endeavour to keep it so for the present. If you wish to amuse yourself by discussing possibilities, I would suggest your consideration of the reason why, if he wanted to disappear quietly, he should leave so obvious a track through the snow of his own lawn. For myself, as I am leaving for Camdon *via* Waterloo Station in ten minutes, I shall hope for more definite data before night."

"Peace," I asked him eagerly, "may I come with you?"

"If you can be ready in time," he said.

It was past two o'clock when we arrived at the old town of Camdon. A carriage met us at the station. Five minutes more and we were clear of the narrow streets and climbing the first bare ridge of the downs. It was a desolate prospect enough—a bare expanse of wind-swept land that rose and fell with the sweeping regularity of the Pacific swell. Here and there a clump of ragged firs showed black against the snow. Under that gentle carpet the crisp turf of the crests and the broad plough lands of the lower ground alike lay hidden. I shivered, drawing my coat more closely about me.

It was half-an-hour later that we topped a swelling rise and saw the grey towers of the ancient mansion beneath us. In the shelter of the valley by the quiet river, that now lay frozen into silence, the trees had grown into splendid woodlands, circling the hall on the further side. From the broad front the white lawns crept down to the road on which we were driving. Dark masses of shrubberies and the tracery of scattered trees broke their silent curves. The park wall that fenced them from the road stood out like an ink line ruled upon paper.

"It must have been there that he disappeared," I cried, with a speculative finger.

"So I imagine," said Peace. "And if he has spent two nights on the Hampshire downs, he will be looking for a fire to-day. You have rather more than your fair share of the rug, Mr. Phillips, if you will excuse my mentioning it."

A man was standing on the steps of the entrance porch when we drove up. As we unrolled ourselves he stepped forward to help us. He was a thin, pale-faced fellow, with fair hair and indeterminate eyes.

"My name is Harbord," he said. "You are Inspector Addington Peace, I believe."

His hand shook as he stretched it out in a

tremulous greeting. Plainly the secretary was afraid, visibly and anxiously afraid.

"Mr. Ransom, the manager of Mr. Ford's London office, is here," he continued. "He is waiting to see you in the library."

We followed him through a great hall into a room lined with books from floor to ceiling. A stout, dark man, who was pacing it like a beast in a cage, stopped at the sight of us. His face, as he turned it towards us, looked pinched and grey in the full light.

"Inspector Peace, eh?" he said. "Well, Inspector, if you want a reward name it. If you want to pull the house down only say the word. But find him for us, or, by heaven, we're done."

"Is it as bad as that?"

"You can keep a secret I suppose. Yes —it couldn't well be worse. It was a tricky time; he hid half his schemes in his own head; he never trusted even me altogether. If he were dead I could plan something, but now——"

He thumped his hand on the table and turned away to the window.

"When you last saw Mr. Ford was he in good health. Did he stand the strain?"

"Ford had no nerves. He was never better in his life."

"In these great transactions he would have his enemies. If his plans succeeded there would be many hard hit, perhaps ruined. Have you any suspicion of a man who, to save himself, might make away with Mr. Ford?"

"No," said the manager after a moment's thought. "No, I cannot give you a single name. The players are all big men, Inspector. I don't say that their consciences would stop them from trying such a trick, but it wouldn't be worth their while. They hold off when gaol is the certain punishment."

"Was this financial crisis in his own affairs generally known?"

"Certainly not."

"Who would know of it?"

"There might be a dozen men on both sides of the Atlantic who would suspect the truth. But I don't suppose that more than four people were actually in possession of the facts."

"And who would they be?"

"His two partners in America; myself, and Mr. Harbord there."

Peace turned to the young man with a smile and a polite bow.

"You have simply trampled them out of existence, between you."

"Can you add any names to the list?" he asked.

"No," said Harbord, staring at the detective with a puzzled look, as if trying to catch the drift of his questions.

"Thank you," said the inspector; "and now will you show me the place where this curious disappearance occurred?"

We crossed the drive, where the snow lay torn and trampled by the carriages, and so to the white, even surface of the lawn. We soon struck the trail, a confused path beaten by many footprints. Peace stooped for a moment, and then turned to the secretary with an angry glance.

"Were you with them?" he said.

"Yes."

"Then why, in the name of common sense, didn't you keep them off his tracks? You have simply trampled them out of existence, between you."

"We were in a hurry, Inspector," said the secretary meekly. "We didn't think about it."

We walked forward, following the broad trail until we came to a circular patch of trodden snow. Evidently the searchers had stopped and stood talking together. On the further side I saw the footprints of a man plainly defined. There were some half-dozen clear impressions and they ended at the base of the old wall, which was some six feet in height.

"I am glad to see that you and your friends have left me something, Mr. Harbord," said the inspector.

He stepped forward and, kneeling down, examined the nearest footprint.

"Mr. Ford dressed for dinner?" he enquired, glancing up at the secretary.

"Certainly! Why do you ask?"

"Merely that he had on heavy shooting boots when he took this evening stroll. It will be interesting to discover what clothes he wore."

The inspector walked up to the wall, moving parallel to the tracks in the snow. With singular activity for his plump and unathletic figure he climbed to the top and seated himself while he stared about him. Then on his hands and knees he began to crawl forward along the coping. It was a quaint spectacle, but the extraordinary care and vigilance of the little man took the farce out of it.

Presently he stopped and looked down at us with a gentle smile.

"Please stay where you are," he said, and disappeared on the further side.

Harbord offered me a cigarette, and we waited with due obedience till the inspector's bullet head again broke the horizon as he struggled back to his position on the coping of the wall.

He seemed in a very pleasant temper when he joined us; but he said nothing of his discoveries, and I had grown too wise to inquire. When we reached the entrance hall he asked for Jackson, the valet, and in a couple of minutes the man appeared. He was a tall, hatchet-faced fellow, very neatly dressed in black. He made a little bow, and then stood watching us in a most respectful attitude.

"A queer business this, Jackson," said Addington Peace.

"Yes, sir."

"And what is your opinion on it?"

"To be frank, sir, I thought at first that Mr. Ford had run away; but now I don't know what to make of it."

"And why should he run away?"

"I have no idea, sir; but he seemed to me rather strange in his manner yesterday."

"Have you been with him long?"

"No, sir. I was valet to the Honourable John Dorn, Lord Beverley's second son. Mr. Ford took me from Mr. Dorn at the time he rented the Hall."

"I see. And now will you show me your master's room. I shall see you again later, Mr. Harbord," he continued; "in the meanwhile I will leave my assistant with you."

We sat and smoked in the secretary's room. He was not much of a talker, consuming cigarette after cigarette in silence. The winter dusk had already fallen when the Inspector joined us, and we retired to our rooms to prepare for dinner. I tried a word with Peace upon the staircase, but he shook his head and walked on.

The meal dragged itself to an end somehow, and we left Ransome with a second decanter of port before him. Peace slipped away again, and I consoled myself with a book in the library until half-past ten, when I walked off to bed. A servant was switching off the light in the hall when I mounted the great staircase.

My room was in the old wing at the further side of the picture gallery, and I had some difficulty in steering my way through the dark corridors. The mystery that hung over the house had shaken my nerves, and I remember that I started at every creak of a board and peered into the shadows as I passed along with, Heaven knows, what ghostly expectations. I was glad enough to close my door upon them and see the wood fire blazing cheerfully in the open hearth.

* * * * *

I woke with a start that left me sitting up in bed, with my heart thumping in my ribs like a piston rod. I am not generally a light sleeper, but, that night, even while I snored, my nerves were active. Someone had tapped at my door—that was my impression.

I listened with the uncertain fear that comes to the newly waked. Then I heard it again—on the wall near my head this time. A board creaked. Someone was groping his way down the dark corridor without. Presently he stopped, and a faint line of illumination sprang out under my door. It winked, and then grew still. He had lit a candle.

Assurance came with the streak of light. What was he doing, groping in the dark, if he had a candle with him? I crept over to the door, opened it, and stared cautiously out.

About a dozen feet away a man was standing, a striking figure against the light he carried. His back was towards me, but I could see that his hand was shading the candle from his eyes while he stared into the shadows that clung about the further end of the corridor.

Presently he began to move forward.

The picture gallery and the body of the house lay behind. The corridor in which he stood terminated in a window, set deep into the stone of the old walls. The man walked slowly, throwing the light to right and left.

His back was towards me, but I could see that his hand was shading the candle.

His attitude was of nervous expectation—that of a man who looked for something that he feared to see.

At the window he stopped, staring about him and listening. He examined the fastenings, and then tried a door on his right. It was locked against him. As he did so I caught his profile against the light. It was Harbord, the secretary. From where I stood he was not more than forty feet away. There was no possibility of a mistake.

As he turned to come back I retreated into my room, closing the door. The fellow was in a state of great agitation, and I could hear him muttering to himself as he walked. When he had passed by I peeped out to see him and his light dwindle, reach the corner by the picture gallery, and fade into a reflection, a darkness.

I took care to turn the key before I got back into bed.

I woke again at seven, and, hurrying on my clothes, set off to tell Peace all about it. I took him to the place, and together we examined the corridor. There were only two rooms beyond mine. The one on the left was occupied by Ransome; that on the right was a large store-room, the door of which was locked. The housekeeper kept the key, we learnt upon inquiry. Whom had Harbord followed? The problem was beyond me. As for Inspector Peace, he did not indulge in verbal speculations.

It was in the central hall that we encountered the secretary on his way to the breakfast-room. The man looked nervous and depressed; he nodded to us and was passing on, when Peace stopped him.

"Good-morning, Mr. Harbord," he said. "Can I have a word with you?"

"Certainly, Inspector. What is it?"

"I have a favour to ask. My assistant and myself have our hands full here. If necessary, could you help us by running up to London and——"

"For the day?" he interrupted.

"No, It may be an affair of three or four days."

"Then I must refuse. I am sorry, but——"

"Don't apologise, Mr. Harbord," said the little man, cheerfully. "I shall have to find someone else, that is all."

We walked into the breakfast-room, and a few minutes later Ransome appeared with a great bundle of letters and telegrams in his hand. He said not a word to any of us, but dropped into a chair, tearing open the envelopes and glancing at their contents. His face grew darker as he read, and once he thumped his hand upon the table with a crash that set the china jingling.

"Well, Inspector?" he said at last.

The little detective's head shook out a negative.

"Perhaps you require an incentive," he sneered. "Is it a matter of a reward?"

"No, Mr. Ransome; but it is becoming one of my personal reputation."

"Then, by thunder, you are in danger of losing it. Why don't you and your friend hustle instead of loitering around as if you were paid by the job? I tell you, man, there are thousands, hundreds of thousands melting, slipping through our fingers, every hour of the day."

He sprang from his seat and started his walk again, up and down, up and down, as we had first seen him.

"Shall you be returning to London?"

At the question the manager halted in his stride, staring sharply down into the Inspector's bland countenance.

"No," he said; "I shall stay here, Mr. Addington Peace, until such time as you have something definite to tell me."

"I have an inquiry to make which I would rather place in the hands of someone who has personal knowledge of Mr. Ford. Neither Mr. Harbord nor yourself desire to leave Meudon. Is there anyone else you can suggest?"

"There is Jackson, Ford's valet," said the manager, after a moment's thought. "He can go if you think him bright enough. I'll send for him."

While the footman who answered the bell was gone upon his errand, we waited in an uneasy silence. There was the shadow of an ugly mystery upon us all. Jackson, as he entered, was the only one who seemed at his ease. He stood there, a tall figure of all the respectabilities.

"The Inspector here wishes you to go to London, Jackson," said the manager. "He will explain the details. There is a fast train from Camdon at eleven."

"Certainly, sir. Do I return to-night?"

"No, Jackson," said Peace. "It will take a day or two."

The man took a couple of steps towards the door, hesitated, and then returned to his former place

"I beg your pardon, sir," he began, addressing Ransome. "But I would rather remain at Meudon under present circumstances."

"What on earth do you mean?" thundered the manager.

"Well, sir, I was the last to see Mr. Ford. There is, as it were, a suspicion upon me. I should like to be present while the search continues, both for his sake—and my own."

"Very kind of you, I'm sure," growled Ransome. "But you either do what I tell you, Jackson, or you pack your boxes and clear out. So be quick and make up your mind."

"I think you are treating me most unfairly, sir. But I cannot be persuaded out of what I know to be my duty."

"You impertinent rascal—!" began the furious manager. But Peace was already on his feet with a chubby hand outstretched.

"Perhaps, after all, I can make other arrangements, Mr. Ransome," he said. "It is natural that Jackson should consider his own reputation in this affair. That is all, Jackson; you may go now."

It was half-an-hour afterwards, when the end of breakfast had dispersed the party, that I spoke to Peace about it, offering to go to London myself and do my best to carry out his instructions.

"I had bad luck in my call for volunteers," he said.

"I should have thought they would have been glad enough to get the chance of work. They can find no particular amusement in loafing about the place all day."

"Doubtless they all had excellent reasons," he said with a smile. "But, anyway, you cannot be spared, Mr. Phillips."

"You flatter me."

"I want you to stay in your bedroom. Write, read, do what you like, but keep your door ajar. If anyone passes down the corridor, see where he goes, only don't let him know that you are watching him if you can help it. I will take my turn at half-past one. I don't mean to starve you."

I obeyed. After all, it was, in a manner, promotion that the Inspector had given me; yet it was a tedious, anxious time. No one came my way, barring a sour-looking housemaid. I tried to argue out the case, but the deeper I got the more conflicting grew my theories. was never more glad to see a friendly face than when the little man came in upon me.

The short winter's afternoon crept on, the Inspector and I taking turn and turn about in our sentry duty. Dinner-time came and went. I had been off duty from nine, but at ten-thirty I poured out a whisky and soda and went back to join him. He was sitting in the middle of the room smoking a pipe in great apparent satisfaction.

"Bed-time, isn't it?" I grumbled, sniffing at his strong tobacco.

"Oh, no," he said. "The fact is, we are going to sit up all night."

I threw myself on a couch by the window without reply. Perhaps I was not in the best of tempers; certainly I did not feel so.

"You insisted on coming down with me," he suggested.

"I know all about that," I told him. "I haven't complained, have I? If you want me to shut myself up for a week I'll do it; but I should prefer to have some idea of the reason why."

"I don't wish to create mysteries, Mr. Phillips," he said kindly; "but believe me there is nothing to be gained in vague discussions."

I know that settled it as far as he was concerned, so I nodded my head and filled a pipe. At eleven he walked across the room and switched off the light.

"If nothing happens you can take your turn in four hours from now," he said. "In the meanwhile get to sleep. I will keep the first watch."

shut my eyes, but there was no rest in me that night. I lay listening to the silence of the old house with a dull speculation. Somewhere far down in the lower floor a great gong-like clock chimed the hours and quarters. I heard them every one, from twelve to one, from one to two. Peace had stopped smoking. He sat as silent as a cat at a mousehole.

It must have been some fifteen minutes after two that I heard the faint, faint creak of a board in the corridor outside. I sat up, every nerve strung to a tense alertness. And then there came a sound I knew well, the soft drawing touch of a hand groping in the darkness as someone felt his way along the panelled walls. It passed us and was gone. Yet Peace never moved. Could he have fallen asleep? I whispered his name.

"Hush!"

The answer came to me like a gentle sigh.

One minute, two minutes more and the room sprang into sight under the steady glow of an electric hand-lamp. The Inspector rose from his seat and slid through the door with me upon his heels. The light he carried searched the clustered shadows; but the corridor was empty, nor was there any place where a man might hide.

"You waited too long," I whispered impatiently.

"The man is no fool, Mr. Phillips. Do you imagine that he was not listening and staring like a hunted beast. A noisy board, a stumble, or a flash of light, and we should have wasted a tiring day."

"Nevertheless he has got clear away."

"I think not."

As we crept forward I saw that a strip of the oak flooring along the walls was grey with dust. If it had been in such a neglected state in the afternoon I should surely have noticed it. In some curiosity I stooped to examine the phenomenon.

"Flour," whispered the little man touching my shoulder.

"Flour?"

"Yes. I sprinkled it myself. Look—there is the first result."

He steadied his light as he spoke, pointing with his other hand. On the powdery surface was the half footprint of a man.

The flour did not extend more than a couple of feet from the walls, so that it was only here and there that we caught up the trail. We had passed the bedroom on the left—yet the footprints still went on; we were at the store-room door, yet they still were visible before us. There was no other egress from the corridor. The tall window at the end was, as I knew, a good twenty feet from the ground. Had this man also vanished off the earth like Silas Ford?

Suddenly the inspector stopped, grasping my arm. The light he held fell upon two footprints close together. They were at right angles to the passage. Apparently the man had passed into the solid wall!

"Peace, what does this mean?"

You, sir, sitting peaceably at home, with a good light and an easy conscience, may think I was a timid fool; yet I was afraid —honestly and openly afraid. The little detective heard the news of it in my voice, for he gave me a reassuring pat upon the back.

"Have you never heard of a 'priest's hole?'" he whispered. "In the days when Meudon Hall was built, no country house was without its hiding-place. Protestants and priests, Royalists and Republicans, they all used the secret burrow at one time or another."

"How did he get in?"

"That is what we are here to discover, and as I have no wish to destroy Mr. Ford's old oak panels I think our simplest plan will be to wait until he comes back again."

The shadows leapt upon us as Peace extinguished the light he carried. The great window alone was luminous with the faint starlight that showed the tracery of its ancient stonework; for the rest, the darkness hedged us about in impenetrable barriers. Side by side, we stood by the wall in which we knew the secret entrance must exist.

It may have been ten minutes or more when from the distance—somewhere below our feet, or so it seemed to me—there came the faint echo of a closing door. It was only in such cold silence that we could have heard it. The time ticked on. Suddenly, upon the black of the floor, there shone a thin reflection like the slash of a sword—a reflection that grew into a broad gush of light as the sliding panel in the wall, six feet from where we stood, rose to the full opening. There followed another pause, during which I could see Peace draw himself together as if for some unusual exertion.

A shadow darkened the reflection on the floor, and a head came peering out. The light but half displayed the face, but I could see that the teeth were bare and glistening, like those of a man in some deadly expectation. The next moment he stepped across the threshold.

With a spring like the rush of a terrier,

With a spring like the rush of a terrier, Addington Peace was upon him.

Addington Peace was upon him, driving him off his balance with the impact of the blow. Before I could reach them, the little detective had him down, though he still kicked viciously until I lent a hand. The click of the handcuffs on his wrists ended the matter.

It was Ford's valet, the man Jackson.

We were not long by ourselves. I heard a key turned in the lock, and Ransome burst out of his room into the corridor like an angry bull. Almost at the same moment there sounded a quick patter of naked feet from behind us, and Harbord, the secretary, came running up, swinging a heavy stick in his hand. They both stopped at the edge of the patch of light in which we were, staring from us to the gaping hole in the wall.

"What in thunder are you about?" cried the manager.

"Finding a solution to your problem," said the little detective, getting to his feet.

"Perhaps, gentlemen, you will be good enough to follow me."

He stepped through the opening in the wall, and lifted the candle which the valet had placed on the floor whilst he was raising the panel from within. By its light I could see the first steps of a flight which led down into darkness.

"We will take Jackson with us," he continued. "Keep an eye on him, Mr. Phillips, if you please."

It was a strange procession that we made. First Peace, with the candle, then Ransome, with the valet, following, while I and Harbord brought up the rear. We descended some thirty steps, formed in the thickness of the wall, opened a heavy door, and so found ourselves in a narrow chamber, some twelve feet long by seven broad. Upon a mattress at the further end lay a man, gagged and bound. As the light fell upon his features, Ransome sprang forward, shouting his name.

"Silas Ford, by thunder!"

With eager fingers we loosened the gag and cut the ropes that bound his wrists. He sat up, turning his long, thin face from one to the other of us as he stretched the cramp from his limbs.

"Thank you, gentlemen," said he. "Well, Ransome, how are things?"

"Bad, sir; but it's not too late."

He nodded his head, passing his hands through his hair with a quick, nervous movement.

"You've caught my clever friend, I see. Kindly go through his pockets, will you? He has something I must ask him to return to me."

We found it in Jackson's pocket-book—a cheque, anti-dated a week, for five thousand pounds, with a covering letter to the manager of the bank. Ford took the bit of stamped paper, twisting it to and fro in his supple fingers.

"It was smart of you, Jackson," he said, addressing the bowed figure before him: "I give you credit for the idea. To kidnap a man just as he was bringing off a big deal—well, you would have earned the money."

"But how did you get down here?" struck in the manager.

"He told me that he had discovered an old hiding-place—a 'priest's hole,' he called it, and I walked into the trap as the best man may do sometimes. As we got to the bottom of that stairway he slipped a sack over my head and had me fixed in thirty seconds. He fed me himself twice a day, standing by to see I didn't holloa. When I paid up he was to have twenty-four hours' start; then he would let you know where I was. I held out awhile, but I gave in to-night. The delay was getting too dangerous. Have you a cigarette, Harbord? Thank you. And who may you be?"

It was to the detective he spoke.

"My name is Peace, Inspector Addington Peace, from Scotland Yard."

"And I owe my rescue to you?"

The little man bowed.

"You will have no reason to regret it. And what did they think had become of me, Inspector?"

"It was the general opinion that you had taken to yourself wings, Mr. Ford."

* * * * *

It was as we travelled up to town next day that Peace told me his story. I will set it down as briefly as may be.

"I soon came to the conclusion that Ford, whether dead or alive, was inside the grounds of Meudon Hall. If he had bolted, for some reason, by-the-way, which was perfectly incomprehensible, a man of his ability would not have left a broad trail across the centre of his lawn for all to see. There was, moreover, no trace of him that our men could ferret out at any station within reasonable distance. A motor was possible, but there were no marks of its presence next morning in the mud of the roads. That fact I learnt from a curious groom who had aided in the search, and who, with a similar idea upon him, had carefully examined the highway at daybreak.

"When I clambered to the top of the wall I found that the snow upon the coping had been dislodged. I traced the marks, as you saw, for about a dozen yards. Where they ended I, too, dropped to the ground outside. There I made a remarkable discovery. Upon a little drift of snow that lay in the shallow ditch beneath were more footprints. But they were not those of Ford. They were the marks of long and narrow boots, which led into the road, where they were lost in the track of a flock of sheep that had been driven over it the day before.

"I took a careful measurement of those footprints. They might, of course, belong to some private investigator; but they gave me an idea. Could some man have walked across the lawn in Ford's boots, changed them to his own on the top of the wall, and so departed? Was it the desire of someone to let it be supposed that Ford had run away?

"When I examined Ford's private rooms I was even more fortunate. From the boot-boy I discovered that the master had three pairs of shooting boots. There were three pairs in the stand. Someone had made a very serious mistake. Instead of hiding the pair he had used on the lawn, he had returned them to their place. The trick was becoming evident. But where was Ford? In the house or grounds, dead or alive, but where?

"I was able, through my friend the boot-boy, to examine the boots on the night of our arrival. My measurements corresponded with those that Jackson, the valet, wore. Was he acting for himself, or was Harbord, or even Ransome, in the secret? That, too, it was necessary to discover before I showed my hand.

"Your story of Harbord's midnight excursion supplied a clue. The secretary had evidently followed some man who had disappeared mysteriously. Could there be the entrance to a secret chamber in that corridor? That would explain the mystification of Harbord as well as the disappearance of Silas Ford. If so Harbord was not involved.

"If Ford were held a prisoner he must be fed. His gaoler must of necessity remain in the house. But the trap I set in the suggested journey to town was an experiment singularly unsuccessful, for all the three men I desired to test refused. However, if I were right about the secret chamber I could checkmate the blackmailer by keeping a watch on him from your room, which commanded the line of communications. But Jackson was clever enough to leave his victualling to the night time. I scattered the flour to try the result of that ancient trick. It was successful. That is all. Do you follow me?"

"Yes," said I; "but how did Jackson come to know the secret hiding place?"

"He has long been a servant of the house. You had better ask his old master."

With eager fingers we loosened the gag and cut the ropes that bound his wrists.

(Next month "The Mystery of the Jade Spear" will appear.)

The Chronicles of Addington Peace.

By B. FLETCHER ROBINSON.

Joint Author with Sir A. Conan Doyle in his best Sherlock Holmes story, "The Hound of the Baskervilles."

THE STRANGE AND STARTLING EXPERIENCES OF THAT FAMOUS DETECTIVE, ADDINGTON PEACE.

EACH STORY IS COMPLETE IN ITSELF.

VI.—THE MYSTERY OF THE JADE SPEAR.

"Are you Inspector Peace, sir?"

He looked what he was, a gardener's boy, and he stood on the platform of Richmond station regarding us with a solemn, if cherubic, countenance. The little Inspector nodded his head as he felt in his pocket for the tickets.

"I have a cab waiting for you, sir."

"Are you from the Elms?"

"Yes, sir. Miss Sherrick sent me to meet you, having heard as you were coming."

We walked up the steps to the roadway, climbed into the cab, and, with the boy on the box, dragged our way up the steep of the narrow street, past the Star and Garter, the hostelry of ancient glories, and so for a mile along the Kingston Road until, at a word from our youthful conductor, the cab drew up at a wicket-gate in a fence of split oak. As we stepped out a girl swung open the gate and stood confronting us.

She was a tall and graceful creature, with the delicacy of the blonde colouring a beautiful face. There was fear in her blue eyes, a fear that widened and fixed them; and a tremor of the full red lips that told of a great calamity.

"Inspector Addington Peace?"

"Yes, Miss Sherrick."

There was that about the little Inspector that ever invited the trust of the innocent, and also, to be frank, no inconsiderable proportion of the guilty, to their special disadvantage. I have noticed a similar confidence inspired by certain of the more famous doctors. So I was not surprised when Miss Sherrick walked up to him and laid her hand on his arm, with a confident appeal in her eyes.

"Do you know they have arrested him?" she said.

"I had not heard. What is his name?"

"Mr. Boyne."

"The man who found the body."

"Yes. The man I intend to marry."

I liked that sentence. It was stronger than any protestations of his innocence that she could have made. Peace marked it, too, for he smiled, watching her with his head to one side in his solemn fashion.

"You cannot think he is guilty," she said quietly. "You are too clever for that, Inspector Peace."

"My dear young lady, at two o'clock I heard that a Colonel Bulstrode, of the Elms, Richmond, had been stabbed to death in a road near his house. That was the single fact telegraphed to Scotland Yard. Taking my friend here, I caught the 2.35 from Waterloo Station. It is now half-past three. As you will observe, my work has not yet commenced."

"I sent the boy to meet you. I wished you to hear my story before you saw—the police up at the house. I should like to tell you all I know."

Copyright in U.S.A., 1905, by The Transatlantic Press Alliance, Ltd.

"That will, doubtless, be very valuable," said the little Inspector. "Can you find us a place where we shall not be disturbed?"

For answer she led the way through the wicket-gate. A couple of turns and the winding walk brought us to an open space in the laurels and rhododendrons. On the further side was a garden bench, and there we seated ourselves, waiting, with great anxiety on my part, at least, for further details of the tragedy.

"My father was a widower," said Miss Sherrick, "and when he died he left as my guardians and trustees my mother's two brothers, Colonel Bulstrode and Mr. Anstruther Bulstrode. Colonel Bulstrode, who had been in the Indian Staff Corps, had retired the year before my father's death, and taken this house. It was with him that I went to live. Richmond suited him, for he could spend the day at his London club and yet be home in plenty of time for dinner.

"My Uncle Anstruther was also an Anglo-Indian. He had been for many years a planter in Ceylon. It was on the Colonel's advice that he took a house near us when he came home this Spring.

"I first met Mr. Boyne last Christmas when we were skating on some flooded meadows by the Thames. He is a lawyer, and though he is doing well, is by no means a rich man. Unfortunately, I am an heiress, Inspector Peace."

"I understand, Miss Sherrick."

"Colonel Bulstrode expected me to make what he called a first-rate marriage. Mr. Boyne and I had been engaged for two weeks, and at last we decided to tell the Colonel. We knew there would be trouble, but there was nothing to be gained by continued postponement. Mr. Boyne made an appointment with him for one o'clock to-day.

"The morning seemed as if it were never to end. As the hour approached I could wait in my room no longer. I slipped out of a side door into the upper garden, which lies at the further side of the house. I wandered about for some time in great misery. When I heard the stable clock chime the half-hour, I started back to the house. It must have been decided between them one way or the other."

"I had reached the drive and was walking up to the front door when I saw Cullen, the butler, come running out of the Wilderness—as we call the shrubberies where we now are—and so across the lawn towards me. He was in an excited state, waving his arms and shouting. Cullen is so stout and respectable that I could only conclude that he had gone mad. When he was some twenty yards off he caught sight of me, and slunk away towards the front door as if trying to avoid me.

"'What is the matter, Cullen?' I called to him.

"He slackened his pace and finally stopped, with his eyes staring at me in an odd fashion.

"'You come in with me, miss,' he stammered. 'It's no mischief of your making. Eh, eh, but it's ugly work, black and ugly work.'

"'What do you mean, Cullen?' I said as boldly as I could, for his manner frightened me.

"'The Colonel has come by an accident, miss, down by the wicket-gate. I was going for a doctor.'

"I did not wait to hear more. I was very fond of my guardian, Mr. Peace. He had a hot temper, but to me he had ever been kind and considerate. As I started, however, Cullen came panting up and tried to turn me back, waving his hands. Lunatic or not, I did not mean to let him frighten me. So I avoided him and set off running across the grass to the Wilderness gate—the one through which we have just come. I had almost reached it when I met Mr. Boyne. I was surprised, for I thought he had already gone home. Beyond him I could see the gate, with two of our gardeners standing on the further side and talking earnestly together.

"I asked Mr. Boyne what was the matter, and for answer he took me by the arm and led me back towards the house. He looked very white and ill. I still begged for an explanation, and at last he told me the truth. My uncle, Colonel Bulstrode, had been found lying in the road stabbed to death with a spear. They had no idea who the murderer might be.

"They brought up the body to the house. Afterwards they let me see him. Even in death his face was convulsed with passion. Oh, it is dreadful, dreadful!"

Her reserve gave way all in a moment, and she burst into a fit of sobbing, hiding her face in her hands. It was some time before she regained her self-control, and when she spoke again it was with difficulty and in detached sentences.

"It was about three o'clock," she said, "Mr. Boyne came into the room where I was. He told me that my uncle had spoken very bitterly to him in their interview, and that there had been a quarrel between them; but Mr. Boyne's sorrow was sincere. I am sure it was sincere. Afterwards he begged me not to believe any rumours I might hear about him. Then he went away. Afterwards, as I was looking from the window, I saw him walking down the drive with a policeman. Several of the servants were gathered at the front door watching and pointing. I don't know how—but the suspicion came to me—perhaps it was through what Cullen had said. I ran down the stairs and ordered them to answer. At last they told me—he had been arrested—for the murder."

We waited for a while, and then the little Inspector rose, and, in his courteous manner, offered her his arm. She took it, looking at him through her tears.

"He is innocent, Mr. Peace," she said.

"I trust so, Miss Sherrick."

They moved off up the walk, I following behind them. We emerged from the shrubbery on to a broad lawn. The house, a sprawling old mansion of red brick, was before us. We crossed the grass, and, turning an angle of the house, came to the porch, from which a drive curled away amongst the foliage of an avenue of elms.

The central hall was better fitted for a museum than a habitation of comfort-loving folk. Bronze gods and goddesses glimmered in the corners, dragons carved in teak glared upon the Eastern arms and armour that lined the walls, the duller hues of ivory and jade contrasted with the brilliant turquoise of old Pekin vases. It was here, among these spoils of the East, that Miss Sherrick left us, walking up the stairs to her room, as fair a figure of beauty in distress as a man might see.

As she disappeared, a tall, thin fellow in plain clothes stepped out of a door on our right and saluted the Inspector.

"Good afternoon, Sergeant Hales," said Addington Peace. "So you have arrested Boyne?"

"Yes, sir."

"Upon good grounds?"

"The evidence is almost complete against him."

"Indeed. I shall be pleased to hear it."

"Well, sir, it stands like this. Mr. Boyne called upon Colonel Bulstrode about one o'clock. He was shown into the library and——"

"One moment," interrupted the Inspector. "Where is the library?"

"That is the door, sir," answered Hales, pointing to the room from which he had emerged.

"Perhaps it would be easier to understand if we go there?"

The library was a long, low room, lined with shelves that were in a great part empty. It projected from the main building—evidently it was of more recent construction—and thus could be lighted by windows on both sides. To our right were two which commanded the drive; to the left two more looked out upon a triangular plot of grass dotted with flower-beds, upon which several windows at the back of the house also faced.

"Pray continue," said Inspector Peace.

"About ten minutes later, Cullen, the butler, heard high words passing. A regular fighting quarrel it sounded—or so he says."

"How could he hear? Was he listening in the hall?"

"No, sir, he was in his pantry, cleaning silver. The pantry is the first of those windows at the back of the house. The library windows being open, he could hear the sound of loud voices, though, as he says, he could not distinguish the words."

The Inspector walked to an open lattice

and thrust out his head. He closed it before he came back to us, as he did to the second window on the same side.

"Mr. Cullen must not be encouraged," he said gently. "He is there now, listening with pardonable curiosity. Well, Sergeant?"

"Presently there came a tremendous peal at his bell, and he hurried to answer it. When he reached the hall, he found the Colonel and Mr. Boyne standing together. 'You understand me, Boyne,' the Colonel was saying, 'If I catch you lurking about here again after my niece's money-bags I'll thrash you within an inch of your life; I will, by thunder!' The young man gave the Colonel an ugly look, but he had seen the butler, who was standing behind his master, and kept silent. 'Show this fellow out, Cullen,' said the Colonel. 'And if he ever calls slam the door in his face.' And with that he stumped back into the library, swearing to himself in a manner that, as the butler declares, gave him the creeps, it was so very imaginative.

"With one thing and another, Cullen was so dumfounded—for he thought that Boyne and Miss Sherrick were as good as engaged already—that he stood in the shadow of the porch watching the young gentleman. Boyne walked down the drive for a hundred yards or so, looked back at the house, and, not seeing the butler as he supposes, turned off to the left along a path that led towards the fruit gardens. Cullen did not know what to make of it. However, it was none of his business, and at last he went back to his pantry. Sticking out his head, he could see the Colonel writing at that desk "—the Sergeant pointed a finger at a knee-hole table littered with papers that was set in the further of the windows looking out upon the grass-plot—"and so concluded that he could not have seen Boyne leave the drive, having had his back to it at the time.

"About twenty minutes later Cullen and Mary Thomas, the parlour-maid, were in the dining-room, getting the table ready for lunch. This room looks out upon the lawn at the front of the house. All of a sudden they heard a shout, and the next moment the Colonel rushed by and made across the lawn to the Wilderness gate. He had a revolver in his hand, and was loading it as he ran. He dropped two cartridges in his hurry, for I found them myself when I was going over the ground. Cullen had been with him for years; he is an old soldier himself, and at the sight of the revolver he dropped the tray he was holding, climbed out of the window, and set off after his master, who had by then disappeared amongst the shubberies.

"He is a slow traveller, is the old man, and he reckons that he was not more than half way across the lawn when he heard a distant scream, which pulled him up in his tracks. It put the fear into him, that scream. He told me that he had seen too much active service not to know the cry that comes from a sudden and mortal wound. It was no surprise to him, when at last he reached the wicket-gate, to find his master lying dead in the road.

"Above him, tugging at the spear that had killed him, stood Boyne.

"There was no one in sight, and though the road curves at that point he could see it for fifty yards and more either way. He had no doubt in his own mind as to who had done the thing. Boyne must have seen the suspicion in his face, for he jumped back, Cullen says, and stood staring at him as white as a table-cloth.

"'Why do you look at me like that, Cullen,' he says. 'You don't think——'

"'If you can explain that away,' says Cullen, pointing to the body, 'you will be, sir, if you'll forgive me for saying it, a devilish clever man.'

"'You're mad,' says Boyne. 'I found him like this.'

"'And where did you spring from, if I may make so bold?' asked the butler. Very sarcastic he was, he tells me.

"'I had been in the upper garden, and as you very well know, Cullen, I wished to avoid the Colonel,' says the young man. 'I walked round the back of the house and entered the Wilderness at the upper end. I was walking down the centre path towards the wicket gate, when I heard someone scream, and set off running. I could not have been here more than half a minute before you.'

"The butler did not argue the matter, but left him standing beside the body, and went to get assistance. On the lawn he met two of the gardeners and sent them back. I believe he also met Miss Sherrick near the porch. It was upon those facts, sir, that I arrested Boyne."

"I don't think," said the Inspector, shaking his head at him, "I don't think that I should have arrested him, Sergeant Hales."

"It looks very black against him, you must allow."

"Which affects his guilt or innocence neither one way nor the other. Has a doctor examined the body?"

"Yes, sir, and extracted the spear."

"Why did you let him do that?" asked the little man sharply.

"I knew you would be vexed about it, but it was done while I was out of the house, examining the road and lawn. He was very careful not to handle it more than was necessary, he said; but he had to saw the shaft in two."

"And why was that?"

"He said that the force used by the thrower must have been very great."

"Very great?"

"Yes, sir, gigantic—that is what he said."

Addington Peace walked to the window and stood there staring out at the elm avenue that swayed softly in the breeze.

"Is the doctor still in the house?" he asked over his shoulder.

"No, sir."

"We have none too much light left. Have you the spear?"

The sergeant opened a side cupboard and drew out two pieces of light-coloured wood. The polished surface was dulled by stains that were self-explanatory. The head was broad and flat, formed of the finest jade, microscopically carved. It had been fashioned for Eastern ceremony, and not for battle. That was plain enough.

Peace returned to the window and examined it with the closest attention. Presently he slipped out a magnifying glass, staring eagerly at a spot on the longer portion of the shaft.

"Do I understand you, Sergeant Hales, that you found Boyne endeavouring to pull out the spear?"

"Yes, sir."

"Who else touched it?"

"No one that I know of, save the doctor."

"And yourself."

"Of course, sir."

"Let me see your hands."

The Sergeant thrust them out with a smile. They had plainly not been washed that afternoon.

"Thank you. Have you discovered the owner of this spear?"

"No, sir; I wish I could."

"Have you tried Cullen or Miss Sherrick?"

"No, sir," said the Sergeant, looking blankly at the Inspector.

The little man walked to the fireplace and touched the electric bell. In a few moments the door opened and a fat, red-faced man walked in. There is no mistaking the attitude and costume of a British butler.

"Colonel Bulstrode was a collector of jade?" said the Inspector in his most innocent manner.

"Yes, sir."

"I noticed the specimens in the hall. Well, Cullen, have you ever seen this spear amongst his trophies?"

The man glanced at it and then shrank back with a shiver.

"It's the thing that killed him," he stammered.

"Exactly. But you do not answer my question."

"There may have been one like it, but I couldn't swear to it, sir. The Colonel would never have his collection touched. He or Miss Sherrick dusted 'em and arranged 'em themselves. He was always buying some new thing."

"Would Miss Sherrick know?"

"Very likely, sir."

"Thank you. That is all."

As the butler closed the door, the Sergeant stepped up to the Inspector and saluted.

"I should have noticed those collections," he said. "I have made a fool of myself, sir."

"A man who can make such an admission is never a fool, Sergeant Hales. And now kindly take me upstairs to the Colonel's room. You can wait here, Mr. Phillips."

It was close upon the half-hour before they came back to me, and I had leisure enough for considering the problem. When Peace had walked into my rooms at lunch-time, mentioning that he had a case with possibilities at Richmond, if I cared to come with him, I had never expected so strange a development. Nor, I fancy, had he.

This Colonel Bulstrode had served many years in India. Had the mysteries of the East followed him home to a London suburb? The gigantic force with which this spear had been thrown—there was something abnormal there, a something difficult to explain. Yet, after all, it might be a simple matter. Boyne was presumably a strong man, and the deadly fury that induces murder in a law-abiding citizen is akin to madness, giving almost a madman's strength. I was still puzzling over it when the door opened and the little Inspector walked in.

"The story of Sergeant Hales?" I asked him. "Is he exaggerating—was the spear thrown with unusual violence?"

"Very unusual. It is the crime of a giant or——"

He did not finish his sentence, but stood tapping the table and staring out at the gold and green of a summer sunset. At last he turned to me with a slow inclination of the head.

"Hales is waiting," he said, "and we must get to work. The light will not last for ever."

The Sergeant led us over the lawn to the Wilderness and through its paths to the wicket-gate. Showers in the early morning had turned the dust of the road into a grey mud that had dried under the afternoon sunshine. The surface was scored into a puzzle of diverging lines by the wheels of carts and carriages, cycles and motors. Yet Peace hunted it over even more closely than he had hunted the paths in the grounds. He was particularly anxious to know the position in which the body had lain, and finally the Sergeant got down in the drying mud to show him.

Apparently the Colonel had walked about ten yards from the gate when the spear struck him. He had fallen almost in the centre of the road, which at that point was broad, with stretches of grass bordering it on either side. His revolver had not been fired, though he had been found with it in his hand.

We walked on down the road, Addington Peace leading, his eyes fixed on its surface, and the Sergeant and I following behind. For myself, I had not the remotest idea of what he hoped to effect by this promenade, nor do I believe had the Sergeant. We circled the outside of the gardens, the road finally curving to the left and bringing us to the entrance-gates. Here we stopped at a word from the Inspector. The little man himself walked on, and finally dropped on his knees close to the hedge. When he joined us again, it was with an expression of benignant satisfaction. He beamed through the gates at the old elm avenue, that rustled sleepily in the gathering dusk.

"What a pretty place it is," he said. "Thank Heaven that these old houses still find owners or tenants who dare to defy the jerry builder and all his works. Hello, and who may this be?"

He had turned to the toot of the horn. The motor was close upon us, for a steam-car moves in silence as compared to the busy hum of a petrol-driven machine. It stopped, and the chauffeur jumped down and ran to open the gates. Of the driver we could see nothing save a peaked cap, goggles, and a long white dust-coat.

As it disappeared up the avenue towards the house I heard a faint bubble of laughter in my ear. I turned in surprise.

"Why, Peace," I said, "what is the joke?"

"There is no joke, Mr. Phillips," he answered. "It was fate that laughed, not I."

There were moments when, to a man of ordinary curiosity, Inspector Addington Peace was extremely irritating.

We walked up the avenue in silence. The

motor was standing at the front door, the chauffeur, a bright-faced youngster, loitering beside it. Peace greeted him politely, entering at once into a dissertation upon greasy roads and the dangers of side-slips. Was there nothing that would prevent them? He had heard that there was a patent, consisting of small chains crossing the tyres, that was excellent.

"It's about the best of them, sir," said the lad. "Mr. Bulstrode uses it on this car sometimes."

"So this is Mr. Anstruther Bulstrode's car?"

"Yes, sir. He was the brother of the poor gentleman inside."

"The roads are fairly dry now," continued Peace, "but if you had been out this morning——"

"Oh, Mr. Bulstrode had the chains on this morning," he interrupted. "I did not go with him, but when he came back he told me he was glad to have them, for the roads were very bad."

"And Mr. Bulstrode thought the roads were dry enough this afternoon to do without them?"

"Yes. He told me to take them off. He——"

"I am glad to see the police interest themselves in motoring," broke in a high-pitched voice behind us. "I was under the impression—false as I now observe—that they were confirmed enemies to the sport."

A yellow husk of a man was Mr. Anstruther Bulstrode, as I knew this stranger must be. Years under the Indian sun had sucked the English blood from his veins and burnt their own dull colour into his cheeks. He stood on the step of the porch with his hands behind him and his little eyes glaring at the Inspector like a pair of black beads. His mouth, twitching viciously under his straggly moustache, proved that the poor Colonel had not been the only member of the Bulstrode family possessed of an evil temper. Over his shoulder I could see Miss Sherrick's white face watching us. And now she stepped forward to explain.

"This is Inspector Peace, uncle," she said nervously.

"I know, my dear, I know. Do you think I can't tell a detective when I see him. So you have caught your man, eh, Inspector?"

"If you will come into the library, Mr. Bulstrode, I will answer what questions I may."

It was now close upon eight o'clock and the pleasant twilight of the long summer evening was drawing into heavier shadows. There was no gas in the old house, but Miss Sherrick ordered lamps to be brought in. We all seated ourselves about the big fireplace save Peace, who stood on the hearthrug with his back to the flowers that filled the empty grate. The shaded lamp dealt duskily with our faces. There was a strain, a vague anxiety in the air that kept me leaning forward in my chair, nervous and watchful.

"Well, Inspector," repeated Mr. Bulstrode, "what is your news?"

For answer, Peace walked up to the lamp and laid beneath it the jade spearhead, now cleaned and polished, with its four inches of broken shaft.

"Do you recognise that, Miss Sherrick?"

The girl bent over it without alarm. She had no idea what part it had played in that grim tragedy.

"Certainly," she said. "It is a unique piece of stone, and Colonel Bulstrode prized it more than anything else in his collection. I know it was hanging in the hall this morning, for I was at work with a duster. How did the shaft come to be broken?"

"An accident, Miss Sherrick."

"My poor uncle would have been dreadfully angry about it, and so must you be, Uncle Anstruther, for I understand you claim it to be yours."

"We did not come here, Mary, to talk about jade collecting," snarled the old planter.

"But does the spear really belong to you, Mr. Bulstrode?" asked the Inspector blandly.

The man stiffened himself in his chair with his fists clenched on his knees, and his beady eyes staring straight before him.

"That spear is mine, Mr. Detective. My brother having practically stolen it from me, threatened me with personal violence if I attempted to reclaim it. It was the most perfect piece of workmanship in my own collection. I shall take legal steps to claim my rightful property in due course."

"Your brother seems to have acted in a very high-handed manner with you, Mr. Bulstrode. I wonder that you did not walk in here one day and recover your property."

The planter rose with a twisted laugh.

"I'm not a housebreaker," he said. "Also I must point out that I don't intend to sit here all night. Can I do anything more for you, Inspector?"

"No, Mr. Bulstrode."

"Or for you, Mary?"

"No, uncle. I have my maid and there is Agatha, the housekeeper."

"So that's all right. Let us thank Heaven the criminal is no longer at large. It didn't take long for our excellent police to make up their minds. Gad! they're clever beggars. They had their hands on him smart enough. It is a pleasure to meet such a man as you, Inspector Addington Peace. A celebrity, by thunder, that's what I call you."

He burst out into a peal of high-pitched laughter, rocking to and fro and clutching the edge of the table with his hand. Then he bowed to us all very low and swaggered out of the room. Peace stepped out after him, and I followed at his heels.

A lamp hung in the roof of the porch, and Mr. Bulstrode stopped beneath it. In its light he looked more fierce and old and yellow than ever.

"It is no good, Mr. Bulstrode," said Addington Peace.

"Exactly; can I give you a lift?" he said quite quietly as he pointed to the car.

"It would certainly be most convenient."

Mr. Bulstrode laughed again, leering back at me over his shoulder, as if my presence afforded an added zest to his merriment. There seemed an understanding between him and the Inspector. Frankly, it puzzled me.

"You do not make confidants of your assistants, Mr. Peace," he said.

The little Inspector bowed.

"At the same time," continued the old planter, "I should like to make a statement before we go. There is no necessity to warn me. I know the law."

"It is just as you like, Mr. Bulstrode."

"If I sneered at the police this evening I now make them my apologies. You have managed this business well. I still do not understand how you come to accuse me. Remember I did not know he was dead until I received a telegram from my niece after lunch. It was rather a shock; perhaps at first I was of a mind not to confess. It would have saved me much inconvenience."

"And endangered an innocent man," said the Inspector.

"Well, well, you couldn't have proved it against him, and I might have escaped. The whole affair was an accident. I had no intention even of wounding him."

"Exactly, Mr. Bulstrode—no more than the excursionist who throws out a glass bottle intends to brain the man walking by the line."

The truth was clear enough now. In some strange fashion this man had killed his brother. I stepped back a pace instinctively.

"You see," he continued, "Brother William had, under circumstances of no immediate importance, appropriated my jade spear. I made up mind to get it back. I knew the hour at which he lunched, and leaving my motor in the road I walked down the avenue, hoping to find the front door open and no one about. I had a successful start. The front door was ajar. I went in, took the spear from the wall, and set off back to my car. I was some fifty yards down the drive when I heard a yell, and there was brother William tumbling out of the porch, revolver in hand.

"It startled me, for I knew he had the very worst of tempers; but though I was the elder man I knew I had the pace of of him, and set off running. When I reached the entrance gates and looked back he was nowhere to be seen. I took it that he had thought better of it and gone back to lunch.

"I was driving the car myself, having left the chauffeur behind, as I did not wish him to know what I was about. I started up the engines, jumped into the seat, put the spear beside me, and let her go. We came round that corner at a good thirty miles an hour, and there was brother William in the road, waving his revolver and cursing me for a thief. He had run down through the Wilderness to cut me off.

"I give you my word I was frightened, for I knew him and his tempers. I took up the spear, and as I passed I threw it at him anyhow. Let him keep it, and be blowed to him, I thought. I wasn't going to have a hole drilled in me for any jade ever carved. I never saw what happened, for in that second I was off the road and only pulled the car straight with difficulty. The spear must have struck him end on, and I was travelling thirty miles an hour.

"My niece sent me a wire. When I received it I understood what had happened. I was in a blue funk about the business. I meant to get out of it if I could. You see I am hiding nothing. I told my man to take the chains off the motor—I had a thought for the tracks I might have left—and came back to find out how the land lay. Well, you know the rest."

"You have done yourself no harm, Mr. Bulstrode, by this confession," said Inspector Addington Peace.

"Thank you. And now, if you will jump in, I will drive you to the police-station. You will want to get Boyne out and put me in, eh, Inspector?"

He was still laughing in that high-pitched voice of his when the car faded into the night.

* * * * *

It was not until next day that Peace gave me his explanation over our pipes in my studio. It is interesting enough to set down, if briefly.

"There were many points in the favour of Boyne," he said. "Miss Sherrick's story not only coincided with that told us by Cullen, but it also explained much that the butler considered suspicious. The young man left the drive hoping to meet Miss Sherrick. Cullen told me that Boyne asked where she was as he left, and was informed somewhere in the upper garden. He failed to find her, however, and probably concluded she had gone in to lunch. Boyne said he was walking down through the Wilderness when he heard the scream. Yet, if this were a lie, how could he have obtained the spear? Was he a man of such phenomenal strength as to use it in so deadly a fashion. You observe the difficulties.

"It was when I was upstairs examining the body that the idea occurred to me. The force used in throwing the spear was abnormal. Either the murderer must have been a man of remarkable physique, or he must have thrown the spear from a rapidly moving vehicle. You remember the notices that are displayed in railway-carriages begging passengers not to throw bottles from the window which will imperil the lives of plate-layers. It is not in the force of the throw but in the pace of the train that the danger lies. It was a possible parallel.

"And here I made a remarkable discovery. On closely inspecting the shaft of the spear, I found a smear of lubricating oil such as motorists use. It suggested that a man who had been lately attending to the machinery of a car had been handling the weapon. Had one of the group under possible suspicion anything to do with motors or machinery? Not one.

"I had noticed the jade collections in the hall. This spearhead was of unusual beauty. Could it have come from the Colonel's own collection? He had not taken it with him when he ran towards the Wilderness, loading his revolver. Why did he so run thus armed? Had he been robbed?

"Yet the thief had not passed that way. Cullen would have seen him if he had done so. Was the Colonel endeavouring to cut him off?

"I found the motor-tracks in the drying mud—unusual tracks, mark you, for the driver had run off the road circling the place where the Colonel had stood. I traced them easily by the chain marks on the tyres. They led to the front gate, and just beyond it the car had stopped for some time close to the hedge. Lubricating oil had dripped on the road while it waited. The case was becoming plainer.

"My talk with Bulstrode's chauffeur made

it self-evident. The information of Miss Sherrick and her uncle's own explanation as to his quarrel with his brother over the spear swept away my last doubt. Do you understand?"

"Yes," I said. "It seems simple now. Bulstrode has had bad luck though. Things look black against him."

"I think he will be all right," said Addington Peace. "His story has the merit of being not only easily understandable, but true."

"And Boyne?"

"I saw him meet Miss Sherrick. It was enough to make an old bachelor repent his ways, Mr. Phillips. Believe me, there is a great happiness of which we cannot guess —we lonely men."

THE END.

THE SCIENTIST.

A SCIENTIST sat in his study,
    Surrounded by learning and lore,
His fingers were messy and ruddy,
    For his hands were all covered with gore;
But his face wore a look of defiance,
    And triumph was plain in his eyes,
As he cried, "I'm a servant of Science,
    And Science has captured the prize!"

    For years he had experimented,
        For years he had tested and toiled,
    And tho' Nature had never relented,
        Still, this savant was not to be foiled.
    And now, in a moment, the mystery
        Of all he had sought was his own,
    His name would be handed to history
        As soon as his secret was known.

"I've found it!" he shouted, "I've found it!
    In this phial 'tis visibly plain,
I've collared the wretch and, confound it!
    'Twill never escape me again;
I've caught it and stained it with carmine,
    Its nature is known to me now,
Its manners and properties are mine,
    And none can deny it, I vow!

    "For twenty long years I have sought it,
        In summer and winter the same,
    But at last all alone I have caught it,
        And corked it up tightly and tame.
    I'm as proud as a peacock this minute,
        Tho' as meek and as mild as a dove,
    For you sent me a flower, and in it
        I've discovered the Microbe of Love!"

ARNOLD HARE.

THE MYSTERY OF THOMAS HEARNE.
A Tale of Dartmoor.
By B. Fletcher Robinson.

"With the police," I said, "to err is inhuman."

Inspector Harbord smiled and threw a pebble into the sea. Even a great detective must have a holiday sometimes, and the Inspector was enjoying his sun bath on the beach just like the ordinary citizen to whom Scotland Yard is a convenient lost property office.

"The papers were very severe on you," I continued.

He brushed the fact away with a shrug of his shoulders.

"I suppose you know more than was ever published?"

"I had the details from an eye-witness," he said, sending a second pebble after the first.

It was a surprising remark, seeing that a year before the whole country, roused by the singular nature of the tragedy, had roundly abused the police for their failure to explain the unexplainable.

"You can't avoid telling me the story after that," I said.

"It's my holiday."

I shook my head with great determination.

"About three months ago," he said, abandoning the contest, "I received a message from Guy's Hospital that there was a patient lying very ill who wished to see me. I recognised him the moment I set foot in the ward—a gentleman born and bred who had slipped down the ladder from running his own horses to dodging the police as a bookmaker's tout. He was a half-and-half man, too lazily clever to be quite honest, and too honest to be quite a criminal. Poor Jack Henderson! A good man gone wrong—let that be his epitaph when it comes to setting up his headstone.

"'Well, Henderson,' I said, 'what's the trouble?'

"'I'm done, Harbord,' he whispered. 'They've no more use for me this side of the black river; but I wanted to see you before I answered the call.'

"'You mustn't talk like that,' I said, though he was looking pretty bad. 'They'll put you on your legs again in a month; don't worry any more about it.'

"'It don't matter much either way,' he smiled, in a quiet way he had, 'so let us get to business. You had your share of trouble, I understand, in the matter of Julius Craig last spring.'

"I nodded.

"'I was in that job,' he said, 'and after what happened I should like to tell you the truth about it. I may have been a pretty bad lot in my time, Inspector, but I had my limits, and murder was one of them.'

"I won't try to give you his exact words, for the poor fellow spoke very slowly, with big pauses in between. But this is close upon the story as he told it to me."

* * * * *

I expect you know the "Blue Shield," in Percher Street. Take them one with another, the customers are about the worst crowd in all London. One Saturday night, towards the end of March, last year, I had joined the gang there, hoping to meet some friend with the price of a drink upon him, for I was broke to the wide, wide world. Bill Redman, who was afterwards lagged for bank note forgeries in Manchester, had just ordered me a whiskey, and I was sitting on a stool watching the bar-tender reach down the special Scotch, when in walked a moon-faced fellow, very fat and prosperous, with a dark blue overcoat and a diamond in his necktie. He looked about him, screwing up his eyes as a near-sighted man will do, and then came over to where I was sitting.

"Mr. Henderson, I believe," he said.

"That's my name," I told him, wondering who he might be.

"I have been recommended to you by a—by a mutual friend," he said, "but I cannot discuss my business here. My carriage is waiting, if you will give me your company for ten minutes."

I hesitated a moment, until Redman, who seemed to know him, leant across, whispering that I should be a fool to refuse. The stranger pushed me into a brougham that was standing by the pavement opposite the door, and we started off at a smart pace. Once in Regent's Park, however, the driver pulled his horse to a walk, and my companion began to do his talking.

"Five hundred sovereigns would be useful to you these days—eh, Mr. Henderson?"

There was a smile all over his fat face as he said the words, and he chuckled softly to himself with a sound like water coming out of a bottle. It seemed an offer of life to me, a promise of everything the lack of which makes each day a torment to the man who has known clean comfort.

"Is it murder?" I asked him, between fear and hope as it were.

"Oh, my dear sir, you surprise me," he cried, lifting his flabby hands. "What a horrible suggestion! Allow me to explain at once. Have you ever heard of Julius Craig?"

"The company promoter, who organised the Spanish mine swindle? Of course I have. He used to come racing. A tall, thin, melancholy looking fellow with a black beard wasn't he?"

"Yes, that is Julius Craig. He is now in the Princetown Prison with six more years to run. The climate of Dartmoor is not suited to his health. He is anxious to change his residence; nor do I blame him, Mr. Henderson, for it is the most desolate spot in all England. I am in a position to offer you the sum I have mentioned if you will arrange his escape. Do you agree?"

"Yes," I told him.

"Ah, that is most satisfactory. To-morrow I will send you half the money with some little suggestions of my own as to your plan of campaign. The second half you will receive when Mr. Craig is free. By the way, there are some curious relics of the Stone Age on the moors. Perhaps you might read up the subject and appear at Princetown as a student—yes, Mr. Henderson, that will suit you well, a student of prehistoric man."

He chuckled until the carriage shook. It was like driving with a good-tempered blanc mange.

"I shall be glad of any advice you can give me," I said.

He pulled a cord, and when the carriage stopped I got out and stood waiting.

"Good-night and good luck to you," he said, his great white face shining upon me from the window as he shook my hand. "I have your address. Drive on, Williams."

As the carriage rolled away I noticed that he raised the little flap at the back to see that I didn't try to follow him.

The packet arrived next morning. The notes I stowed away in an inside pocket. The typewritten instructions were unsigned and undated.

According to them Craig was a member of gang D, employed on the convict farm in draining and inclosing a portion of moor by a stream known as the Black brook. Above the stream rose a small hill on which was an ancient cairn and stone circle that in my character as a student would offer an excuse for my presence.

Though communication with Craig could not be established, he knew that an attempt was in preparation. The sight of a man in a white waterproof loitering on the cairn hill would be his signal that all was ready. Sudden fogs were frequent upon the moor, and when they came while the convicts were at work in the fields, the chance of escape was excellent; for the authorities did not chain their men, and the warders rarely used their rifles. They trusted to the huge moors upon which men who escaped were easily retaken, half dead from fatigue and starvation.

Craig would make a rush for the cairn hill. From thence it was my duty to convey him to Torquay, thirty miles away on the coast. Once there, he would know where to go, and my responsibility ended. A letter to the Torquay Post Office, under the name of W. Slade, would be forwarded to the writer if I required further assistance.

That was all; but it was enough for me. Here was a scheme into which I could put my heart. There was no low-down swindling, no dirty work about it. I felt as gay as a schoolboy off for a holiday.

And so in three days' time that ragged rascal Jack Henderson disappeared from London, and the well dressed Mr. Abel Kingsley, vaguely described in the visitors' book of the "Princetown Arms" as of Harvard University, U.S.A., was sitting on the cairn hill above the great prison that held Julius Craig.

To the far horizon there stretched the melancholy moors, deserted wastes of rushy marshes and stunted heather, broken here and there by outcrops of granite, that crowned the rolling ground like the ruins of a hundred feudal castles. For Dartmoor is a huge granite tableland, and on its barren surface no corn will grow nor tree flourish.

Beneath the rampart of its containing hills lies the garden of Devon, a land of orchards and pleasant woods, of cornfields and pasture farms; but the moors have defied the farmer and remain the same sad wilderness that prehistoric man inhabited four thousand years ago.

The huge prison was built on the opposite slope of the shallow valley, and the farm which the convicts had won field by field stretched down from its walls to a brook at the foot of the cairn hill where I sat. On the further edge of the brook a gang was at work inclosing some new ground, and through my glasses I soon made out the man I was after. The last time I had seen him was on his own coach at Ascot, with the girls buzzing round him like wasps after sugar, and there he was digging trenches with a spade. It's a funny world!

About twenty men were in the gang. On the outer side a couple of warders strolled up and down with rifles under their arms. There was nothing but a low hedge to stop the convicts if they knocked down the guards with their spades and made a run for it. But when I looked back across the wastes of the moor I understood. In a city a man may vanish in a crowd, but on Dartmoor he must tramp a dozen miles before he can find even a bush to hide him. In clear weather the mounted warders of the pursuit would ride him down in half-an-hour.

The "Princetown Arms," a grey, weather-beaten square of granite, was a pleasant

I routed out the landlord and engaged a private room. I had had enough of taking meals with a Neolithic expert.

country inn standing near the centre of the village. It was too early in the year for tourists; indeed, as I discovered, there was only one man beside myself staying in the house, a Mr. Thomas Hearne, whose address in the visitors' book was briefly "London." When I came down to dinner that night I found him already seated at a little table with my knife and fork laid opposite. I wasn't anxious to make new acquaintances, but I couldn't very well ask them to lay another table for my benefit. So I took my chair and wished him good evening as politely as possible.

He was a small, grey-bearded man of over sixty, as I reckoned, and he seemed as disinclined for conversation as ever I was. For that I thanked my luck, and worked through the dinner with my brain busy with one plan after another. It was just as coffee was served that he asked the question which startled me.

"The landlord tells me you are studying the stone remains on the moor," he said. "Is it your opinion that they're Neolithic or Druidical?"

I cursed the landlord under my breath. I

had told him my story, but I had forgotten he might pass it on to others.

"The latter, undoubtedly," I said; though, if the truth be told, I had no opinion whatever.

"I cannot agree with you. They were here before ever the Druids came over the sea. May I ask what arguments you adduce in support of your theory?"

Everything I had read about those confounded stones slipped out of my mind in an instant. There was no good trying to bluff him, for he probably had the subject at his fingers' ends. So I nodded my head wisely, and suggested it was a bit too big a subject to start after dinner.

"I saw you by the cairn and circle above the Black brook this afternoon," he went on. "Is that to be the scene of your first investigations?"

"I have no definite plan at present," I said with a snap.

He took a long look at me and stopped his questions. I left the table as soon as I could do so decently, routed out the landlord, and engaged a private room. I had had enough of taking meals with a Neolithic expert.

It was blowing hard next day, a fierce north-wester that cleaned the clouds out of the sky like a sponge washes a slate.

Just after eleven I started out to make a further examination of the position. I wasn't such a fool as to march up to the cairn with old Hearne and a warder or two, as it might be, spying on me from another hillock, so I went down the high road that lay as white and clear across the grey moor as a streak of paint, until I had left the place some distance behind me. No one, so far as I could see, was in sight, and presently I turned off the road along a disused cart track that seemed to lead in the direction I wanted. Its ancient ruts were filled with bunches of heather, and the short moor turf had covered up the hoof-marks with a velvet surface.

I had walked a good quarter of a mile, when, rounding a curve of the hill, I found the old road explained in the ruins of a small farm, one of those melancholy memorials of a time when frozen meat was unknown, and it paid a man to breed cattle and sheep and cultivate a wheatfield or two, even on Dartmoor. The roof had fallen in, and the woodwork had been carried away, but the stone walls of the house and outbuildings still remained undefeated by a hundred years of storm. A weather-beaten cherry tree was pushing out its spring leafage before the door.

Leaving the farm I began to climb the cairn hill, as I must call it for want of a better name, which sheltered the farm from the north and west.

It was rough walking, for the heather was set thick with granite boulders. At last I reached the top, skirted the mound set about with stones where the prehistoric chief lay sleeping, and very nearly stepped upon the body of that confounded old fellow, Thomas Hearne.

Luckily for me he never turned his head. The wind on the face of the hill was blowing in great gusts like the firing of a cannon, and my footsteps had been drowned in its thunder. I crept back behind a heap of tumbled rocks and dropped on my hands and knees, watching him through a convenient crevice. He lay flat on his chest, while he covered the gang at work in the new ground below with a small telescope.

It might be curiosity of course, for many men regard a convict as something abnormal, something that is pleasant to stare at as if he were the cannibal king at a fair. And yet that seemed a weak explanation. Was he in with the police? Had they got news that an attempt at rescue was to be made? If so, I stood the best chance in the world of finding myself in the county gaol within the week.

There was nothing to be gained by imagining bad luck. I walked back to the inn, and sat down to a study of the district with maps I had brought with me. There was only one railroad within easy reach, and that was the single track that ran up from Plymouth to Princetown village. At the first signal that a convict had escaped the station would be full of warders; so that outlet was barred. South of the moor, fifteen miles away, ran another branch line ending at Ashburton. But I was determined to leave the railroad alone. The stations would be the first places to be watched by the police. Torquay, some thirty miles off, might easily be reached by a good horse and trap within the day. I could hire one for a month through the landlord, with the excuse that I wanted it for my exploring expeditions amongst the stone remains. It would surprise no one if it were seen off the roads with a luncheon basket prominently displayed. So I decided, and welcomed dinner with enthusiasm.

I questioned the girl who brought the meal to my sitting-room as to old Hearne, but she could give me little information. He had arrived at the inn a couple of days before I appeared, and had spent most of his time in long walks on the moors. She thought he had a friend amongst the prison officials, for she had twice seen him coming out of the great gates down the street. That was all—and it left me more anxious about him than before.

After dinner, I walked into the inn bar to buy a smoke, and found Hearne with his back to the fire, talking to the landlord. As I entered, they both dropped into an uneasy silence. I was certain they had been discussing me, but I didn't want to let them know it, and so began to talk big about the scenery. I stayed down for about half-an-hour, and then allowed that I would get back to some writing I had to do.

"I'm glad you admire the moor, Mr. Kingsley," said the landlord, holding back the door for me. "Nothing quite like it in the States, I should think."

Upon my soul, I was as near as may be to owning I had never been there. But I remembered that I was Abel Kingsley, of Harvard, just in time.

"No," I said, "it's something quite unique."

"It's a wild place, sir," he went on. "Very wild and desolate. You should take a walk one night when the moon is full, as it is now. Then you would understand how the stories of ghost hounds and headless riders and devils in the mires first started. Mr. Hearne here is going to take my advice."

"To-night?" I asked, turning to the old fellow.

"No, Mr. Kingsley, I am too tired to think of it to-night," he said. "To-morrow or the next day, perhaps."

I wished them a good evening and tramped up the stairs to my sitting-room, which looked over the moors at the back of the inn. It was certainly a splendid night, with a great searchlight of a moon drawing the strange

I crept behind a heap of tumbled rocks, and dropped on my hands and knees, watching him through a convenient crevice.

tors—as they call the granite caps of the hills—in black silhouette upon the luminous skyline. I lit a pipe and sat there in the shadows, thinking, thinking. It was pleasant to be a decent man again, to wear clean linen and boots with real soles; to wash and shave and brush myself daily. I was back in my Eden days before the fall, when six hunters were in my stable, and men and women were glad to know Jack Henderson of Lowood Hall in the best of counties; yes, I was away from Princetown village in the midst of happy memories when I came to my senses with the sound of a soft tap-tapping under the window. There were tip-toe skulking footsteps on the gravel of the yard.

I crept softly to my window and peered out. The man was almost across the yard, moving in the shadow of the pig-sties. As he stopped at the wicket-gate that opened on to the moor, he turned his head to the moon. It was Hearne again.

I decided on that instant. I slipped on my boots and ran down the stairs. The landlord was locking up for the night as I came to the front door.

"I'm going to take your advice," I said with a laugh.

"Very good, sir, I will sit up for you."

"No, no, give me the key. Has Mr. Hearne gone to bed?"

"Yes, sir, about ten minutes ago."

"His room is on the first floor, isn't it?"

"No, sir, he chose one on the ground floor. He preferred it."

When I got to the back of the inn Hearne was a good four hundred yards away, climbing a low ridge. As he disappeared over its edge I set off running at top speed, for I saw that in so broken and rugged a place I should have to keep close on his heels or I should lose him altogether. It was well I did so, for when I reached the crest of the rise he had vanished.

Presently, however, I caught sight of him again walking very fast down a hollow at right angles to the line he first took. It led in the direction of the cairn hill.

It was hard work, that two miles' stalk across the moor. Sometimes I ran, sometimes crawled, sometimes lay flat on my chest with my head buried in the heather like an ostrich. Once I tried to cut a corner across what seemed a plot of level turf and struggled back, panting, from the grasp of the bog with the black slime almost to my waist. But I took great credit for my performance since the old man tramped steadily forward showing no sign of having seen me.

He did not climb the cairn hill as I had half expected, but skirted along the base until he came to the track which led to the ruined farm. Down this he walked quickly and passed through the doorway of the main building. I remained upon the slope of the hill, waiting for him to reappear. Five, ten minutes went by, and then my curiosity got the better of prudence. I determined to go down and see what he was about.

The place was sheltered from the gale, but I could hear it yelping and humming in the rocks above, while now and again a gust came curling up the valley, setting the heather whispering around me. I crept forward over the soft turf of the cart track, reached the gap where the door had been, hesitated, listened, and then stuck in my head.

I had been a boxer in my time, or that would have been the end of me. As I ducked, the heavy stick flicked off my cap and crashed into the wall with a nasty thud. I jumped back, and he came storming out through the doorway like a madman. I never saw a deadlier fury in a man's eyes. I side-stepped, and he missed me again—it was a knife this time. Then I woke up, and let him have it with my right under the ear. He staggered, dropping his knife. As he stooped to pick it up, I jumped for him, and in ten seconds more was sitting on his chest, pegging out his arms on the turf. He tried a struggle or two; but he soon saw that I was far the stronger man, and so lay panting, with a hopeless despair in his face that, in a man of his age, was shocking to witness. He had tried to kill me, but, on my honour, I felt sorry for him.

"Well, Mr. Hearne," I said, "and what does this mean?"

"Too old," he gasped. "Twenty years ago—different. How did you suspect? It was justice—nothing but bare justice, by heaven!"

"Now, what in the world do you think I am?" I asked him, in great surprise.

"A detective. You couldn't deceive me."

I got to my feet with a curse at the muddle I had made of it, and he sat up, staring at me as if he thought I had gone clean crazy of a sudden.

"I'm no detective," I said angrily, "though I was fool enough to believe you were one."

"Then why did you follow me to-night," he asked with a quick suspicion.

"Why did you try to kill me?" I said. "The truth is, Mr. Hearne, you and I are playing a risky game. Is it to be cards on the table, or are we to separate and say no more about it?"

He sat watching me for a time with a puzzled look. Plainly he was in great uncertainty of mind.

"Perhaps I have nothing to tell," he said at last.

"A man does not attempt to murder detectives unless he has a crime to conceal."

"That is true," he said, nodding his head; "very just and true."

There was nothing to be gained by a long bargaining of secrets with him. Whatever his business he could speedily discover mine if he chose. If I were honest with him he might return the confidence.

"I am arranging for the escape of Julius Craig, now doing his time in the prison yonder," I told him.

"Julius Craig!" he echoed with wild eyes. "The escape of Julius Craig?"

"Yes. Do you know him?"

Then I woke up and let him have it with my right under the ear. He staggered, dropping his knife.

He burst into a scream of hysterical laughter, swaying his body to and fro, and pressing his hands to his sides as if trying to crush the uncanny merriment out of him; and then, before I guessed what he was about, the old fellow was upon me, with his arms about my neck in a mad embrace.

"Welcome, comrade," he cried. "I too have come to find a way out of Princetown Gaol for Julius Craig."

It took a good five minutes and a pull out of a flask to get him back to hard sense.

Then he told me his story sitting on a fallen stone under the old cherry tree.

Craig was dearer to him than any brother, he said with a burst of open sincerity. There was that between them that he could never forget while life remained to him. He had heard how the man was pining under prison discipline, and had come to help him escape if that were humanly possible. Of me or my London employers he knew nothing whatever.

He had been shown over the prison, having

obtained a pass from an influential friend, and while there had learnt the place where Craig was daily employed. Yesterday from the cairn hill he had satisfied himself that the convict was working in the gang.

He had crept out this evening to examine the stream and hedge which divided the new inclosure from the moor. When he saw me on his track, his suspicions as to my business were confirmed. Either he must give up his project or my mouth must be stopped. So he tempted me into the ruined farm. The rest I knew.

He spoke in an easy, pleasant voice with a perfect frankness and good humour. It never seemed to occur to him that he had done anything unreasonable, anything to which a level-headed man could object. I stared at him in a growing amazement.

There seemed, indeed, only one solution before me—that he had become partially insane.

"You must understand my position, Mr. Kingsley," he concluded, "I am not a lunatic; but I have made up my mind in this matter of Julius Craig. Anyone who is foolish enough to come between us must stand aside or take the consequences. Towards yourself, for example, I had no ill will. In fact, I rather liked you. But you must admit that as a detective your presence was excessively inconvenient. Now that I know the truth, I welcome you as a most valuable ally. I am prepared to trust you absolutely. Come, what are your plans?"

I told him as we walked back to the inn. He expressed himself an admirer of their simplicity as we parted for the night. Mad or not, I had found an assistant who would be of great help to me. So I let it stay at that and slept like a rock till nine next morning.

Matters moved quickly with us. I hired a stout horse and a two-wheeled cart for a month from the landlord to whom I talked Neolithic man of an evening, impressing him with a learning, acquired from the reports of that worthy society the Devonshire Association. I preferred to drive myself, declining the boy offered for that purpose.

There were no other preparations to make; and so, on the day following, that earnest student, Mr. Abel Kingsley, might have been seen smoking his pipe on the cairn hill in a new white mackintosh, for was there not a threat of rain in the air? while Mr. Thomas Hearne lay hid amongst the stones watching the effect of the signal through his pocket telescope. He reported all well; Julius Craig had undoubtedly noticed the white waterproof and understood that we were waiting for him.

I could talk to you for an hour of our doings in the next three weeks. We lived on the edge of a powder-barrel in which we had set the fuse. Never a morning but we were up with the sun staring to windward for signs of the weather. Would it be to-day, to-morrow—not at all? A nervous man would never have stood that strain; but we were not a neurotic couple, the old chap and I.

As hard and keen and clever as a lad of twenty-one was Thomas Hearne. It was he who spent the day in Plymouth, returning with a wig and long overcoat that might temporarily conceal the convict's identity until he could change his yellow prison uniform for the clothes I had already bought; it was he who gathered to himself all the weather lore of the village until he had become a better prophet than the wisest veteran of the moors. Two fogs we had, but during the first the convicts were kept within the walls; while before the other caught them the warders had time to rush the gangs back to their cells. Yet Hearne never lost temper at these delays, cheering me back into patience with the strength of his own certainty.

"Don't you worry, Kingsley," he would say; "what is fated to happen cannot be prevented, and Providence will see to it that Julius Craig comes to us soon."

His affection for the convict seemed to fill his life. No risk, no labour was too heavy; no storm would drive him from his post. Often when I was smoking by the inn fire, he was crouching patiently amongst the rocks on the cairn hill, as if it were his only son for whom he waited. There was something inhuman in his merciless self-sacrifice; but I had no reason to complain, for it lightened the burden on my shoulders.

It was at three o'clock on Tuesday, May 9th, that Julius Craig escaped. Poor devil! if he had but known!

We had quarrelled that morning over the eternal weather question. Perhaps both our tempers were wearing thin, but that was no excuse for his dropping from argument to insults. I daresay he thought my language just as bad; but that didn't make the trouble any lighter. There was fog in the air, he said, though even the landlord laughed at the idea when I put the question to him. Finally, the old man walked off in a huff, though I had so far given way as to promise that I would bring the cart to the ruins by lunch time.

I sulked about the inn until the papers came from Plymouth. When I had finished reading them it was nigh one o'clock. A leg of lamb was cooking in the kitchen. Just because Hearne preferred cold ham sandwiches on a draughty hill there was no reason why I should not have my meal in comfort. I would lunch before I started and he could wait for his sandwiches.

It was a selfish thing to do, but he had irritated me that morning more than I now can understand. I was finishing off with cheese when the landlord thrust his head through the door of my sitting-room.

"I gave fool's wisdom this morning, sir," he said. "The fog be blowing up proper from the eastward. "I'm feared that Mr. Hearne——"

He got no further, for I was past him like a flash and out into the open.

The moors had gone; utterly vanished away. In their place there lay a blanket of billowy white that sent wild streamers upwards to the flying veil of clouds. Only a quarter mile of the main road was visible, and up it the first wave of the misty inundation was marching like a lofty wall. I ran towards the stable cursing myself in my mad disappointment.

I galloped for two hundred yards, and then the fog gathered me to itself, and I had just enough sense to pull the horse to a slow trot.

I could still see the road for a dozen paces, but all sense of proportion and distance had gone from me. The fog was not stationary, but curled in broad confusing wreaths, or poured sideways upon me in avalanches of denser mist. Sometimes the cart was on the road, sometimes off it. Twice I nearly capsized. In the end I climbed down and went to the horse's head, leading it forward at the run. I made better progress after that.

Yet I was not more than half way to the cairn hill when from the whirling shadows to my left there came a sound that set my heart leaping in my breast. It was the muffled crack of a rifle.

I stopped, listening and staring into the mist. A second shot followed. And then, as if raised by these echoes there clanged a distant bell, a deep voice of loud alarm from the prison tower telling the moor that a convict had escaped, that Julius Craig was free and that I—I, miserable fool that I was, had failed in the trust which had been placed upon me.

I tried not to think, but ran stubbornly on beside the horse with that infernal bell rioting in my ears. My life on the moors had put me in sound condition, and I never slackened my pace till I had trotted up the rise to where the track to the ruined farm began. I checked the horse and walked slowly forward studying the edge of the moor beside the highway for the mark of the grass grown ruts I knew so well.

I heard his footsteps long before I saw him, a quick patter upon the hard surface behind me. As he came out of the fog he shouted, bringing his rifle to his hip with an easy swing. He was a stoutly built man in the neat dark uniform that marks the prison warder.

"Be careful with that gun," I said, for he still had me covered.

"I beg your pardon, sir," he panted, "but we were close to him and—"

"Close to whom?"

"There's a convict escaped," he explained. "You haven't seen him?"

"No, nor likely to in this weather."

He had got his breath by this time and stood leaning on his rifle, looking vaguely about him.

"You're right, sir. We stand a far better chance of losing ourselves than of finding him in a fog like this. But one thing is equally certain, he can't get far either."

It was while he spoke that I heard it, the clink of a boot striking a stone and that not a score of yards away.

"I'm afraid you are only wasting time," I said as carelessly as I was able. "A needle in a haystack is easy compared to a convict in a fog."

"I think I must take your advice, sir," he laughed.

We wished each other good afternoon and he melted away as a man might slide behind a curtain. His footsteps died out down the road by which he had come as I moved forward.

"That was a near thing, Kingsley," said a voice in the shadows, and I humbly thanked my luck as old Hearne stepped out on the road.

"I've no excuse," I began. "It was all my fault, and——"

"Hush, keep quiet."

He stood for a moment listening like a dog at the door.

"If that fool of a warder had not gone back we were done," he whispered. "The guards chased us right into the ruins. While they searched them we slipped down the track. Come along, Craig, all's well."

The convict rose from the heather where he had lain and stumbled towards us. He was shaking like a man with the ague, and the sweat was running off his forehead and down his cheeks in narrow streaks.

"Am I safe," he stuttered, grabbing my arm. "I've money, man, money. You shall have it, I swear you shall have it all. But I won't go back there—not alive."

"Come, pull yourself together," said Hearne with a hand on his shoulder. "We have no time to waste, remember."

The convict rose from the heather, where he had lain, and stumbled towards us. He was shaking like a man with the ague.

We wrapped the long coat over his yellow clothes, stuck the wig over his cropped head, and helped him to the front seat. I took my place beside him, Hearne clambered up behind, and our journey began.

The horse was of the old moor breed. He could have bowled us along at a good ten miles an hour if the fog had allowed it; but as it was we rarely exceeded half that speed. It was a miserable time. Craig sat huddled by my side, now cursing me for the delay, now peering back along the road while he implored us to tell him if it were galloping hoofs that he heard. He was an evil-tempered, petulant man, and I did not waste either politeness or sympathy upon him. It was not until we had passed over some miles of rolling uplands and dropped down a steep descent to a moss-grown bridge that the fog showed signs of breaking. As we strained up the opposing hill it began to tear away in flying wisps like the smoke of great guns, giving us glimpses of a narrow slope of turf ending in a cliff at the foot of which an unseen river moaned and chuckled.

"I helped you loyally—you have no complaint against me?" asked old Hearne, tapping me suddenly on the shoulder.

"I could never wish a better comrade," I told him.

"That is how I hope you will always think of me."

He was not the kind of man to talk

sentiment, and I glanced back in surprise. There was an expression of peace upon him, such as I have never seen in a human countenance either before or since. He smiled and, reaching over, gave my hand a squeeze.

"You have the making of a good fellow in you," he said. "May the fates forget your follies."

We drove on in silence for a while; and then the old man rose, kneeling upon the cushions of the back seat.

"Here comes the sun, Julius Craig," he said. "The mists are scattering, and the world comes peeping through to welcome you back to freedom. Women and wine and cards—does the old spirit stir within you?"

"And who the devil may you be?" asked the convict, turning upon him.

"Have five years changed me so much? Perhaps my beard is whiter than it was the night you fled with her to the yacht in Cadiz Bay."

The convict gave a miserable cry, like a beast in pain, shrinking back, with his face one grey mask of fear.

"Not Mortimer?" he whispered. "It can't be Mortimer. He died."

"You are quite mistaken," said Hearne politely.

It all happened very swiftly—in one long breath or so, it seemed to me. Craig sprang from his seat and ran wildly down the slope; but the old man was not five yards behind him. I believe that the convict had the pace of him, but the cliff turned Craig to the right, and the next moment they had closed, and hung, swaying, upon the edge.

The flicker of a knife, a shrill, piping cry, and they were gone.

I was alone in a great silence save for the faint murmurs of the stream as it fought the rocks below.

It took me ten minutes and more to reach them, for I had to skirt the cliff until a slide of granite boulders gave me a path to the bottom. Craig was dead, the knife had done its work; but the old man was alive though his grave blue eyes were glazing fast. He recognised me and smiled very very faintly. I raised his head upon my arm and wiped his wrinkled face with my handkerchief.

"Is he dead?"

"Yes," I told him.

"I was—manager—his mines in Spain," he whispered. "My daughter—he took her to his yacht—scoundrel was married already —she died in London."

There was no vengeance in his face now; he faltered on as simply as a little child.

"Long search—found he was in prison— came to kill him. I met you—to help him escape seemed a better way. Then he would know why he had to die—if I had shot him over a hedge he would—never have understood —sorry for you—had to do my duty—by him."

His head fell back with a long sigh so that I thought all was over; but presently he rallied again, in the last blind effort at life which even a man with a broken back will make.

"Not a sin, Mary dear," he called. "How can they tell you it was murder when they know——"

He finished his explanation in another world.

That is about all I need tell you. I found the horse grazing by the road side and drove to Ashburton with no great care whether they caught me or not. I was back in London before they found the bodies.

* * * * *

So ended the story of John Henderson as Inspector Harboard told it to me.

"And you?" I asked.

"I suspected that 'Kingsley' had helped in the escape, but I never identified him with Jack Henderson. Who Thomas Hearne might be or why he killed the convict I could never find out. So I failed, but I don't know that I am ashamed of it, all things considered."

"Did Henderson die in hospital?"

"No, they pulled him round. Some old friends found him a place in some racing stables. He is there now."

"Surely he had broken several sorts of laws," I suggested. "When he recovered didn't you——"

"No, I didn't," said the Inspector firmly.

The Return of Oliver Manton

By

B. FLETCHER ROBINSON
Author of "The Vanished Billionaire," etc.

THEY acquitted William Fenton Bennett without leaving the jury-box. In truth he walked from the dock with a cleaner reputation than we who had borne witness against him. His counsel took pains to make that fact plain to us, and there was an echo of his speech in the summing up of old Gregory; and though Gregory may be a cynic, he is a fair-minded judge, or has that reputation. He assured us, with a sneer in every wrinkle of his face, that we were three centuries late with our evidence; that in Puritan days we should doubtless have proved valued allies in the smelling out of wizards with whom, as he understood, England was at that period much infested. I believe we were hooted as we left the court. The evening papers were pleased to be very funny, in four headlines, over our theory; and one of them published a cartoon of us dressed as Familiars of the Inquisition, dancing around a bonfire.

If you walk through Hyde Park to the head of the Serpentine you will find a stone arbor that faces to the southward. Hardly a fine day but noon sees William Fenton Bennett settle himself on the stone slab or on a seat near by, turning his lean, yellow face to catch the sun. Nurse-maids and their little wards expend much sympathy on the poor, blind gentleman. To any one who addresses him he will speak with an old-fashioned courtesy. Strangers have often wondered at his resignation under his affliction. Yet had justice its rights, he would have passed from the Newgate dock to the Newgate jail and from that place to the gallows two years or more ago. Had a hundred juries acquitted him, my belief in his guilt would go unshaken.

I will tell you the story, then you can judge for yourselves:

Oliver Manton was one of the most pugnacious, self-willed, muddle-headed men that ever ruined his own career. He had his enemies by the score who will tell you this and that against him; but under his bluster he was as honest a fellow as ever stepped. I ought to know, seeing that I lived with him for five years.

We had a set of chambers in the Temple—that ancient rambling home of London's law and literature—and our windows looked dustily out on the old church where the crusaders lie asleep. A quiet back-water it was during the day. By night the murmur of the roaring Strand hung faint in the air, just as a spray of lavender will scent a room.

When the courts were up for the day and king's counsel and junior had drifted homeward, a footstep on the flagged court below would ring loud enough to bring me to the window to see who was passing so late.

One evening in November it was, I had a chop at my club, and after playing two rubbers at bridge, came home to find that Oliver had not returned. We were an independent couple habitually incurious as to each other's engagements. I didn't give a thought to him but smoked a last pipe and walked off to bed.

It was about one in the morning that I woke to find him standing over me with a candle in his hand. He was by nature a florid, full-blooded man, but now his cheeks were very pale and his mouth pulled down at the corners as I had seen it once or twice before when he was "up against it," as he used to term it.

"Get up," he said, "I want a talk."

I slipped on a dressing gown and followed him out into the sitting-room. There was a spark of fire in the grate and I drew a chair before it, wondering what in the world could be the matter. He was pacing up and down the room with his hands behind him and I knew him well enough by this time to leave him the first word.

"I'm not responsible! I can't be responsible!" he burst out suddenly. "It's some thundering trick they are playing upon me. Blackmail, that's what it is."

I gave him a sympathetic nod, having no remark worthy of the making.

"I never thought Jim Stonham was such a fool," he went on, "but he's become a spiritualist. Imagine a leading lawyer at the Chancery bar a spiritualist! It's enough to make a dog laugh. For weeks past he's been trying to persuade me into going to one of the meetings of his 'Circle' up at Hampstead. I told him I'd see him smothered in his own brief bag before I'd do any such thing. But he stuck to it and, to cut the story short, I went—to-night. In the cab he began a lecture on how I must behave. I was not to break the linked hands or insult a spook if I saw one, or do anything likely to prove him and his friends to be the set of fat-headed idiots they are. I began to explain my opinion of him and his 'Circle,' and he lost his temper. We were not on the best of terms when we arrived.

"They were holding their show in an artist's studio. I suppose there were about a dozen of us—men and women—all told. They had hung a curtain in one corner, behind which the spirits were to be precipitated, as they called it. I was introduced to the medium, a withered little man with bulging eyes. I asked him if the business paid and he made out that I had insulted him. The women had to coo around him quite a time before he cooled down. The whole thing simply reeked of fraud.

"Presently we sat down in a half-circle facing the curtain. Stonham was on my left and an elderly woman on the other side. Some one switched off the electric lights and we joined hands. The place was dark as pitch, save for a special sort of candle in a red lantern that gave a feeble flicker. The electric switch, by the way, was just behind me.

"I don't say that medium was not worth his money. He did well. It was the best bit of ventriloquism I ever heard. There were half a dozen voices going on at once, or so it seemed, from a high piping squeal to the rumble of a basso profundo in a bad temper. They died away after a while. I waited to see the next turn with some amusement.

"I take it that five minutes had gone by, when there came a snarl from behind the curtain like an angry dog and on the top of it a burst of some infernal lingo I could make nothing of whatever. The old lady next to me was shaking like a jelly. I asked her what was the matter. 'It's the Ghazi,' she said; 'if you see him, please do not speak. He is not under full control. We never know if——' She stopped short with a quick gasp of fear. Not that I blame her. It was cleverly done, let me tell you.

"The face came peering out from the deepest black of the shadows. It was lit by some device so that it glowed in a soft, uncertain brilliance. A bushy, black beard, sullen eyes and full red lips with a glint of white teeth at the corners—as brutal and cruel a face as I ever saw. It made me mad to think how many poor women the fellow had frightened out of their wits, and in thinking the impulse came upon me. The thing wasn't right. The fraud ought to be exposed. By sitting there I was passively aiding in the imposture. I made one jump from my chair to the switch behind me and flashed on the lights."

Oliver stopped his talk for a moment while he walked to the sideboard and poured himself out a whisky. His hand was none too steady for the bottle, and the rim of the glass clattered like a pair of castanets.

"And what then?" I said.

"There was the devil's own row. The women began to yelp and chatter; but drowning them all, there came, from within the curtain a horrible gasping cry like an animal in a trap. I could see nothing of the Ghazi. Wherever he hid, he was brisk about it. I give him that credit.

"A couple of the men ran behind the curtain and dragged out the medium. He wasn't a pleasant sight. His eyes were twisted up and his neck jerked on one side and his legs and arms anywhere but where they ought to have been. They sponged his face and shoved smelling salts under his nose, all to no purpose. I was left to myself, as if I'd been some sort of a leper. No one so much as looked at me. Stonham was as nasty as the rest. Presently I took him by the arm, but he shook me off, saying that I might have killed the man. If the whole fraud hadn't been so unutterably absurd I should have lost my temper. As it was, I asked him, with a grin, what I was supposed to have done. He made out that I had short circuited the medium, so to speak, chucking his spirit back into him with a thump that had knocked him silly. It was medieval superstition at its very worst.

"It was the best part of an hour before they brought him around. I saw him stretching out his hands to them and moaning. One of the women went off into hysterics there and then, and several of the others burst out sobbing and crying. Finally Stonham came up to the chair where I was sitting. He was looking black as thunder. 'You may be sorry to learn that you have blinded him, Mr. Manton,' he began.

"'Humbug, Mr. Jim Stonham,' said I.

"'I suggest that you go home,' he said, and I could see he was shivering with the rage that was on him. 'Your presence is resented by every man and woman here.'

"I never argue with a crank. I found a cab at the top of the road and here I am."

"But was the medium really blinded?" I asked him.

"Stonham said so. But if the man is blind as a barn full of owls it doesn't affect me. He may try blackmail, but if he does he'll see the inside of a jail pretty smart. Damages to a medium for injury caused by sudden interference in the precipitation of an Afghan—think of it, Sanderson! Some judges would give a week's pay for the advertisement of their humor that such a case would give them. No, no, my friend, we shall hear no more about the medium. You can bet on that for a certainty."

He burst out into a great laugh; but all the same I fancy he was far from comfortable in his mind.

"Well, Sanderson," said he presently, "you've heard the story. What's your opinion?"

Whether the thing had been a fraud or no, I thought that he had acted like a fool; but it was waste of time to tell Oliver Manton a thing like that.

"Probably he is trying to frighten you. He must be mad with you for turning up the lights," I suggested. "But, all the same, I should give him a call in the morning."

He broke out against me for that; indeed I believe he had only been waiting for the excuse. I was as bad as the rest. I was sympathizing with an imposter. He would see the whole lot of us in Hades before he would so much as inquire after the scoundrel. If they intended to blackmail him, he was ready for them. So he went on with a lot of much wilder talk, until I could stand it no longer and went back to bed. A wordy warrior was Oliver Manton.

I had a big case in the Appeal Court next day and I did not see Manton until after dinner. He never mentioned the medium, so I left the subject alone. After all, it was none of my business and, to be frank, I had more than a suspicion that Manton was right in suspecting an attempt at blackmail. It was six weeks and more before the subject turned up again between us.

Manton and I had dined at the club and brought some men back with us for a mild game of poker. There was James Leslie, the editor of the *Evening Gazette*, Malcolm Neill and "Digger" Osborne, both of them lawyers, and Henry Fordyce, who was on the Stock Exchange. We had just settled ourselves down around the table, and Oliver was handing out the chips, when there came a gentle tap at the door and a red-headed boy stepped into the room leading a man by the hand. As I found out afterward, we had left the outer door ajar. The boy had knocked, and receiving no answer had led his companion down the short passage to where he could hear the chatter of our voices.

The man was below middle height, with a yellow, wrinkled face and a way of stretching out his neck and lifting his nose as if he were hunting by scent. From the shade he wore over his eyes I guessed his infirmity, and with the knowledge came the realization of whom he might be. I glanced across at Oliver. He had stopped in his counting, a bunch of chips in his hand, and was staring at the pair by the door.

"I am sorry if I disturb you, gentlemen," said the blind man, with an air of cringing humility, "but I desire to see Mr. Oliver Manton. Is he here?"

"What do you want, Mr. Bennett?" said Oliver in a gentler tone than I had expected.

"I came to thank you, sir, for your great kindness to me. They tell me that you have paid my doctor's bill. You were under no legal liability, Mr. Manton. I am well aware of that. And as I understand that you hold yourself in no way responsible for my— for my trifling misfortune, it seems the more generous of you. I have been ill, sir, a form of nervous prostration, or I should have been here before."

Oliver made no reply. He stood dropping the counters one by one into the box before him. We were all watching him now, I in some anxiety and the rest in open wonder.

"The Circle have been very kind," continued the blind man. "I am glad to say that I am still of use to them. To a medium, Mr. Manton, there is neither light nor darkness."

Oliver let the remaining counters fall with a clatter, and turned on him with a very red face and a squaring of the shoulders.

"Your infirmity, Mr. Bennett, is my sole excuse for not running you down the stairs," he said. "For the help I gave you I do not wish to be thanked. You are under no obligation to me whatever. I consider that you have been earning your living in a contemptible manner. I am sorry to hear that you are continuing to do so. Good-evening."

But Bennett did not go; nor did he seem to resent Oliver's vehemence. Instead he waved his hand with a gesture of deprecation.

"Abuse is not logic, Mr. Manton," he said. "You accuse me of fraud. On what evidence? Simply that you saw a thing which you could not understand. You made an effort to expose me, by which I suffered a heavy misfortune. Did you discover evidence of trickery when you turned up the lights?"

"I am not an expert in conjuring," said Oliver with a sneer.

"You evade my question, Mr. Manton."

"Oh, I can be frank enough if you desire it. I did not observe the precise method of the fraud, and yet I am certain that it existed. Do you imagine, my good man, that you can impose on me with your curtains and your dark rooms? Your materialized spirits are sensible to the touch, I am told. Then from what are they formed? From good British flesh and blood at a pound a week, beer included, or so I venture to suggest. Keep to your old women and neurotic boys, my friend, but don't come proselyting among grown men who are regular in their exercise and hearty at their meals. Take it from me, that you will be wasting your time."

"Yet I do not despair of you, Mr. Oliver Manton."

The blind man stepped forward as he spoke, thrusting out his arms toward us with his long fingers outstretched, and so stood fixed in a sudden rigidity like a pointer dog at the hot scent of a covey. Oliver gave a loud laugh which smelt rather of an intentional insult than of merriment. For myself there came upon me so strong a repulsion and disgust for the fellow that I turned my back on him and walked over to the fire. When I looked around I found that he had fallen back into his pose of exaggerated humility.

"In the studio you imagined wires, trapdoors, paid assistants," he said, "you would not suspect your friends here of collusion? If they will assist in forming a circle, I may be able to convince you that I am no imposter. I find there is power among them. Perhaps we might have some striking manifestation."

Harry Fordyce, the easy cynic, led a chorus of assent. He was already dragging the chairs into position when Oliver stopped him.

"Leave those chairs alone, Harry," he said. "I have told the fellow my opinion of him, and he must go."

They protested loudly. Malcolm Neill, who from the fact that he had a ghost in his father's place near Nairn professed a general belief in the supernatural, began an argument in his penetrating Highland voice. Jim Leslie, as I suspect with an eye to a column in the *Evening Gazette*, joined warmly in support. Even old "Digger" Osborne grumbled against his host for spoiling a bit of fun. Oliver stood it in silence for a while; but at last he turned about and walked to the inner door which communicated with our little dining-room. As he opened it he looked back at us with a flushed face and angry eyes.

"So long as you don't expect me to be present you can play what tricks you please," he said. "When you have quite finished and Mr. Bennett has been so good as to leave my rooms, you can give me a call."

He slammed the door behind him and left us staring.

I had half a mind to follow him, but while I hesitated the others had got the room fixed for the séance and I did not like to seem inhospitable. They had stuck a three-leaf screen in a corner and set chairs before it in a semi-circle, Bennett directing them what to do. We sat down upon the chairs and the red-headed boy, who had stood silent in the shadow of the door all through the argument with Oliver, led the medium behind the screen and then took a place among us. We joined hands, the boy sitting in the center with Fordyce on one side of him and

I on the other. I was determined to keep an eye on him, for he seemed uncommon smart for his age, which I put at about fifteen.

"I think my uncle will have passed into his trance," said the lad presently. "If we are to see Them, there must be darkness."

The shadows sprang out upon us as Fordyce extinguished the two gas jets which lit the room. The fire had sunk away to a glow that stared out like a dull red eye set in the black of the darkness that hedged us in. For the first time in my life I understood why a nervous woman burns a night-light.

Fordyce came groping his way back to his seat and we all joined hands once more. I sat staring straight in front of me into the gloom with vague apprehension. How long it was that I so remained I cannot say. It may have been three or thirty minutes. But, whatever the period, I experienced throughout it, a sensation of nervous exhaustion, a sapping of vitality that left me flaccid and depressed. And it was to this cause that I attribute my extreme terror at the first manifestation.

It was an uncanny sound, a low chuckle of laughter that came bubbling out of the darkness like water out of a bottle. Coward that I was, I cried out at it. And the laugh answered me with a sudden mocking malignity that pressed me shivering against the back of my chair as if in expectation of a blow. Then silence fell again like the slamming of a door.

"They are angry to-night," said the boy, and I felt his hand quiver in mine. "Let us trust that He does not come."

"What do you mean?" asked Fordyce from his other side.

"There is one spirit whom we cannot control. In life he was a Ghazi. If he should appear, do not speak to him. For one can never tell."

Almost as if in answer to him from somewhere within the narrow circle of the chairs there rose a voice, a low guttural snarl in some dialect unknown to me. And with it came a cold air that touched my cheek and fluttered my hair and so was gone. I looked about me, expectant of heaven knows what ghastly apparition. Something was there, I knew, something which I could not see. I was seized by an indefinable dread, a sensation as of the presence of some inhuman Thing, some unnamable horror. What was the secret which the silence and the darkness held? I felt a trickle of sweat on my face. The boy beside me strained at my hand and I heard my fears repeated in his panting breath.

"He has not gone," he whispered, "but He has left the circle, and I am afraid."

"I don't like this, you men," said Fordyce. "I think there's something beastly happening. Let's turn up the lights."

"It would kill my uncle, sir!" cried the boy. "There can be no danger to us from the Ghazi while we keep the circle. It is only that I do not understand."

"All right," grunted Fordyce. "We'll see it through. But I don't like it, not at all."

And so we waited.

There were noises now from behind the screen, though the words themselves were never distinguished. Sighs I heard and little trills of laughter and once a sullen rumble, as of protestation. After a while they ceased, and for a second time the cold wind came, the wind which, as I afterward learned, precedes the materialized spirit. Again I felt a presence which I could not see.

And then out from the gloom there grew the shadow of a face.

Shadow, I have called it, but the word is not correct, for it was luminous with a pale shine. Nor did it immediately define itself. It was the eyes alone that were first distinguishable, nothing but those cold, intolerable eyes. Gradually, as if building itself up line by line, the brow and nose and bearded, sensual lips formed themselves into visibility, and stamped upon them was an expression of hate and mockery that had in it something human, something that served to show that this unknown horror partook of matter sufficient to make it a deadly and fearful enemy to material forms.

The grotesque fancies of medieval monks never created a fiend with an aspect so remorseless, so malign.

The face drew nearer, and now its expression had changed. The eyes glittered with exultation; triumph curled the red lips.

I tore myself from that appalling gaze with a gasp of agony, and as I did so I became aware that a second face was rising beside the first, a face with a wild and hopeless terror in every lineament. It was that of my friend, Oliver Manton—and I knew that he was dead.

It is a confused remembrance that I have. The circle broke into stumbling, shouting segments of panic. At last a gas jet flared up upon the disordered room.

The medium was lying on the ground beside the overturned screen. His eyes were upturned and he was breathing in heavy, stentorous gasps. The red-headed lad was kneeling beside him. So much I saw, before I sprang to the inner door and burst into the little dining-room.

Huddled in the farthest corner, behind the big armchair, with such a look upon his face as will ever be remembered in grief and horror by those who witnessed it, was Oliver Manton, stone dead.

That is all. You will have seen the trial in the papers. There was no mark upon Oliver's body. Heart disease or death from shock or syncope, the doctors wrote it down, as it seemed best to them. And William Fenton Bennett went into the world again. Men still tap their foreheads and smile when they speak of that famous trial. Yet the evidence I gave, I now repeat. For sure am I, and ever shall be, that Bennett came to find his revenge that night; that it was by his influence that the Thing he created drew the life from Oliver Manton, and that he brought the spirit of the newly dead back among us to bear witness to his triumph.

The Greatness of Billy

By

RALPH HENRY BARBOUR

Author of "The Father of a Hero," etc.

Drawing by William Oberhardt

I THINK he might ask me down for a week or two," said Mr. William—to his intimates, Billy—Mellidge in aggrieved tones. He was only five feet five inches from the soles of his small feet to the top of his round, sandy-thatched head, was Billy, but he could look aggrieved enough for the Cornish giant.

Patience Boyd laughed softly in that delicious, "gurgly," way of hers that Billy loved.

"Dad knows when he's well off, Billy. He told me last night that Brae Mere Park was pretty steep as a summer resort, but that it was worth every cent of what it would cost to get somewhere where he wouldn't stumble over you every ten minutes."

"I don't see why he's so down on me lately," said Billy; "we used to be rather thick two years ago."

"I fancy you have begun to pall on him, Billy; you know even caviar loses its piquancy after a prolonged diet of it."

"But I don't see—Why, I'm not tired of him!"

"Oh, Billy," she gasped, "you're too ridiculous!"

"I suppose I must be," he admitted dolefully. "I'm too something, anyway; all my friends are turning away from me nowadays; even you, Pat."

"Billy! I'm not! You've no business to say such things! I can't help it if dad is grouchy, can I? I've said lots of good things about you, and stood up for you right along."

"Have you, Pat? Honest Injun?" he asked eagerly.

She nodded. "Why, last week after you'd told him—that—you know—that you wanted to marry me——" She paused and laughed reminiscently. "Gee, Billy, but he was in an awful pickle!"

"I know," said Billy gloomily; "you told me."

"Well, I said then that I didn't see why he need be so peppery; it wasn't as though you were a coachman or one of those imitation counts, such as Amy Bowditch got herself engaged and almost married to."

"Oh, you said that? Thanks terribly, Pat."

HOW MR. DENIS O'HALLORAN TRANSGRESSED HIS CODE

By B. FLETCHER ROBINSON

ILLUSTRATED BY ARTHUR BECHER

R. DENIS O'HALLORAN paused in the shelter of the inn porch, clasping his long horseman's cloak about him. He was a man below the middle height and of a spare and active figure. His expression was resolute and his eyes of a merry audacity. The light from behind him threw his shadow in gigantic relief upon the spreading puddles of the highway. Above him the gale roistered among the chimneys and gables of the old house. An April moon, sailing clear in a hurrying sky, showed him where, to the southward, his road crept up from the village into the shadows of the hills.

"'Tis no night for travelers, sir," said the landlord, pushing forward. "A young gentleman would be safer employed with a bowl of punch, or it might be a spike of mulled claret, than in riding the moors."

"Safer, ye say?" The brogue betrayed him.

"Indeed, sir," urged the landlord, "if you were of this country you would know that we have been much plagued of late by knaves that the late unhappy rebellion has let loose upon us. 'Twas not a week since that Sir Francis Grove, of Oakdale, was waylaid."

"Pish, man, I know ye've a bed to let," grinned Mr. O'Halloran.

"There be yet worse things than a cutpurse," said the landlord, wagging his head.

"Faith, but I'd make their acquaintance."

"The powers of evil, young gentleman. For when a body is freshly swung by the Beacon Hill, which I would have you remember that you must pass, there have been substantial folk come riding here, calling loudly for strong drink and telling of things that crouched beneath the tree like toads, and things that screamed and chattered in the air. The Lord preserve us."

"Let me be plain with ye, landlord," said Mr. O'Halloran. "On to York I must. As f'r what I may meet by the way, I take it that a sword an' pistol will serve f'r the wan and a clane conscience f'r the other. My horse, if ye plase."

"'Tis here, sir, 'tis here," said the landlord. He bustled out into the road as he spoke, waving an arm to an advancing hostler.

Denis O'Halloran rode swiftly through the village street, easing his mount as he met the shoulder of the hill. To right and left, as his horse stumbled and grunted up the ill-kept road, there spread a succession of vast and melancholy moorlands that rose and fell in long undulations until they were merged in the gloom of the middle distance. From the ridges above him the gusts swooped down in sudden squalls like the firing of cannon. Not a cottage, not a barn, nor any creature that might house therein, was to be seen. Bold as he might be, his courage did not save him from uneasy glances toward the shifting pools of shadow which the scattered bushes threw upon the track. It was an age when the wayfarer had still to rely upon his own weapon for safety, and he knew that after nightfall such waste places must have their perils.

He reached the crown of the hill and pushed forward at a livelier gait. It was a rolling country, however, and within a mile he found himself descending a sharp incline into a valley deep in shadow. Once his hand slipped round to his sword; but it was no more than the cry of a distant owl, and he was jeering at himself for a coward as his horse stumbled among the bowlders of a ford and breasted the opposing slope.

"Mr. O'Halloran looked 'round just in time."

The wind was still blowing in fitful gusts, but the high crest of the hill, beneath which he now found himself, afforded him an absolute shelter. Moreover, it hid the moon. Silence on a solitary and dangerous way is ever suggestive in its possibilities. He found himself leaning forward with eager ears. Suddenly he drew rein, cocking his head with a queer trick he had, like a dog at a door. From somewhere beyond the bend of the road there came a faint sound as of metal on metal or metal on stone. Yet it was neither beat of hoof nor clink of stirrup iron.

For man Denis O'Halloran had little fear. He had already acquired some reputation in campaigns under an alien flag. But it was a superstitious age and he came of a superstitious people. The tales of the landlord had not left him unaffected. Therefore, when pushing warily forward he rounded the spur of the hill into the full light of the moon, the spectacle which met his gaze shook his heart into his mouth and his hand to the pistol in his holster.

On a little plateau some fifty paces from the road and circled by a rising slope, stood a gallows whereon hung the body of a man. The sight was familiar; by such means were the highways rightfully protected. But the corpse did not swing unattended. A few paces from the foot of the gibbet were two figures, the one erect, wrapped in a trailing cloak, the other crouching to some labor. And there fell on him the conviction that these creatures were not of earth nor of God.

The crouching figure moved; the light gleamed on a pick as it rose, and the clicking sound came again to his ears. It was digging a grave painfully and slowly. Presently it stopped, dropping the tool, and as it did so the other struck it so that it raised a loud wail of pain. A woman's voice, thought the traveler, and his blood stirred within him. He glanced about him like a man waking from a dream. On the road two hundred yards away was the blurred outline of a coach. These were neither ghosts nor wizards then; but a man and with him a woman suffering distresses. With an oath he set spurs to his horse and galloped headlong toward them.

The man never moved from where he stood, but the woman ran toward him, crying, with outstretched arms. The traveler was out of the saddle in a flash and slipped an arm about her, for she seemed near to falling.

"Save me," she said, "for the love of heaven."

"Faith, madam, an' I will be blithe to do so," said Mr. O'Halloran. He looked down at her with satisfaction. She was indeed a fine woman, though not in her first youth.

The man advanced from beneath the shadow of the corpse, dropping his cloak as he did so. The moon showed him tall and lean, with a long face and a stern and melancholy expression. He carried himself with an air of dignity. Plainly he was of gentle breeding.

"It would be well, sir, if you do not interfere in that which nowise concerns you," he said sternly.

"By the blessed saints, but did ye ever hear the like!" cried Mr. O'Halloran, clasping the lady a thought more closely.

"I perceive you are an Irishman," sneered the tall man.

"An' I perceive that ye ar-re an impertinent scoundrel," returned Mr. O'Halloran.

"I do not desire to brawl with you, my good fellow. Let it suffice you that I have an explanation for what I am about."

"An explanation, have ye?" cried Mr. O'Halloran in vast indignation. "Then let me tell ye that amongst Irish gentlemen the striking iv a lady admits no explanation. Sor, ye lack gentility. If I had the time I would tache ye manners with a cane. Is that your coach, madam?" He turned, pointing a finger to where it stood. She nodded her head, watching him with eager eyes.

"Then permit me to escort ye to it."

"That you shall not do, by heaven," cried the tall man.

The Irishman made him a mock reverence. Plainly the situation pleased him greatly.

"'Tis the first word iv sinse that ye've spoken," he said. "The moon shines bravely, sir, though the company"—he glanced at the gallows—"might well be bethered."

"My preserver," whimpered the lady, clinging to his arm.

"That, madam, is as the saints may direct," he said. "Though our melancholy friend yonder seems more apt with his tongue than with his weapon."

"What are you?" said the tall man. "Jacobite fugitive, cutthroat, or an Irish bogtrotter on a journey? Pray give me so much of your confidence."

"I hold a captain's commission," replied Mr. O'Halloran with becoming dignity, "though in what ar-rmy it is not precisely convanient f'r me to mention. Does that content ye?"

"I am at your service," said the other.

"May heaven aid you," murmured the lady.

Mr. O'Halloran stooped and kissed her hand.

"Ye do me great honor, madam," said he.

"My knight in time of need," she smiled into his eyes.

"I account meself the more fortunate," he said, and then in a lower tone, "While we ar-re engaged, I pray you, madam, away to your coach. 'Twill be safer—in case——"

"Sir," she said very loud and bold, "I stay here that I may see you kill him."

Mr. O'Halloran slipped off his cloak, drew his sword, and stepped forward with a lean activity. He made a pretty figure of a man as he stood in the moonlight, examining the ground. The moor was rough with tufted heather, save for a level patch in the midst of which the gibbet had been planted. A score of feet to the right he marked the open grave with its banks of dark mold. He did not dwell upon so suggestive a spectacle.

"It must be here or nowhere," he said. "May the poor lad yonder pardon us."

"For his pardon I will answer, sir," said the tall man with a sad sort of smile. "He would not have wished it otherwise."

Mr. O'Halloran did not reply save by a fencing-room salute.

"The moon shines justly for both," said the tall man; and the swords rang together.

In the French capital there was not a *maître d'armes* but spoke well of the sword of the Irishman. Yet before the sudden and infernal onslaught of his opponent he gave back five paces and more. The man crowded in upon him with a contained and glowing fury, so that he fought for his life, making no effort beyond the parrying of the deadly stabs hurled at him. Blue shone the blades as they flickered under the moon, save when now and again a spark sprang from a fiercer thrust met by a stronger parry. The ground was bad, the light was bad, and if O'Halloran was by far the more accomplished swordsman, he knew too much to risk an attack against a man to whom death seemed a matter of no concern at all.

In that first mad rush of his opponent the Irishman had been forced back to the very foot of the gallows tree, so that it almost seemed that he fought with his back against it. Above them the corpse swung in its chains so that now its shadow fell upon the blades as if to lend its aid to the fiercer, if less expert, of the duelists. He noticed it and laughed aloud in a high, inhuman note. Yet it was the renewed strength that it seemed to lend him which proved his undoing. He lunged too wildly—too far; the Irishman met him by a keen *riposte*. He stopped with an oath, dropping his sword to the ground.

"Again, again!" screamed the woman.

Mr. O'Halloran paid her no attention, but stepped back, lowering his point. The other swayed where he stood, plucking at his shoulder with red and dripping fingers. In another moment the Irishman was beside him, supporting him.

"It was the charge iv a bull," he panted. "Man, ye were beside yourself. Are ye badly hurted?"

"The shoulder, not the lung, I think," said the tall man. "May I ask you, sir, to keep that woman off me?"

Mr. O'Halloran looked round just in time. The lady had picked up his sword and was running in upon them. She halted, gesticulating.

"You fool!" she cried. "Kill him!"

Mr. O'Halloran was by her side in two strides and recovered his weapon. He moreover took the precaution of picking up that of his adversary before he returned to him. It was a disabling but not a dangerous wound. In three minutes he had triced it up so as to stop the bleeding. He rose from his knees. The woman was standing beside him. He met her eyes without flinching.

"Madam," said he, "I have found this gentleman a very brave and iligant fighter. To be thruthful with ye, I would know more iv this business."

"Then I will bid you good night, sir," she said coldly. "I can find my way to the coach."

"I must ask ye, with due submission, to remain where ye ar-re," replied Mr. O'Halloran. "At least until such time as I have inquired further iv this gentleman."

The tall man was seated on the ground, nursing his arm, his back propped against the gallows. He regarded them curiously.

"I can trust my story to an antagonist who is as honorable as he is bold," he said. "If you can induce the lady to remain——"

"It would only be right," interrupted Mr. O'Halloran.

She laughed defiantly.

"And if I disobey?" she inquired.

"I trust ye will not," he said with a sharp decision.

She made no reply, but seated herself, drawing her cloak about her.

"I am at your service, sor-r," said Mr. O'Halloran.

The tall man bent his head for a moment, plucking at the grass with his uninjured hand.

"My name is Yorke," he said. "Colonel Francis Yorke. You may have heard it?"

"It was tolerably familiar after Fontenoy," laughed the Irishman. "I am proud to make your betther acquaintance."

"What I now have to tell you is the truth—upon my honor."

"That is sufficient for me," replied Mr. O'Halloran.

"An old man with grown sons about him married again," said the colonel. "Heavens, sir, does not the devil's opportunity lie in old men's follies? He had met the lady at a rout at York. He knew naught of her but that she was bold in spirit and pleasing to the eye. His elder son, a soldier serving abroad, saw neither the wooing nor the wedding; the younger did that which he could to check his father's doting desires. She met the lad and defeated him at every turn of the game. She laughed away his evidence of her past as malicious talebearing. So he perforce must watch this jade come flaunting into his home, knowing full well with what hatred she regarded him and what little hope of joy in life under his father's roof remained to him."

"Ye speak bitterly, sir," said Mr. O'Halloran.

"Is it a merry tale? Come, hear it out. Within a year of the marriage, over the border came the Highland cattle lifters with that Papist adventurer, Charles Stuart—What? Do I touch your politics? Forget it, sir, or I shall never have done. The lad was of an age for romance. His father's wife had raffish friends who made a pothouse boast of it to drink to their king over the water. Together they beguiled him until in the end he rode away to join—pshaw, but I must be careful—to join the most valiant army of the only true and puissant monarch of these islands, then about to retreat from Derby. 'Twas a pretty plot, worthy of the sex to which, I observe, sir, you are a devoted champion. The old man was a Whig who hated the Pretender as he would the devil. To him comes his good wife with loud lamentations. The prodigal son had ridden away to join the invaders, a Jacobite declared. She hinted at fines and sequestrations. Whereat the father swore that his son should never darken his doors again; and this may I say of him, that the sterner the vow the more closely he ever held to it. He had been a strong man in his day, both of mind and body.

"I will not tire you, sir, with needless particulars. The lad was in hiding for six months, starving for a year. He crept back to his home, was turned from the doors, and in his desperation he stopped a coach here upon the moors. Information against him was already out, through whose agency you may best guess. He was apprehended and hanged in chains near by the scene of his offense as a warning to malefactors."

"Ye should have told me iv this before—before we fell to disputing," said Mr. O'Halloran.

"You understand, then?"

For answer the Irishman whipped out his sword and saluted the corpse where it clanked and swung.

"He died for his king," he said, "though I had rather it had been at Culloden. God save the king!"

"You do us honor, sir," said the colonel. "In my brother's name I thank you."

The lady rose from where she sat, throwing back her cloak with an angry gesture.

"Do you believe this man?" she cried.

"Faith, madam, but I do," said Mr. O'Halloran.

"This woman beater?"

She scored a hit. He hung undecided, with a toe scratching the turf.

"Permit me to finish my tale, sir," said the colonel. "I learnt that my good stepmother was journeying home this evening. Wherefore I took the occasion to invite her to my brother's funeral. I could not leave him here, poor lad. As she had hung my brother, it seemed but in due course that she should help me to dig his grave. Finding her opposed to the suggestion, I used the argument most likely to appeal to her. Our work was well-nigh ended when you appeared. Upon its termination it was my intention to escort her to her coach."

"You hear this villain," cried the lady. "He forced me to dig, to dig till my hands were blistered!"

"It would be a better grave were it a few inches deeper," said the colonel, "and the soil is light."

Mr. Denis O'Halloran thrust out his chest, fingered his sword hilt, and scowled at the gallows, the moon, and the moors.

"By the honor of me house, sor-r," he said, "but I think that your stepmother will do well if she takes to the spade again."

Footnotes and Sources

1

Black Magic - The Story of the Spanish Don: *Cassell's Magazine*, July 1899 (pp. 178-189), illustrated by F.H. Townsend, edited by Max Pemberton and published by Cassell & Co. Ltd. (London). This standard-sized British monthly was a continuation of *Cassell's Family Magazine* (December 1874-November1897). Bertram Fletcher Robinson began writing non-fiction for that title during March 1897. However, under the editorship of Pemberton, the magazine began to publish more fiction and it grew to resemble *The Strand Magazine*. References to nautical terms, kerosene and palm-oil, suggest that Fletcher Robinson based this story upon a tale that was told to him by his father, Joseph Fletcher Robinson. Joseph had visited South American during the 'Guerra Grande' (1839-1851) and he was befriended by Giuseppe Garibaldi (commander of the Uruguayan fleet). Thereafter, Joseph returned to Liverpool and founded a merchant business that traded molasses, oil and kerosene. This was the only story that Fletcher Robinson wrote prior to his collaboration with Arthur Conan Doyle over *The Hound of the Baskervilles* (1901). This implies that Fletcher Robinson was inspired anew by that experience. During 1907, Pemberton completed a novel entitled *Wheels of Anarchy* (London: Cassell & Co. Ltd.) using notes that were bequeathed to him by the then deceased Fletcher Robinson. During 1928, Pemberton was knighted for his contribution to both writing and journalism.

2

The Laughter of Dr. Marais: *Cassell's Magazine*, May 1902 (pp. 653-661), illustrated by Allan Stewart, edited by Max Pemberton and published by Cassell & Co. Ltd. (London). This story is Fletcher Robinson's second story and it was also the first to appear after the publication of both the first British and American book editions of *The Hound of the Baskervilles* (March 1902 and April 1902 respectively). The opening scene is reminiscent of seascape paintings of the Breton Coast by the French Impressionist, Henri Moret (1856-1913). Certainly, this area (once referred to as 'Lesser Britain') resembles the Cornish coast, where Fletcher Robinson had set the start to his first story. Furthermore, the principal character in this second story is called Henri Marsac, a name that resonates with Henri Moret. In any event, Fletcher Robinson was a Francophile and he had visited France during 1897. Moreover, Fletcher Robinson also wrote reviews of books that were written in French for the *Daily Express* newspaper (1900-1904). One such article (21st May 1901), was for a book entitled *La Guerre Transvaal – En Pleine Epopée* by Jean Carreres, a correspondent for the French newspaper, *Le Matin*. This book is generally critical of British foreign attitudes in relation to the Second Boer War (1899-1902), but it is complimentary about Conan Doyle, a point that Fletcher Robinson stresses within his review. Shortly thereafter, Conan Doyle used the name 'Carere' for an incidental character in *The Hound of the Baskervilles*.

The Strange Experience of Dr. Robert Harland (with John Malcolm Fraser): *The Windsor Magazine*, December 1902–May 1903. All six stories were illustrated by Adolf Thiede, edited by Arthur Hutchinson and published by Ward, Lock & Co. Ltd. (London). This standard-sized British monthly was a rival to *The Strand Magazine* within which, many of the Sherlock Holmes tales were first published (including *The Hound of the Baskervilles*). This serialization of six tales is about an insane professor who leaves a trail of murdered critics strewn across Europe. Each episode is based about a location that Fletcher Robinson had visited whilst researching a non-fictional six-part serialization entitled *Capitals at Play* for *Cassell's Magazine* (1897). All six episodes were republished in a book entitled *The Trail of the Dead* in both Britain and Canada (February 1904) and also as a serialization in two American newspapers, *The Sumner Gazette* (Sumner, Iowa; May-August 1906) and *Daily Herald* (Chicago, Illinois; May-August 1906). Fraser (1878-1949) worked with Fletcher Robinson as 'Day Editor' of the *Daily Express* between 1902 and 1904. Later, Fraser was knighted (1919), created a baronet (1921) and awarded the Knight Grand Cross of the Order of the British Empire (1922).

[**3**] *I.-The Hairy Caterpillar*: *The Windsor Magazine*, December 1902 (pp. 121-129). This first episode opens at Heidelberg University and it introduces the reader to the three principal protagonists; Sir Henry Graden (hero, scientist and explorer), Doctor Robert Harland (narrator, physician, student and Graden's cousin) and Professor Rudolf Marnac (villain, scientist, lecturer and skilled linguist). There is a repetition here between Graden's title and Christian name and a major character in *The Hound of the Baskervilles* (Sir Henry Baskerville). Fletcher Robinson also makes references to both South Africa and Berlin. Conan Doyle wrote that his friendship with Fletcher Robinson was 'cemented' in July 1900 during a voyage between Cape Town and Southampton. Moreover, both men had previously visited Berlin during 1890 and 1897 respectively. There are also some parallels between the characters of Professor Marnac and Professor Moriarty, the latter of whom is featured in the Holmes story, *The Adventure of the Final Problem* (1893). Moriarty is also mentioned in another Holmes story to which, Fletcher Robinson made a contribution, *The Adventure of the Norwood Builder* (1903).

[**4**] *II.-The Mystery of the Lemsdorf Ham*: *The Windsor Magazine*, January 1903 (pp. 264-274). This second episode is set predominantly within a West Prussian village called 'Lemsdorf', close to what is now the border between Poland and Russia. In this story, Graden and Harland speed to the home of Professor Peter Mechersky from St. Petersburg University in a fruitless bid to prevent his murder. It is worth noting that in 1897, Fletcher Robinson had visited both St. Petersburg and Livadia Palace in Livadiya where he was received by the entourage of Tsar Nicholas II. Pemberton wrote that during this visit, Fletcher Robinson met the 'Emperor's Great Chamberlain' and was subjected to persistent surveillance by the 'Russian Secret Police'. It is feasible that the Tsar's entourage also included the then Deputy Foreign Minister, Vladimir Lambsdorff (pronounced 'Lamsdorf' in vernacular British English). Later, Lambsdorff succeeded Mikhail Muravyov as the Russian Foreign Minister and he

presided in that office during the Russo-Japanese War (1904-1905). This was a topic that Fletcher Robinson wrote about during his editorship of *Vanity Fair* (1904-1907).

[5] *III.-The Chase in the Snow*: *The Windsor Magazine*, February 1903 (pp. 370-379). In this third episode, Professor Marnac attempts to escape from Lemsdorf to the Prussian town of 'Gnessen', close to what is now the border between Poland and Germany. However, Marnac's plan to escape by train is thwarted and so he escapes by sleigh instead, committing a third murder in the process. It is worth noting that Marnac had originally planned to use the 'Posen-Frankfurt' train for the final stage of his journey to Gnessen. Between 1869 and 1938, a silversmith company by the name of Lazarus Posen traded at Frankfurt-am-Main in Germany. This company specialized in the design of ornate plates, cups and beakers that were sometimes awarded as trophies to the winners of sports competitions. It is feasible that Fletcher Robinson had competed for a 'Posen-Frankfurt' trophy during his time as either a rugby player or rower at Cambridge University (1890-1894).

[6] *IV.-The Anonymous Article*: *The Windsor Magazine*, March 1903 (pp. 477-486). In this fourth episode, Graden and Harland travel from Berlin to London in order to ascertain the identity of Marnac's next victim. Thereafter, they travel to the fictional village of 'Polleven' in Cornwall and avert the murder of a Cambridge don called Professor Weston. However, Marnac (alias Mr. Hermann) is able to make good his escape by fishing-boat. The core part of this tale is narrated from a diary that is owned by the intended victim's daughter, Miss Mary Weston. Conan Doyle had employed a similar narrative technique for the Dartmoor-based chapters of *The Hound of the Baskervilles*, which are related from letters that were written by Dr. John H. Watson and sent to Sherlock Holmes. Moreover, in both stories, the principal characters undertake their journey to the West Country by a train that departs from Paddington Station in London.

[7] *V.-The Ammonia Cylinder*: *The Windsor Magazine*, April 1903 (pp. 627-638). In this fifth and penultimate episode, Graden and Harland procure a sailing ship and set-off in pursuit of Marnac who is fleeing towards the French coast. However, a violent storm sinks Marnac's boat and he alone is saved by Graden. The three men are then picked-up by a Portuguese ship and Marnac, a skilled linguist, manages to convince the ship's captain that Graden and Harland are fugitives. Marnac then attempts to murder both men but he is disturbed and kills a servant boy instead. He then manages to escape from the ship when it docks at Southampton, the same port to which, Fletcher Robinson and Conan Doyle had returned from South Africa during July 1900. The Portuguese ship is called *San Joseph* and it was on-route to Hamburg from Buenos Ayres [sic]. There is here, the repetition of the Christian name of Fletcher Robinson's father, who once made a solitary 800 mile trek by horse from Buenos Aires to Santiago across the Andes. It seems likely that Joseph recounted such adventures to Fletcher Robinson and thereby prompted his son's passion for story-telling.

[8] *VI.-The End of the Trail*: *The Windsor Magazine*, May 1903 (pp. 734-743). This sixth and final episode opens at 'Polleven' where it is decided that the ailing Weston and his daughter, the future Mrs. Harland, should over-winter at Pontresina in Switzerland. They are placed in the protective custody of 'Reski', the father of Marnac's third victim. However, the plan is betrayed by Marnac's accomplice, 'Penruman' who is courting Weston's housekeeper (her name changes from 'Marjory' to 'Martha' in this episode). When Graden and Harland are summoned to Switzerland they are hijacked by Marnac. Reski sacrifices his own life to kill Marnac and to prevent him from driving the coach carrying Graden and Harland into a deep gorge called 'Berguner Stein'. It is feasible that Fletcher Robinson derived this name from a fictitious Swiss gorge named 'Bergunerstein' that features in the novel, *Samuel Brohl et Cie* (1877) by Charles Victor Cherbuliez (1829-1899). In any event, the fate of Professor Marnac bares some resemblance to that of Professor Moriarty who was seemingly killed after falling from a ledge at the nearby Reichenbach Falls in *The Adventure of the Final Problem* (1893). It appears that Fletcher Robinson visited the Engadine area of Switzerland during a trip to neighboring Austria in 1897.

9

The Battle of Fingle's Bridge: *Pearson's Magazine*, May 1903 (pp. 530-536), illustrated by Nathan Dean, edited by Percy Everett and published by C. Arthur Pearson Ltd. (London). This standard-sized British monthly was the leading rival to *The Strand Magazine*. The story is a fairy tale, narrated by a boy who falls asleep upon a moor and witnesses a battle between the 'people of the ferns and rushes' and the 'people of the gorse and heather'. All the characters are six inches tall and they are dressed in medieval garb and armour and equipped with miniature horses and weapons. The boy, aided by a fairy, becomes involved in the battle and finally awakens to find signs of the battle on the moor. There is a Fingle Bridge over the River Teign, which is a famous tourist beauty spot near Drewsteignton, on the north-eastern border of Dartmoor. On 24th February 1923, Conan Doyle reportedly told a reporter from *The Western Morning News and Mercury* that he believed in Devonshire fairies. It is also worth noting that during 1903, Fletcher Robinson and Percy Everett were each employed by Cyril Arthur Pearson to work for the *Daily Express* newspaper as the debut editor and literary editor respectively. Moreover, Fletcher Robinson was Godfather to Everett's daughter, Geraldine 'Winn' Everett (6th February 1903–21st January 1998). In 1930, Percy Everett was knighted for his work with the Boy Scouts and Girl Guides Association.

10

Fog Bound (with John Malcolm Fraser): *The London Magazine*, August 1903 (pp. 47-56), illustrated by A.J. Gough, edited by Charles Sisley and published by The Amalgamated Press Ltd. (London). This standard-sized British monthly specialized in the publication of popular adventure and mystery fiction. The story centers upon an Irish-born British Army officer called Captain Francis Delaney VC, who has recently served in the Second Anglo-Afghan War. He is captured by revengeful Nihilists who mistakenly believe him to be their former jailer, Prince Michael Pavaloff of Little Russia, an area that Fletcher Robinson had visited during 1897.

Ironically, Delaney is saved by Pavaloff but the two men later duel with pistols after Pavaloff threatens to harm a Radical called Madame Paula. Afghanistan was also the location of The Battle of Maiwand (1880), a conflict that is mentioned on page one of the first Sherlock Holmes story, *A Study in Scarlet* (1886). During this battle, Dr. Watson is wounded and he is forced to retire from the British Army and return to England where he meets Sherlock Holmes. A real-life survivor of The Battle of Maiwand called Gunner Loosemore was also forced to return to England because of his injuries. Following his retirement from the army during the 1880's, Loosemore resided in Exeter, whilst Fletcher Robinson lived at nearby Ipplepen (20 miles).

11

The Debt of Heinrich Hermann: *Pearson's Magazine*, October 1903 (pp. 432-440), illustrated by C. Lawson Wood, edited by Percy Everett and published by C. Arthur Pearson Ltd. (London). In this London-based story, a young electrician (Cecil Ransome) is imprisoned with a savage gorilla by a jilted love-rival and animal-dealer (Heinrich Hermann). However, both man and beast eventually come to some 'understanding' and conspire to escape. Later, Ransome's ordeal is discovered by a physician (Sir Richard) who after treating him, reads a diary that he kept during the captivity. This aspect of the story resonates with the true-life discovery during 1884, of 'The Elephant Man' by the physician, Frederick Treeves. This might indicate that Fletcher Robinson was opposed to both 'freak shows' and zoos. However, the story goes beyond this and it also conflicts the 'humanity' shown by the ape towards Ransome with the inhumanity shown to him by Hermann. It minds a modern reader of the relationship between Ann Darrow and the ill-fated giant gorilla in the film, *King Kong* (1933). This was in turn influenced by Conan Doyle's novel, *The Lost World* (1912), within which, Fletcher Robinson appears thinly disguised as the heroic narrator, Edward E. Malone. There is also a repetition between the villain's name and that of the famous German physician and bacteriologist, Heinrich Hermann Robert Koch (1843-1910). During 1890, Conan Doyle went to Berlin to investigate Koch's claim that he had discovered a cure for tuberculosis, a condition suffered by his wife (see [**15**]). However, this declaration proved unfounded and there was for a short time, a furious backlash against Koch.

12-18

The Chronicles of Addington Peace: *The Lady's Home Magazine*, August 1904–October 1904 and thereafter, in the renamed *Home Magazine of Fiction*, November 1904–January 1905. All six stories were illustrated by Thomas Heath Robinson, edited by K. Maud Bennett and published by C. Arthur Pearson Ltd. (London). This monthly magazine was a pulp alternative to *The Strand Magazine*. Each episode features Inspector Addington Peace, who is described as 'a tiny slip of a fellow, of about five and thirty years of age'. Peace works for Scotland Yard's Criminal Investigation Department and he is partnered by a Watson-like biographer called James Phillips (a neighboring artist). During June 1905, revised versions of all six stories were republished in a book that is also entitled *The Chronicles of Addington Peace* (London: Harper & Brother). This book edition includes two additional episodes, *The Story of Amaroff the Pole* and *The Mystery of Thomas Hearne* and it is listed in the influential *Queen's Quorum: A History of the Detective-Crime Short Story as Revealed by the 106 Most Important Books Published in this Field Since 1845* (Boston: Little, Brown & Co., 1951). Thomas Heath Robinson was the elder brother of the more-famous William Heath Robinson. Both men were illustrators, as was a third brother, their father, uncle and grandfather. Pearson had previously employed Fletcher Robinson as a journalist for the *Daily Express* (1900-1904). During 1916, Pearson was granted a baronetcy in recognition of his charitable work on behalf of the blind.

[12] *I. The Terror in the Snow*: *The Lady's Home Magazine*, August 1904 (pp. 114-127). This first episode (Chapter 2 in the book edition) opens in Phillips' flat at Keble Street in Westminster in London. Phillips informs Peace that he will be spending Christmas Eve at the Norfolk home of his wealthy financier friend, Baron Steen. During this visit, Phillips learns that Steen leases the estate from an old family called de Laune and that the gardens are reputedly haunted by the ghost of an albino wolf. Later, Phillips hears Steen's death cries and he also sees what he believes to be the ghost on a nearby pathway that is bordered by yew trees. There is some repetition here with the events and circumstances that surrounded the death of Sir Charles Baskerville in *The Hound of the Baskervilles*. Moreover, this story was written shortly after Fletcher Robinson and Conan Doyle had visited Norfolk together during late April 1901. Later, Peace concludes that Steen was killed by his secretary, Maurice Terry in revenge for ruining his father. It was Conan Doyle's secretary, Major Charles Terry, who wrote from dictation a letter that acknowledges Fletcher Robinson's assistance with *The Hound of the Baskervilles* for the first American book edition of that story (New York: McClure, Phillips & Co. Ltd., 15th April 1902). This letter was written on 26th January 1902 and it is now held by the Berg Collection at the New York Public Library.

[13] *II. Mr. Taubery's Diamond*: *The Lady's Home Magazine,* September 1904 (pp. 220-230). In this second episode (Chapter 3 in the book edition), Peace is asked to investigate the disappearance of a valuable diamond on behalf of one Julius Taubery. The gem is substituted for a worthless imitation during a luncheon party that is held shortly before Taubery is due to relocate to France. Despite the rapid detection of this theft and a meticulous search of the assembled guests, the diamond is not located. Thereafter, an auction takes place at Taubery's home and a 'bicycle-horse' sells for far more than was anticipated. It transpires that the missing diamond was concealed in the saddle of this toy by a guest called The Honourable George Carstairs. Both this title and surname are shared by a character in a Sherlock Holmes film entitled *Terror by Night* (Universal Studios, 1946). This film is loosely based upon the plot of two Holmes stories, *The Adventure of the Blue Carbuncle* (1892) and *The Disappearance of Lady Frances Carfax* (1911). In the film, The Honourable Roland Carstairs employs Holmes to prevent the theft of a valuable diamond that belongs to his mother, Lady Margaret. Holmes suspects that she might be robbed on a train as it travels between London and Edinburgh. Shortly after the train departs from Euston Station, his suspicion is confirmed and Carstairs is also murdered.

[14] *III. Mr. Coran's Election*: *The Lady's Home Magazine,* October 1904 (pp. 326-336). In this third episode (Chapter 7 in the book edition), Peace foils a plot to discredit a political candidate called James Coran at a public meeting on the eve of a county council election. Fletcher Robinson had been shortlisted to be the Liberal Party Parliamentary Candidate for Mid Devonshire during the run-up to a by-election that was contested in January 1904. During July of that same year, he wrote an article entitled *On Political Lies – A Growing Danger in British Politics* for *Vanity Fair*. In this item, Fletcher Robinson condemned the way in which some political parties were using misinformation to further their cause. He dismissed claims that food prices were rising, immigration was spiralling and the British Army had committed atrocities during The Second Boer War (1899-1902). He exemplified this point further through a reference to Conan Doyle who had stood in the General Election of 1900. Fletcher Robinson wrote that Conan Doyle's election had seemed certain but that on 'the day of the poll, however, the constituency was placarded with posters, stating in four-feet letters that Conan Doyle was a Roman Catholic, and that the Church of Scotland was in danger…An honourable method of winning an election surely!'. Evidently, Fletcher Robinson was dissatisfied with the political process in Britain when he wrote this story.

[15] *IV. The Mystery of the Causeway*: *Home Magazine of Fiction,* November 1904 (pp. 431-440). In this fourth episode (Chapter 4 in the book edition), a character called Sir Andrew Cheyne (nephew of Sir William Cheyne) is killed whilst tampering with a 'spring gun' that he intends to use to kill a blackmailer. It is possible that Fletcher Robinson derived the name for this character from a Scottish merchant of that same name. Captain Andrew Cheyne undertook numerous trading voyages to the Western Pacific region and he wrote about them in a book entitled *A Description of Islands in the Western Pacific Ocean, North and South of the Equator: with Sailing Directions* (London: J.D. Potter, 1852). It is conceivable that this book was owned by the former shipping merchant, Joseph Fletcher Robinson and that his son, Bertram, had read it too. Certainly, Fletcher Robinson wrote about sea voyages and explorers on several occasions. Captain Andrew Cheyne was also the father of Sir William Watson Cheyne, a British surgeon and bacteriologist. William Cheyne was interested in preventative medicine and he trained at Koch's laboratory in Berlin during 1886 (see **[11]**). Later, William Cheyne conducted trials with a drug called tuberculin upon tuberculosis patients and reported that repeated doses led to an improved condition. He also served as a consulting surgeon for the British military in South Africa between 1900 and 1901. Hence, it is possible that Fletcher Robinson and Conan Doyle had each met William Cheyne during their own visits to that country (April 1900-July 1900).

[16] *V. The Vanished Millionaire*: *Home Magazine of Fiction,* December 1904 (pp. 577-587). This fifth and penultimate episode (Chapter 6 in the book edition) is the most 'popular' of Fletcher Robinson's short stories in so much that it has been republished on at least eleven occasions. There are various versions of this original story and several of these were published under the inflationary title of *The Vanished Billionaire* within American publications (see *B. Fletcher Robinson Bibliography*).

This episode centers upon the kidnapping of an American businessman during the execution of an important business deal. Although this crime is committed upon an estate on the Hampshire downs, the general setting is reminiscent of Dartmoor in Devon. Furthermore, like Conan Doyle's two Dartmoor-based Sherlock Holmes stories, *Silver Blaze* (1892) and *The Hound of the Baskervilles* (1901), the case hinges upon a set of tracks that were made by the victim and then subsequently disturbed. Such parallels have prompted the noted Sherlockian scholar, Philip Weller to speculate that *The Vanished Millionaire* might be based upon some 'Proto-Hound' story that was written during the collaboration between Conan Doyle and Fletcher Robinson over *The Hound of the Baskervilles*. However, there is, as of yet, no documentary evidence to support this theory.

[17] *VI. The Mystery of the Jade Spear*: *Home Magazine of Fiction*, January 1905 (pp. 79-88). In this sixth and final episode (Chapter 8 in the book edition), one Colonel William Bulstrode is inadvertently killed by his brother, Anstruther Bulstrode following a dispute over the ownership of a valuable jade spear. The surname of both the victim and culprit might be derived from Bulstrode Park in northwest Buckinghamshire. This is the site of a former house that was built for the infamous 'Hanging Judge', George Jeffreys (1645-1689). He was the son John Jeffreys (1608-1691), a notable Royalist during the English Civil War (1642-1651). Fletcher Robinson was a history graduate with a special interest in the English Civil War and he is known to have visited Buckinghamshire. The use of the Christian name Anstruther is also noteworthy because it was later used by P.G. Wodehouse within a short story entitled *The Love That Purifies* from *Very Good, Jeeves* (1930). Wodehouse collaborated with Fletcher Robinson on at least three occasions (1903-1905) and Mr. Anstruther remains one of his most famous incidental characters.

[18] *The Mystery of Thomas Hearne*: *Pearson's Magazine*, May 1905 (pp. 497-507), illustrated by C. Lawson Wood, edited by Percy Everett and published by C. Arthur Pearson Ltd. (London). This Dartmoor-based tale features an escaped convict and an act of murderous revenge. It was probably intended to be a stand-alone tale but it was swiftly revised and then incorporated into the book edition of *The Chronicles of Addington Peace* (Chapter 5). Perhaps for this reason, the structure of this story differs from the previous six Peace episodes (see **[12-17]**). Most notably, the police character, Inspector Harbord and his unnamed assistant appear only in the introduction and conclusion to this adventure. The majority of the story is narrated by a non-police hero called Jack Henderson formerly of Lowood Hall ('Lowood School' features in *Jane Eyre* by Charlotte Bronte, 1847). Much of the plot revolves about a fictional hotel called the 'Princetown Inn' that resembles the former Duchy Hotel in Princetown where Fletcher Robinson and Conan Doyle had stayed whilst researching the setting for *The Hound of the Baskervilles* (31st May 1901-2nd June 1901). Interestingly, both of these stories also include references to 'Princetown Prison', a 'stone circle', a 'telescope', stories of 'ghost hounds' and a character called 'Mortimer'. Conan Doyle featured Princetown Prison to varying degrees in three other stories; *The Sign of Four* (February 1890), *How the King Held the Brigadier* (April 1895) and *How the Brigadier Triumphed in England* (March 1903*)*. The first of these was the second Sherlock Holmes novella (October 1890) and the other two stories featured a fictional hero called Brigadier Gerard.

19

The Return of Oliver Manton: *Pearson's Magazine* (US), November 1905 (pp. 500-505), edited by Arthur W. Little and published by J.J. Little & Co. (New York). This standard-slick American monthly was originally a like-for-like republication of the British periodical of that same name. However, beyond January 1903, it diverged considerably and began running original American material together with reprints from other British periodicals. This story is about a blinded medium called William Fenton Bennett who seeks revenge against Oliver Manton for disrupting a séance. Fletcher Robinson was a devout Christian throughout his life but like many middle-class Edwardians, he was also interested in Spiritualism. Indeed, Pemberton is quoted as having remarked that 'Fletcher Robinson was always a little psychic' in an anonymous newspaper article that was entitled *Sidelights on Great Crime Stories (No 10) – "Ghost Hound" of the Marshes – Was it the Inspiration of Conan Doyle's Story?* (*The Evening News*: 25th May 1939). Conan Doyle was also interested in both Spiritualism and Occultism. This fascination began during 1880 and it eventually led him to renounce his Catholicism. In November 1916, Conan Doyle publically declared his conversion to Spiritualism within an article entitled *A New Revelation. Spiritualism and Religion* that was published by the psychic magazine, *Light*.

20

How Mr. Denis O'Halloran Transgressed His Code: *Appleton's Magazine* (US), January 1907 (pp. 16-20), illustrated by Arthur Becher, edited by Trumbull White and published by D. Appleton & Co. (New York). This standard-sized American monthly ran serialized tales, short stories and literary discussion. The story centers upon a tragic domestic dispute between one Colonel Francis Yorke and his stepmother. At the time of its publication, Fletcher Robinson was working as the editor of *The World: a Journal for Men and Women*. This periodical was managed by Pemberton and it was both owned and printed by the newspaper magnate, Alfred Harmsworth (1865-1922). On 11th December 1906, '*The World*' published a literary supplement entitled *Boot and Stocking Fund Supplement*, in which it was announced that Fletcher Robinson had recently completed a story entitled *An Episode of 1746: Being the Unchivalric Conduct of an Irish Gentleman*. It appears that for editorial reasons, this title was subsequently altered to *How Mr. Denis O'Halloran Transgressed His Code*. This was the last of fifty-four short stories that Fletcher Robinson had published prior to his death on 21st January 1907, aged just 36 years and 153 days. Later, Conan Doyle lamented that Fletcher Robinson was a 'fine fellow' whose premature death was 'a loss to the world'.

Source Acknowledgements

The stories featured in this book are no longer copyright material. Most of the stories have been reproduced from original items owned by the compiler of this work. However, both *The Mystery of Thomas Hearne. A Tale of Dartmoor* (18) and *How Mr. Denis O' Halloran Trangressed his Code* (20) have been reproduced using copyrighted images that were supplied by the British Library (all rights reserved). Permission for reproducing these images was kindly secured from the British Library Board by Shelah Duncan (Research Service, British Library).

B. FLETCHER ROBINSON BIBLIOGRAPHY

The following abbreviations in square brackets denote:

[ar] = article;
[ss] = short story;
[pm] = poem;
[pl] = playlet;
[ly] = lyric;
(US) = American Publication.

1887-1889

BFR edited issues 98 - 115 of Volumes 13 and 14 of his school magazine entitled *The Newtonian*. This periodical was produced by a local printer and stationer called G.H. Hearder of Wolborough Street in Newton Abbot and was periodically collated and leather-bound.

1893:

18th February.	*The Granta*: A Compromise [pm] (p. 210).
22nd April.	*The Granta*: A Chess Player's Chortle [pm] (p. 265).
6th May.	*The Granta*: A Craven Attack [pm] (p. 302).
15th June.	*The Granta*: Chuck Her Up! [pm] (p. 395).
14th October.	*The Granta*: The Female Extensionist [pm] (pp. 10-11).
14th October.	*The Granta*: Spectator Inops [pm] (p. 15).
21st October.	*The Granta*: A Quid Pro Quo [pm] (p. 29).

1894:

20th January.	*The Granta*: "How To Be Happy Though Married" [pm] (p. 133).
20th January.	*The Granta*: A Memory [pm] (p. 143).
27th January.	*The Granta*: To The Muse Of Poetry [pm] (p. 149).
10th February	*The Granta*: An Appeal [pm] (p. 187).
3rd March.	*The Granta*: Solvitur Ambulando [pm] (pp. 236-237).
28th April.	*The Granta*: Scene Elysium [pl] (pp. 278-279).
28th April.	*The Granta*: A Woman's Revenge [pm] (pp. 283-284).
26th May.	*The Granta*: A Protest [pm] (p. 348).
3rd November.	*The Granta*: To An Old Friend [pm] (pp. 36-37).

1895:

16th November	*The Granta*: Irish Beauties Of The Last Century [pm] (p. 76).

1896:

October.	Robinson, B.F., (ed. Pemberton, M.), *Rugby Football*, (London: A.D. Innes & Co.).

1897:

23rd January.	*The Granta*: Ye Ancient Ballade [ly] (p. 144).
March.	*Cassell's Family Magazine*: A Day With The Hounds [ar] (pp. 355-364).
April.	*Cassell's Family Magazine*: The New Railway To London [ar] (pp. 492-500).
April.	Pemberton, A.C. & others, (ed. Robinson, B.F.), *The Complete Cyclist*, (London: A.D. Innes & Co.).
June.	*Cassell's Family Magazine*: Through The Flames [ar] (pp. 42-50).
July/August.	*The Railway Magazine*: The Great Railway Extension [ar] (Vol. 1).
November.	Winn, R.A., (ed. Robinson, B.F.), *Boxing*, (London: A.D. Innes & Co.).
24th November.	Lehmann, R.C., (ed. Robinson, B. F.), *Rowing*, (London: A.D. Innes & Co.).
27th November.	Budd, A.J. & Fry, C.B., *Football*, (London: Lawrence & Bullen) [with contributions by Bertram Fletcher Robinson].
December.	*Cassell's Magazine*: Capitals At Play - St. Petersburg [ar] (pp. 18-29).

1898:

January.	*Cassell's Magazine*: Capitals At Play - Copenhagen [ar] (pp. 178-187).
February.	*Cassell's Magazine*: Capitals At Play - Berlin [ar] (pp. 227-236).
March.	*Cassell's Magazine*: Capitals At Play - The Hague [ar] (pp. 398-407).
April.	*Cassell's Magazine*: Capitals At Play - Vienna [ar] (pp. 496-505).
May.	*Cassell's Magazine*: Capitals At Play - London [ar] (pp. 627-637).
28th July.	McLean, D.H. & Grenfell, W.H., *Rowing & Punting*, (London: Lawrence & Bullen) [with contributions by Bertram Fletcher Robinson].
30th September.	Smith, G.G., (ed. Robinson, B.F.), *The World of Golf*, (London: A. D. Innes & Co.).
22nd November.	Monier-Williams, M.S., (ed. Robinson, B.F.), *Figure-Skating*, (London: A.D. Innes & Co.).
December.	*Cassell's Magazine*: The Guards Of Europe [ar] (pp. 53-61).

1899:

January.	*Cassell's Magazine*: The Duke's Hounds A Chat About The Badminton [ar] (pp. 206-210).
May.	*Cassell's Magazine*: Emperors' Gardens [ar] (pp. 665-672).
June.	*Cassell's Magazine*: London Night By Night – I. The Next Day's Dinner [ar] (pp. 48-56).
July.	*Cassell's Magazine*: Black Magic – The Story Of The Spanish Don [ss] (pp. 178-189).

1899

July.	*Cassell's Magazine*: London Night By Night – II. The Next Day's Paper [ar] (pp. 142-149).
27th July.	Williams, L.B., (ed. Robinson, B.F.), *Croquet*, (London: A.D. Innes & Co.).
August.	*Cassell's Magazine*: London Night By Night – III. On The River [ar] (pp. 313-320).
September.	*Cassell's Magazine*: London Night By Night – IV. The Next Day's Letters [ar] (pp. 404-411).
October.	*Cassell's Magazine*: London Night By Night – V. Late Suppers And Early Breakfasts [ar] (pp. 529-537).
November.	*Cassell's Magazine*: London Night By Night – VI. The Streets [ar] (pp. 632-639).
15th November.	Smith, J.N. & Robson, P.A., (ed. Robinson, B.F.), *Hockey: Historical and Practical*, (London: A.D. Innes & Co.).
December.	*Cassell's Magazine*: The Better Part Of Valour – Dedicated To All Sportsmen in Love [pm] (pp. 24-27).
December.	*Cassell's Magazine*: Famous Regiments – I. The Royal Horse Artillery [ar] (pp. 121-129).

1900:

January.	*Cassell's Magazine* – New Year's Day [pm] (p. 245).
January.	*Cassell's Magazine*: Famous Regiments – II. The Royal Dragoons [ar] (pp. 182-188).
25th January.	Robinson, B.F, & others, *Britain's Sea-Kings and Sea-Fights*, (London: Cassell & Company Limited) [Bertram Fletcher Robinson contributed 4/35 chapters and 139/756 pages].
February.	*Cassell's Magazine*: Famous Regiments – III. The Black Watch [ar] (pp. 310-318).
March.	*Cassell's Magazine*: Famous Regiments – IV. The Connaught Rangers [ar] (pp. 386-393).
March.	*Pearson's Magazine*: A True Story (Wherein all golfers may learn something to their advantage) [pm] (pp. 118-120).
March.	*Pearson's Magazine* (US): A True Story (Wherein all golfers may learn something to their advantage) [pm] (pp. 235-237).
April.	*Cassell's Magazine*: Famous Regiments – V. The Tenth (Prince Of Wales' Own Royal) Hussars [ar] (pp. 529-535).
May.	*Cassell's Magazine*: Famous Regiments – VI. The Corps Of Royal Engineers [ar] (pp. 610-619).
4th May.	*Daily Express*: Capetown For Empire [ar].
8th May.	*Daily Express*: In A Cape Hotel [ar].
14th May.	*Daily Express*: High Treason [ar].
16th May.	*Daily Express*: Boer Newspapers [ar].
21st May.	*Daily Express*: Puffing Billy At The War [ar].
22nd May.	*Daily Express*: Gate Of The War [ar].
26th May.	*Daily Express*: Behind The Veil [ar].

1900

29th May.	*Daily Express*: Nursing An Army [ar].
5th June.	*Daily Express*: A Question Of Language [ar].
7th June.	*Daily Express*: Real Nurses Or Mere Trippers? [ar].
22nd June.	*Daily Express*: The Parcels Of Mr. H. Gatliff [ar].
25th June.	*Daily Express*: How I Nearly Became A Rebel [ar].
30th June.	*Daily Express*: How The Bond Promotes Peace [ar].
28th September.	*Daily Express*: The Danger In South Africa [ar].
8th October.	*Daily Express*: In Kruger's Pavilion [ar].
11th October.	*Daily Express*: That Censor Again [ar].
19th November.	*Daily Express*: Riding To Hounds [ar].
December.	*Pearson's Magazine*: The Sarcastic Caddie [pm] (pp. 614-616).
December.	*Pearson's Magazine* (US): The Sarcastic Caddie [pm] (pp. 646-650).
5th December.	*Daily Express*: American Slang [ar].
26th December.	*Daily Express*: About Bullies [ar].

1901:

4th January.	*Daily Express*: Is Cape Colony In Danger? [ar].
6th February.	*Daily Express*: The Queen And Her Poets [ar].
18th March.	*Daily Express*: How the Yankees Advertise [ar].
22nd March.	*Daily Express*: The Fate Of The Wild Things [ar].
1st April.	*Daily Express*: A Race Worth Watching [ar].
6th April.	*Daily Express*: A Dream Of A Boat-Race [ar].
23rd April.	*Daily Express*: What Is Doing At Glasgow [ar].
24th April.	*Daily Express*: An Exhibition In The Making [ar].
May.	*Pearson's Magazine*: Big Ben And Little Ben [pm] (pp. 567-568).
1st May.	*Daily Express*: War's Brighter Side [ar].
18th May.	*Daily Express*: From The Jaws Of Death [ar].
21st May.	*Daily Express*: "Truthful Jean" On The War [ar].
29th May.	*Daily Express*: The Grim Tragedy In China [ar].
10th June.	*Daily Express*: Memories Of The May Week [ar].
19th June.	*Daily Express*: Pro-Boers, Please Note! [ar].
July.	*Pearson's Magazine*: Up the River – The Humours and Terrors of It [ar] (pp. 117 – 120).
2nd July.	*Daily Express*: The Battle On The Thames [ar].
27th July.	*Daily Express*: A Talk With Max Adeler [ar].
August.	*Pearson's Magazine*: Concerning Cricket – The Humour of the Game [ar] (pp. 228-232).
13th August.	*Daily Express*: Last Scene At Potsdam [ar].
27th August.	*Daily Express*: The Confessions Of A Pro-Boer [ar].
September.	*Pearson's Magazine*: On Card Games And Others [ar] (pp. 340-344).
October.	*Pearson's Magazine*: On Shooting [ar] (pp. 451-456).
November.	*Pearson's Magazine*: Article: The Humour of Football [ar] (pp. 564-568).
November.	*Pearson's Magazine*: Article: Deceitful Appearances - A true story of Golfers and other Virtuous Folk [ar] (pp. 591-593).

1901:

19th November.	Cook, T.A. & others, (ed. Robinson, B.F.), *Ice Sports*, (London: Ward, Lock & Co., Ltd).
30th November.	*Daily Express*: A Book Of The Moment – War as it was Under the Iron Duke [ar].
December.	*Pearson's Magazine*: Christmas Games old and new [ar] (pp. 740-744).
21st December.	*Daily Express*: A Book Of The Moment – A Peep Into the Future According to Mr. H.G. Wells [ar].

1902:

January.	*Pearson's Magazine*: The Hunting of the Fox [ar] (pp. 115-120).
8th January.	*Daily Express*: According To The Prophets [ar].
February.	*Pearson's Magazine*: Concerning Golf [ar] (pp. 228-232).
28th February.	*Daily Express*: At The Saturday Supper Club [ar].
March.	*Pearson's Magazine*: Motor-Cars and Bicycles [ar] (pp. 340-344).
15th March.	*Daily Express*: A Book Of The Hour [ar].
20th March.	*Daily Express*: A Battle At The N.S.C. [ar].
24th March.	*Daily Express*: The Coronation Boat Race [ar].
April.	*Pearson's Magazine*: Sporting and Athletic Girls [ar] (pp. 452-456).
23rd April.	Robinson, B.F., (ed. Savory, E.W.) *Sporting Pictures*, (London: Cassell & Co. Ltd.).
May.	*Cassell's Magazine*: The Laughter of Dr. Marais – A Story of the Breton Coast [ss] (pp. 653-661).
May.	*Pearson's Magazine*: Concerning Yachts – A Nautical Story or Two [ar] (pp. 564-568).
June.	*Pearson's Magazine*: Croquet and Tennis [ar] (pp. 674-678).
1st July.	*Daily Express*: A Ride With Fifty Horses [ar].
17th July.	*Daily Express*: The Riflemen Of An Empire [ar].
29th July.	*Daily Express*: The Man That Was [ar].
31st July.	*Daily Express*: From Friday To Monday [ar].
7th August.	*Daily Express*: The Boers At The Seaside [ar].
September.	*Pearson's Magazine* (US): Concerning Yachts – A Nautical Story or Two [ar] (pp. 950-954).
1st September.	*Daily Express*: Two Shooting Memories - A Day with a Pointer in Devonshire and a Great Partridge Drive [ar].
25th September	*The Treasury*: "A Day of My Life." No.1. – The Journalists (pp. 30-33) [ar].
30th September.	*Daily Express*: Tales For The Children [ar].
October.	*Pearson's Magazine* (US): Up the River – The Humours and Terrors of it [ar] (pp. 1067-1070).
1st October.	*Daily Express*: The Bird Of The Autumn [ar].
8th October.	*Daily Express*: A Pair Of Humorists [ar].
18th October.	*Daily Express*: The Sagacious Lieutenant [ar].
29th November.	*Daily Express*: A Play People Love [ar].

1902:

December.	*Cassell's Magazine*: Ghosts and Their Funny Ways [ss] (pp. 107-110).
December.	*The Windsor Magazine*: The Trail Of The Dead: The Strange Experience Of Dr. Robert Harland - I. The Hairy Caterpillar [ss] (pp. 121-129) [with J. Malcolm Fraser].
1st December.	*Daily Express*: De Wet On The War [ar].
13th December.	*Daily Express*: The Story Of M. Beacaire [ar].
20th December.	*Daily Express*: Where We Hold Our Own [ar].

1903:

Bertram Fletcher Robinson wrote the lyrics to a song entitled *The John Bull Store*. The music was composed by Robert Eden. The score was arranged by George W. Byng and the sheet music was published by Elkin and Co. Ltd. of London.

January.	*The Windsor Magazine*: The Trail Of The Dead: The Strange Experience of Dr. Robert Harland - II. The Mystery Of The Lemsdorf Ham, [ss] (pp. 264-274) [with J. Malcolm Fraser].
1st January.	*Daily Express*: Story Of The Brave [ar].
3rd January.	*Daily Express*: Highway To Success [ar].
8th January.	*Daily Express*: Master And The Man [ar].
17th January.	*Daily Express*: For Collectors Only [ar].
23rd January.	*Daily Express*: The Acres Of Alien Shame [ar].
28th January.	*Daily Express*: A Fight At The N.S.C [ar].
February.	*The Windsor Magazine*: The Trail Of The Dead: The Strange Experience of Dr. Robert Harland – III. The Chase In The Snow, [ss] (pp. 370-379) [with J. Malcolm Fraser].
4th February.	*Daily Express*: Pity The Pro-Boer! [pm].
4th February.	*Daily Express*: Circulation By The Million [ar].
7th February.	*Daily Express*: In The Eye Of The Public [ar].
16th February.	*Daily Express*: Alien Thief To Britisher [ar].
March.	*The Windsor Magazine*: The Trail Of The Dead: The Strange Experience of Dr. Robert Harland - IV. The Anonymous Article, [ss] (pp. 477- 486) [with J. Malcolm Fraser].
21st March.	*Daily Express*: Where To Dine In Paris [ar].
26th March.	*Daily Express*: Talk About The Boat Race [ar].
April.	*The Windsor Magazine*: The Trail Of The Dead: The Strange Experience of Dr. Harland - V. The Ammonia Cylinder, [ss] (pp. 627-638) [with J. Malcolm Fraser].
9th April.	*Daily Express*: A Question Of Good Taste [ar].
15th April.	*Daily Express*: A Country's Resurrection [ar].
28th April.	*Daily Express*: The Return Of A Hero [ar].
May.	*The Windsor Magazine*: The Trail Of The Dead: The Strange Experience of Dr. Harland - VI. The End Of The Trail, [ss] (pp. 734-743) [with J. Malcolm Fraser].

1903:

May	*Pearson's Magazine*: The Battle of Fingle's Bridge: How the Ferns and Rushes Fought the Gorse and the Heather, And What Came of the Battle, [ss] (pp. 530-536).
23rd May.	*Daily Express*: The Man In The Cage [ar].
June.	*Pearson's Magazine*: The Romance of Motor Racing [ar] (pp. 604-610).
4th June.	*Daily Express*: The China Collector [ar].
August.	*The London Magazine*: Fog Bound [ss] (pp. 47-56) [with J. Malcolm Fraser].
8th August.	*Daily Express*: The Great French Trial [ar].
25th September.	*Daily Express*: A Peaceful Revolution [ar].
October.	*Pearson's Magazine*: The Debt Of Heinrich Hermann, [ss] (pp. 432-440).
20th October.	*Daily Express*: A Leader Of Men [ar].
29th October.	*Daily Express*: Helping A Good Cause [ar].
14th November.	*Daily Express*: The People Of The Abyss [ar].
18th November.	*Daily Express*: On The Roof Of The World [ar].
27th November.	*Daily Express*: The Food Of The Gods [ar].
December.	*Pearson's Magazine*: Cupid = Billiard Marker [pm] (pp. 585-588).
December.	*Cassell's Magazine*: Clowns [ss] (pp. 88-90).
5th December.	*Daily Express*: A Quarter-Mile Of Death [ar].
24th December.	*Daily Express*: A Champion Of British Art [ar].
28th December.	*Daily Express*: A Fiscal Pantomime. The Sleeping Beauty, [pl] (with P.G. Wodehouse).

1904:

Bertram Fletcher Robinson wrote the lyrics to a song entitled *The Little Loafer*. The music was composed by Robert Eden and the sheet music was published by Elkin and Co. Ltd. of London.

14th January.	*Daily Express*: The Future Of The Very Rich [ar].
22nd January.	*Daily Express*: Not Playing The Game [ar].
February.	B. F. Robinson & J. M. Fraser, *The Trail of the Dead*, (London: Ward, Lock & Company Limited). [This book features all five episodes of *The Trail of the Dead: The Strange Experience of Dr. Robert Harland* from *The Windsor Magazine*. A Canadian edition was also published by and Langton Hall of Toronto. Both the British and Canadian editions were illustrated by Adolf Thiede].
9th February.	*Daily Express*: The Czar's Responsibility [ar].
23rd February.	*Daily Express*: Common-Sense v. Propriety [ar].
3rd March.	*Daily Express*: Mischief For Idle Hands [ar].
10th March.	*Daily Express*: A War That Will Decide [ar].
18th April.	*Daily Express*: A True Ghost Story [ar].

1904:

21st April.	*Daily Express*: Old West Surrey [ar].
5th May.	*Daily Express*: A Question For The Nation [ar].
10th May.	*Daily Express*: The Continent And The War [ar].
13th May.	*Daily Express*: The Black Coat Fetish [ar].
19th May.	*Daily Express*: The Future Of The Nations [ar].
26th May.	*Vanity Fair*: Women Of Civilisation [ar] (pp. 664-665).
31st May.	*Daily Express*: The Home Of Islam [ar].
9th June.	*Vanity Fair*: Spain And Her King – The Royal Guest Of 1905 [ar] (p. 730).
14th June.	*Daily Express*: A Pagan Metropolis [ar].
15th June.	*Daily Express*: Mr. Beckles' Invention [ar].
28th June.	*Daily Express*: "Unreliability Tests" [ar].
30th June.	*Vanity Fair*: Pagan London - Miss Corelli's Libel On The Clergy [ar] (pp. 831-832).
7th July.	*Vanity Fair*: On Political Lies – A Growing Danger In British Politics [ar] (pp. 15-16).
14th July.	*Vanity Fair*: For Ladies Only [pl] (p. 41).
14th July.	*Vanity Fair*: The Policy Of Honesty – An Old Proverb With New Applications [ar] (p. 48).
21st July.	*Vanity Fair*: A Sensation Per Diem [ar] (pp. 79-80).
28th July.	*Vanity Fair*: The Quick And The Dead – Being A Ghost Story, With Comments Thereon [ar] (p. 105).
August.	*The Lady's Home Magazine*: The Chronicles Of Addington Peace – I. The Terror In The Snow [ss] (pp. 114-127).
11th August.	*Vanity Fair*: Pity Poor Agriculture! [ar] (pp. 175-176).
18th August.	*Vanity Fair*: Out Of The Depth [ar] (pp. 207-208).
25th August.	*Vanity Fair*: The Country – Second Hand [ar] (p. 240).
September.	*The Lady's Home Magazine*: The Chronicles of Addington Peace – II. Mr. Taubery's Diamond [ss] (pp. 220-230).
September.	*Pearson's Magazine*: Historic Monuments of Britain. III. The Fortress Of The First Britons. A Description of the Fortress of Grimspound, on Dartmoor [ar] (pp. 273-280).
1st September.	*Vanity Fair*: Upon Popular Agitations [ar] (pp. 271-272).
8th September.	*Vanity Fair*: The God Of Irony [ar] (pp. 304-305).
29th September.	*Vanity Fair:* As We Fight Elections [ar] (pp. 400-401).
October.	*The Lady's Home Magazine*: The Chronicles of Addington Peace – III. Mr. Coran's Election [ss] (pp. 326-336).
27th October.	*Vanity Fair*: The Good Old Times [ar] (pp. 527-528).
November.	*Home Magazine of Fiction*: The Chronicles of Addington Peace – IV. The Mystery Of The Causeway [ss] (pp. 431-440).
10th November.	*Vanity Fair*: "The Standard" And The New Journalism [ar] (pp. 591-592).
17th November.	*Vanity Fair*: Satire — Not Undeserved [ar] (pp. 625-626).
December.	*Home Magazine of Fiction*: The Chronicles of Addington Peace – V. The Vanished Millionaire [ss] (pp. 577-587).
December.	*Pearson's Magazine*: Legend Of Bess The Mare [pm] (pp. 719-722).

1904:

8th December. *Vanity Fair*: Our Christmas Pantomime – Little Red Riding Hood; or, The Virtuous British Public And The Smart Set Wolf, [pl] (pp. 731-734) [with P.G. Wodehouse].

1905:

January. *Home Magazine of Fiction*: The Chronicles of Addington Peace – VI. The Mystery Of The Jade Spear [ss] (pp. 79-88).

12th January. *Vanity Fair*: The German War Scare And 'Vanity Fair' [ar] (p. 48).

19th January. *Vanity Fair*: 'Vanity Fair' And Its Critics [ar] (pp. 83-84).

26th January. *Vanity Fair*: Russia And France – An Historic Parallel In Revolutions [ar] (p. 120).

February. *Pearson's Magazine* (US): The Vanished Billionaire: One of Inspector Hartley's Famous Cases [ss] (pp. 140-147). [Republication of *The Vanished Millionaire*].

2nd February. *Vanity Fair*: False Economy [ar] (pp. 155-156).

9th February. *Vanity Fair*: The Franco=Russian Alliance [ar] (pp. 191-192).

May. *Pearson's Magazine*: The Mystery Of Thomas Hearne [ss] (pp. 497-507).

18th May. *Vanity Fair*: The Pick of the Bookstall – "Rose Of The World" [ar] (p. 708).

June. B. F. Robinson, *The Chronicles of Addington Peace*, (London: Harper & Brother). [This book features all six episodes of the serialization of the same name from *The Lady's Home Magazine* and *Home Magazine of Fiction*. It also includes two additional stories entitled: *The Story of Amaroff the Pole* and *The Mystery of Thomas Hearne*. All eight stories were illustrated by Thomas Heath Robinson (no relation)].

29th June. *Vanity Fair*: The Discomforts Of English Racing [ar] (pp. 897-898).

6th July. *Vanity Fair*: The Problem Of National Degeneracy [ar] (pp. 15-16).

27th July. *Vanity Fair*: "The Valley Of Peace" [ar] (p. 114).

17th August. *Vanity Fair*: The Messenger Bhoys – A Political Extravaganza [pl] (p. 209).

17th August. *Vanity Fair*: The Chronicles Of Pen – I. The Tact Of Anne [ss] (p. 210). [Set in the village of Ipplepen where Robinson lived as a child].

31st August. *Vanity Fair*: The Chronicles Of Pen – II. The Unchivalric Conduct Of M. Paul [ss] (pp. 275-276).

7th September. *Vanity Fair*: The Chronicles Of Pen – III. The Return Of Gilbert Hare [ss] (pp. 306-307).

21st September. *Vanity Fair*: The Chronicles Of Pen – IV. The Curious Coincidence Of The Three Sermons [ss] (pp. 373-374).

5th October. *Vanity Fair*: Vain Tales – No. DCLXL. The Woman's Point Of View [ss] (pp. 434-435).

12th October. *Vanity Fair*: The Chronicles Of Pen – V. Mr. Mathers, Sportsman [ss] (p. 469).

1905:

November.	*Pearson's Magazine* (US): The Return of Oliver Manton [ss] (pp. 500-505).
December.	*The Windsor Magazine*: Chronicles In Cartoon – I. Royalty [ar] (pp. 35-51).
7th December.	*Vanity Fair*: II. A Tale Of Mystery – The Return Of Oliver Manton [ss] (pp. 733-735). [A republication with slight amendments].
11th December.	*The Detroit News* (US): Inspector Grey Stories. The Czarnecki Tragedy, [ss] (p. 8). [Part 1: a republication of the Addington Peace story, *Amaroff the Pole*].
12th December.	*The Detroit News* (US): Inspector Grey Stories. The Czarnecki Tragedy, [ss] (p. 7). [Part 2].
13th December.	*The Detroit News* (US): Inspector Grey Stories. The Czarnecki Tragedy, [ss] (p. 6). [Part 3].
14th December.	*The Detroit News* (US): Inspector Grey Stories. The Terror in the Snow, [ss] (p. 8). [Part 1: a republication of the Addington Peace story of that same title].
14th December.	*Vanity Fair*: A Winters Tale – King Arthur And His Court, [pl] (pp. 778-781) [with P. G. Wodehouse].
15th December.	*The Detroit News* (US): Inspector Grey Stories. The Terror in the Snow, [ss] (p. 8). [Part 2].
16th December.	*The Detroit News* (US): Inspector Grey Stories. The Terror in the Snow, [ss] (p. 7). [Part 3].
18th December.	*The Detroit News* (US): Inspector Grey Stories. The Theft of the Pavaloff Diamond, [ss] (p. 4). [Part 1: a republication of the Addington Peace story, *Mr. Taubery's Diamond*].
19th December.	*The Detroit News* (US): Inspector Grey Stories. The Theft of the Pavaloff Diamond, [ss] (p. 6). [Part 2].
20th December.	*The Detroit News* (US): Inspector Grey Stories. The Theft of the Pavaloff Diamond, [ss] (p. 4). [Part 3].
21st December.	*The Detroit News* (US): Inspector Grey Stories. Who Killed Andrew Cheyne?, [ss] (p. 8). [Part 1: a republication of the Addington Peace story, *The Mystery of the Causeway*.].
22nd December.	*The Detroit News* (US): Inspector Grey Stories. Who Killed Andrew Cheyne? (p. 7). [Part 2].
23rd December.	*The Detroit News* (US): Inspector Grey Stories. Who Killed Andrew Cheyne? [ss] (p. 10). [Part 3].
25th December.	*The Detroit News* (US): Inspector Grey Stories. The Dartmoor Tragedy, [ss] (p. 4). [Part 1: a republication of the Addington Peace story, *The Mystery of Thomas Hearne*].
26th December.	*The Detroit News* (US): Inspector Grey Stories. The Dartmoor Tragedy, [ss] (p. 4). [Part 2].
27th December.	*The Detroit News* (US): Inspector Grey Stories. The Dartmoor Tragedy, [ss] (p. 4). [Part 3].
28th December.	*The Detroit News* (US): Inspector Grey Stories. A Blackmailing Incident, [ss] (p. 8). [Part 1: a republication of the Addington Peace story, *Mr. Coran's Election*].

1905:

28th December.	*Vanity Fair*: Vain Tales - No. DCCI – The Sentiment Of Self-Sacrifice, (pp. 846-847).
29th December.	*The Detroit News* (US): Inspector Grey Stories. A Blackmailing Incident, [ss] (p. 7). [Part 2].
30th December.	*The Detroit News* (US): Inspector Grey Stories. A Blackmailing Incident, [p. 6). [Part 3].

1906:

Great Short Stories, Volume 1 (1): Detective Stories edited by William Patten, published by P. F. Collier & Sons of New York. This anthology (the first of three volumes) includes twelve short stories by Broughton Brandenburg (1), Arthur Conan Doyle (2), Anna Katherine Green (1), Edgar Allan Poe (3) and Robert Louis Stevenson (4). The final tale is *The Vanished Millionaire* by Bertram Fletcher Robinson (pp. 411-429). [A republication].

January.	*The Windsor Magazine*: Chronicles In Cartoon – II. Potentates, Princes and Presidents [ar] (pp. 261-276).
11th January.	*Vanity Fair*: Vain Tales – No. DCCIII – Love And An Election [ss] (pp. 50-51).
25th January.	*Vanity Fair*: When Labour Rules (c.1920) The Amazing Adventure Of Mr. Hiram K. Paddle [ss] (pp. 114-115).
February.	*The Windsor Magazine*: Chronicles In Cartoon – III. Politics: First Series [ar] (pp. 383-398).
1st February.	*Vanity Fair*: When Labour Rules (c.1920) In The House Of Commons [ss] (pp. 145-146).
8th February.	*Vanity Fair*: Vain Tales – No. DCCVII - A Sentimental Episode [ss] (pp. 178-179).
March.	*The Windsor Magazine*: Chronicles In Cartoon – IV. Politics: Second Series [ar] (pp. 489-506) [with Wilfrid Meynell].
1st March.	*Vanity Fair*: Vain Tales – No. DCCX - A Jest Of Fate [ss] (pp. 275-276) [with Dion Clayton Calthrop].
15th March.	*Vanity Fair*: Vain Tales – No. DCCXII - The Last Of The Mad Lindores [ss] (pp. 339-340).
29th March.	*Vanity Fair*: Vain Tales – No. DCCXIV - The Return Of "Piccadilly" [ss] (pp. 403-404).
April.	*The Windsor Magazine*: Chronicles In Cartoon – V. Bench And Bar [ar] (pp. 611-630).
5th April.	*Vanity Fair*: The New Privileged Class [ar] (pp. 431-432).
12th April.	*Vanity Fair*: Vain Tales – No. DCCXVI - Mr. Andrew Perkins–Knight Errant [ss] (pp. 466-467).
19th April.	*Vanity Fair*: Vain Tales – No. DCCXVII - The End Of The Chapter [ss] (pp. 498-499).
May.	*The Windsor Magazine*: Chronicles In Cartoon – VI. The Army [ar] (pp. 733-752) [with Evan Ashton].
3rd May.	*Vanity Fair*: Vain Tales – No. DCCXIX - Miss Bulpit's Wooing [ss] (pp. 562-563).

1906:

10th May.	*Vanity Fair*: Vain Tales – No. DCCXX - West Africa Comes To Town [ss] (pp. 594-595).
18th May.	*Daily Herald* (US): The Trail of the Dead – The Strange Experience of Dr. Robert Harland [ss] (p. 4) (with J. Malcolm Fraser) [Chapters I & II].
24th May.	*Vanity Fair*: Contentment [pm] (p. 656).
24th May.	*The Sumner Gazette* (US): The Trail of the Dead – The Strange Experience of Dr. Robert Harland [ss] (p. 6), (with J. Malcolm Fraser) [Chapters I & II].
25th May.	*Daily Herald* (US): The Trail of the Dead – The Strange Experience of Dr. Robert Harland [ss] (p. 4) (with J. Malcolm Fraser) [Chapters III & IV].
31st May.	*The Sumner Gazette* (US): The Trail of the Dead – The Strange Experience of Dr. Robert Harland [ss] (p. 6) (with J. Malcolm Fraser) [Chapters III & IV].
31st May.	*Vanity Fair*: Vain Tales – No. DCCXXIII - Romance And A Racing Fraud [ss] (pp. 691-692).
June.	*The Windsor Magazine*: Chronicles In Cartoon – VII. Music [ar] (pp. 35-52).
1st June.	*Daily Herald* (US): The Trail of the Dead – The Strange Experience of Dr. Robert Harland [ss] (p. 4) (with J. Malcolm Fraser) [Chapters V & VI].
7th June.	*The Sumner Gazette* (US): The Trail of the Dead – The Strange Experience of Dr. Robert Harland [ss] (p. 3) (with J. Malcolm Fraser) [Chapters V & VI].
7th June.	*Vanity Fair*: Wastminster Vair [ly] (p. 721).
7th June.	*Vanity Fair*: Vain Tales – No. DCCXXIV - The Mystery Of Mr. Nicholas Boushaw [ss] (pp. 725-726). [An Addington Peace story].
8th June.	*Daily Herald* (US): The Trail of the Dead – The Strange Experience of Dr. Robert Harland [ss] (p. 4) (with J. Malcolm Fraser) [Chapters VI (cont.) & VII].
14th June.	*The Sumner Gazette* (US): The Trail of the Dead – The Strange Experience of Dr. Robert Harland [ss] (p. 3) (with J. Malcolm Fraser) [Chapters VI (cont.) & VII].
14th June.	*Vanity Fair*: How We Entertain [pl] (p. 756-757).
15th June.	*Daily Herald* (US): The Trail of the Dead – The Strange Experience of Dr. Robert Harland [ss] (p. 10) (with J. Malcolm Fraser) [Chapters VIII & VIX].
21st June.	*The Sumner Gazette* (US): The Trail of the Dead – The Strange Experience of Dr. Robert Harland [ss] (p. 3) (with J. Malcolm Fraser) [Chapters VIII & IX].
21st June.	*Vanity Fair*: Vain Tales – No. DCCXVI - A Story Of The Ascot Stakes [ss] (pp. 789-791).
22nd June.	*Daily Herald* (US): The Trail of the Dead – The Strange Experience of Dr. Robert Harland [ss] (p. 6) (with J. Malcolm Fraser) [Chapters X & XI].

1906:

28th June. *The Sumner Gazette* (US): The Trail of the Dead – The Strange Experience of Dr. Robert Harland [ss] (p. 3) (with J. Malcolm Fraser) [Chapters X & XI].

29th June. *Daily Herald* (US): The Trail of the Dead – The Strange Experience of Dr. Robert Harland [ss] (p. 3) (with J. Malcolm Fraser) [Chapters XII & XIII].

July. *The Windsor Magazine*: Chronicles In Cartoon – VIII. Cricket [ar] (pp. 157-178) [with Home Gordon].

4th July. *Vanity Fair*: Vain Tales – No. DCCXXVIII - In Which A Hero Of Henley Suffers Adversity [ss] (pp. 18-19).

5th July. *The Sumner Gazette* (US): The Trail of the Dead – The Strange Experience of Dr. Robert Harland [ss] (p. 6) (with J. Malcolm Fraser) [Chapters XII & XIII].

7th July. *Daily Herald* (US): The Trail of the Dead – The Strange Experience of Dr. Robert Harland [ss] (p. 10) (with J. Malcolm Fraser) [Chapters XIII (cont.) & XIV].

11th July. *Vanity Fair*: Vain Tales – No. DCCXXIX - How Inspector Bullen Respected The Ends Of Justice [ss] (pp. 51-52).

12th July. *The Sumner Gazette* (US): The Trail of the Dead – The Strange Experience of Dr. Robert Harland [ss] (p. 3) (with J. Malcolm Fraser) [Chapters XIII (cont.) & XIV].

13th July. *Daily Herald* (US): The Trail of the Dead – The Strange Experience of Dr. Robert Harland [ss] (p. 10) (with J. Malcolm Fraser) [Chapters XIV (cont.), XV & XVI].

19th July. *Daily Herald* (US): The Trail of the Dead – The Strange Experience of Dr. Robert Harland [ss] (p. 3) (with J. Malcolm Fraser) [Chapters XVI (cont.), XVII & XVIII].

19th July. *The Sumner Gazette* (US): The Trail of the Dead – The Strange Experience of Dr. Robert Harland [ss] (p. 3) (with J. Malcolm Fraser) [Chapters XIV (cont.), XV & XVI].

25th July. *Vanity Fair*: Vain Tales – No. DCCXXXI - The Moth [ss] (pp. 115-116).

26th July. *The Sumner Gazette* (US): The Trail of the Dead – The Strange Experience of Dr. Robert Harland [ss] (p. 6) (with J. Malcolm Fraser) [Chapters XVI (cont.), XVII & XVIII].

27th July. *Daily Herald* (US): The Trail of the Dead – The Strange Experience of Dr. Robert Harland [ss] (p. 6) (with J. Malcolm Fraser) [Chapters XVIII (cont.), XIX & XX].

August. *The Windsor Magazine*: Chronicles In Cartoon – IX. Rowing, Games, and Athletics [ar] (pp. 279-296).

2nd August. *The Sumner Gazette* (US): The Trail of the Dead – The Strange Experience of Dr. Robert Harland [ss] (p. 3) (with J. Malcolm Fraser) [Chapters XVIII (cont.), XIX & XX].

3rd August. *Daily Herald* (US): The Trail of the Dead – The Strange Experience of Dr. Robert Harland [ss] (p. 6) (with J. Malcolm Fraser) [Chapters XX (cont.) & XXI].

1906

9th August.	*The Sumner Gazette* (US): The Trail of the Dead – The Strange Experience of Dr. Robert Harland [ss] (p. 6) (with J. Malcolm Fraser) [Chapters XX (cont.) & XXI].
10th August.	*Daily Herald* (US): The Trail of the Dead – The Strange Experience of Dr. Robert Harland [ss] (p. 4) (with J. Malcolm Fraser) [Chapters XXII & XXIII].
16th August.	*The Sumner Gazette* (US): The Trail of the Dead – The Strange Experience of Dr. Robert Harland [ss] (p. 6) (with J. Malcolm Fraser) [Chapters XXII & XXIII].
17th August.	*Daily Herald* (US): The Trail of the Dead – The Strange Experience of Dr. Robert Harland [ss] (p. 5) (with J. Malcolm Fraser) [Chapters XXIII (cont.), XXIV & XXV].
22nd August.	*Vanity Fair*: Vain Tales – No. DCCXXXV - The Inadvisability Of Laying Your Cards On The Table [ss] (p. 244).
23rd August.	*The Sumner Gazette* (US): The Trail of the Dead – The Strange Experience of Dr. Robert Harland [ss] (p. 6) (with J. Malcolm Fraser) [Chapters XXIII (cont.), XXIV & XXV].
24th August.	*Daily Herald* (US): The Trail of the Dead – The Strange Experience of Dr. Robert Harland [ss] (p. 6) (with J. Malcolm Fraser) [End].
29th August.	*Vanity Fair*: Vain Tales – No. DCCXXXVI - The Major And The Lady [ss] (pp. 275-276).
30th August.	*The Sumner Gazette* (US): The Trail of the Dead – The Strange Experience of Dr. Robert Harland [ss] (p. 3) (with J. Malcolm Fraser) [Chapters XXV & XXVI].
September.	*The Windsor Magazine*: Chronicles In Cartoon – X. Empire-Builders [ar] (pp. 401-420).
5th September.	*Vanity Fair*: Vain Tales – No. DCCXXXVII - The First Case Of Dr. Edwin Maples [ss] (pp. 306-307).
12th September.	*Vanity Fair*: Vain Tales – No. DCCXXXVIII – "Dreams And Visions" – A Racing Story [ss] (pp. 339-340).
19th September.	*Vanity Fair:* The Gospel of Recreation – The Good Advice In The Speech of James Crichton Browne [ar] (pp. 367-368).
26th September.	*Vanity Fair*: Vain Tales – No. DCCXL - The Thirteenth Stone [ss] (pp. 404-405).
October.	*The Windsor Magazine*: Chronicles In Cartoon – XI. Science And Medicine [ar] (pp. 539-560) [with Charles R. Hewitt].
3rd October.	*Vanity Fair*: Vain Tales – No. DCCXLI - The Misfortunes Of William Henry Eagles, J.P. [ss] (pp. 437-438).
10th October.	*Vanity Fair*: Vain Tales – No. DCCXLII - A Dramatic Engagement [ss] (pp. 467-468).
17th October.	*Vanity Fair*: An Over-Married Man [pm] (p. 498).
17th October.	*Vanity Fair*: Vain Tales – No. DCCXLIII - Two Soft Things [ss] (pp. 501-503).
24th October.	*Vanity Fair*: The Gathering of the Government, Or, How They Loved Each Other [pl] (pp. 529-530).

1906:

November.	*The Windsor Magazine*: Chronicles In Cartoon – XII. Explorers And Inventors [ar] (pp. 645-660).
5th November.	*Oelwein Daily Register* (US): Inspector Grey Stories. I. The Czarnecki Tragedy, [ss] (p. 2). [Part 1: a republication of the Addington Peace story, *Amaroff the Pole*].
6th November.	*Oelwein Daily Register* (US): Inspector Grey Stories. I. The Czarnecki Tragedy, [ss] (p. 2). [Part 2].
10th November.	*Oelwein Daily Register* (US): Inspector Grey Stories. I. The Czarnecki Tragedy, [ss] (p. 3). [Part 3].
14th November.	*Oelwein Daily Register* (US): Inspector Grey Stories. II. The Terror in the Snow, [ss] (p. 2). [Part 1: a republication of the Addington Peace story of that same title].
15th November.	*Oelwein Daily Register* (US): Inspector Grey Stories. II. The Terror in the Snow, [ss] (p. 2). [Part 2].
16th November.	*Oelwein Daily Register* (US): Inspector Grey Stories. II. The Terror in the Snow, (p. 2). [Part 3].
19th November.	*Oelwein Daily Register* (US): Inspector Grey Stories. III. The Theft of the Pavaloff Diamond, [ss] (p. 2). [Part 1: a republication of the Addington Peace story, *Mr. Taubery's Diamond*].
20th November.	*Oelwein Daily Register* (US): Inspector Grey Stories. IV. Who Killed Sir Andrew Cheyne?, [ss] (p. 2). [Part 1: a republication of the Addington Peace story, *The Mystery of the Causeway*. Strangely, this item was published prior to the conclusion of the previous story].
21st November.	*Oelwein Daily Register* (US): Inspector Grey Stories. III. The Theft of the Pavaloff Diamond, [ss] (p. 2). [Part 2].
27th November.	*Oelwein Daily Register* (US): Inspector Grey Stories. V. The Dartmoor Tragedy, [ss] (p. 2). [Part 1: a republication of the Addington Peace story, *The Mystery of Thomas Hearne*. Once again, this item was published prior to the conclusion of the previous story].
28th November.	*Oelwein Daily Register* (US): Inspector Grey Stories. IV. Who Killed Sir Andrew Cheyne?, [ss] (p. 2). [Part 2].
30th November.	*Oelwein Daily Register* (US): Inspector Grey Stories. V. The Dartmoor Tragedy, [ss] (p. 2). [Part 2].
December.	*The Windsor Magazine:* Chronicles In Cartoon – Leaders Of Religion [ar] (pp 83-100).
3rd December.	*Oelwein Daily Register* (US): Inspector Grey Stories. VI. A Blackmailing Incident, [ss] (p. 2). [A republication of the Addington Peace story, *Mr. Coran's Election*].
4th December.	*Oelwein Daily Register* (US): Inspector Grey Stories. VII. The Diasppearance of Silas Ford, [ss] (p. 2). [Part 1: a republication of the Addington Peace story, *The Vanished Millionaire*].
6th December.	*Oelwein Daily Register* (US): Inspector Grey Stories. VII. The Diasppearance of Silas Ford, [ss] (p. 2). [Part 2].
10th December.	*Oelwein Daily Register* (US): Inspector Grey Stories. VII. The Diasppearance of Silas Ford, [ss] (p. 2). [Part 3].

1906:

11th December.	*Oelwein Daily Register* (US): Inspector Grey Stories. VIII. The Indian Spear Mystery, [ss] (p. 2). [Part 1: a republication of the Addington Peace story, *The Mystery of the Jade Spear*].
14th December.	*Oelwein Daily Register* (US): Inspector Grey Stories. VIII. The Indian Spear Mystery, [ss] (p. 2). [Part 2].

1907:

January.	*Appleton's Magazine* (US): How Mr Denis O'Halloran Transgressed His Code [ss] (pp. 16-20).
January.	*The Windsor Magazine:* Chronicles In Cartoon – XIV. The Universities And Public Schools [ar] (pp 262-278).
February.	*The Windsor Magazine:* Chronicles In Cartoon – XV. Men of Letters [ar] (pp 367-386).
May.	*Munsey's Magazine* (US): People Much Talked About in London [ar] (pp. 135-145). [Vol. XXXVII, No. II].
4th May.	*The Penny Magazine*: Addington Peace of the "Yard" – I. The Terror in the Snow [ss] (pp. 145-153). [Republication].
11th May.	*The Penny Magazine*: Addington Peace of the "Yard" – II. Mr Taubery's Diamond [ss] (pp. 215-222). [Republication].
18th May.	*The Penny Magazine*: Addington Peace of the "Yard" – III. Mr Coran's Election [ss] (pp. 277-284). [Republication].
25th May.	*The Penny Magazine*: Addington Peace of the "Yard" – IV. The Mystery of the Causeway [ss] (pp. 340-347). [Republication].
1st June.	*The Penny Magazine*: Addington Peace of the "Yard" – V. The Vanished Millionaire [ss] (pp. 408-415). [Republication]
8th June.	*The Penny Magazine*: Addington Peace of the "Yard" – VI. The Mystery of the Jade Spear [ss] (pp. 471-479). [Republication].

1912:

9th September.	*The Daily Courier* (US): The Chronicles of Addington Peace. The Terror in the Snow, [ss] (p. 7). [Part 1].
9th September.	*The Daily Courier* (US): The Chronicles of Addington Peace. The Terror in the Snow, [ss] (p. 7). [Part 2].
10th September.	*The Daily Courier* (US): The Chronicles of Addington Peace. Mr. Taubery's Diamond, [ss] (p. 7). [Part 1].
11th September.	*The Daily Courier* (US): The Chronicles of Addington Peace. Mr. Taubery's Diamond, [ss] (p. 7). [Part 2].
12th September.	*The Daily Courier* (US): The Chronicles of Addington Peace. The Mystery of the Causeway, [ss] (p. 7).
13th September.	*The Daily Courier* (US): The Chronicles of Addington Peace. The Tragedy of Thomas Hearne, [ss] (p. 7). [Part 1].
14th September.	*The Daily Courier* (US): The Chronicles of Addington Peace. The Tragedy of Thomas Hearne, [ss] (p. 7). [Part 2].

1912:

14th September.	*The Gettysburg Times* (US): The Chronicles of Addington Peace. The Story of Amaroff the Pole, [ss] (p. 4). [Part 1].
16th September.	*The Daily Courier* (US): The Chronicles of Addington Peace. The Vanished Millionaire, [ss] (p. 7). [Part 1].
17th September.	*The Daily Courier* (US): The Chronicles of Addington Peace. The Vanished Millionaire, [ss] (p. 7). [Part 2].
17th September.	*The Fort Wayne Daily News* (US): The Chronicles of Addington Peace, [ss] (p. 11). [Part 1].
17th September.	*The Gettysburg Times* (US): The Chronicles of Addington Peace. The Story of Amaroff the Pole, [ss] (p. 4). [Part 2].
18th September.	*The Daily Courier* (US): The Chronicles of Addington Peace. TheVanished Millionaire, [ss] (p. 7). [Part 3].
18th September.	*The Daily Courier* (US): The Chronicles of Addington Peace. Mr Coran's Election, [ss] (p. 7). [Part 1].
19th September.	*The Daily Courier* (US): The Chronicles of Addington Peace. Mr Coran's Election, [ss] (p. 7). [Part 2].
19th September.	*The Fort Wayne Daily News* (US): The Chronicles of Addington Peace, [ss] (p. 11). [Part 2].
19th September.	*The Gettysburg Times* (US): The Chronicles of Addington Peace. The Terror in the Snow, [ss] (p. 4). [Part 1].
20th September.	*The Daily Courier* (US): The Chronicles of Addington Peace. The Mystery of the Jade Spear, [ss] (p. 7). [Part 1].
20th September.	*The Fort Wayne Daily News* (US): The Chronicles of Addington Peace, [ss] (p. 16). [Part 3].
20th September.	*The Gettysburg Times* (US): The Chronicles of Addington Peace. The Terror in the Snow, [ss] (p. 4). [Part 2].
20th September.	*The Indiana Evening Gazette* (US): The Chronicles of Addington Peace, [ss] (p. 2). [Republication of *The Mystery of the Jade Spear*].
21st September.	*The Daily Courier* (US): The Chronicles of Addington Peace. The Mystery of the Jade Spear, [ss] (p. 7). [Part 2].
21st September.	*The Fort Wayne Daily News* (US): The Chronicles of Addington Peace, [ss] (p. 9). [Part 4].
21st September.	*The Janesville Daily Gazette* (US): The Chronicles of Addington
23rd September.	*The Gettysburg Times* (US): The Chronicles of Addington Peace. Mr. Taubery's Diamond, [ss] (p. 4). [Part 1].
24th September.	*The Janesville Daily Gazette* (US): The Chronicles of Addington Peace, [ss] (p. 9). [Part 2].
25th September.	*The Fort Wayne Daily News* (US): The Chronicles of Addington Peace, [ss] (p. 23). [Part 5].
25th September.	*The Janesville Daily Gazette* (US): The Chronicles of Addington Peace, [ss] (p. 9). [Part 3].
26th September.	*The Fort Wayne Daily News* (US): The Chronicles of Addington Peace, [ss] (p. 9). [Part 6].

1912:

26th September.	*The Janesville Daily Gazette* (US): The Chronicles of Addington Peace, [ss] (p. 11). [Part 4].
27th September.	*The Gettysburg Times* (US): The Chronicles of Addington Peace. Mr. Taubery's Diamond, [ss] (p. 4). [Part 2].
27th September.	*The Janesville Daily Gazette* (US): The Chronicles of Addington Peace, [ss] (p. 11). [Part 5].
28th September.	*The Janesville Daily Gazette* (US): The Chronicles of Addington Peace, [ss] (p. 11). [Part 6].
30th September.	*The Fort Wayne Daily News* (US): The Chronicles of Addington Peace, [ss] (p. 18). [Part 7].
30th September.	*The Janesville Daily Gazette* (US): The Chronicles of Addington Peace, [ss] (p. 11). [Part 7].
1st October.	*The Fort Wayne Daily News* (US): The Chronicles of Addington Peace, [ss] (p. 5). [Part 8].
1st October.	*The Janesville Daily Gazette* (US): The Chronicles of Addington Peace, [ss] (p. 9). [Part 8].
2nd October.	*The Janesville Daily Gazette* (US): The Chronicles of Addington Peace, [ss] (p. 11). [Part 9].
3rd October.	*The Janesville Daily Gazette* (US): The Chronicles of Addington Peace, [ss] (p. 11). [Part 10].
7th October.	*The Gettysburg Times* (US): The Chronicles of Addington Peace. The Mystery of the Causeway, [ss] (p. 4). [Part 1].
7th October.	*The Janesville Daily Gazette* (US): The Chronicles of Addington Peace, [ss] (p. 11). [Part 11].
8th October.	*The Janesville Daily Gazette* (US): The Chronicles of Addington Peace, [ss] (p. 11). [Part 12].
9th October.	*The Gettysburg Times* (US): The Chronicles of Addington Peace. The Mystery of the Causeway, [ss] (p. 4). [Part 2].
9th October.	*The Janesville Daily Gazette* (US): The Chronicles of Addington Peace, [ss] (p. 13). [Part 13].
10th October.	*The Janesville Daily Gazette* (US): The Chronicles of Addington Peace, [ss] (p. 11). [Part 14].
12th October.	*The Janesville Daily Gazette* (US): The Chronicles of Addington Peace, [ss] (p. 13). [Part 15].
14th October.	*The Janesville Daily Gazette* (US): The Chronicles of Addington Peace, [ss] (p. 11). [Part 16].
15th October.	*The Janesville Daily Gazette* (US): The Chronicles of Addington Peace, [ss] (p. 13). [Part 17].
17th October.	*The Janesville Daily Gazette* (US): The Chronicles of Addington Peace, [ss] (p. 13). [Part 18].
18th October.	*The Gazette And Bulletin* (US): The Chronicles of Addington Peace, [ss] (p. 10). [Part 1].
19th October.	*The Gazette And Bulletin* (US): The Chronicles of Addington Peace, [ss] (p. 10). [Part 2].

1912:

21st October.	*The Gazette And Bulletin* (US): The Chronicles of Addington Peace, [ss] (p. 7). [Part 3].
22nd October.	*The Gazette And Bulletin* (US): The Chronicles of Addington Peace, [ss] (p. 8). [Part 4].
23rd October.	*The Gazette And Bulletin* (US): The Chronicles of Addington Peace, [ss] (p. 8). [Part 5].
24th October.	*The Gazette And Bulletin* (US): The Chronicles of Addington Peace, [ss] (p. 10). [Part 6].
25th October.	*The Gazette And Bulletin* (US): The Chronicles of Addington Peace, [ss] (p. 10). [Part 7].
26th October.	*The Gazette And Bulletin* (US): The Chronicles of Addington Peace, [ss] (p. 10). [Part 8].
28th October.	*The Gazette And Bulletin* (US): The Chronicles of Addington Peace, [ss] (p. 8). [Part 9].
29th October.	*The Gazette And Bulletin* (US): The Chronicles of Addington Peace, [ss] (p. 10). [Part 10].
30th October.	*The Gazette And Bulletin* (US): The Chronicles of Addington Peace, [ss] (p. 10). [Part 11].
31st October.	*The Gazette And Bulletin* (US): The Chronicles of Addington Peace, [ss] (p. 10). [Part 12].
1st November.	*The Gazette And Bulletin* (US): The Chronicles of Addington Peace, [ss] (p. 8). [Part 13].
2nd November.	*The Gazette And Bulletin* (US): The Chronicles of Addington Peace, [ss] (p. 10). [Part 14].
4th November.	*The Gazette And Bulletin* (US): The Chronicles of Addington Peace, [ss] (p. 8). [Part 15].
5th November.	*The Gazette And Bulletin* (US): The Chronicles of Addington Peace, [ss] (p. 12). [Part 16].
5th November.	*The Gettysburg Times* (US): The Chronicles of Addington Peace. The Tragedy of Thomas Hearne, [ss] (p. 4). [Part 1].
6th November.	*The Gazette And Bulletin* (US): The Chronicles of Addington Peace, [ss] (p. 8). [Part 17].
6th November.	*The Gettysburg Times* (US): The Chronicles of Addington Peace. The Tragedy of Thomas Hearne, [ss] (p. 4). [Part 2].
7th November.	*The Gazette And Bulletin* (US): The Chronicles of Addington Peace, [ss] (p. 8). [Part 18].
7th November.	*The Gettysburg Times* (US): The Chronicles of Addington Peace. The Tragedy of Thomas Hearne, [ss] (p. 4). [Part 3].
7th November.	*The Gettysburg Times* (US): The Chronicles of Addington Peace. The Vanished Millionaire, [ss] (p. 4). [Part 1].
8th November.	*The Gazette And Bulletin* (US): The Chronicles of Addington Peace, [ss] (p. 8). [Part 19].
8th November.	*The Gettysburg Times* (US): The Chronicles of Addington Peace. The Vanished Millionaire, [ss] (p. 4). [Part 2].

1912:

9th November.	*The Gazette And Bulletin* (US): The Chronicles of Addington Peace, [ss] (p. 10). [Part 20].
11th November.	*The Gazette And Bulletin* (US): The Chronicles of Addington Peace, [ss] (p. 7). [Part 21].
11th November.	*The Gettysburg Times* (US): The Chronicles of Addington Peace. The Vanished Millionaire, [ss] (p. 4). [Part 3].
12th November.	*The Gazette And Bulletin* (US): The Chronicles of Addington Peace, [ss] (p. 8). [Part 22].
12th November.	*The Gettysburg Times* (US): The Chronicles of Addington Peace. Mr Coran's Election, [ss] (p. 4). [Part 1].
13th November.	*The Gazette And Bulletin* (US): The Chronicles of Addington Peace, [ss] (p. 8). [Part 23].
13th November.	*The Gettysburg Times* (US): The Chronicles of Addington Peace. Mr Coran's Election, [ss] (p. 4). [Part 2].
14th November.	*The Gazette And Bulletin* (US): The Chronicles of Addington Peace, [ss] (p. 8). [Part 24].
15th November.	*The Gazette And Bulletin* (US): The Chronicles of Addington Peace, [ss] (p. 10). [Part 25].
15th November.	*The Gettysburg Times* (US): The Chronicles of Addington Peace. Mr Coran's Election, [ss] (p. 4). [Part 3].
16th November.	*The Gazette And Bulletin* (US): The Chronicles of Addington Peace, [ss] (p. 10). [Part 26].
18th November.	*The Gazette And Bulletin* (US): The Chronicles of Addington Peace, [ss] (p. 7). [Part 27].
18th November.	*The Gettysburg Times* (US): The Chronicles of Addington Peace. The Mystery of the Jade Spear, [ss] (p. 4). [Part 1].
19th November.	*The Gazette And Bulletin* (US): The Chronicles of Addington Peace, [ss] (p. 8). [Part 28].
20th November.	*The Gettysburg Times* (US): The Chronicles of Addington Peace. The Mystery of the Jade Spear, [ss] (p. 4). [Part 2].

1913:

9th August.	*Mountain Democrat* (US): The Chronicles of Addington Peace. The Story of Amaroff the Pole, [ss] (p. 7). [Part 1].
16th August.	*Mountain Democrat* (US): The Chronicles of Addington Peace. The Story of Amaroff the Pole, [ss] (p. 7). [Part 2].
23rd August.	*Mountain Democrat* (US): The Chronicles of Addington Peace. The Story of Amaroff the Pole, [ss] (p. 7). [Part 3].
30th August.	*Mountain Democrat* (US): The Chronicles of Addington Peace. The Story of Amaroff the Pole, [ss] (p. 7). [Part 4].
6th September.	*Mountain Democrat* (US): The Chronicles of Addington Peace. The Terror in the Snow, [ss] (p. 7). [Part 1].

1913:

13th September. *Mountain Democrat* (US): The Chronicles of Addington Peace. The Terror in the Snow, [ss] (p. 7). [Part 2].

20th September. *Mountain Democrat* (US): The Chronicles of Addington Peace. The Terror in the Snow, [ss] (p. 7). [Part 3].

27th September. *Mountain Democrat* (US): The Chronicles of Addington Peace. The Terror in the Snow, [ss] (p. 8). [Part 4].

4th October. *Mountain Democrat* (US): The Chronicles of Addington Peace. Mr. Taubery's Diamond, [ss] (p. 8). [Part 1].

11th October. *Mountain Democrat* (US): The Chronicles of Addington Peace. Mr. Taubery's Diamond, [ss] (p. 8). [Part 2].

18th October. *Mountain Democrat* (US): The Chronicles of Addington Peace. Mr. Taubery's Diamond, [ss] (p. 8). [Part 3].

25th October. *Mountain Democrat* (US): The Chronicles of Addington Peace. The Mystery of the Causeway, [ss] (p. 8). [Part 1].

1st November. *Mountain Democrat* (US): The Chronicles of Addington Peace. The Mystery of the Causeway, [ss] (p. 8). [Part 2].

8th November. *Mountain Democrat* (US): The Chronicles of Addington Peace. The Mystery of the Causeway, [ss] (p. 8). [Part 3].

15th November. *Mountain Democrat* (US): The Chronicles of Addington Peace. The Tragedy of Thomas Hearne, [ss] (p. 8). [Part 1].

22nd November. *Mountain Democrat* (US): The Chronicles of Addington Peace. TheTragedy of Thomas Hearne, [ss] (p. 8). [Part 2].

29th November. *Mountain Democrat* (US): The Chronicles of Addington Peace. The Tragedy of Thomas Hearne, [ss] (p. 8). [Part 3].

6th December. *Mountain Democrat* (US): The Chronicles of Addington Peace. The Vanished Millionaire, [ss] (p. 8). [Part 1].

13th December. *Mountain Democrat* (US): The Chronicles of Addington Peace. The Vanished Millionaire, [ss] (p. 8). [Part 2].

20th December. *Mountain Democrat* (US): The Chronicles of Addington Peace. The Vanished Millionaire, [ss] (p. 6). [Part 3].

21st December. *Mountain Democrat* (US): The Chronicles of Addington Peace. Mr Coran's Election, [ss] (p. 8). [Part 1].

1914:

3rd January. *Mountain Democrat* (US): The Chronicles of Addington Peace. Mr Coran's Election, [ss] (p. 7). [Part 2].

10th January. *Mountain Democrat* (US): The Chronicles of Addington Peace. Mr Coran's Election, [ss] (p. 8). [Part 3].

17th January. *Mountain Democrat* (US): The Chronicles of Addington Peace. The Mystery of the Jade Spear, [ss] (p. 8). [Part 1].

27th January. *Mountain Democrat* (US): The Chronicles of Addington Peace. The Mystery of the Jade Spear, [ss] (p. 8). [Part 2].

1914:

31st January. *Mountain Democrat* (US): The Chronicles of Addington Peace. The Mystery of the Jade Spear, [ss] (p. 8). [Part 3].

1928:

March. *Secret Service Stories* (US): Addington Peace of the 'Yard' – The Vanished Billionaire [ss] (pp. 5-16). [A republication of *The Vanished Millionaire*].

June. *Secret Service Stories* (US): The Return of Oliver Manton, [ss] (p. 121 126).

1936:

December. *The Witch's Tales* (US): The Return of Oliver Manton – A Tragic Sequence to a Spiritualistic Séance, [ss] (Vol. 1, No. 2, pp. 52-55). [Republication].

1973:

July. *Mike Shayne Mystery Magazine* (US): The Vanished Billionaire [ss] (Vol. 33, No. 2, pp. 69-85). [A republication of *The Vanished Millionaire*].

1995:

Sherlock Publications (Fareham, Hampshire) republished *The Terror in the Snow* with textual annotations by Philip Weller.

1998:

Oxford University Press (Oxford & New York) republished *Fog Bound* as '*Fogbound*' in a compendium of short stories entitled *Twelve Tales of Murder* (pp. 36-49) [edited by Jack Adrian].

The Battered Silicon Dispatch Box (Ontario, Canada) republished both *The Trail of the Dead* and *The Chronicles of Addington Peace* as a single volume. [This book contains numerous transcription errors within the story narratives].

2008:

Wordsworth Editions Ltd. (Hertfordshire) republished *The Terror in the Snow* in a compendium of short stories entitled *The Werewolf Pack* [edited by Mark Valentine].

Also from MX Publishing:

Brian W. Pugh and Paul R. Spiring

Bertram Fletcher Robinson

A Footnote to the Hound of the Baskervilles

Also from MX Publishing:

Alistair Duncan

Close To Holmes

A Look at the Connections Between Historical London, Sherlock Holmes and Sir Arthur Conan Doyle

Also from MX Publishing:

Alistair Duncan

Eliminate the Impossible

An Examination of the World of Sherlock Holmes on stage and screen

Also from Paul R. Spiring

Brian W. Pugh and Paul R. Spiring

On the Trail of Arthur Conan Doyle

An Illustrated Devon Tour

**Available also
in German ISBN-13: 978-3981132755
and Spanish ISBN-13: 978-1904312482**

www.ingramcontent.com/pod-product-compliance
Lightning Source LLC
Chambersburg PA
CBHW081833170426
43199CB00017B/2715